Shojo Beat

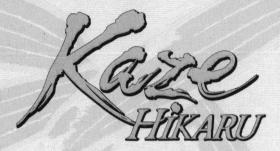

12

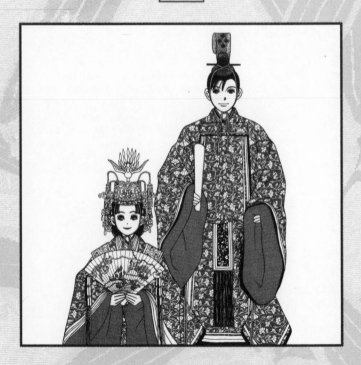

Story & Art by
Taeko Watanabe

Contents

Story Thus Far

It is the end of the Bakufu era, the 3rd year of Bunkyu (1863) in Kyoto. The Shinsengumi is a band of warriors formed to protect the Shogun.

Tominaga Sei, the daughter of a former Bakufu bushi, joined the Shinsengumi disguised as a boy by the name of Kamiya Seizaburo to avenge her father and brother. She has continued her training under the only person in the Shinsengumi who knows her true identity, Okita Soji, and she aspires to become a true *bushi*.

The Shinsengumi prove their worth through their success in the Ikedaya Affair and the *Kinmon no Hen*. Ito Kashitaro and his men join the Shinsengumi. His disdain for violence and lofty approach to *sonno joi* gain the sympathy of Captain Yamanami.

Unfortunately, Yamanami loses faith in the Bakufu when it mercilessly condemns the rebels of the Tengu-to. Unwilling to betray the Shinsengumi, Yamanami chooses *seppuku*. The mystery surrounding his sudden choice of death causes great anxiety in the rest of the troop.

Characters

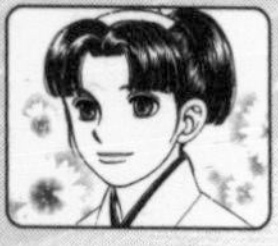

Tominaga Sei
She disguises herself as a boy to enter the Mibu-Roshi. She trains under Soji, aspiring to become a true *bushi*. But secretly, she is in love with Soji.

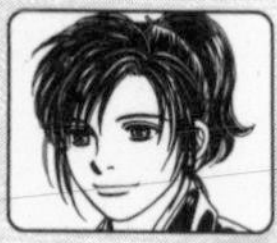

Okita Soji
Assistant vice captain of the Shinsengumi, and licensed master of the Ten'nen Rishin-Ryu. He supports the troop alongside Kondo and Hijikata and guides Seizaburo with a kind yet firm hand.

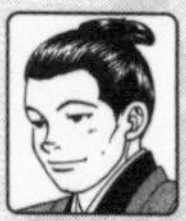

Kondo Isami
Captain of the Shinsengumi and fourth grandmaster of the Ten'nen Rishin-ryu. A passionate, warm and well-respected leader.

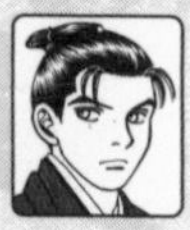

Hijikata Toshizo
Vice captain of the Shinsengumi. He commands both the group and himself with a rigid strictness. He is also known as the "Oni vice captain."

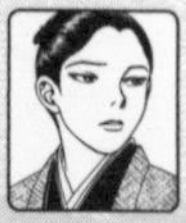

Ito Kashitaro
Councilor of the Shinsengumi. A skilled swordsman yet also an academic. A theorist with an inclination towards anti-Bakufu sentiments.

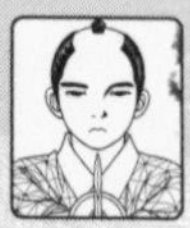

Saito Hajime
Assistant vice captain. He was a friend of Sei's older brother. Sei is attached to him in place of her lost brother.

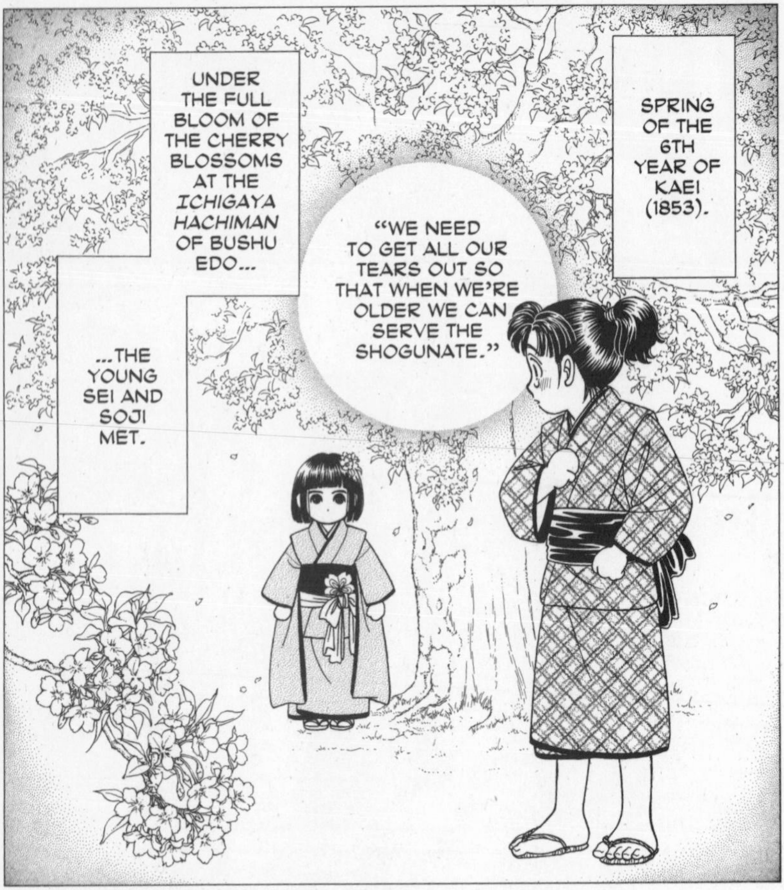
SPRING OF THE 6TH YEAR OF KAEI (1853).
UNDER THE FULL BLOOM OF THE CHERRY BLOSSOMS AT THE *ICHIGAYA HACHIMAN* OF BUSHU EDO...
"WE NEED TO GET ALL OUR TEARS OUT SO THAT WHEN WE'RE OLDER WE CAN SERVE THE SHOGUNATE."
...THE YOUNG SEI AND SOJI MET.

EDO IROHA KARUTA GAME

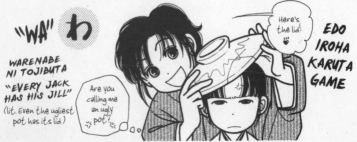

"WA" わ

WARENABE NI TOJIBUTA

"EVERY JACK HAS HIS JILL"

(lit. Even the ugliest pot has its lid)

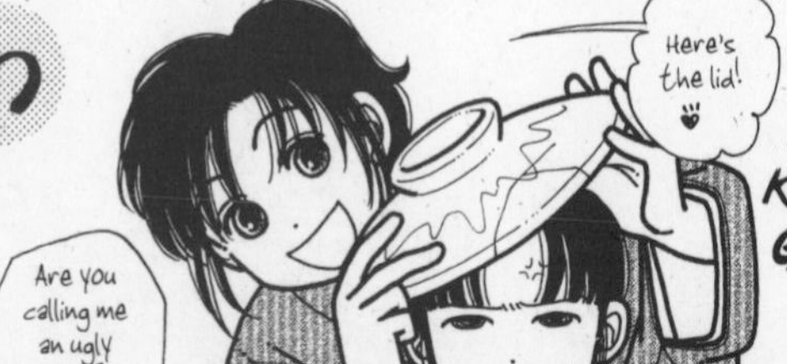
Here's the lid!
Are you calling me an ugly pot?

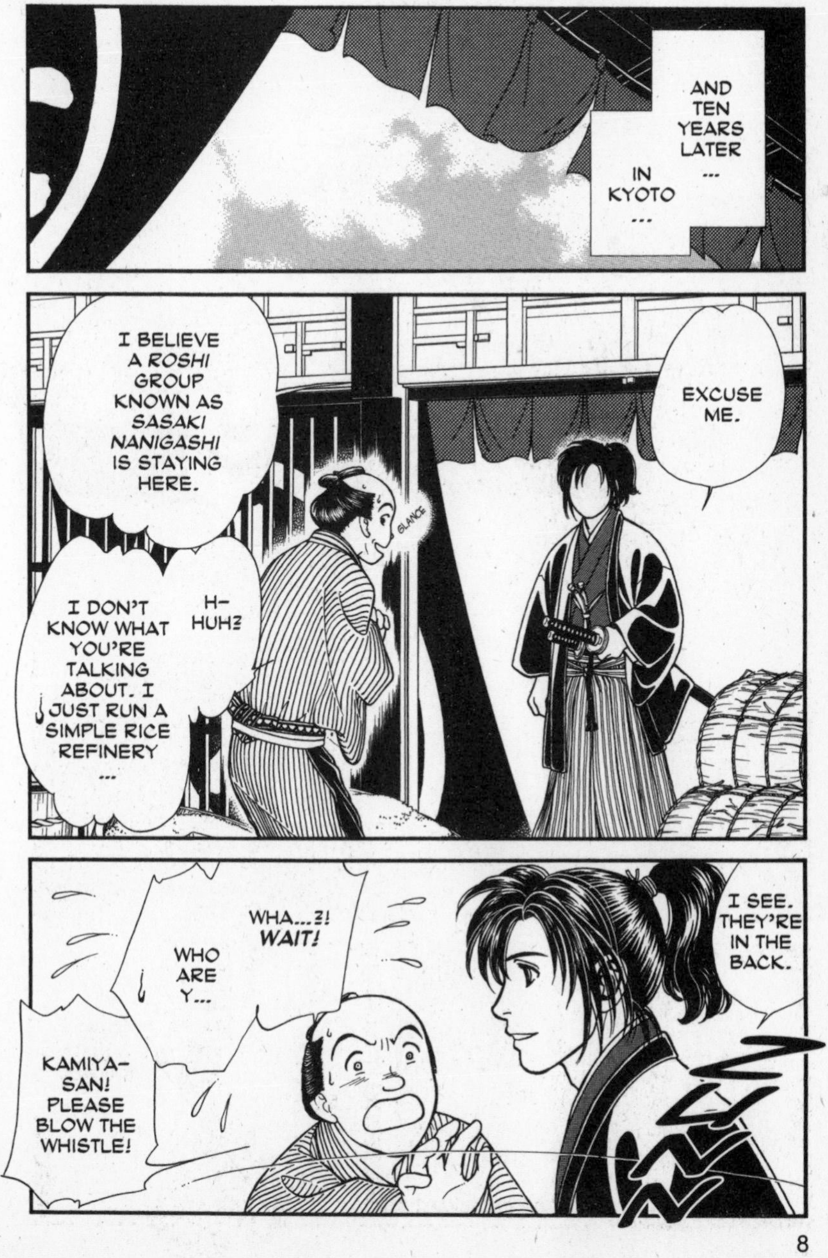
AND TEN YEARS LATER ...
IN KYOTO ...
EXCUSE ME.
I BELIEVE A *ROSHI* GROUP KNOWN AS *SASAKI NANIGASHI* IS STAYING HERE.
GLANCE
H-HUH?
I DON'T KNOW WHAT YOU'RE TALKING ABOUT. I JUST RUN A SIMPLE RICE REFINERY ...
I SEE. THEY'RE IN THE BACK.
WHA...?! ***WAIT!***
WHO ARE Y...
KAMIYA-SAN! PLEASE BLOW THE WHISTLE!

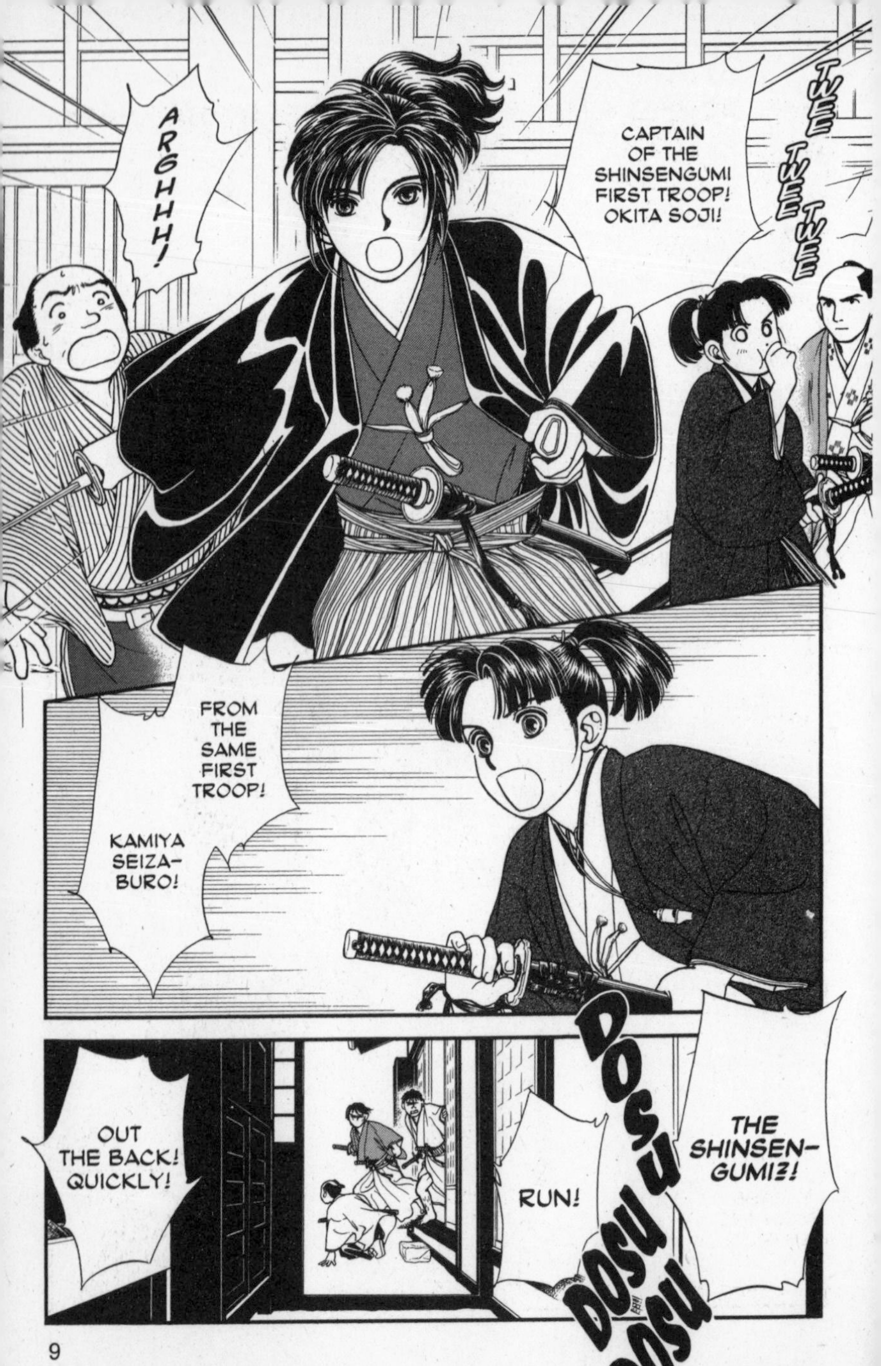
TWEE TWEE TWEE
CAPTAIN OF THE SHINSENGUMI FIRST TROOP! OKITA SOJI!
ARGHHH!
FROM THE SAME FIRST TROOP!
KAMIYA SEIZA-BURO!
THE SHINSEN-GUMI!?!
DOSU DOSU DOSU DOSU
RUN!
OUT THE BACK! QUICKLY!

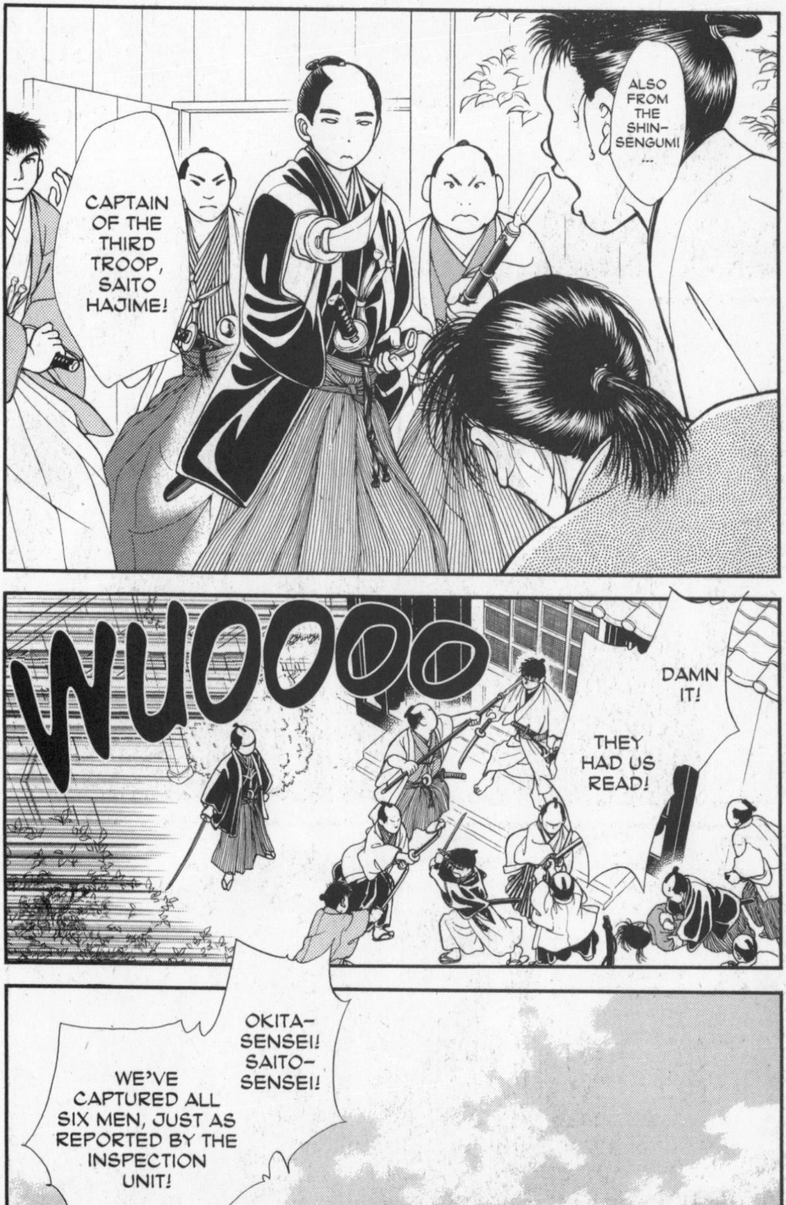
ALSO FROM THE SHIN-SENGUMI! ...
CAPTAIN OF THE THIRD TROOP, SAITO HAJIME!
DAMN IT!
THEY HAD US READ!
WUOOOO
OKITA-SENSEI! SAITO-SENSEI!
WE'VE CAPTURED ALL SIX MEN, JUST AS REPORTED BY THE INSPECTION UNIT!

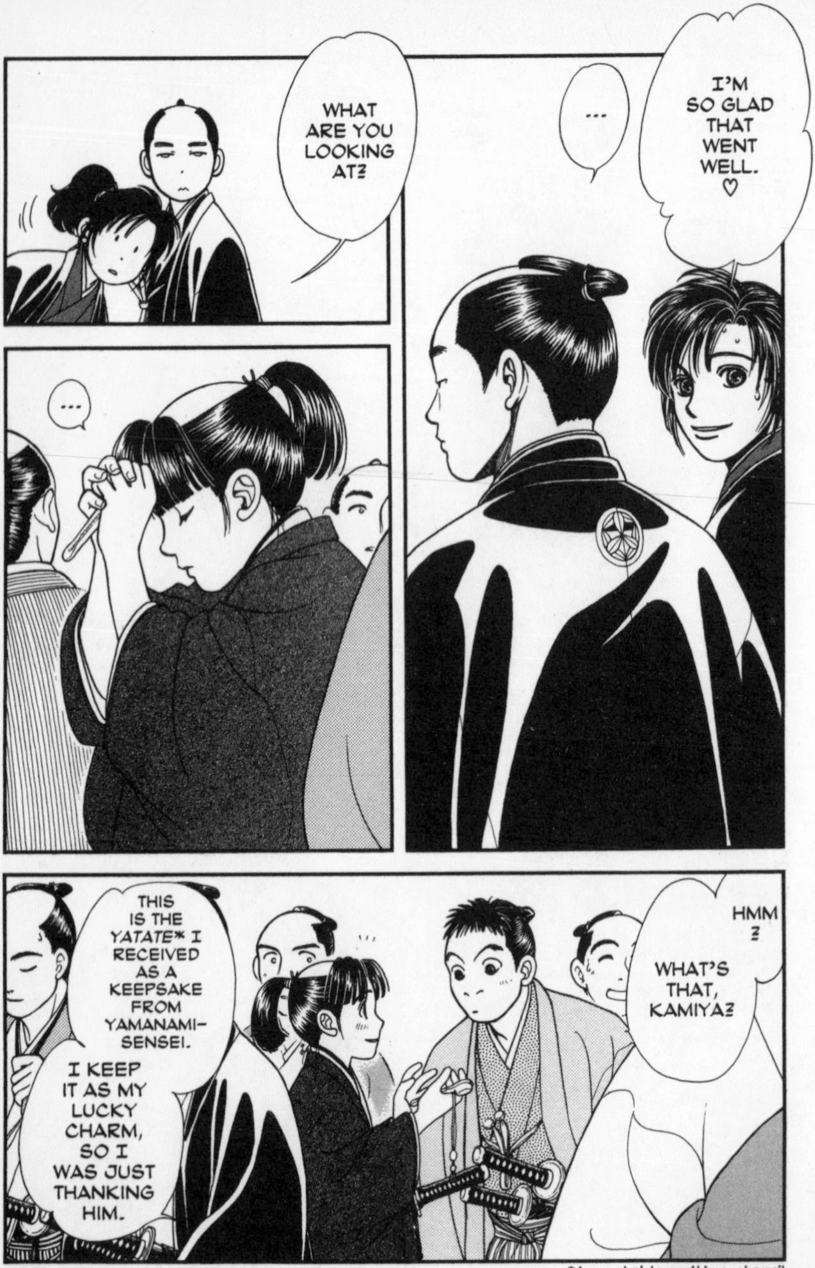
I'M SO GLAD THAT WENT WELL. ♡
...
WHAT ARE YOU LOOKING AT?
...
HMM?
WHAT'S THAT, KAMIYA?
THIS IS THE YATATE* I RECEIVED AS A KEEPSAKE FROM YAMANAMI-SENSEI.
I KEEP IT AS MY LUCKY CHARM, SO I WAS JUST THANKING HIM.

*A portable writing utensil.

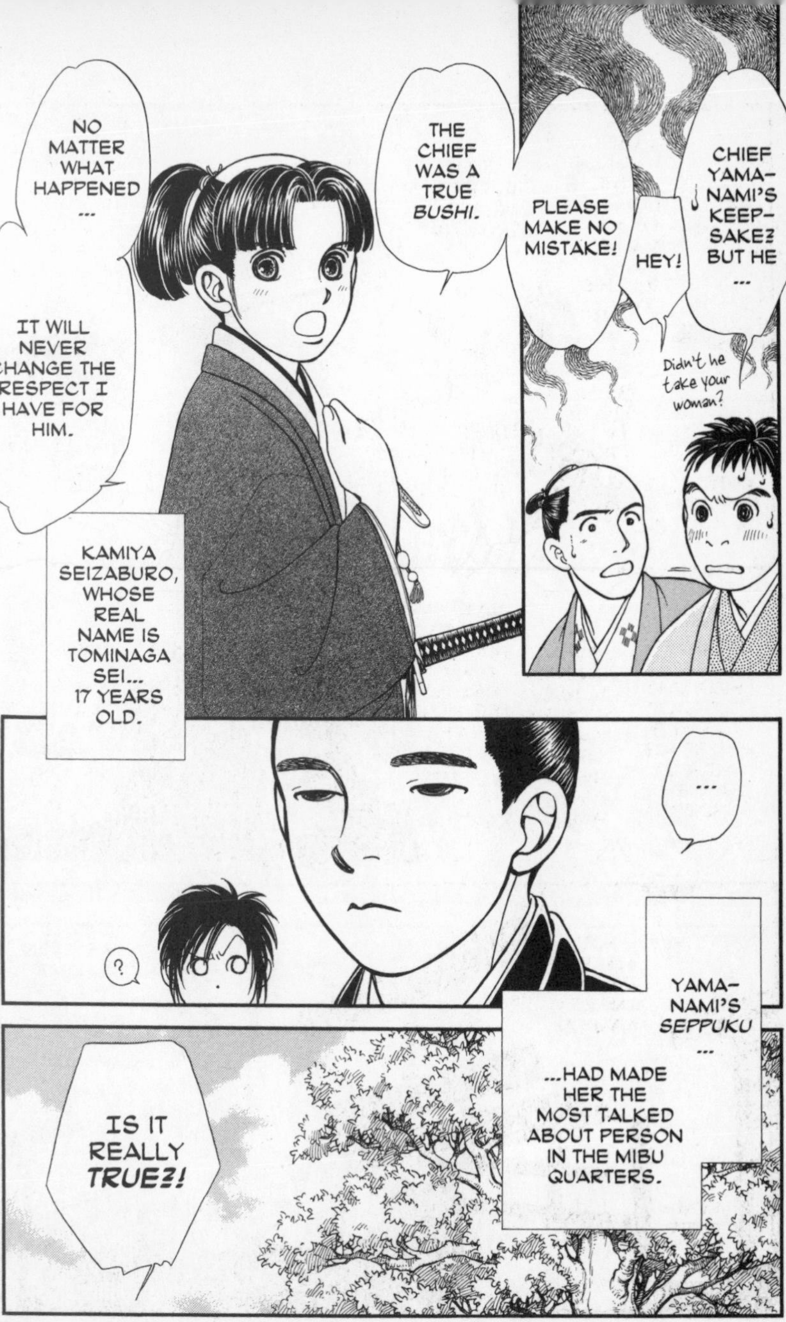
CHIEF YAMANAMI'S KEEPSAKE? BUT HE ...
Didn't he take your woman?
HEY!
PLEASE MAKE NO MISTAKE!
THE CHIEF WAS A TRUE *BUSHI*.
NO MATTER WHAT HAPPENED ...
IT WILL NEVER CHANGE THE RESPECT I HAVE FOR HIM.
KAMIYA SEIZABURO, WHOSE REAL NAME IS TOMINAGA SEI... 17 YEARS OLD.
...
?
YAMANAMI'S *SEPPUKU* ...
...HAD MADE HER THE MOST TALKED ABOUT PERSON IN THE MIBU QUARTERS.
IS IT REALLY ***TRUE?!***

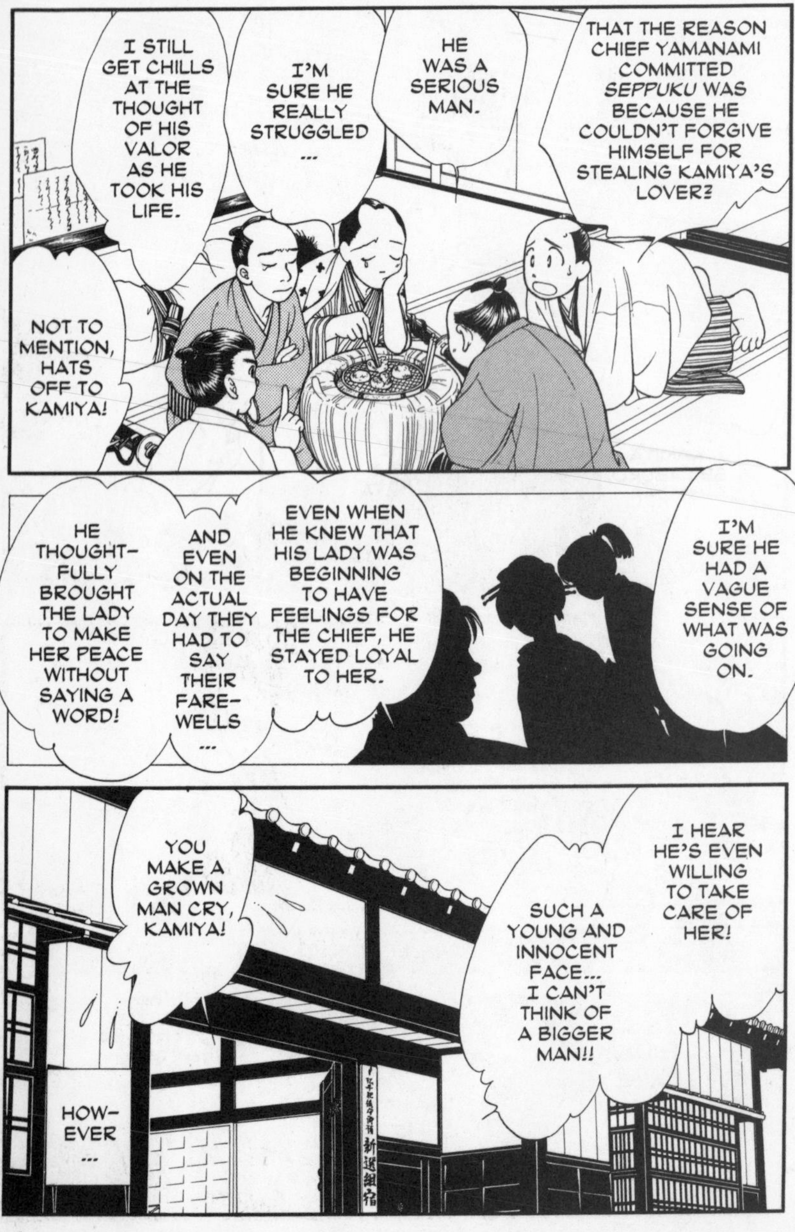
THAT THE REASON CHIEF YAMANAMI COMMITTED *SEPPUKU* WAS BECAUSE HE COULDN'T FORGIVE HIMSELF FOR STEALING KAMIYA'S LOVER?
HE WAS A SERIOUS MAN.
I'M SURE HE REALLY STRUGGLED...
I STILL GET CHILLS AT THE THOUGHT OF HIS VALOR AS HE TOOK HIS LIFE.
NOT TO MENTION, HATS OFF TO KAMIYA!
I'M SURE HE HAD A VAGUE SENSE OF WHAT WAS GOING ON.
EVEN WHEN HE KNEW THAT HIS LADY WAS BEGINNING TO HAVE FEELINGS FOR THE CHIEF, HE STAYED LOYAL TO HER.
AND EVEN ON THE ACTUAL DAY THEY HAD TO SAY THEIR FARE-WELLS...
HE THOUGHT-FULLY BROUGHT THE LADY TO MAKE HER PEACE WITHOUT SAYING A WORD!
I HEAR HE'S EVEN WILLING TO TAKE CARE OF HER!
SUCH A YOUNG AND INNOCENT FACE... I CAN'T THINK OF A BIGGER MAN!!
YOU MAKE A GROWN MAN CRY, KAMIYA!
新選組宿
HOW-EVER...

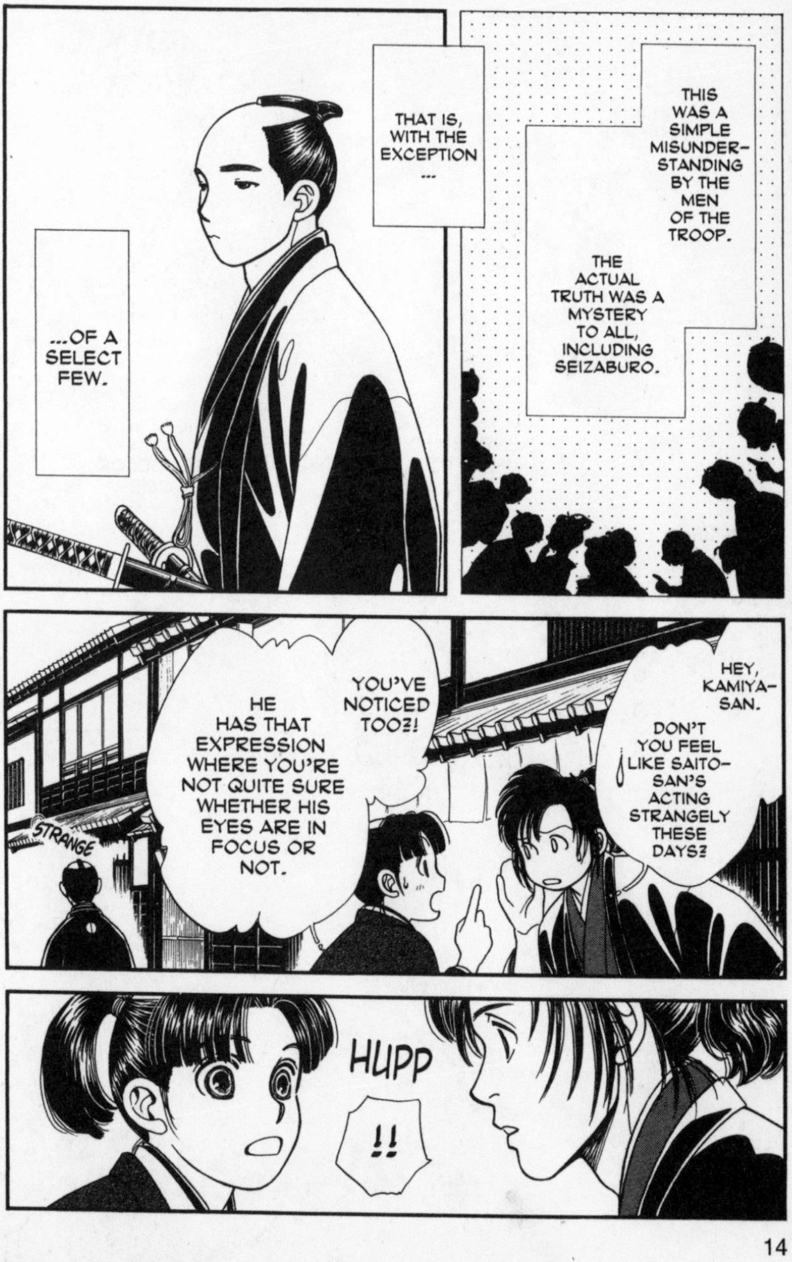
THIS WAS A SIMPLE MISUNDERSTANDING BY THE MEN OF THE TROOP.
THE ACTUAL TRUTH WAS A MYSTERY TO ALL, INCLUDING SEIZABURO.
THAT IS, WITH THE EXCEPTION ...
...OF A SELECT FEW.
HEY, KAMIYA-SAN.
DON'T YOU FEEL LIKE SAITO-SAN'S ACTING STRANGELY THESE DAYS?
YOU'VE NOTICED TOO?!
HE HAS THAT EXPRESSION WHERE YOU'RE NOT QUITE SURE WHETHER HIS EYES ARE IN FOCUS OR NOT.
STRANGE
HUPP
!!

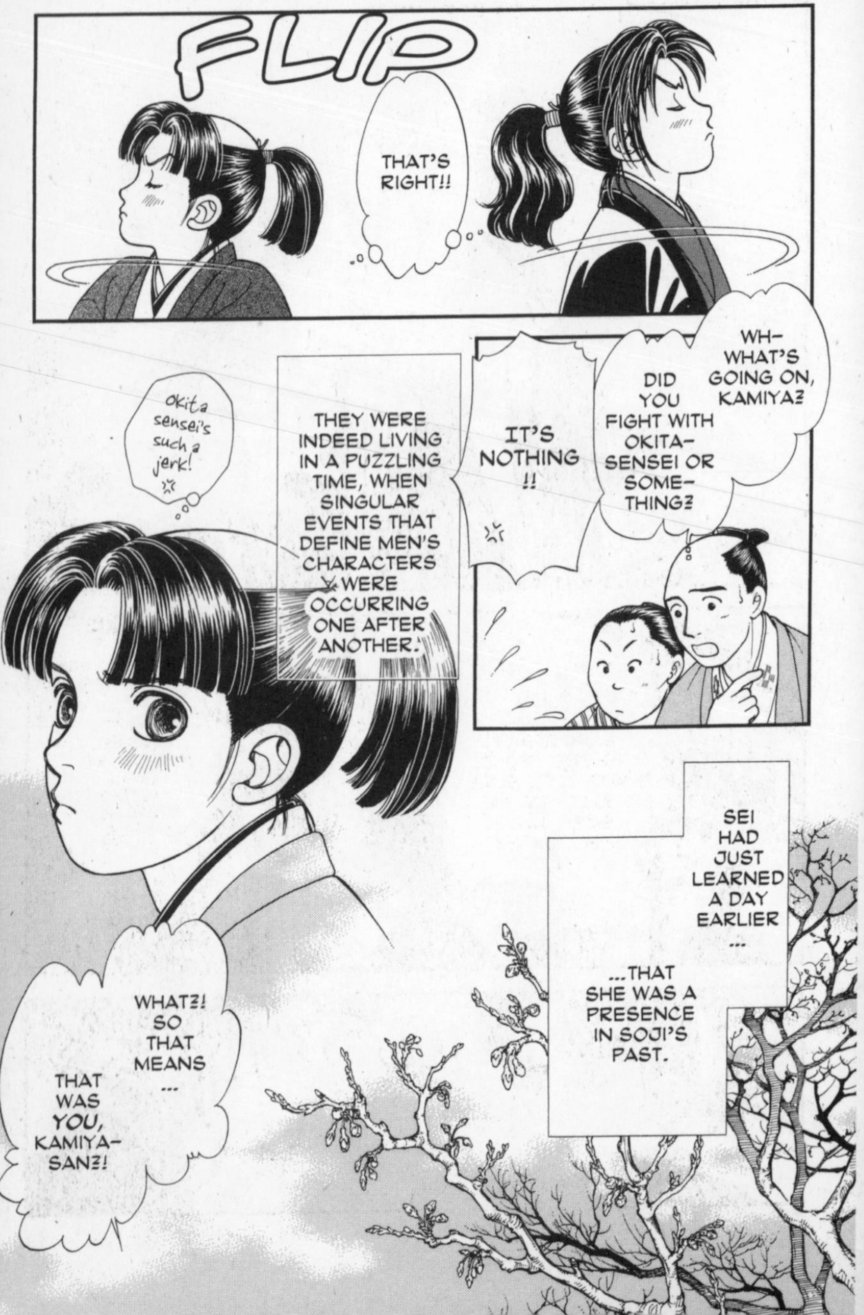
FLIP
THAT'S RIGHT!!
WH- WHAT'S GOING ON, KAMIYA?
DID YOU FIGHT WITH OKITA-SENSEI OR SOMETHING?
IT'S NOTHING!!
THEY WERE INDEED LIVING IN A PUZZLING TIME, WHEN SINGULAR EVENTS THAT DEFINE MEN'S CHARACTERS WERE OCCURRING ONE AFTER ANOTHER.
Okita sensei's such a jerk!
SEI HAD JUST LEARNED A DAY EARLIER...
...THAT SHE WAS A PRESENCE IN SOJI'S PAST.
WHAT?! SO THAT MEANS...
THAT WAS YOU, KAMIYA-SAN?!

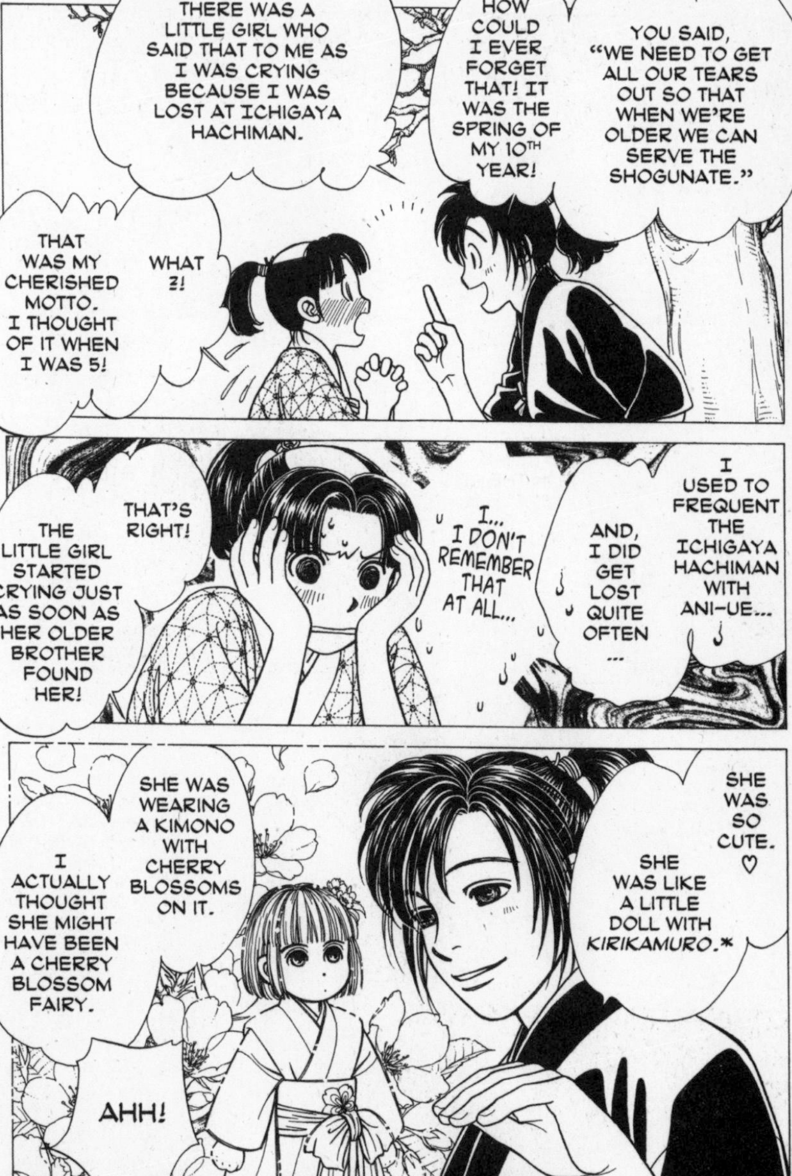
YOU SAID, "WE NEED TO GET ALL OUR TEARS OUT SO THAT WHEN WE'RE OLDER WE CAN SERVE THE SHOGUNATE."
HOW COULD I EVER FORGET THAT! IT WAS THE SPRING OF MY 10TH YEAR!
THERE WAS A LITTLE GIRL WHO SAID THAT TO ME AS I WAS CRYING BECAUSE I WAS LOST AT ICHIGAYA HACHIMAN.
WHAT ?!
THAT WAS MY CHERISHED MOTTO. I THOUGHT OF IT WHEN I WAS 5!
I USED TO FREQUENT THE ICHIGAYA HACHIMAN WITH ANI-UE...
AND, I DID GET LOST QUITE OFTEN ...
I... I DON'T REMEMBER THAT AT ALL...
THAT'S RIGHT!
THE LITTLE GIRL STARTED CRYING JUST AS SOON AS HER OLDER BROTHER FOUND HER!
SHE WAS SO CUTE. ♡
SHE WAS LIKE A LITTLE DOLL WITH *KIRIKAMURO*.*
SHE WAS WEARING A KIMONO WITH CHERRY BLOSSOMS ON IT.
I ACTUALLY THOUGHT SHE MIGHT HAVE BEEN A CHERRY BLOSSOM FAIRY.
AHH!

*A kind of children's haircut with bangs

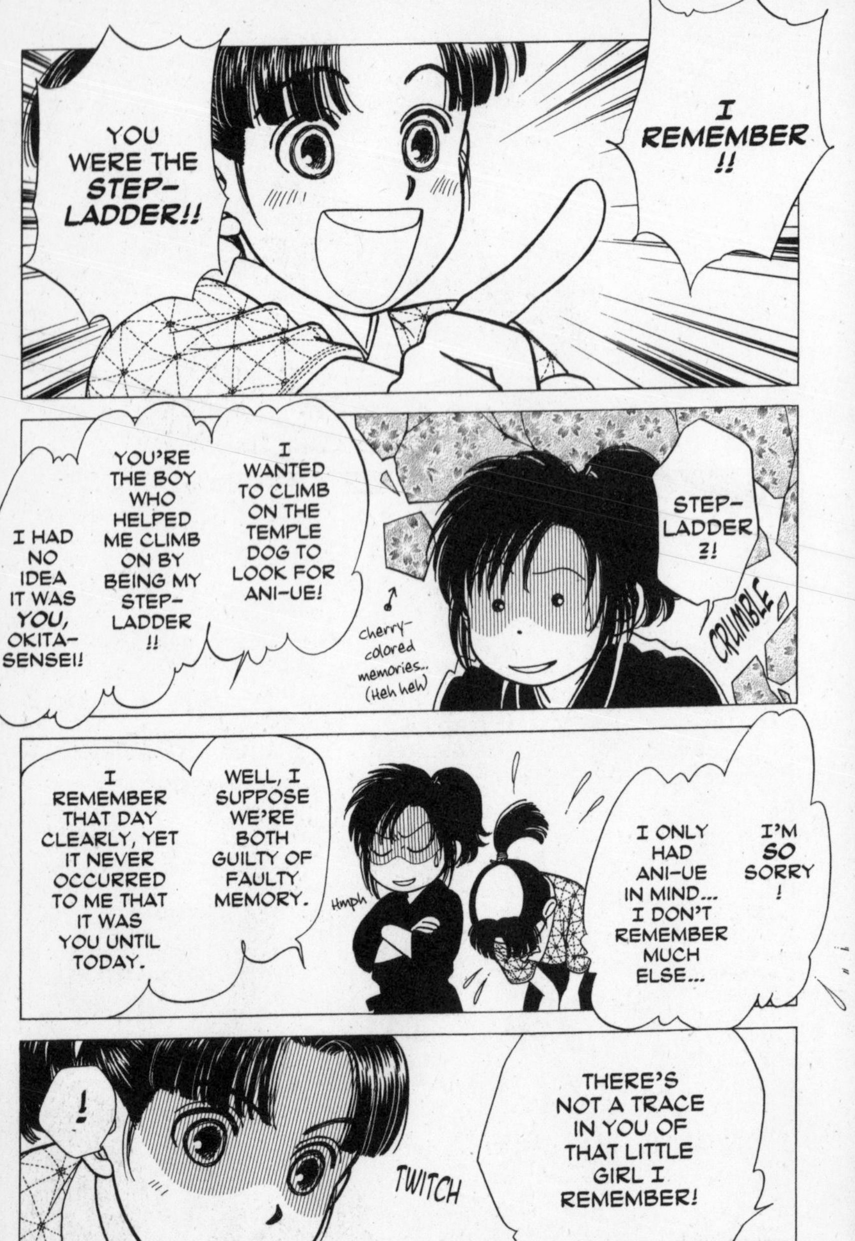
I REMEMBER!!
YOU WERE THE STEP-LADDER!!
STEP-LADDER?!
CRUMBLE
cherry-colored memories.. (Heh heh)
I WANTED TO CLIMB ON THE TEMPLE DOG TO LOOK FOR ANI-UE!
YOU'RE THE BOY WHO HELPED ME CLIMB ON BY BEING MY STEP-LADDER!!
I HAD NO IDEA IT WAS YOU, OKITA-SENSEI!
I'M SO SORRY!
I ONLY HAD ANI-UE IN MIND... I DON'T REMEMBER MUCH ELSE...
Hmph
WELL, I SUPPOSE WE'RE BOTH GUILTY OF FAULTY MEMORY.
I REMEMBER THAT DAY CLEARLY, YET IT NEVER OCCURRED TO ME THAT IT WAS YOU UNTIL TODAY.
THERE'S NOT A TRACE IN YOU OF THAT LITTLE GIRL I REMEMBER!
TWITCH
!

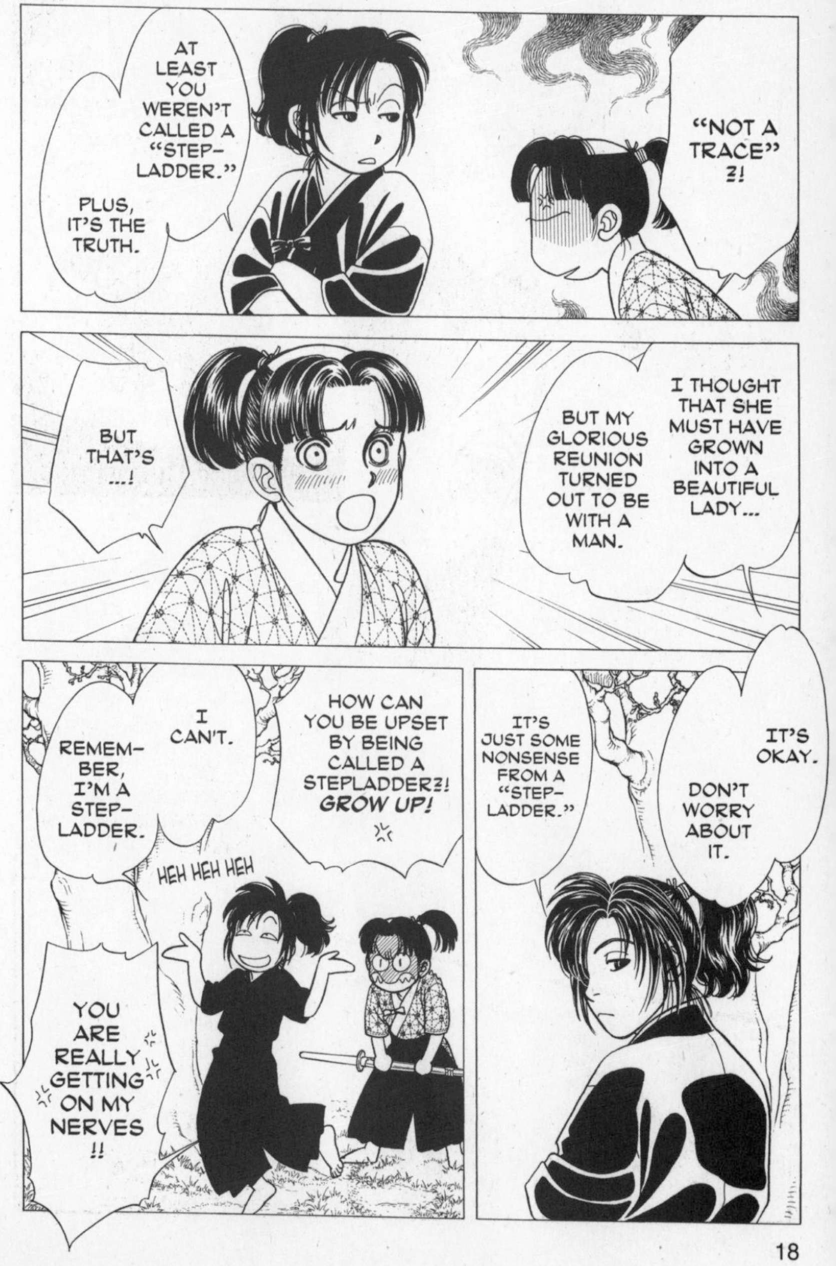
"NOT A TRACE"?!
AT LEAST YOU WEREN'T CALLED A "STEP-LADDER."
PLUS, IT'S THE TRUTH.
I THOUGHT THAT SHE MUST HAVE GROWN INTO A BEAUTIFUL LADY...
BUT MY GLORIOUS REUNION TURNED OUT TO BE WITH A MAN.
BUT THAT'S ...!
IT'S OKAY.
DON'T WORRY ABOUT IT.
IT'S JUST SOME NONSENSE FROM A "STEP-LADDER."
HOW CAN YOU BE UPSET BY BEING CALLED A STEPLADDER?! GROW UP!
I CAN'T.
REMEMBER, I'M A STEP-LADDER.
HEH HEH HEH
YOU ARE REALLY GETTING ON MY NERVES!!

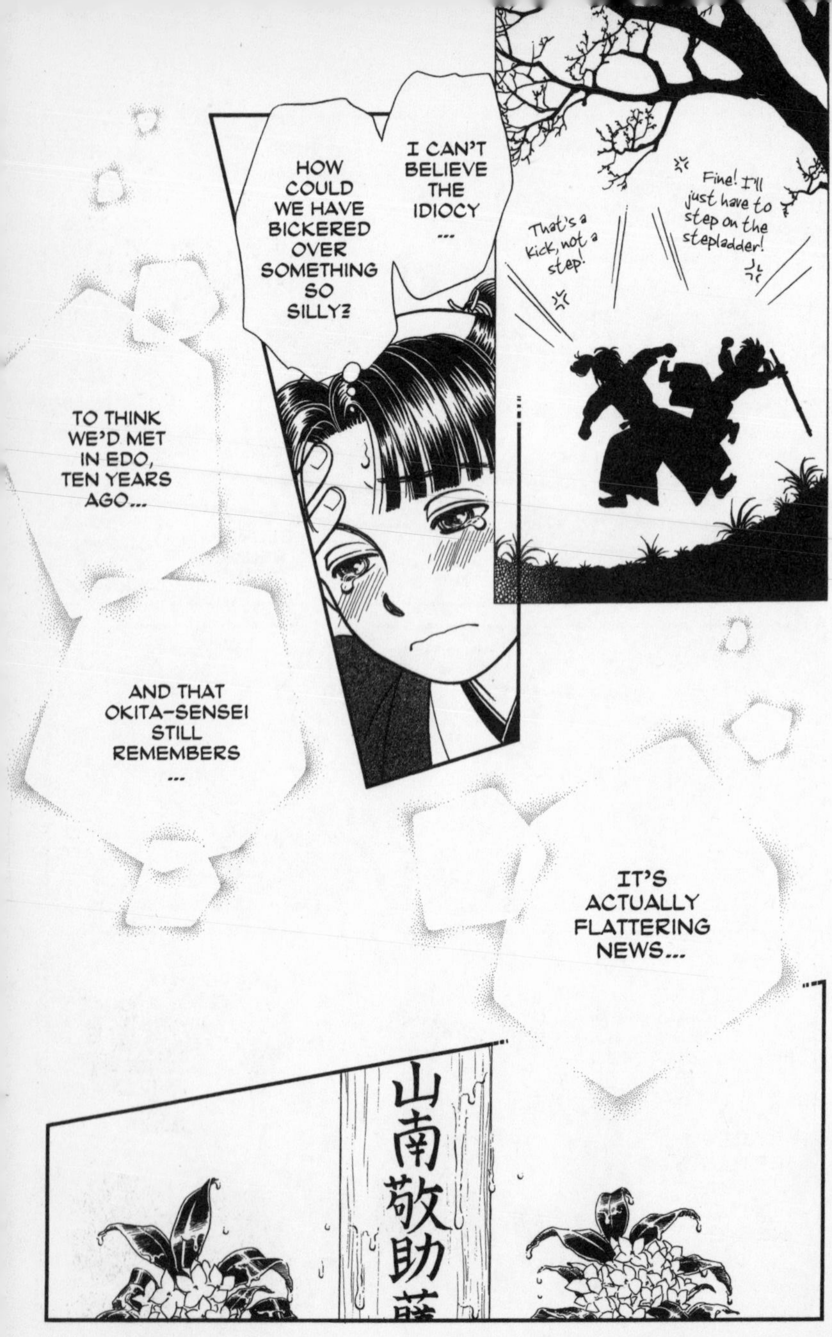
Fine! I'll just have to step on the stepladder!
That's a kick, not a step!
I CAN'T BELIEVE THE IDIOCY...
HOW COULD WE HAVE BICKERED OVER SOMETHING SO SILLY?!
TO THINK WE'D MET IN EDO, TEN YEARS AGO...
AND THAT OKITA-SENSEI STILL REMEMBERS...
IT'S ACTUALLY FLATTERING NEWS...
山南敬助

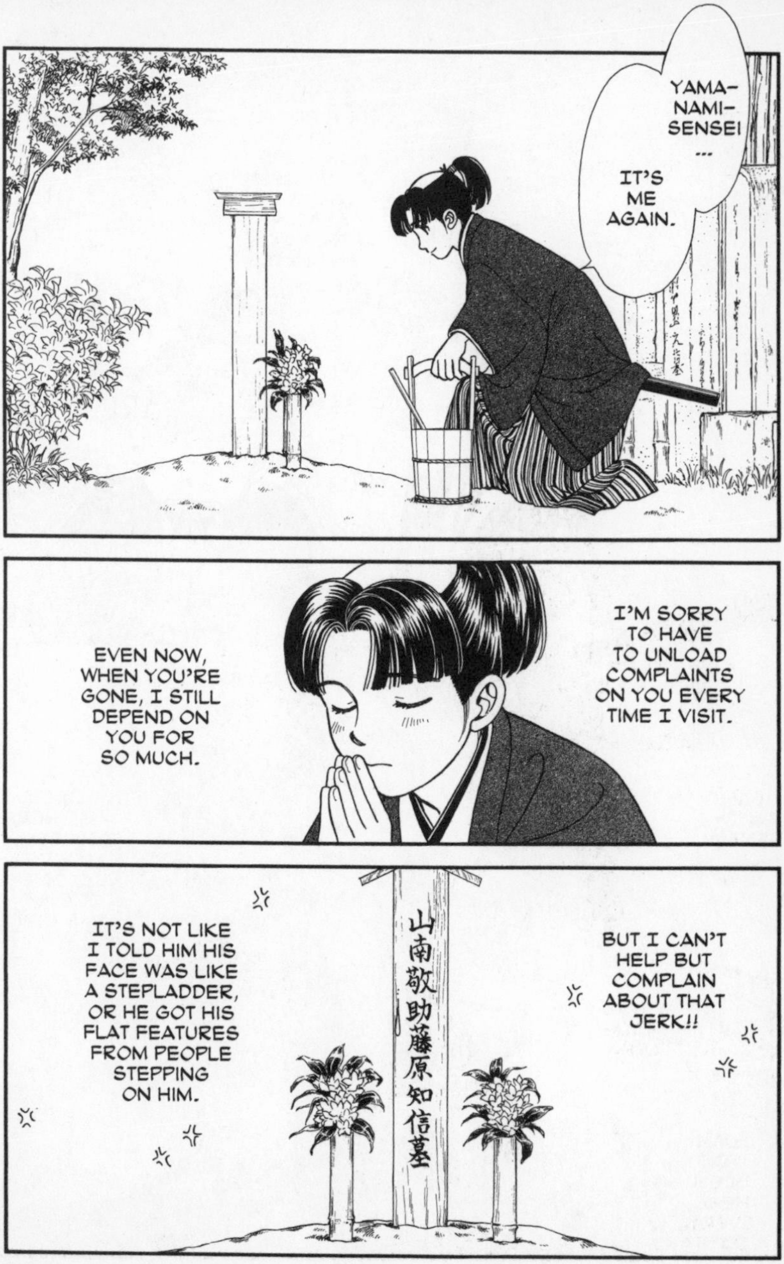
YAMA-NAMI-SENSEI ... IT'S ME AGAIN.
I'M SORRY TO HAVE TO UNLOAD COMPLAINTS ON YOU EVERY TIME I VISIT.
EVEN NOW, WHEN YOU'RE GONE, I STILL DEPEND ON YOU FOR SO MUCH.
山南敬助藤原知信墓
BUT I CAN'T HELP BUT COMPLAIN ABOUT THAT JERK!!
IT'S NOT LIKE I TOLD HIM HIS FACE WAS LIKE A STEPLADDER, OR HE GOT HIS FLAT FEATURES FROM PEOPLE STEPPING ON HIM.

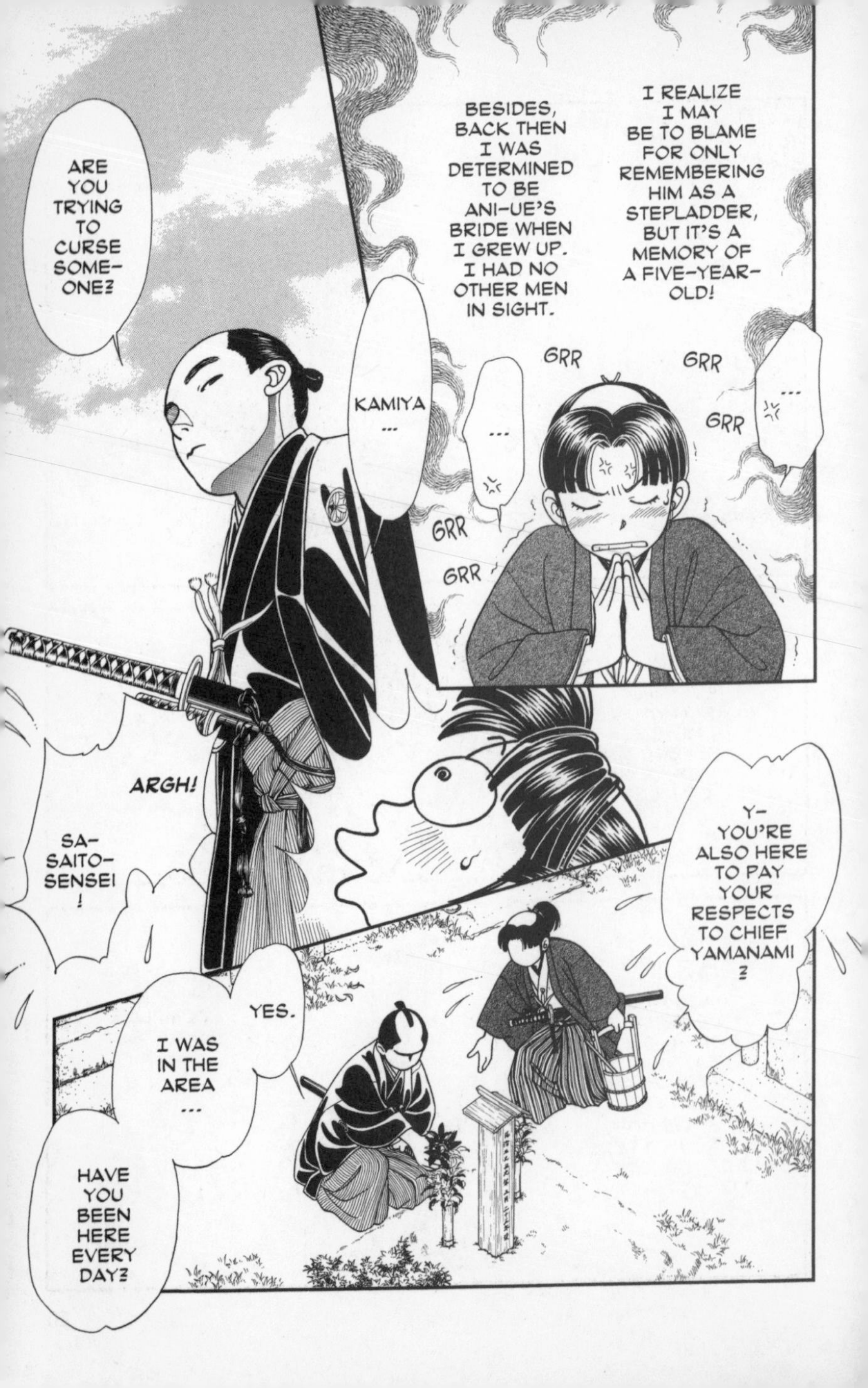

I REALIZE I MAY BE TO BLAME FOR ONLY REMEMBERING HIM AS A STEPLADDER, BUT IT'S A MEMORY OF A FIVE-YEAR-OLD!
BESIDES, BACK THEN I WAS DETERMINED TO BE ANI-UE'S BRIDE WHEN I GREW UP. I HAD NO OTHER MEN IN SIGHT.
GRR
GRR
GRR
...
...
GRR
GRR
KAMIYA ...
ARE YOU TRYING TO CURSE SOMEONE?
ARGH!
SA-SAITO-SENSEI!
Y-YOU'RE ALSO HERE TO PAY YOUR RESPECTS TO CHIEF YAMANAMI?
YES.
I WAS IN THE AREA ...
HAVE YOU BEEN HERE EVERY DAY?

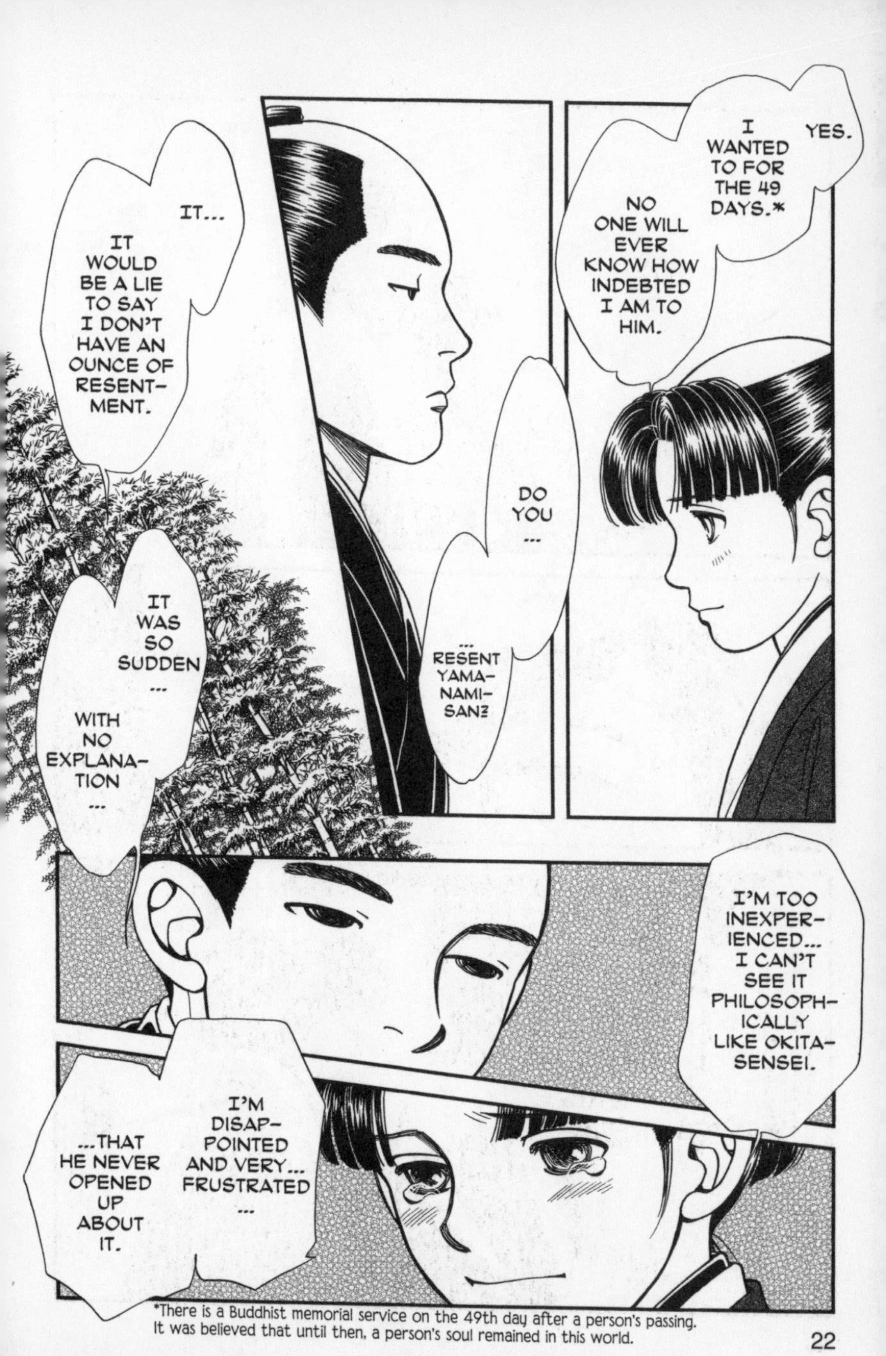
YES.
I WANTED TO FOR THE 49 DAYS.*
NO ONE WILL EVER KNOW HOW INDEBTED I AM TO HIM.
DO YOU ...
... RESENT YAMANAMI-SAN?
IT...
IT WOULD BE A LIE TO SAY I DON'T HAVE AN OUNCE OF RESENTMENT.
IT WAS SO SUDDEN ... WITH NO EXPLANATION ...
I'M TOO INEXPERIENCED... I CAN'T SEE IT PHILOSOPHICALLY LIKE OKITA-SENSEI.
I'M DISAPPOINTED AND VERY... FRUSTRATED ...
...THAT HE NEVER OPENED UP ABOUT IT.

*There is a Buddhist memorial service on the 49th day after a person's passing. It was believed that until then, a person's soul remained in this world.

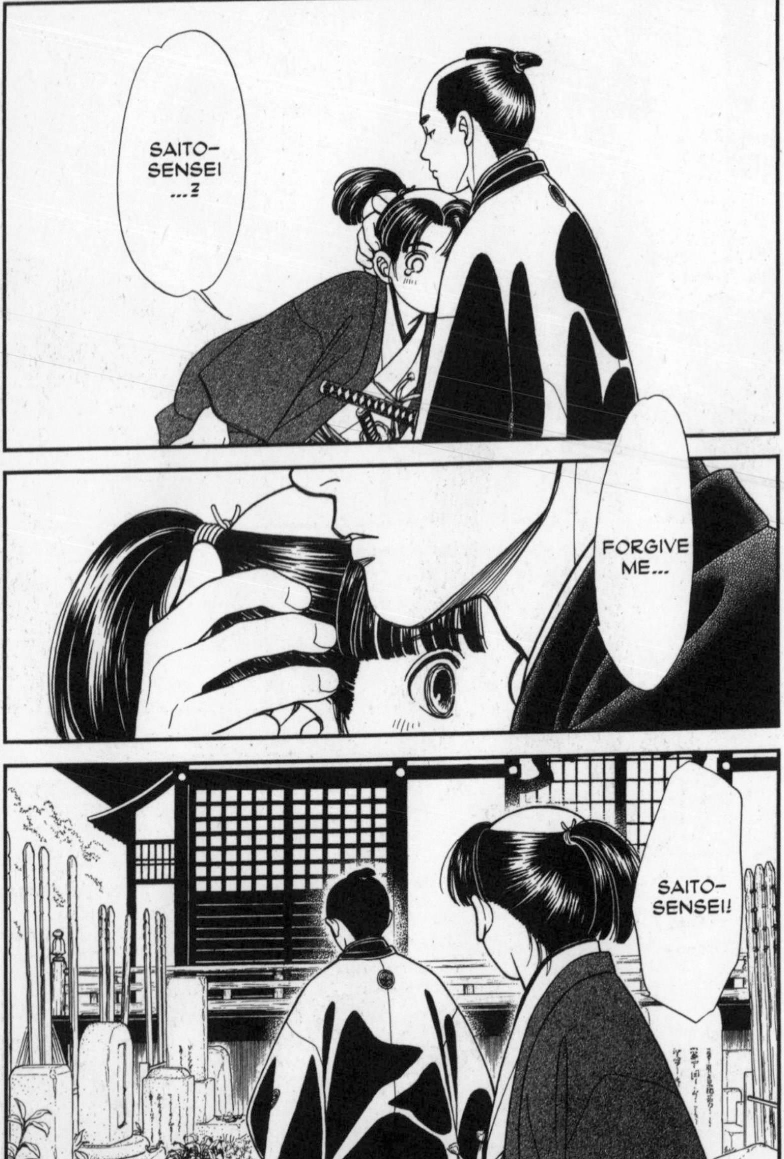
SAITO-SENSEI ...?
FORGIVE ME...
SAITO-SENSEI!

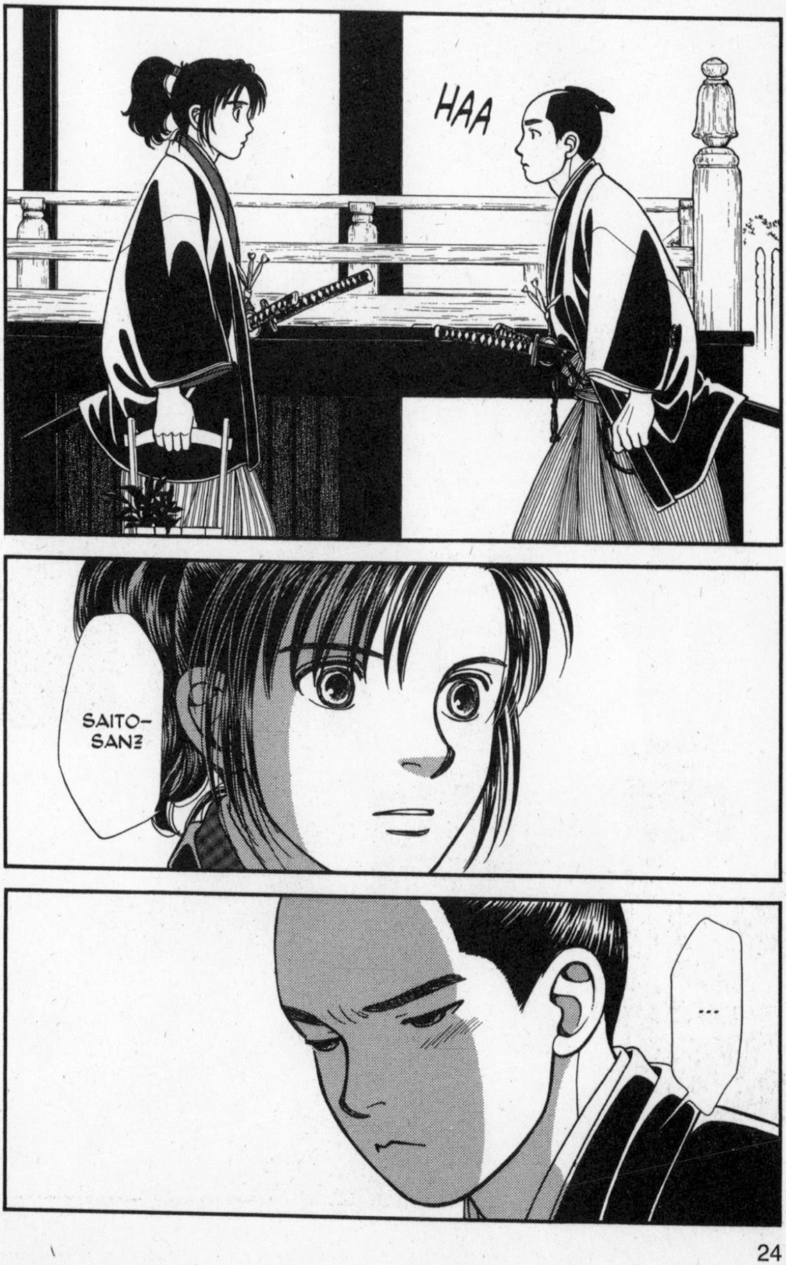
HAA
SAITO-SAN?
...

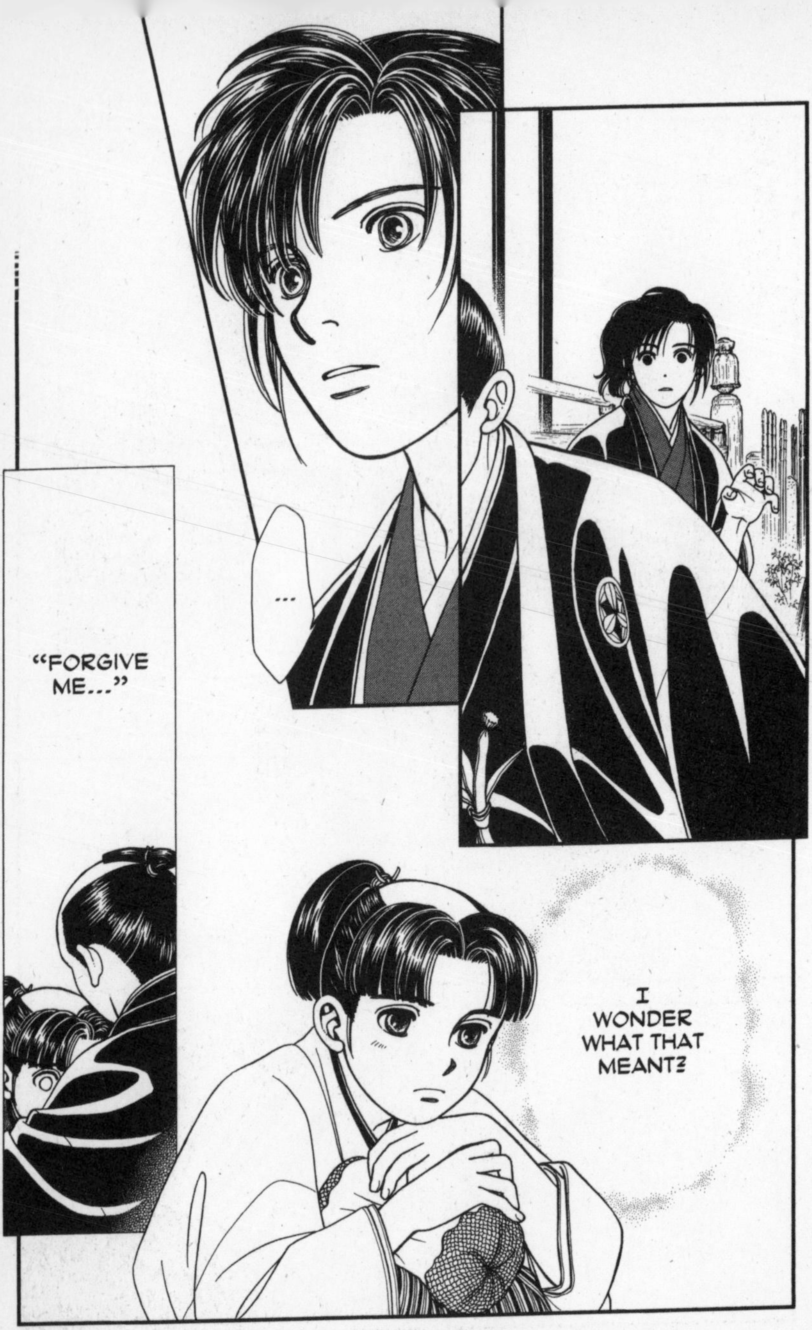
...
"FORGIVE ME..."
I WONDER WHAT THAT MEANT?

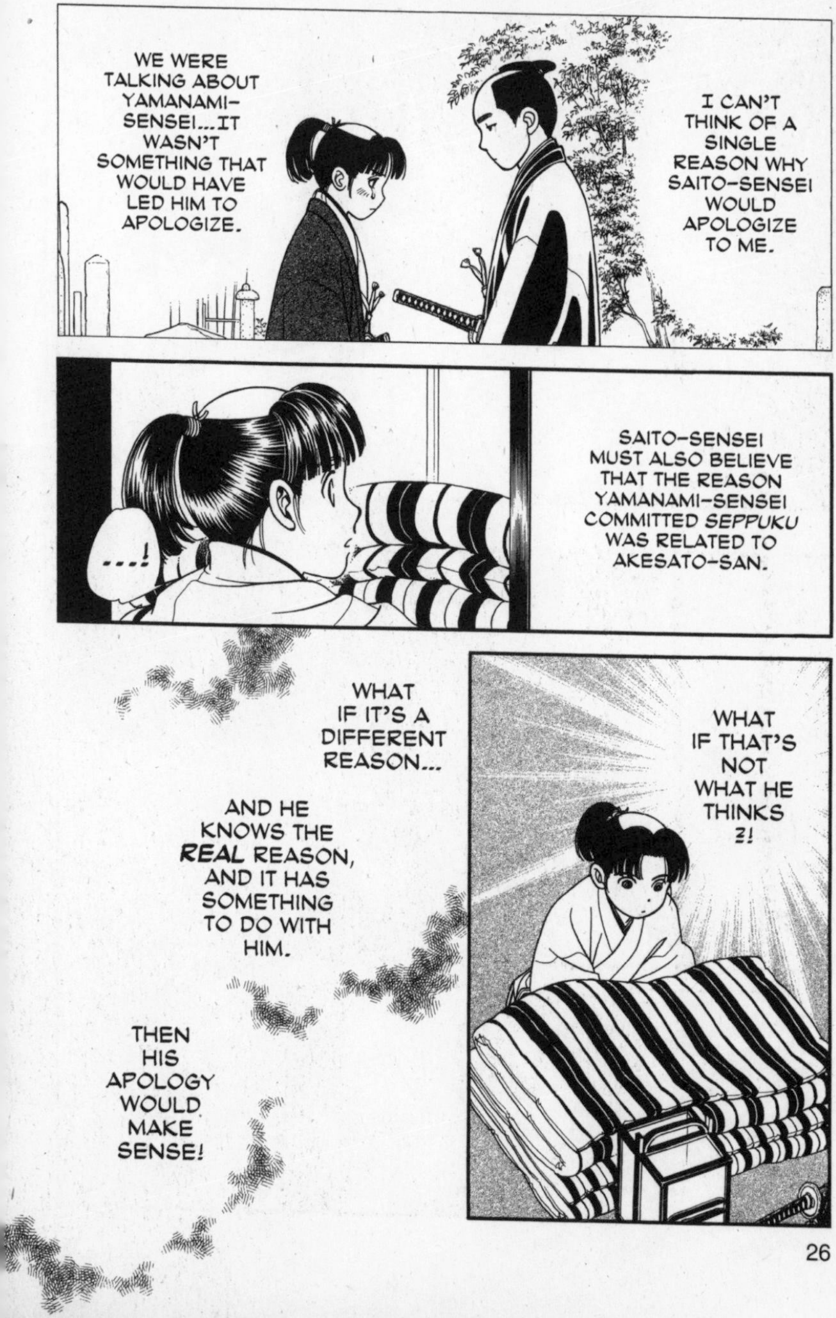
I CAN'T THINK OF A SINGLE REASON WHY SAITO-SENSEI WOULD APOLOGIZE TO ME.
WE WERE TALKING ABOUT YAMANAMI-SENSEI...IT WASN'T SOMETHING THAT WOULD HAVE LED HIM TO APOLOGIZE.
SAITO-SENSEI MUST ALSO BELIEVE THAT THE REASON YAMANAMI-SENSEI COMMITTED *SEPPUKU* WAS RELATED TO AKESATO-SAN.
...!
WHAT IF THAT'S NOT WHAT HE THINKS?!
WHAT IF IT'S A DIFFERENT REASON...
AND HE KNOWS THE ***REAL*** REASON, AND IT HAS SOMETHING TO DO WITH HIM.
THEN HIS APOLOGY WOULD MAKE SENSE!

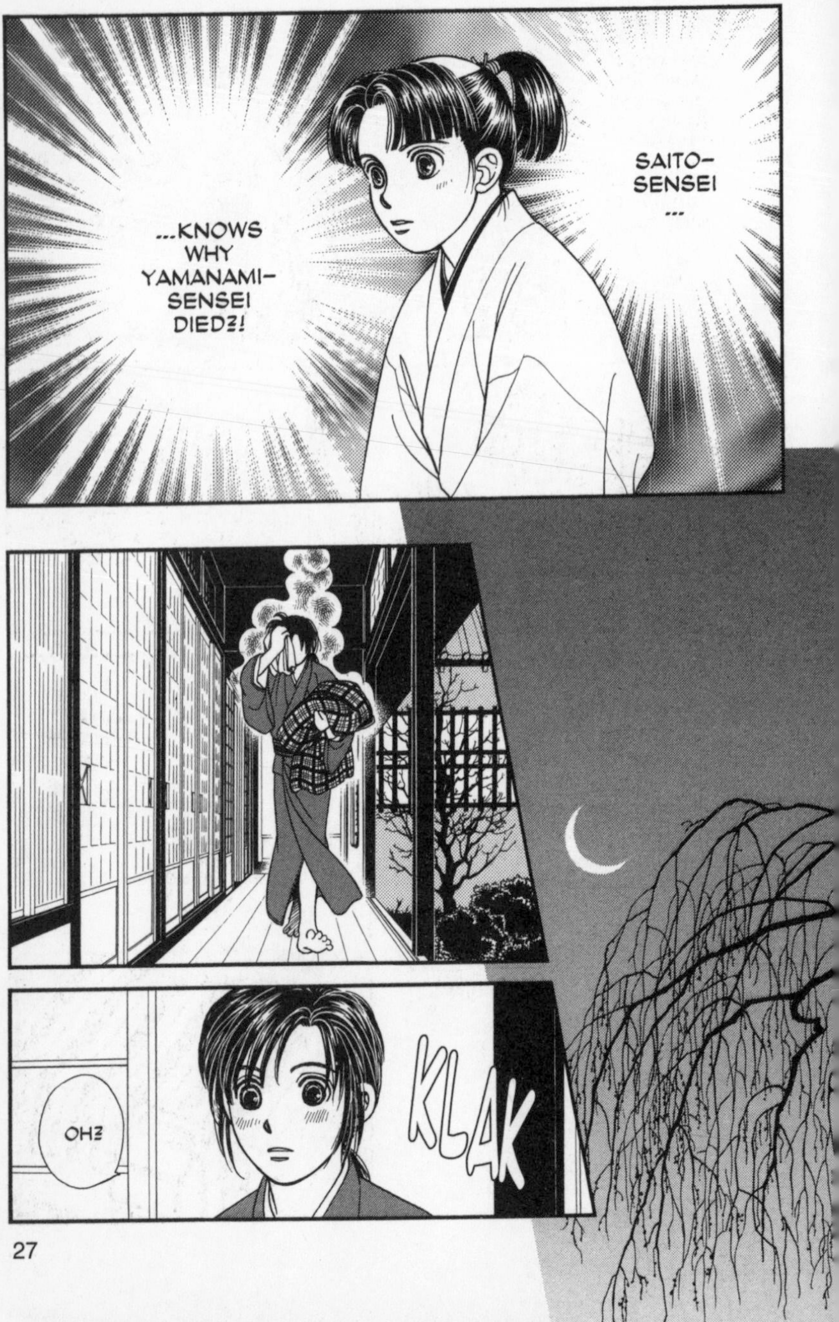
SAITO-
SENSEI
...
...KNOWS
WHY
YAMANAMI-
SENSEI
DIED?!
KLAK
OH?

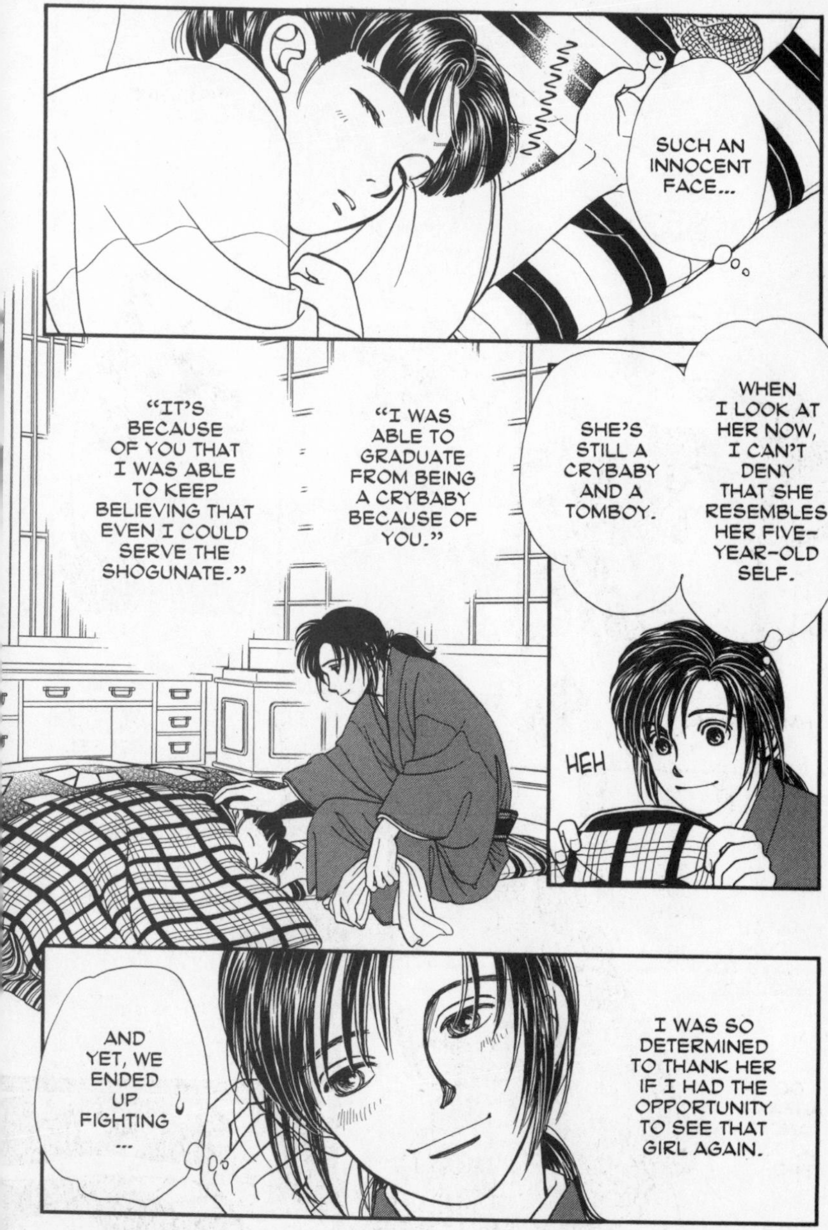
SUCH AN INNOCENT FACE...
WHEN I LOOK AT HER NOW, I CAN'T DENY THAT SHE RESEMBLES HER FIVE-YEAR-OLD SELF.
SHE'S STILL A CRYBABY AND A TOMBOY.
HEH
"I WAS ABLE TO GRADUATE FROM BEING A CRYBABY BECAUSE OF YOU."
"IT'S BECAUSE OF YOU THAT I WAS ABLE TO KEEP BELIEVING THAT EVEN I COULD SERVE THE SHOGUNATE."
I WAS SO DETERMINED TO THANK HER IF I HAD THE OPPORTUNITY TO SEE THAT GIRL AGAIN.
AND YET, WE ENDED UP FIGHTING ...

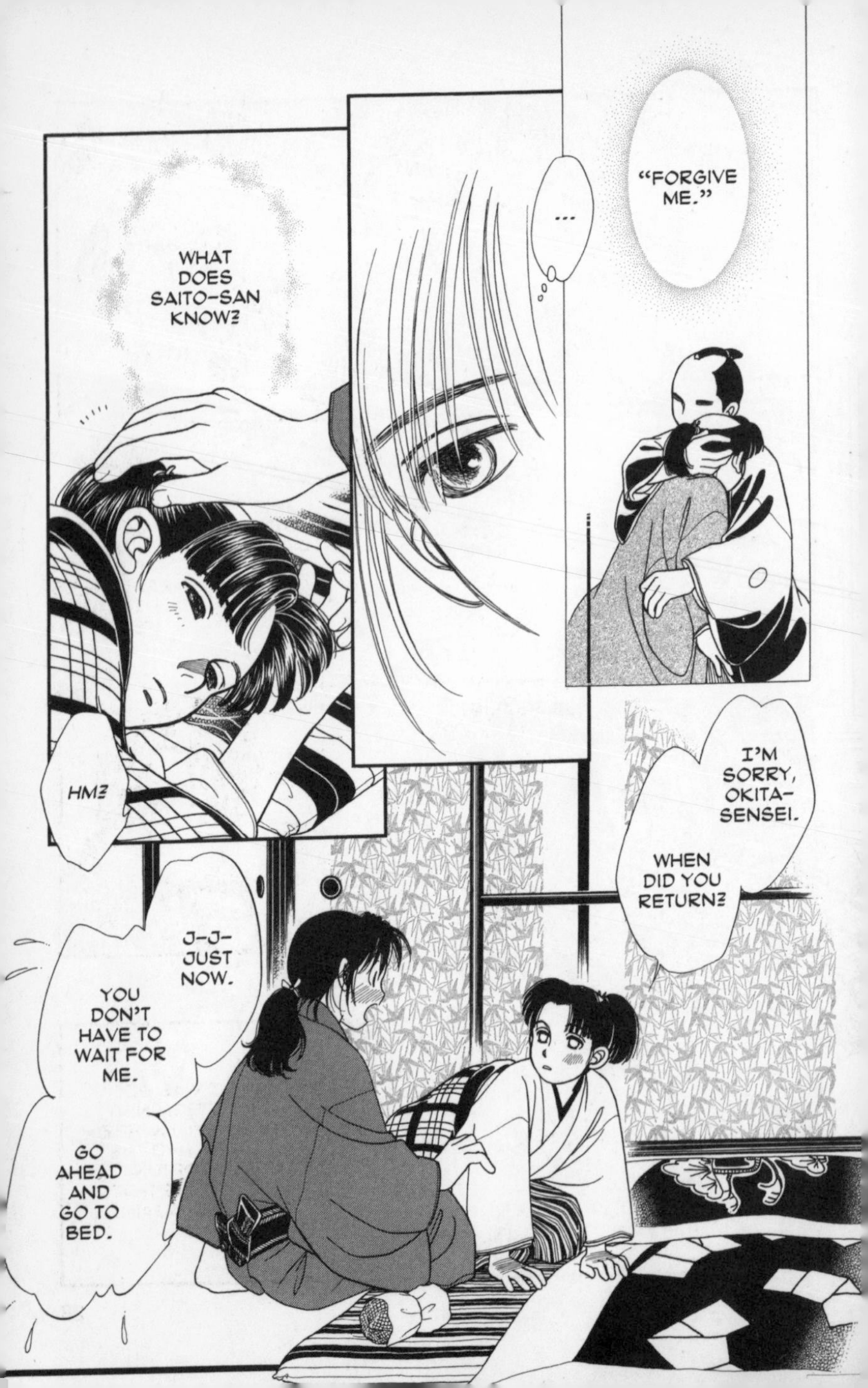
"FORGIVE ME."
...
WHAT DOES SAITO-SAN KNOW?
HM?
I'M SORRY, OKITA-SENSEI.
WHEN DID YOU RETURN?
J-J-JUST NOW.
YOU DON'T HAVE TO WAIT FOR ME.
GO AHEAD AND GO TO BED.

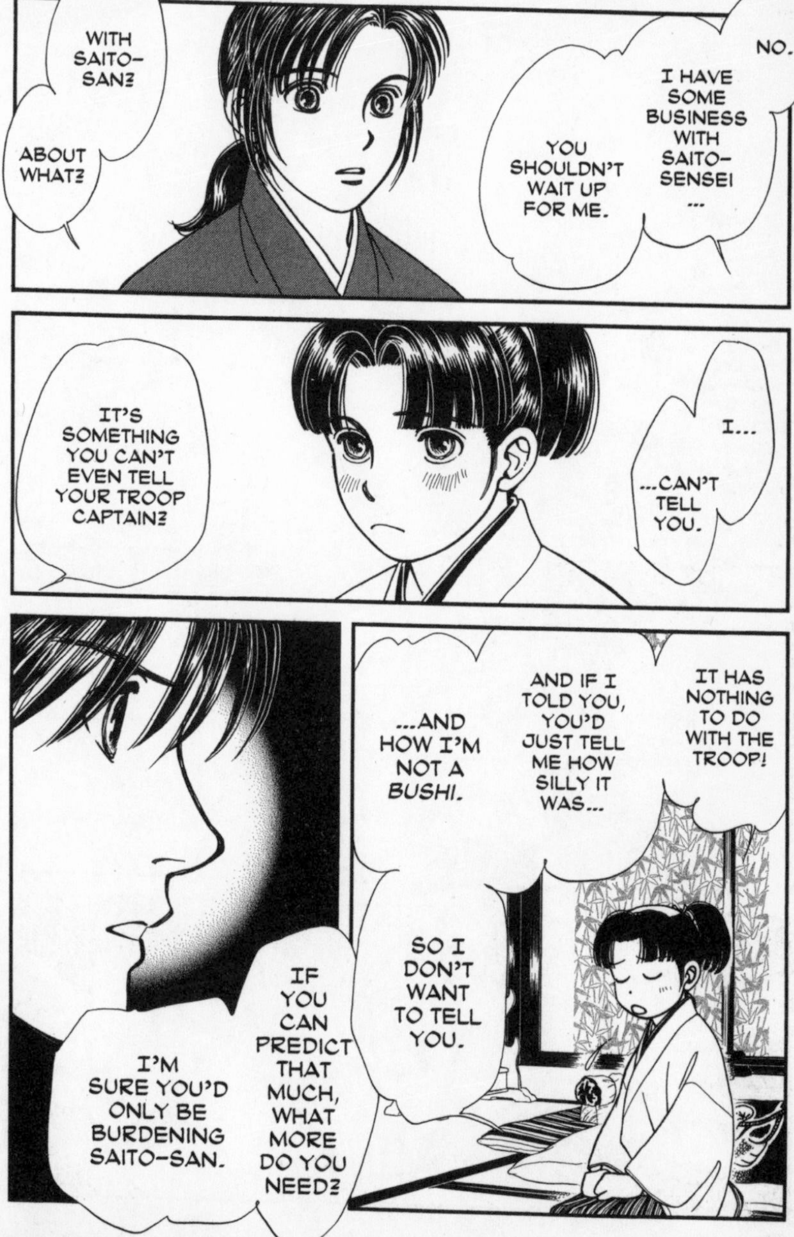
NO.
I HAVE SOME BUSINESS WITH SAITO-SENSEI ...
YOU SHOULDN'T WAIT UP FOR ME.
WITH SAITO-SAN?
ABOUT WHAT?
I...
...CAN'T TELL YOU.
IT'S SOMETHING YOU CAN'T EVEN TELL YOUR TROOP CAPTAIN?
IT HAS NOTHING TO DO WITH THE TROOP!
AND IF I TOLD YOU, YOU'D JUST TELL ME HOW SILLY IT WAS...
...AND HOW I'M NOT A *BUSHI*.
SO I DON'T WANT TO TELL YOU.
IF YOU CAN PREDICT THAT MUCH, WHAT MORE DO YOU NEED?
I'M SURE YOU'D ONLY BE BURDENING SAITO-SAN.

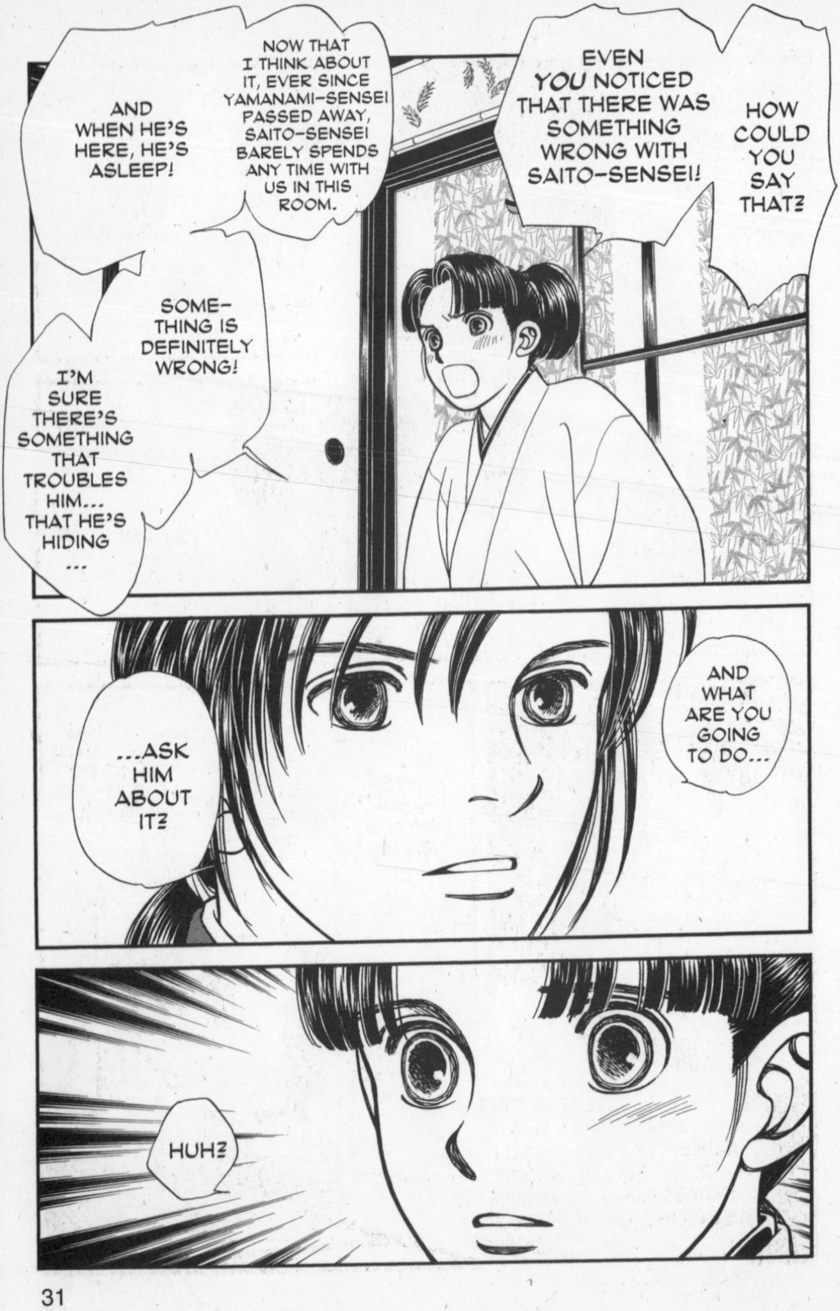
HOW COULD YOU SAY THAT?
EVEN *YOU* NOTICED THAT THERE WAS SOMETHING WRONG WITH SAITO-SENSEI!
NOW THAT I THINK ABOUT IT, EVER SINCE YAMANAMI-SENSEI PASSED AWAY, SAITO-SENSEI BARELY SPENDS ANY TIME WITH US IN THIS ROOM.
AND WHEN HE'S HERE, HE'S ASLEEP!
SOME-THING IS DEFINITELY WRONG!
I'M SURE THERE'S SOMETHING THAT TROUBLES HIM... THAT HE'S HIDING ...
AND WHAT ARE YOU GOING TO DO...
...ASK HIM ABOUT IT?
HUH?

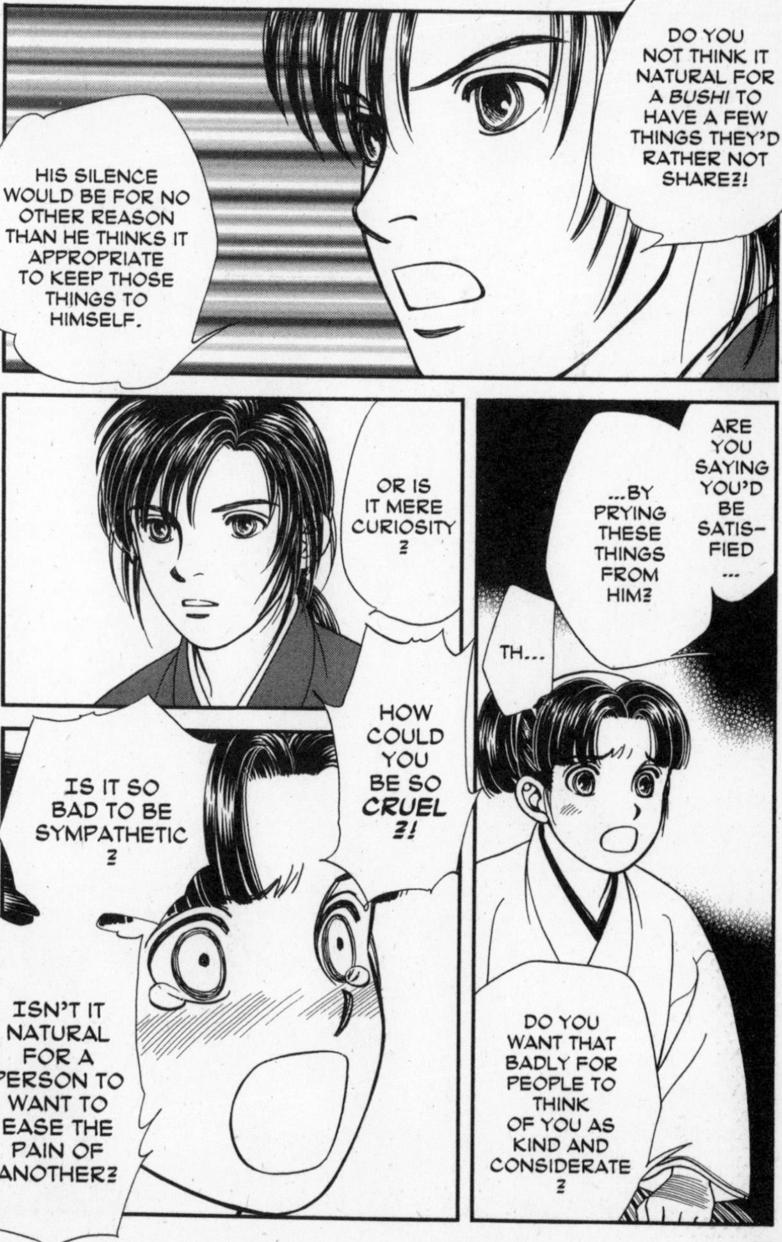
DO YOU NOT THINK IT NATURAL FOR A *BUSHI* TO HAVE A FEW THINGS THEY'D RATHER NOT SHARE?!
HIS SILENCE WOULD BE FOR NO OTHER REASON THAN HE THINKS IT APPROPRIATE TO KEEP THOSE THINGS TO HIMSELF.
ARE YOU SAYING YOU'D BE SATISFIED...
...BY PRYING THESE THINGS FROM HIM?
TH...
DO YOU WANT THAT BADLY FOR PEOPLE TO THINK OF YOU AS KIND AND CONSIDERATE?
OR IS IT MERE CURIOSITY?
HOW COULD YOU BE SO **CRUEL**?!
IS IT SO BAD TO BE SYMPATHETIC?
ISN'T IT NATURAL FOR A PERSON TO WANT TO EASE THE PAIN OF ANOTHER?

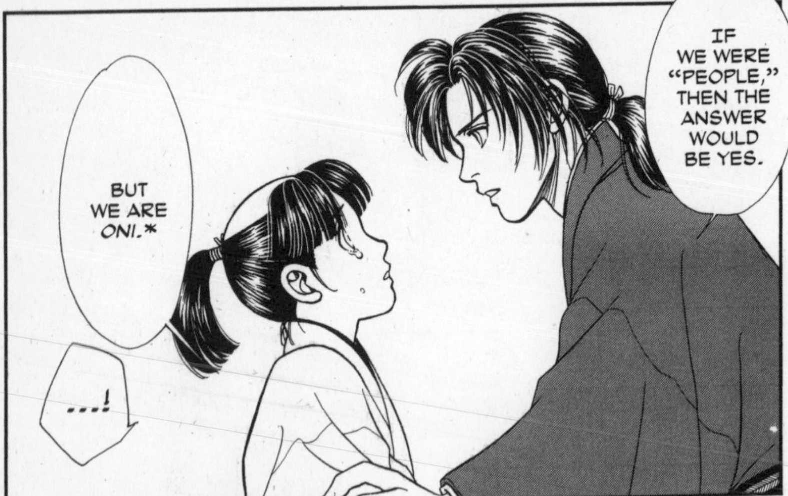
IF WE WERE "PEOPLE," THEN THE ANSWER WOULD BE YES.
BUT WE ARE ONI.*
...!

*An ogre or devil

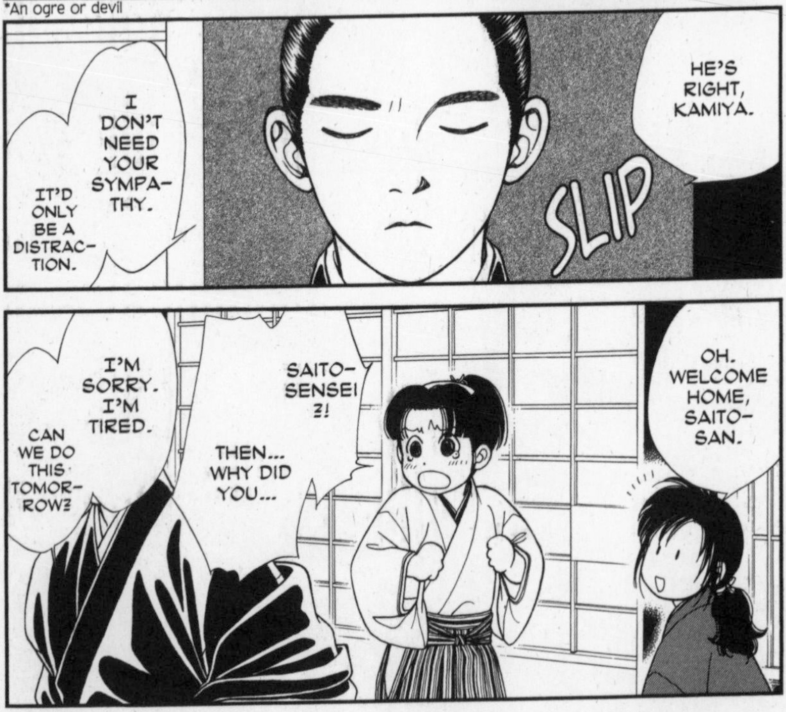
HE'S RIGHT, KAMIYA.
SLIP
I DON'T NEED YOUR SYMPATHY.
IT'D ONLY BE A DISTRACTION.
OH. WELCOME HOME, SAITO-SAN.
SAITO-SENSEI?!
THEN... WHY DID YOU...
I'M SORRY. I'M TIRED.
CAN WE DO THIS TOMORROW?

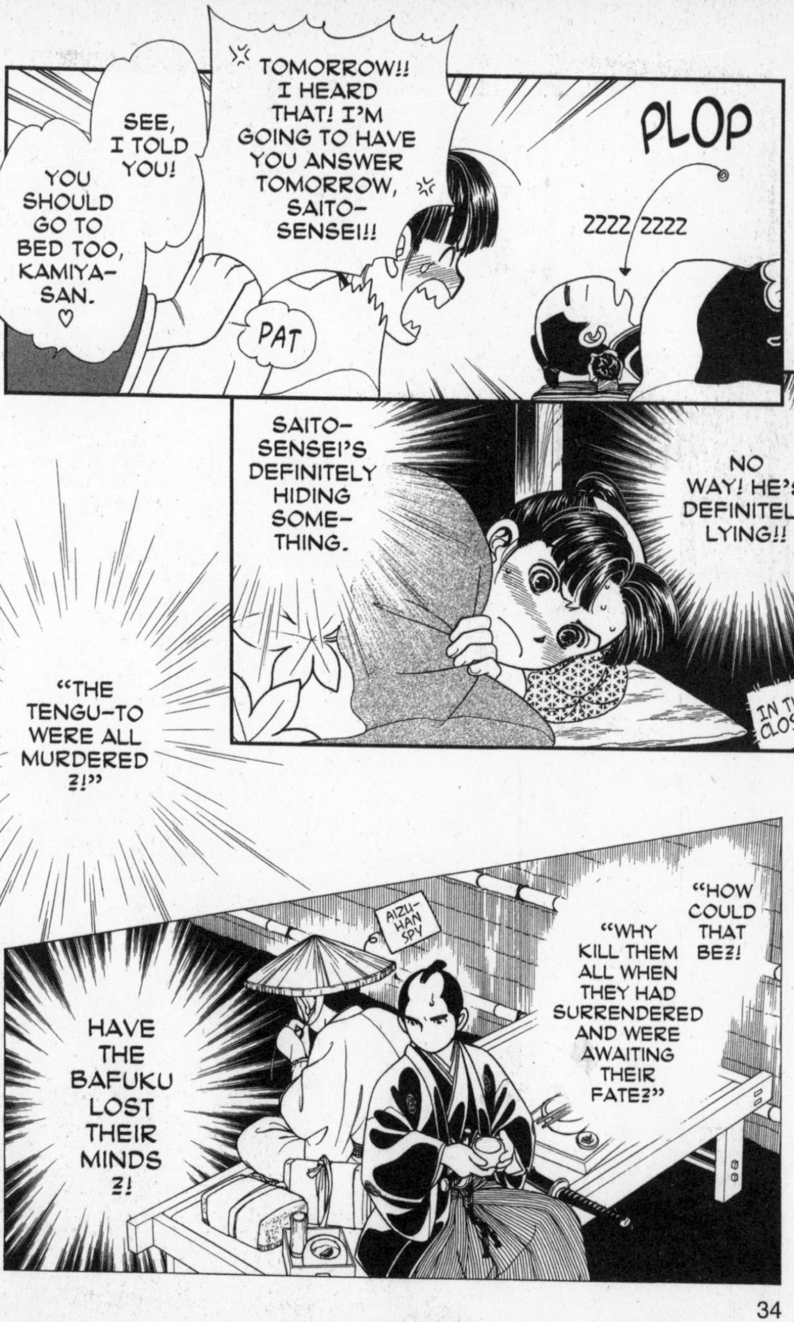
PLOP
ZZZZ ZZZZ
TOMORROW!! I HEARD THAT! I'M GOING TO HAVE YOU ANSWER TOMORROW, SAITO-SENSEI!!
SEE, I TOLD YOU!
YOU SHOULD GO TO BED TOO, KAMIYA-SAN. ♡
PAT
NO WAY! HE'S DEFINITELY LYING!!
SAITO-SENSEI'S DEFINITELY HIDING SOME-THING.
IN THE CLOSET.
"THE TENGU-TO WERE ALL MURDERED?!"
"HOW COULD THAT BE?!
"WHY KILL THEM ALL WHEN THEY HAD SURRENDERED AND WERE AWAITING THEIR FATE?"
AIZU-HAN SPY
HAVE THE BAFUKU LOST THEIR MINDS?!

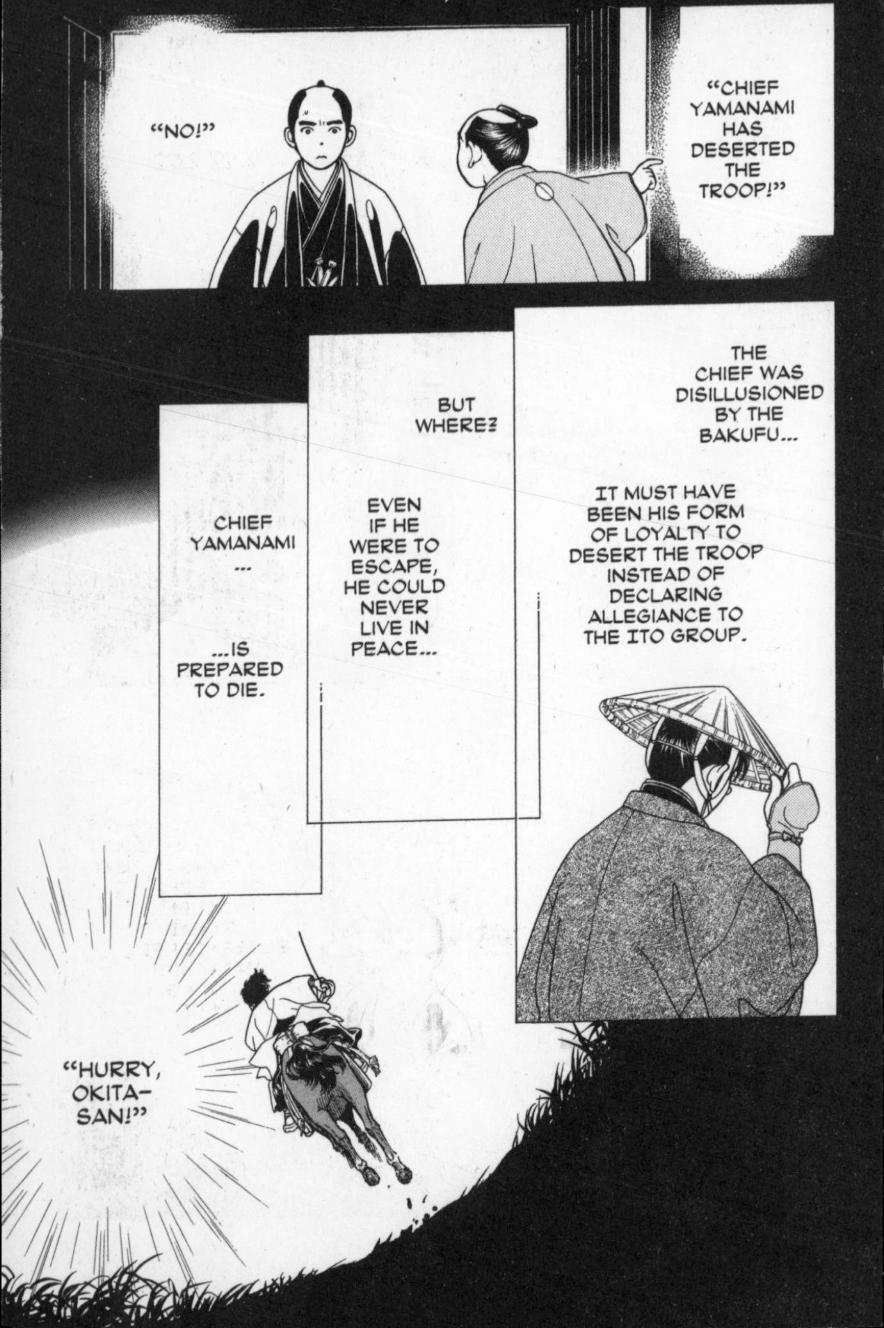
"CHIEF YAMANAMI HAS DESERTED THE TROOP!"
"NO!"
THE CHIEF WAS DISILLUSIONED BY THE BAKUFU...
IT MUST HAVE BEEN HIS FORM OF LOYALTY TO DESERT THE TROOP INSTEAD OF DECLARING ALLEGIANCE TO THE ITO GROUP.
BUT WHERE?
EVEN IF HE WERE TO ESCAPE, HE COULD NEVER LIVE IN PEACE...
CHIEF YAMANAMI ...
...IS PREPARED TO DIE.
"HURRY, OKITA-SAN!"

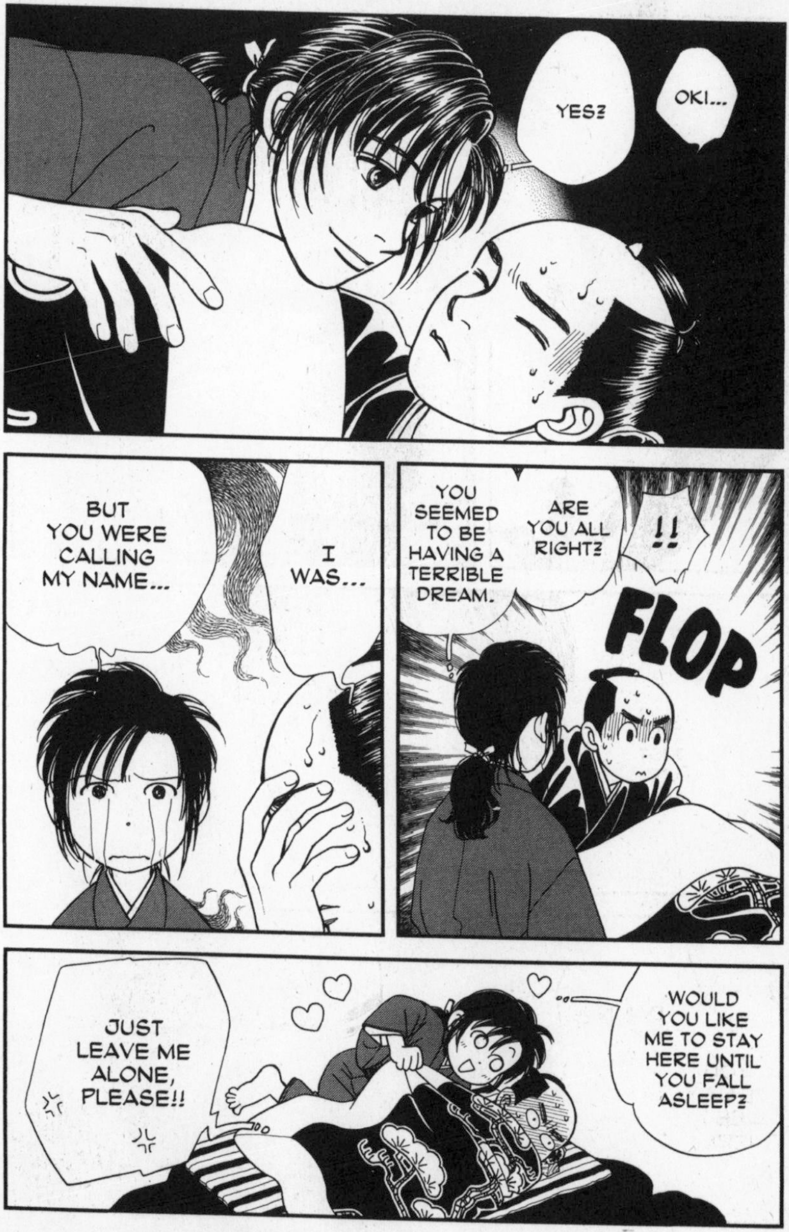
OKI...
YES?
!!
ARE YOU ALL RIGHT?
YOU SEEMED TO BE HAVING A TERRIBLE DREAM.
FLOP
I WAS...
BUT YOU WERE CALLING MY NAME...
WOULD YOU LIKE ME TO STAY HERE UNTIL YOU FALL ASLEEP?
JUST LEAVE ME ALONE, PLEASE!!

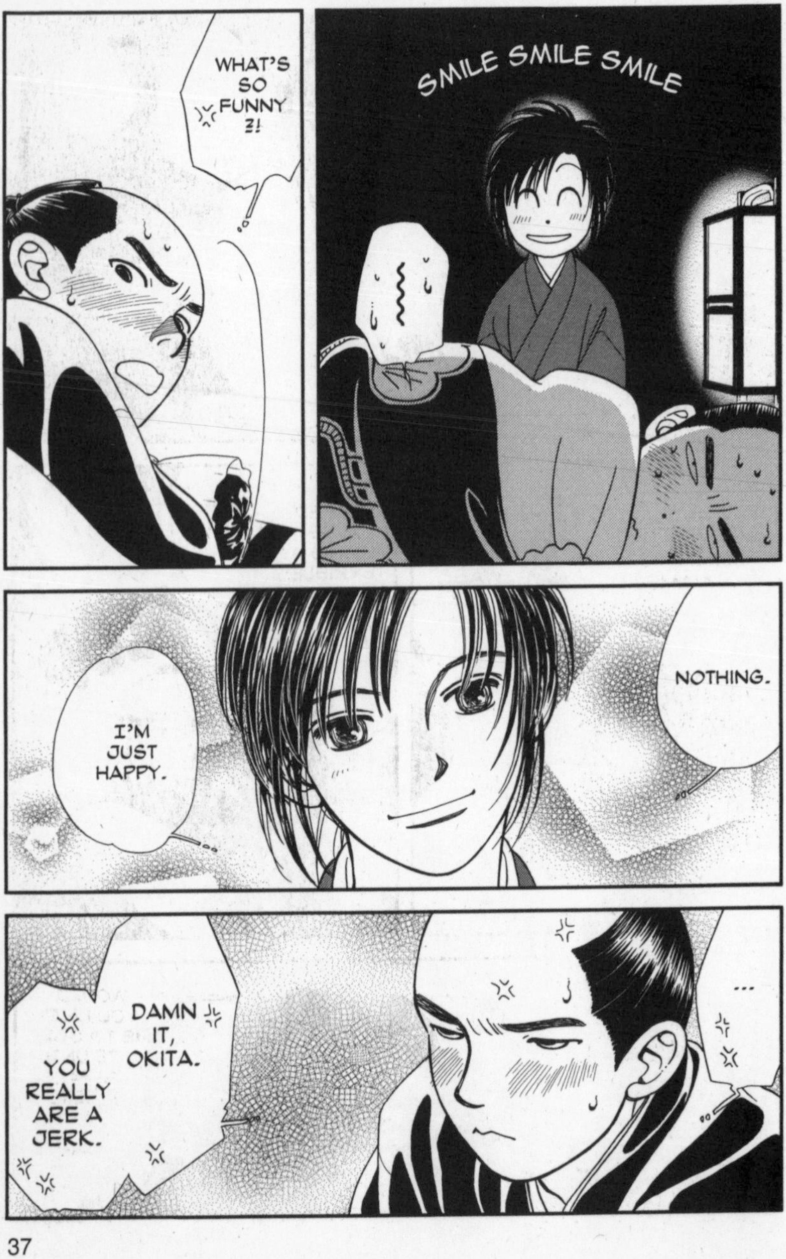
SMILE SMILE SMILE
WHAT'S SO FUNNY ?!
NOTHING.
I'M JUST HAPPY.
...
DAMN IT, OKITA.
YOU REALLY ARE A JERK.

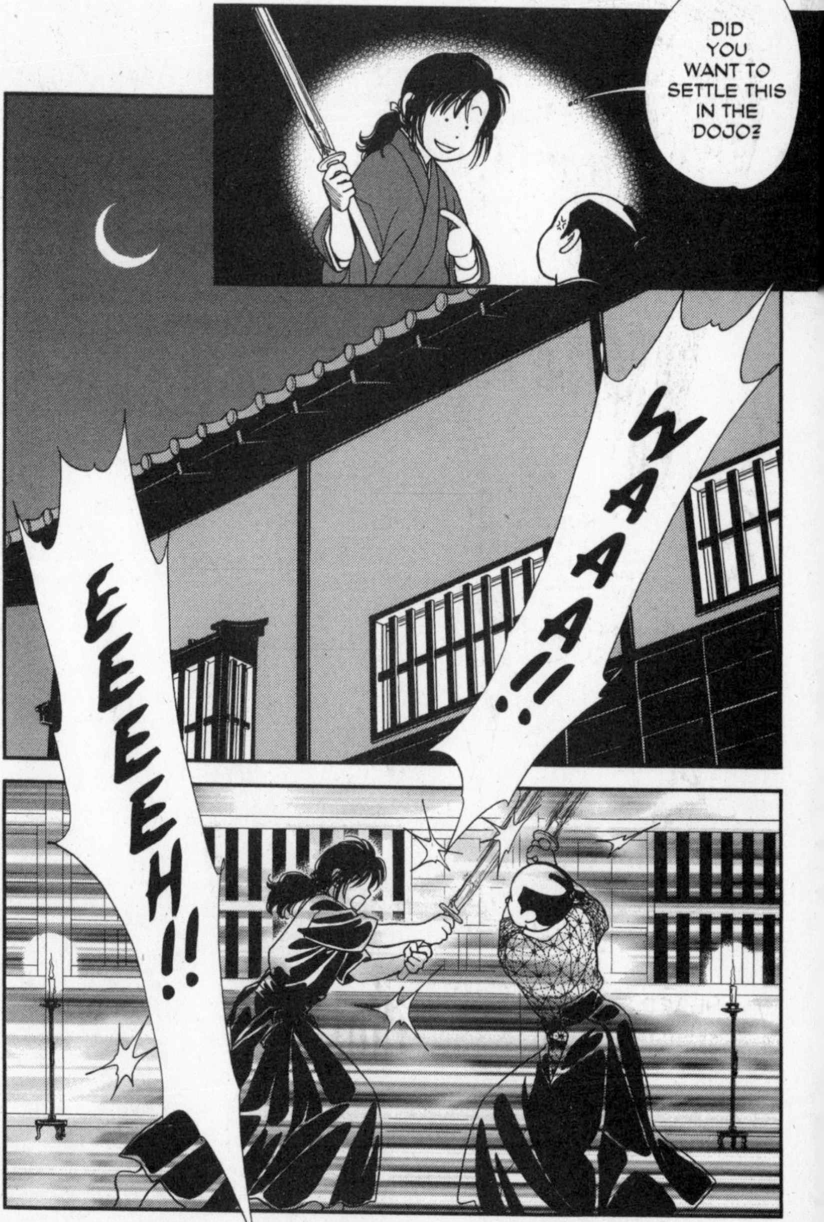
DID YOU WANT TO SETTLE THIS IN THE DOJO?
WAAAA!!
EEEEEH!!

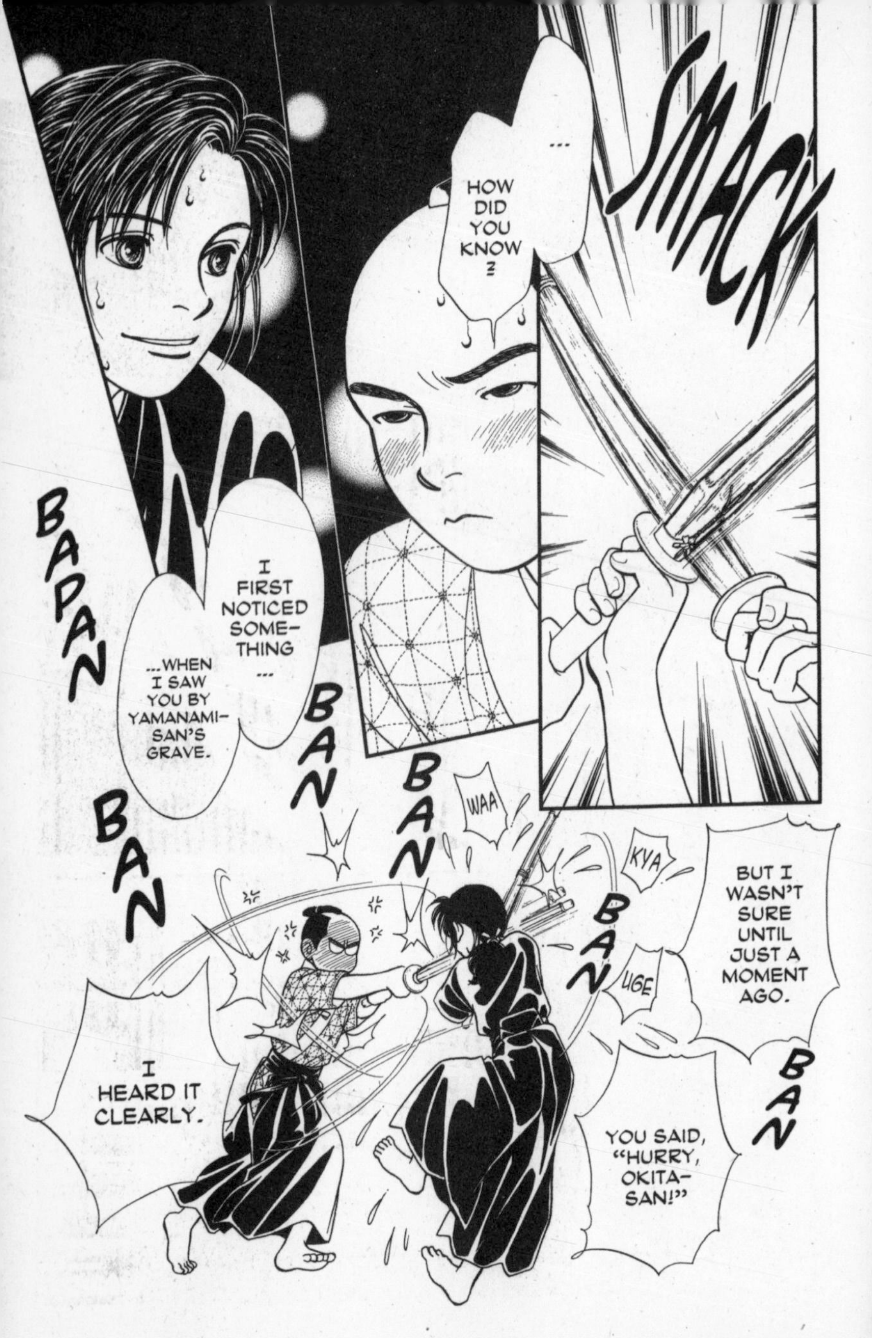
SMACK
...
HOW DID YOU KNOW?
I FIRST NOTICED SOME-THING ...
...WHEN I SAW YOU BY YAMANAMI-SAN'S GRAVE.
BAPAN
BAN
BAN
BAN
BAN
BAN
WAA
KYA
UGE
BUT I WASN'T SURE UNTIL JUST A MOMENT AGO.
BAN
YOU SAID, "HURRY, OKITA-SAN!"
I HEARD IT CLEARLY.

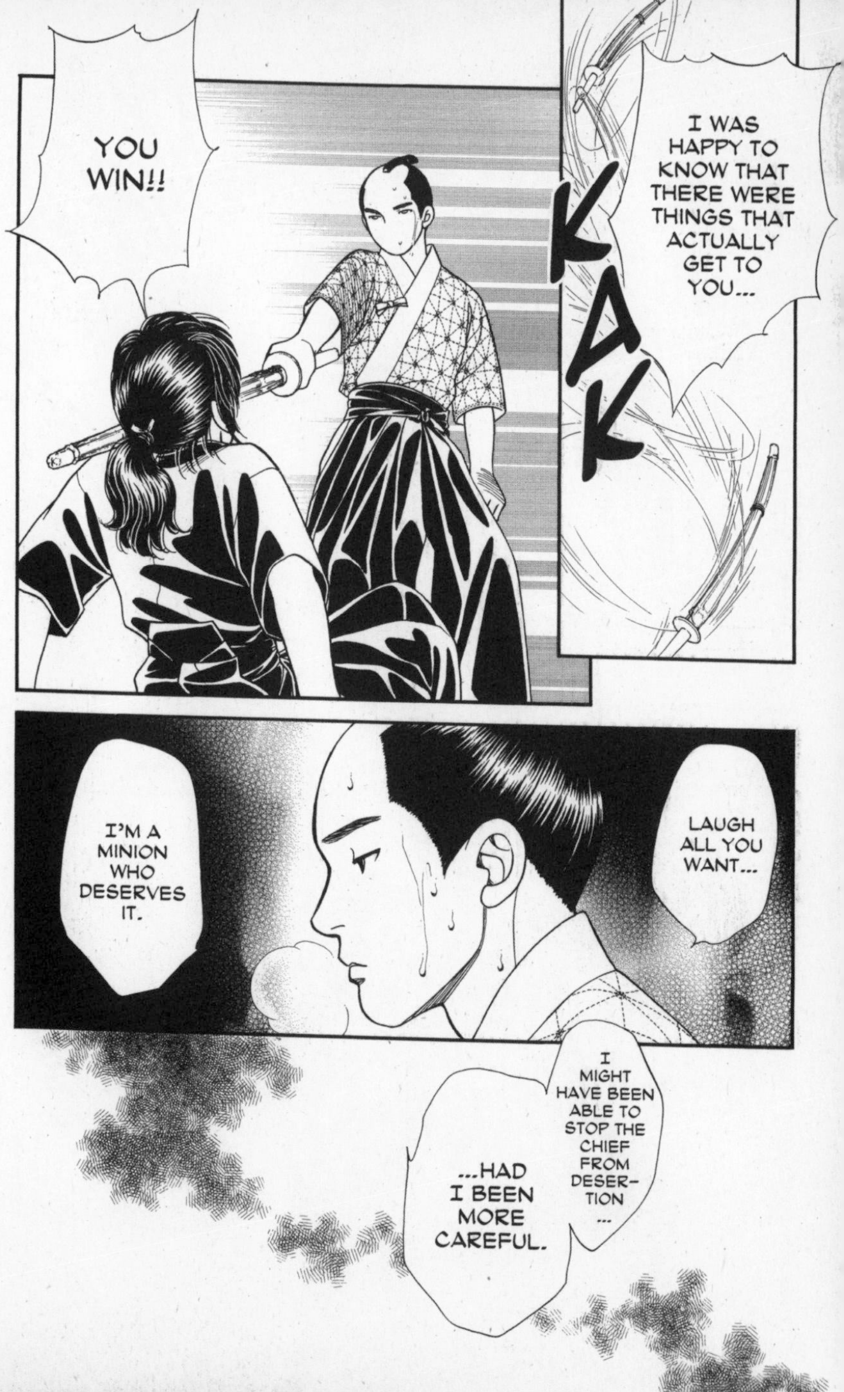
I WAS HAPPY TO KNOW THAT THERE WERE THINGS THAT ACTUALLY GET TO YOU...
KAK
YOU WIN!!
LAUGH ALL YOU WANT...
I'M A MINION WHO DESERVES IT.
I MIGHT HAVE BEEN ABLE TO STOP THE CHIEF FROM DESERTION...
...HAD I BEEN MORE CAREFUL.

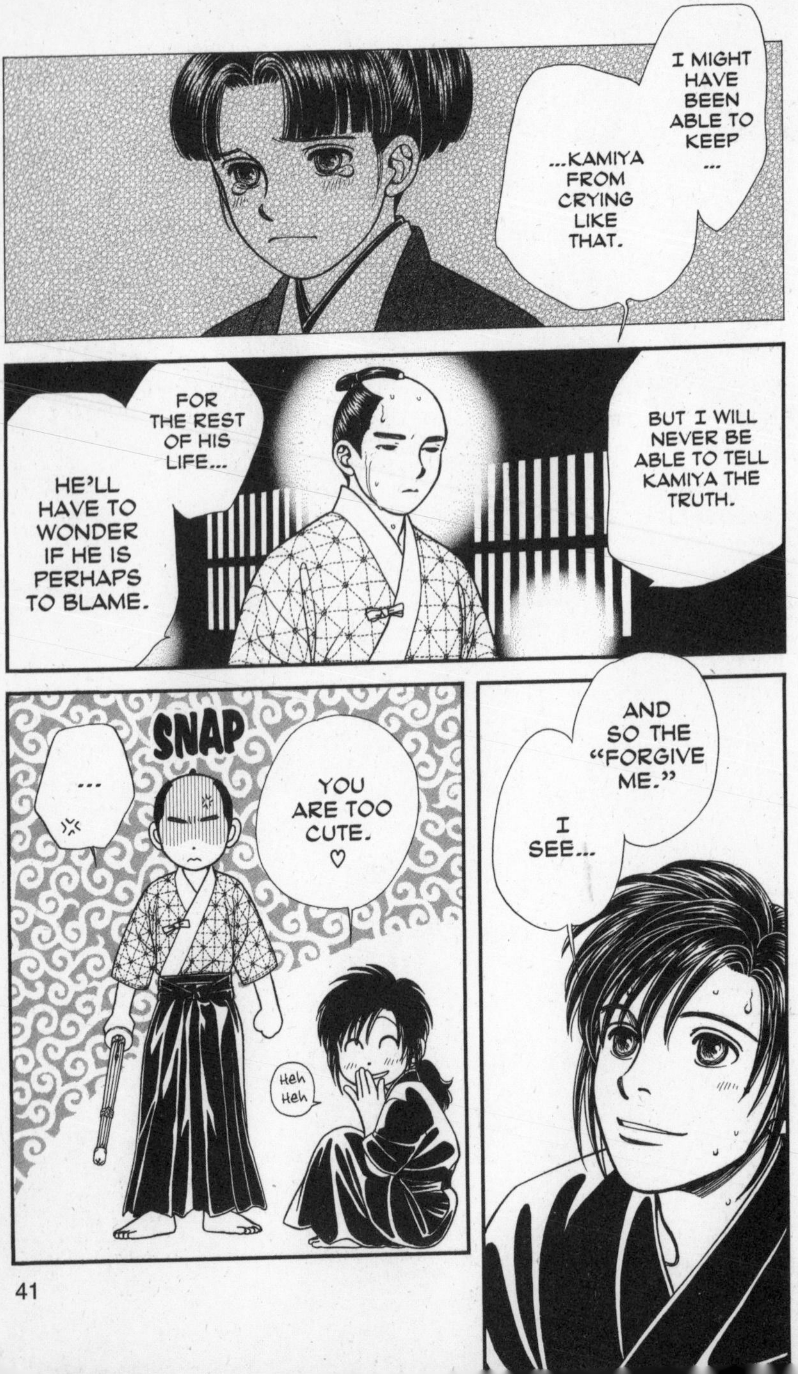
I MIGHT HAVE BEEN ABLE TO KEEP ...
...KAMIYA FROM CRYING LIKE THAT.
BUT I WILL NEVER BE ABLE TO TELL KAMIYA THE TRUTH.
FOR THE REST OF HIS LIFE...
HE'LL HAVE TO WONDER IF HE IS PERHAPS TO BLAME.
AND SO THE "FORGIVE ME."
I SEE...
YOU ARE TOO CUTE. ♡
SNAP
...
Heh Heh

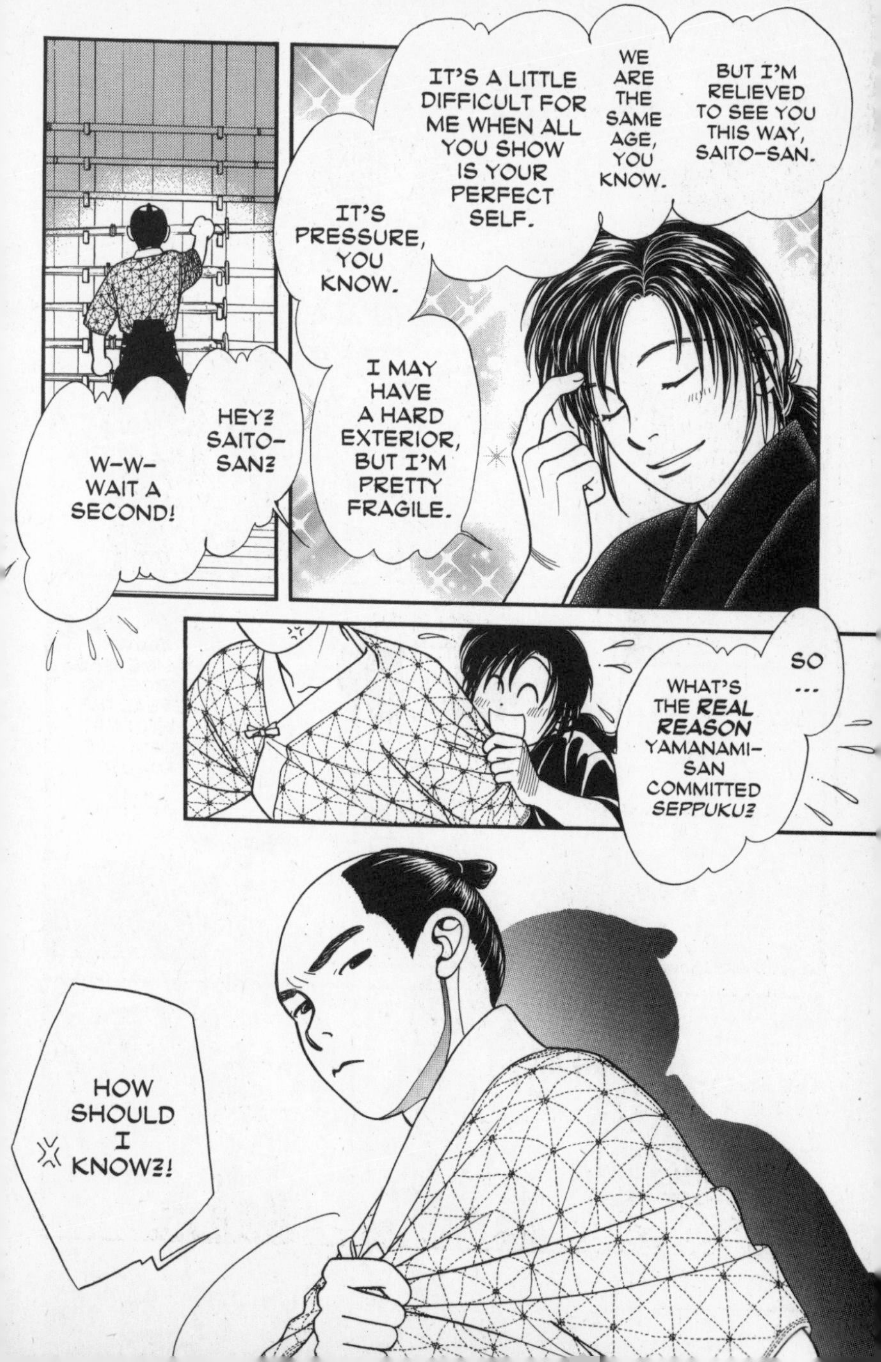
BUT I'M RELIEVED TO SEE YOU THIS WAY, SAITO-SAN.
WE ARE THE SAME AGE, YOU KNOW.
IT'S A LITTLE DIFFICULT FOR ME WHEN ALL YOU SHOW IS YOUR PERFECT SELF.
IT'S PRESSURE, YOU KNOW.
I MAY HAVE A HARD EXTERIOR, BUT I'M PRETTY FRAGILE.
HEY? SAITO-SAN?
W-W-WAIT A SECOND!
SO ...
WHAT'S THE *REAL REASON* YAMANAMI-SAN COMMITTED *SEPPUKU*?
HOW SHOULD I KNOW?!

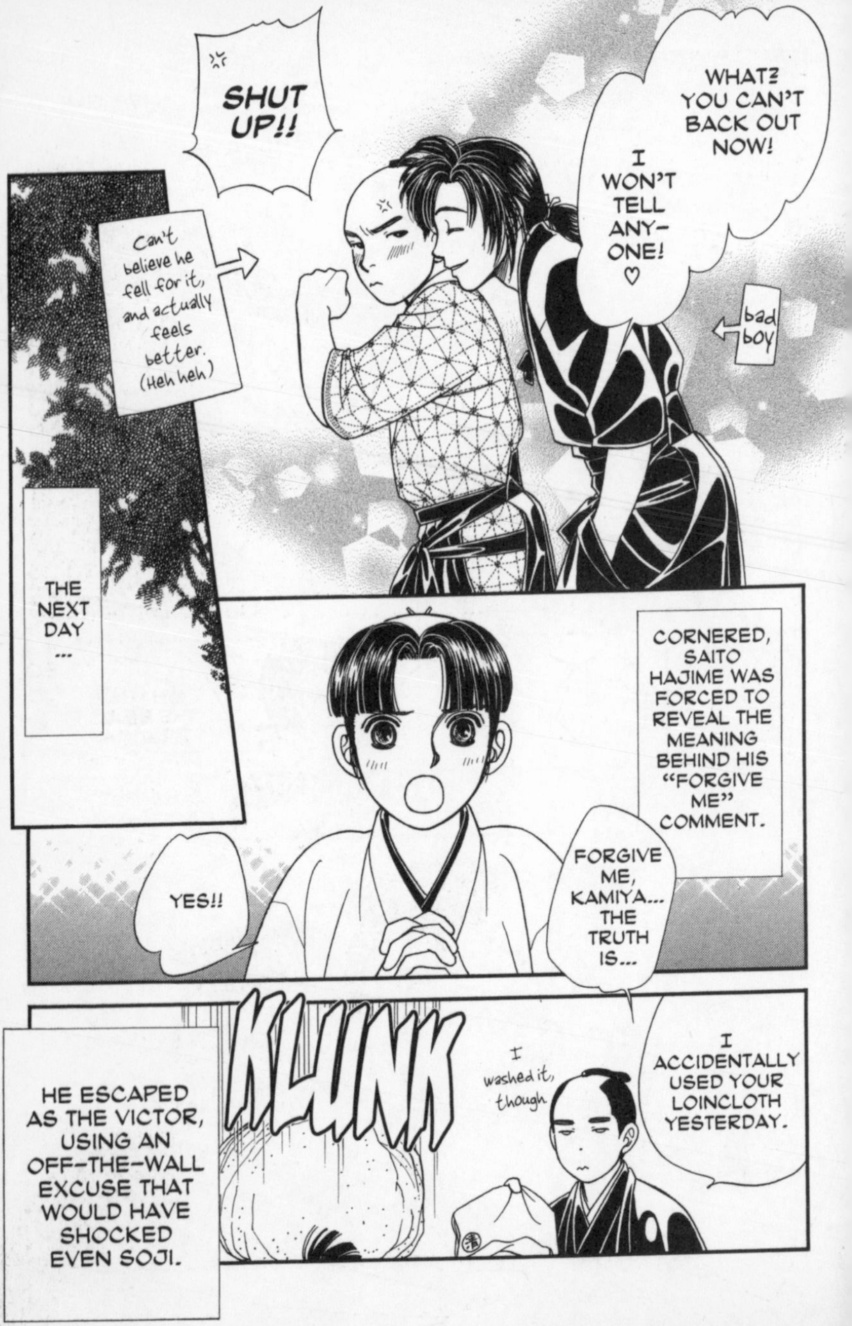
WHAT? YOU CAN'T BACK OUT NOW!
I WON'T TELL ANY-ONE! ♡
bad boy
SHUT UP!!
Can't believe he fell for it, and actually feels better. (Heh heh)
THE NEXT DAY ...
CORNERED, SAITO HAJIME WAS FORCED TO REVEAL THE MEANING BEHIND HIS "FORGIVE ME" COMMENT.
FORGIVE ME, KAMIYA... THE TRUTH IS...
YES!!
I ACCIDENTALLY USED YOUR LOINCLOTH YESTERDAY.
I washed it, though.
KLUNK
HE ESCAPED AS THE VICTOR, USING AN OFF-THE-WALL EXCUSE THAT WOULD HAVE SHOCKED EVEN SOJI.

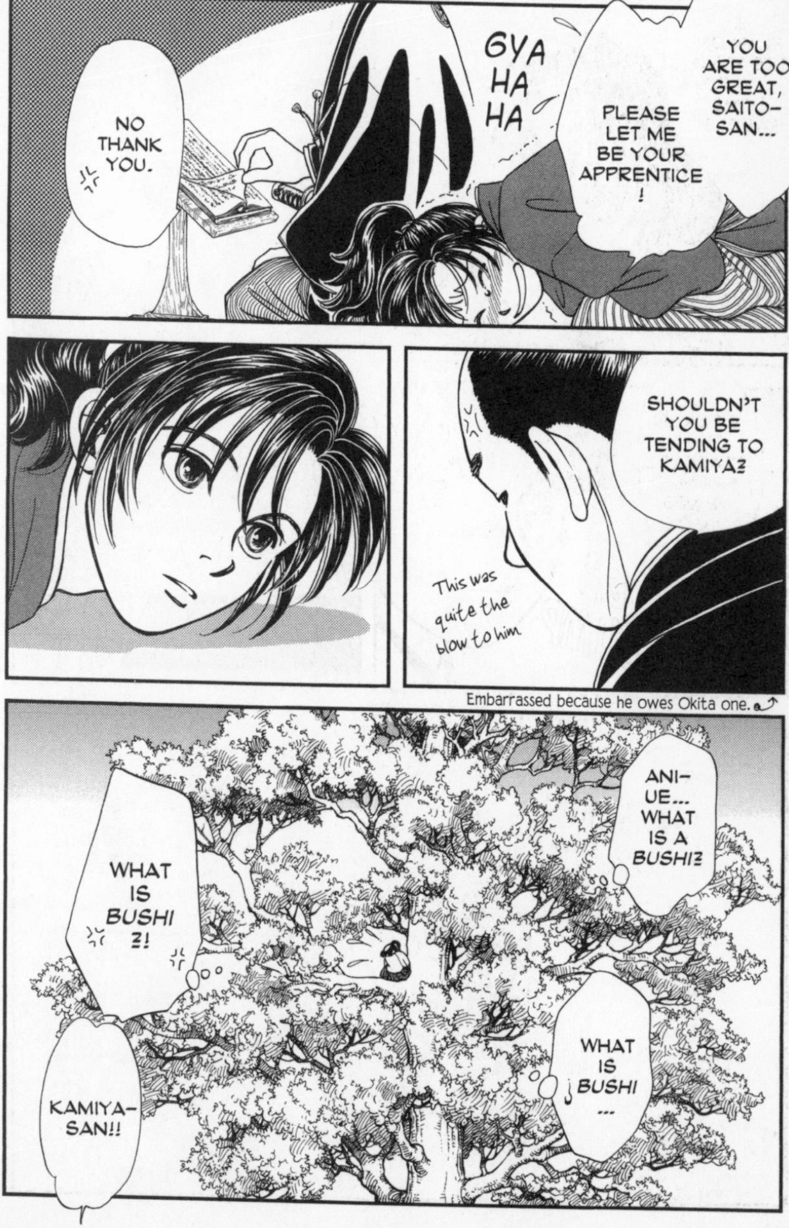
YOU ARE TOO GREAT, SAITO-SAN...
PLEASE LET ME BE YOUR APPRENTICE!
GYA HA HA
NO THANK YOU.
SHOULDN'T YOU BE TENDING TO KAMIYA?
This was quite the blow to him
Embarrassed because he owes Okita one.
ANI-UE... WHAT IS A BUSHI?
WHAT IS BUSHI...
WHAT IS BUSHI?!
KAMIYA-SAN!!

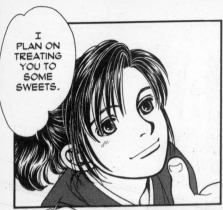

C'MON! YOUR STEPLADDER IS HERE! IT'S TIME TO COME DOWN.
ARE YOU HERE TO PICK A FIGHT?
I PLAN ON TREATING YOU TO SOME SWEETS.
AS A TOKEN OF MY GRATITUDE FROM 12 YEARS AGO.
BA BUMP
HUH?
17-YEAR-OLD SEI, AND 22-YEAR-OLD SOJI...
THIS SPRING MARKS EXACTLY 12 YEARS SINCE THEIR FIRST ENCOUNTER.
C'MON!
ARGH
I-I-I'M ... GONNA ...

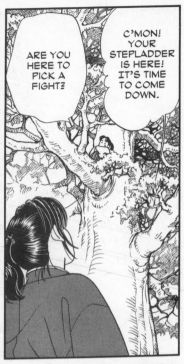

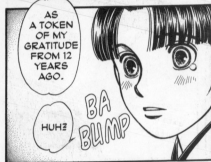

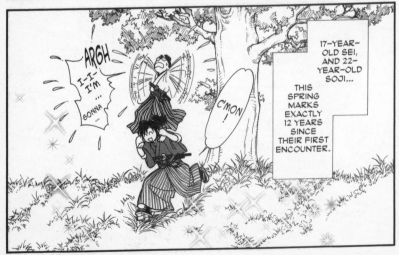

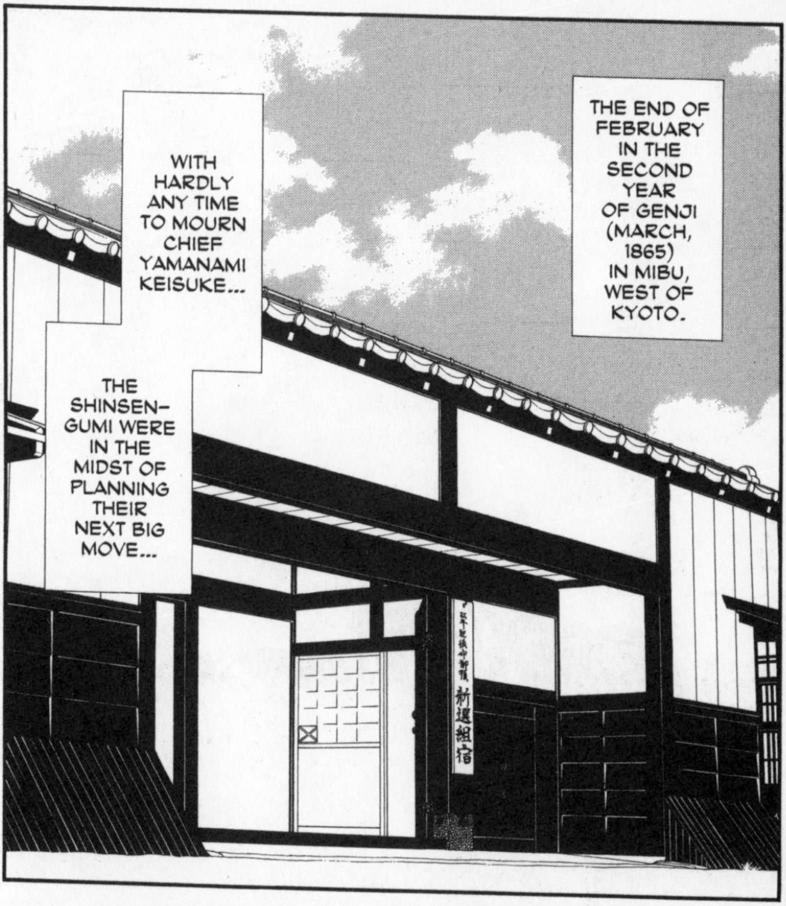
THE END OF FEBRUARY IN THE SECOND YEAR OF GENJI (MARCH, 1865) IN MIBU, WEST OF KYOTO.
WITH HARDLY ANY TIME TO MOURN CHIEF YAMANAMI KEISUKE...
THE SHINSEN-GUMI WERE IN THE MIDST OF PLANNING THEIR NEXT BIG MOVE...
新選組宿

か "KA"

EDO IROHA KARUTA GAME

*As a result of discussions with editors regarding the clear derogatory nature of the proverb associated with "ka," it has been removed from this publication. We appreciate your understanding.

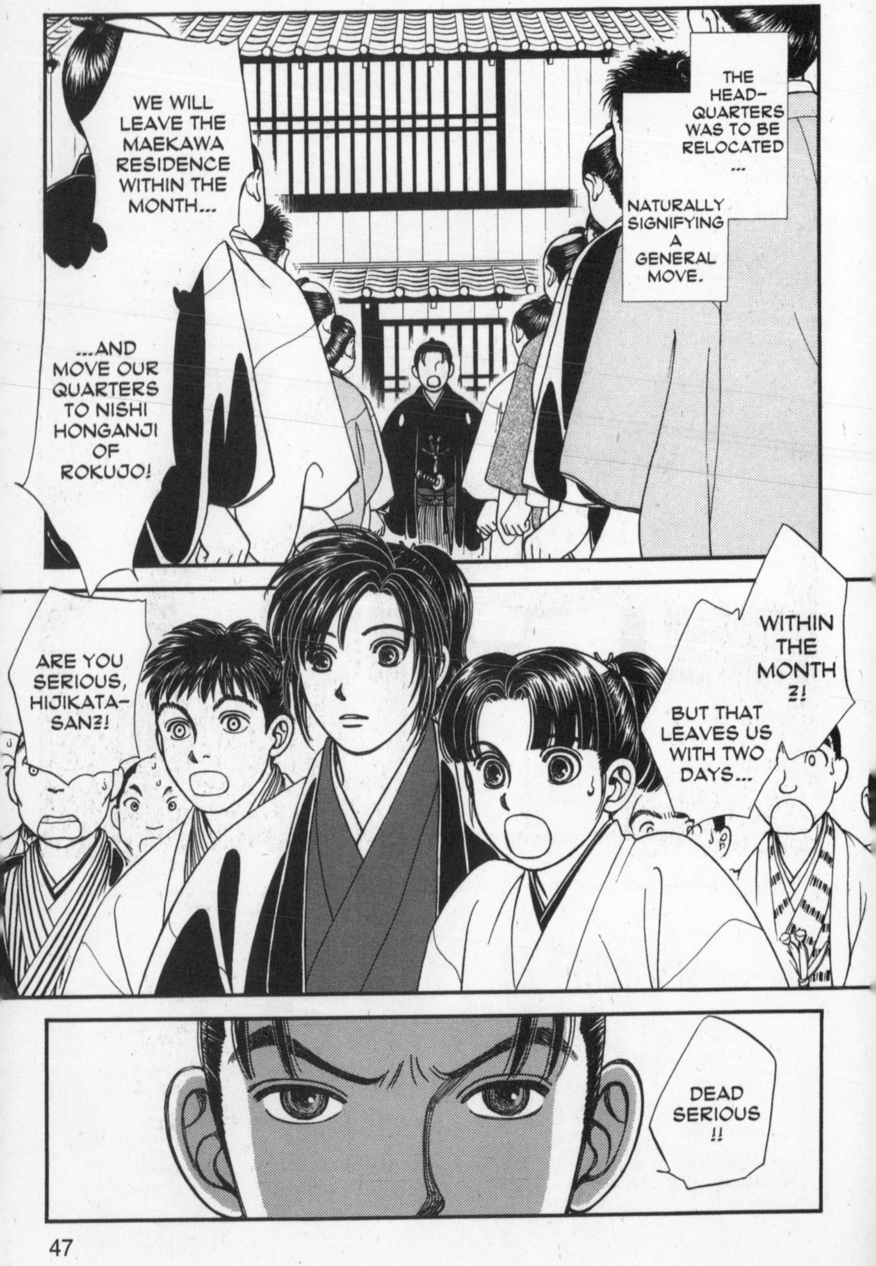
THE HEAD-QUARTERS WAS TO BE RELOCATED ... NATURALLY SIGNIFYING A GENERAL MOVE.
WE WILL LEAVE THE MAEKAWA RESIDENCE WITHIN THE MONTH...
...AND MOVE OUR QUARTERS TO NISHI HONGANJI OF ROKUJO!
WITHIN THE MONTH ?!
BUT THAT LEAVES US WITH TWO DAYS...
ARE YOU SERIOUS, HIJIKATA-SAN?!
DEAD SERIOUS !!

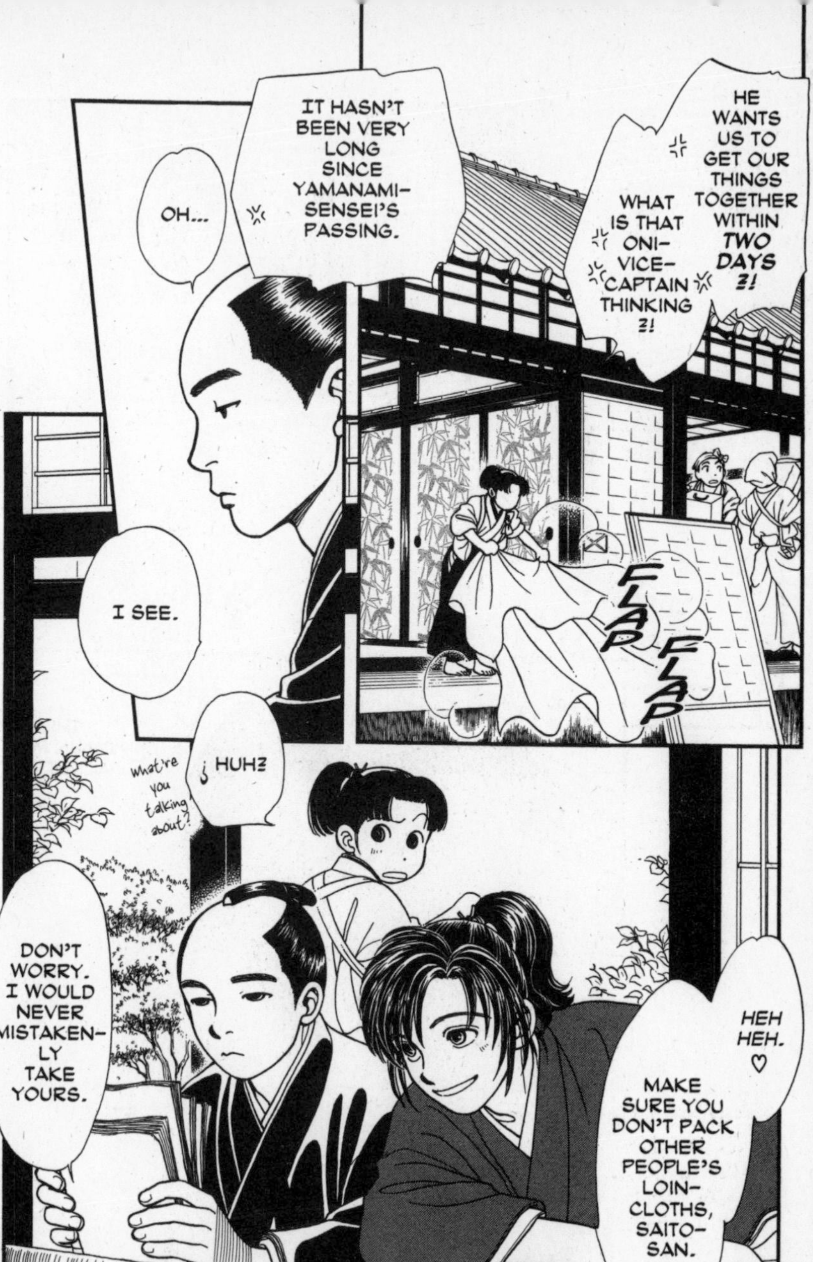
HE WANTS US TO GET OUR THINGS TOGETHER WITHIN TWO DAYS?!
WHAT IS THAT ONI-VICE-CAPTAIN THINKING?!
FLAP FLAP FLAP
IT HASN'T BEEN VERY LONG SINCE YAMANAMI-SENSEI'S PASSING.
OH...
I SEE.
HEH HEH. ♡
MAKE SURE YOU DON'T PACK OTHER PEOPLE'S LOIN-CLOTHS, SAITO-SAN. ♡
¿HUH?
what're you talking about?
DON'T WORRY. I WOULD NEVER MISTAKEN-LY TAKE YOURS.

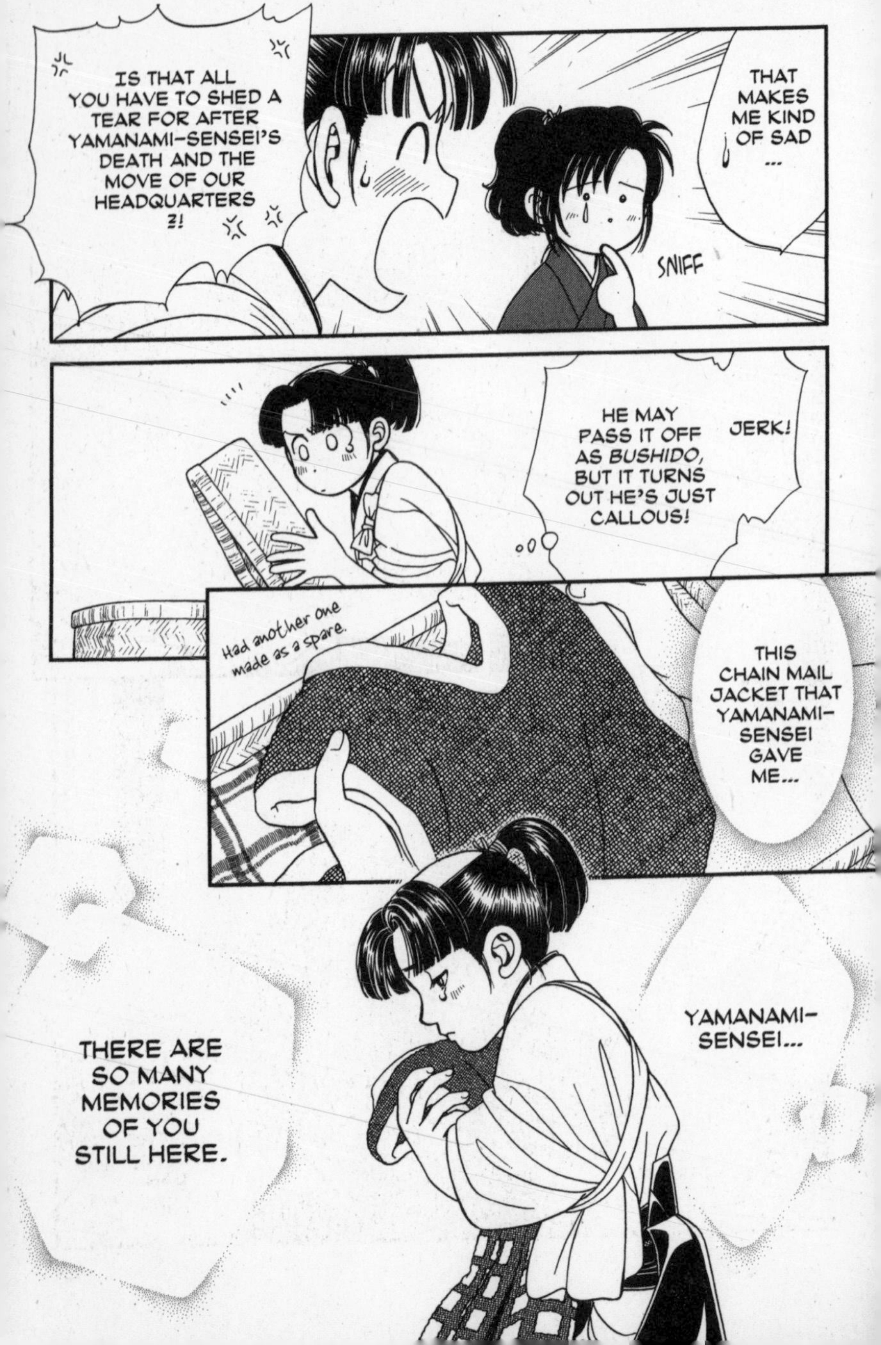
THAT MAKES ME KIND OF SAD ...
SNIFF
IS THAT ALL YOU HAVE TO SHED A TEAR FOR AFTER YAMANAMI-SENSEI'S DEATH AND THE MOVE OF OUR HEADQUARTERS ?!
JERK!
HE MAY PASS IT OFF AS *BUSHIDO*, BUT IT TURNS OUT HE'S JUST CALLOUS!
THIS CHAIN MAIL JACKET THAT YAMANAMI-SENSEI GAVE ME...
Had another one made as a spare.
YAMANAMI-SENSEI...
THERE ARE SO MANY MEMORIES OF YOU STILL HERE.

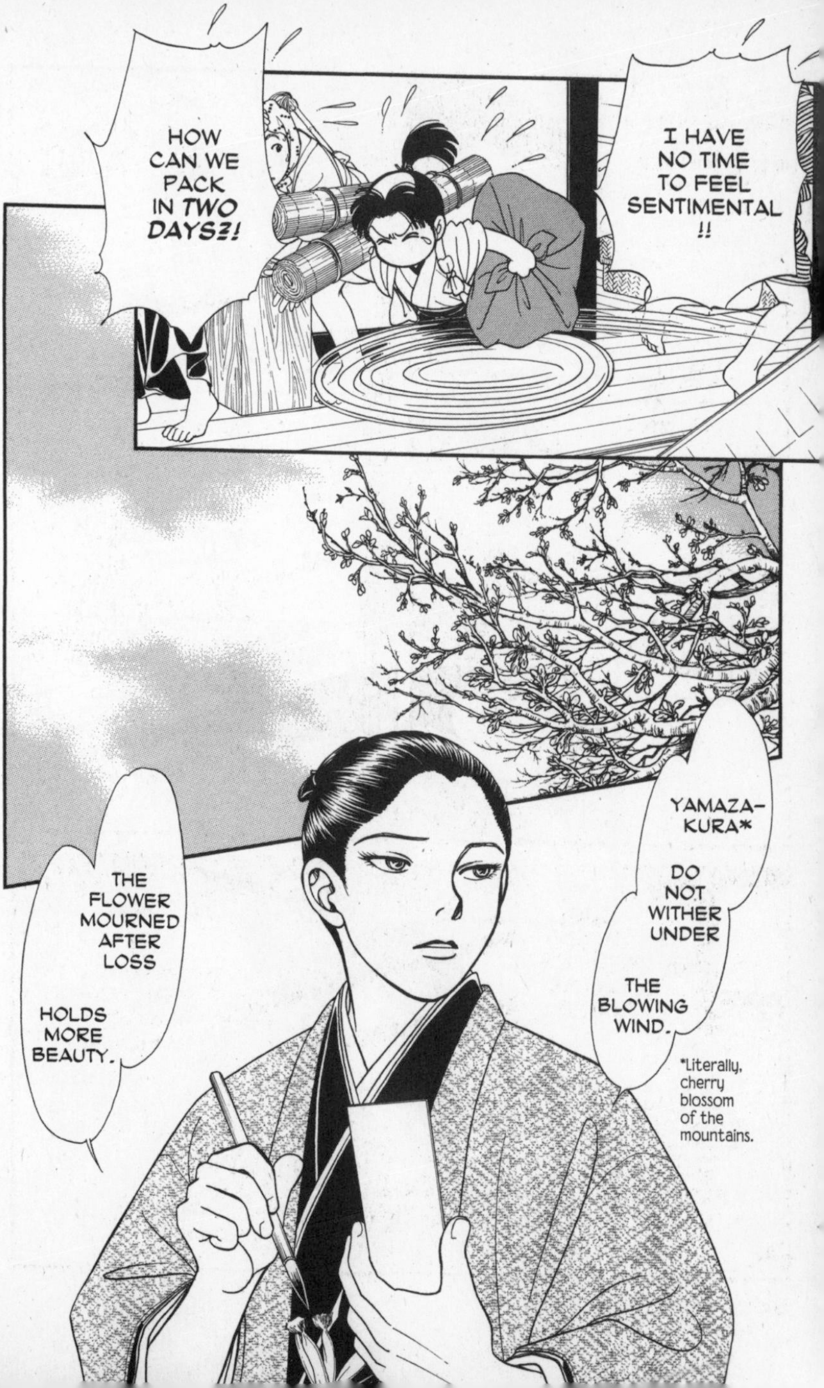
I HAVE NO TIME TO FEEL SENTIMENTAL !!
HOW CAN WE PACK IN TWO DAYS?!
YAMAZA-KURA*
DO NOT WITHER UNDER
THE BLOWING WIND.
THE FLOWER MOURNED AFTER LOSS
HOLDS MORE BEAUTY.
*Literally, cherry blossom of the mountains.

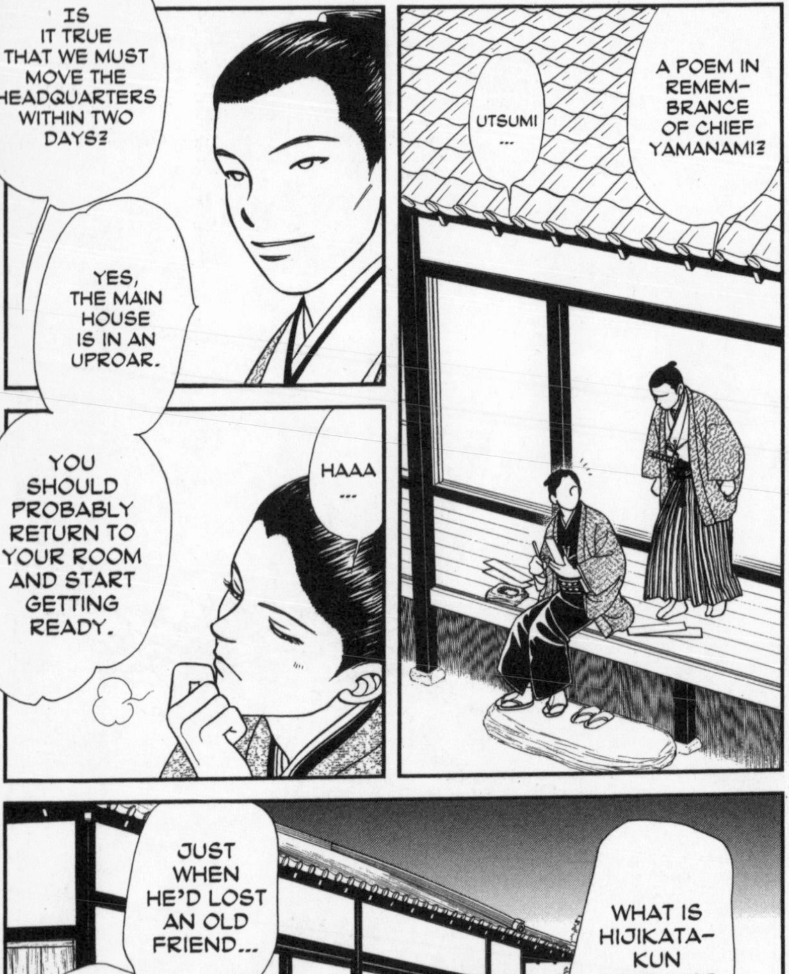
A POEM IN REMEMBRANCE OF CHIEF YAMANAMI?
UTSUMI ...
IS IT TRUE THAT WE MUST MOVE THE HEADQUARTERS WITHIN TWO DAYS?
YES, THE MAIN HOUSE IS IN AN UPROAR.
YOU SHOULD PROBABLY RETURN TO YOUR ROOM AND START GETTING READY.
HAAA ...
WHAT IS HIJIKATA-KUN THINKING?
JUST WHEN HE'D LOST AN OLD FRIEND...
HE HASN'T EVEN TRIED TO FIND OUT WHY, AND HE'S PREPARING TO MOVE.

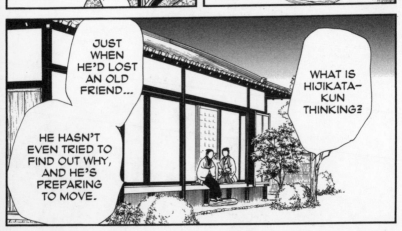

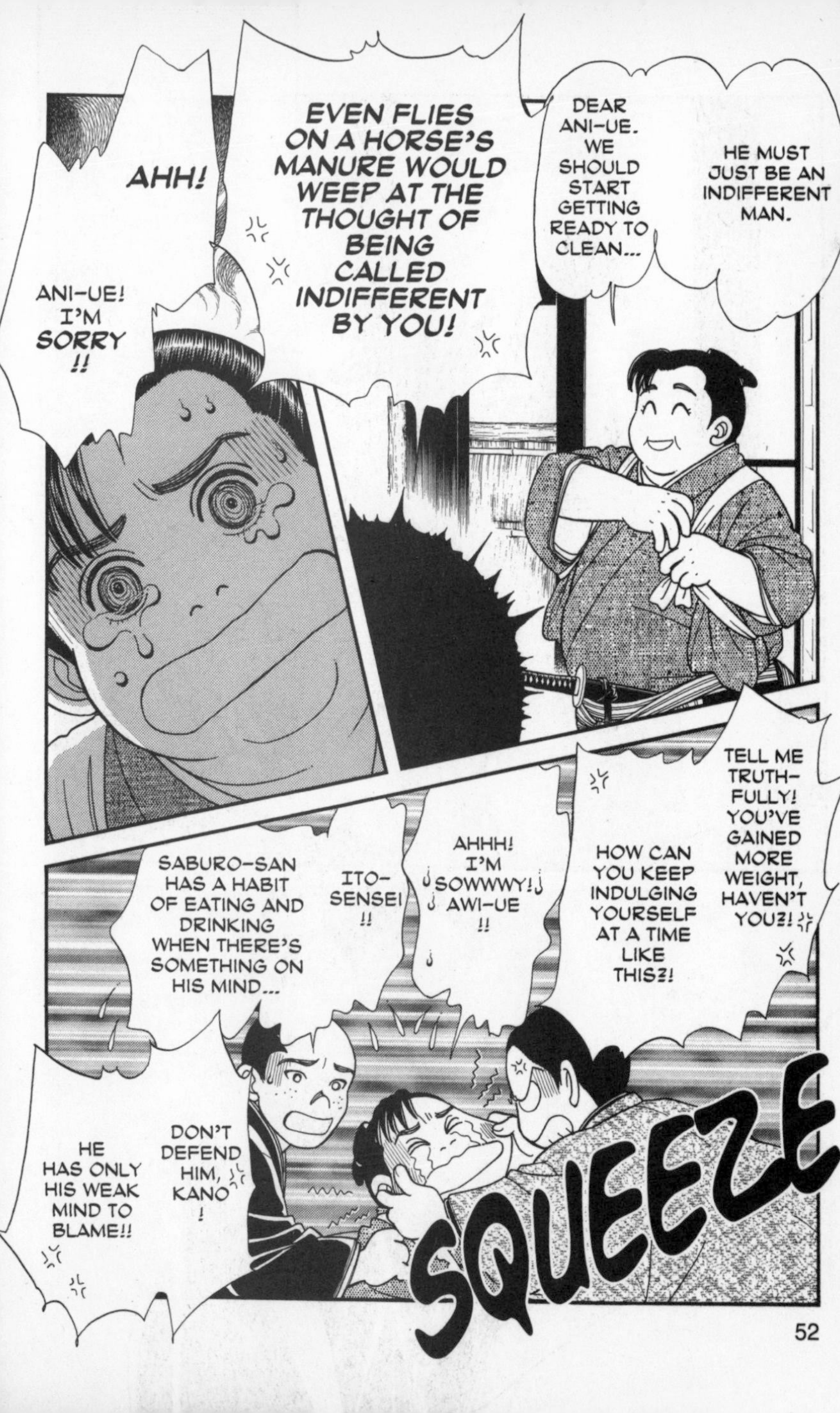
HE MUST JUST BE AN INDIFFERENT MAN.
DEAR ANI-UE. WE SHOULD START GETTING READY TO CLEAN...
EVEN FLIES ON A HORSE'S MANURE WOULD WEEP AT THE THOUGHT OF BEING CALLED INDIFFERENT BY YOU!
AHH!
ANI-UE! I'M SORRY!!
TELL ME TRUTH-FULLY! YOU'VE GAINED MORE WEIGHT, HAVEN'T YOU?!
HOW CAN YOU KEEP INDULGING YOURSELF AT A TIME LIKE THIS?!
AHHH! I'M SOWWWY! AWI-UE!!
ITO-SENSEI!!
SABURO-SAN HAS A HABIT OF EATING AND DRINKING WHEN THERE'S SOMETHING ON HIS MIND...
DON'T DEFEND HIM, KANO!
HE HAS ONLY HIS WEAK MIND TO BLAME!!
SQUEEZE

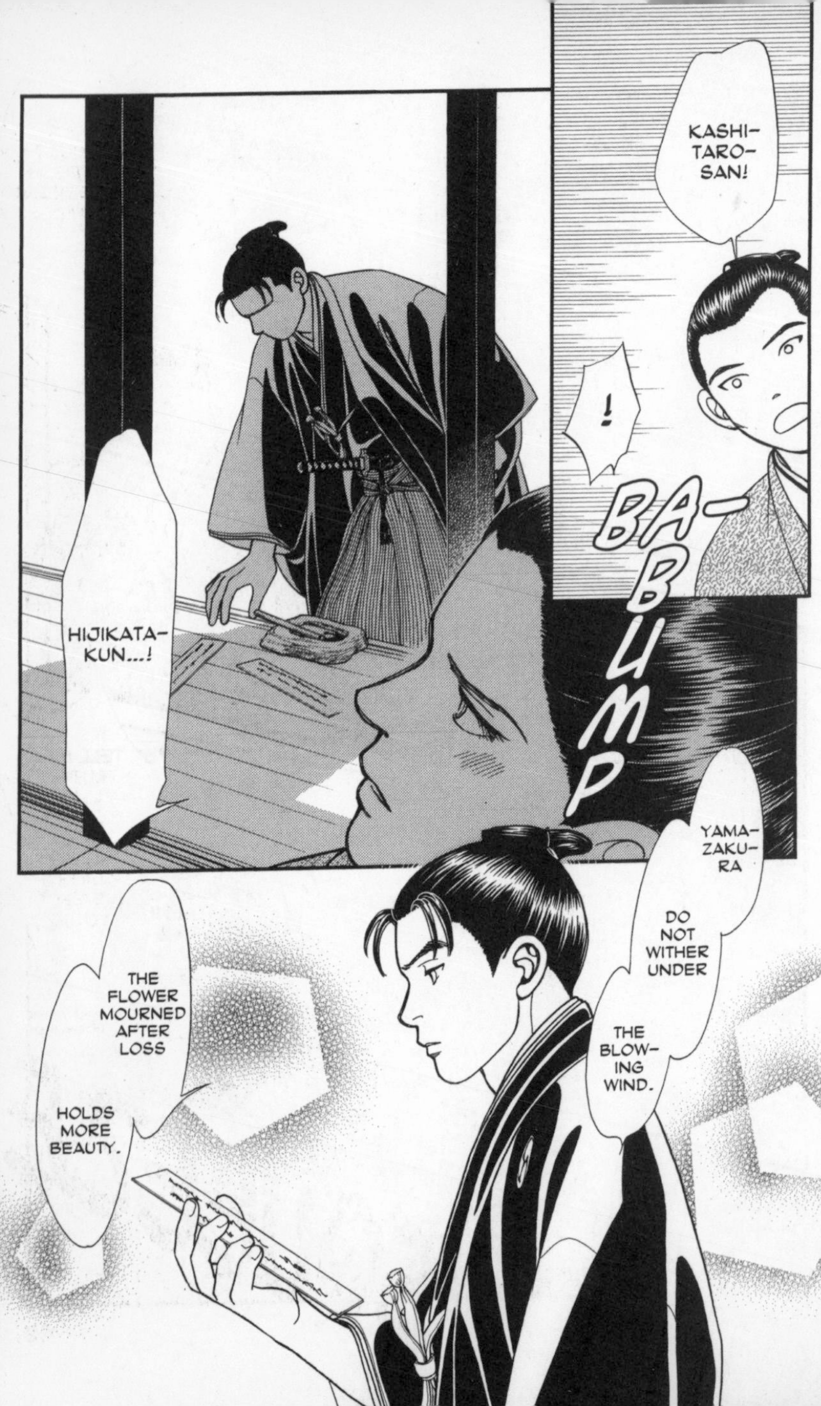
KASHI-TARO-SAN!
!
BA-BUMP
HIJIKATA-KUN...!
YAMA-ZAKU-RA
DO NOT WITHER UNDER
THE BLOW-ING WIND.
THE FLOWER MOURNED AFTER LOSS
HOLDS MORE BEAUTY.

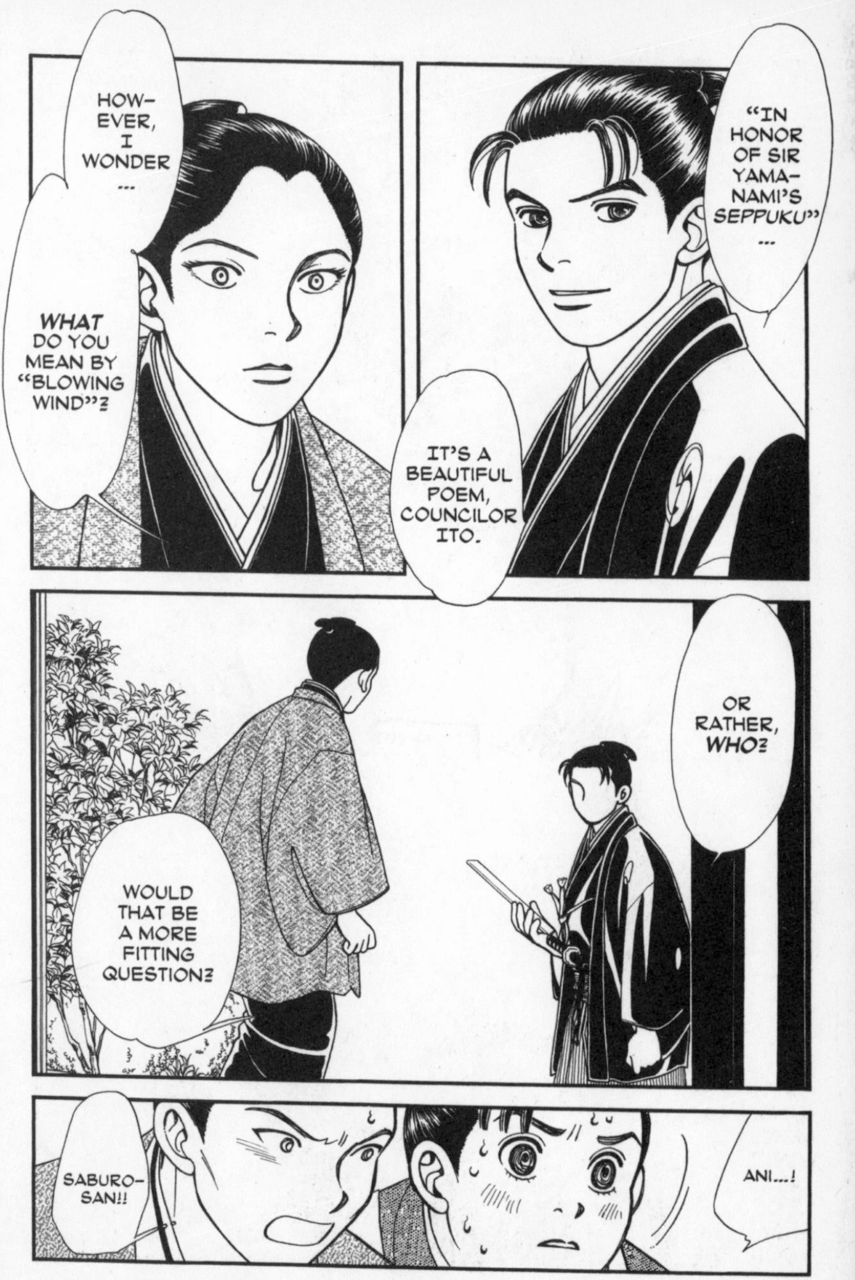
"IN HONOR OF SIR YAMA-NAMI'S SEPPUKU"...
IT'S A BEAUTIFUL POEM, COUNCILOR ITO.
HOW-EVER, I WONDER...
WHAT DO YOU MEAN BY "BLOWING WIND"?
OR RATHER, WHO?
WOULD THAT BE A MORE FITTING QUESTION?
ANI...!
SABURO-SAN!!

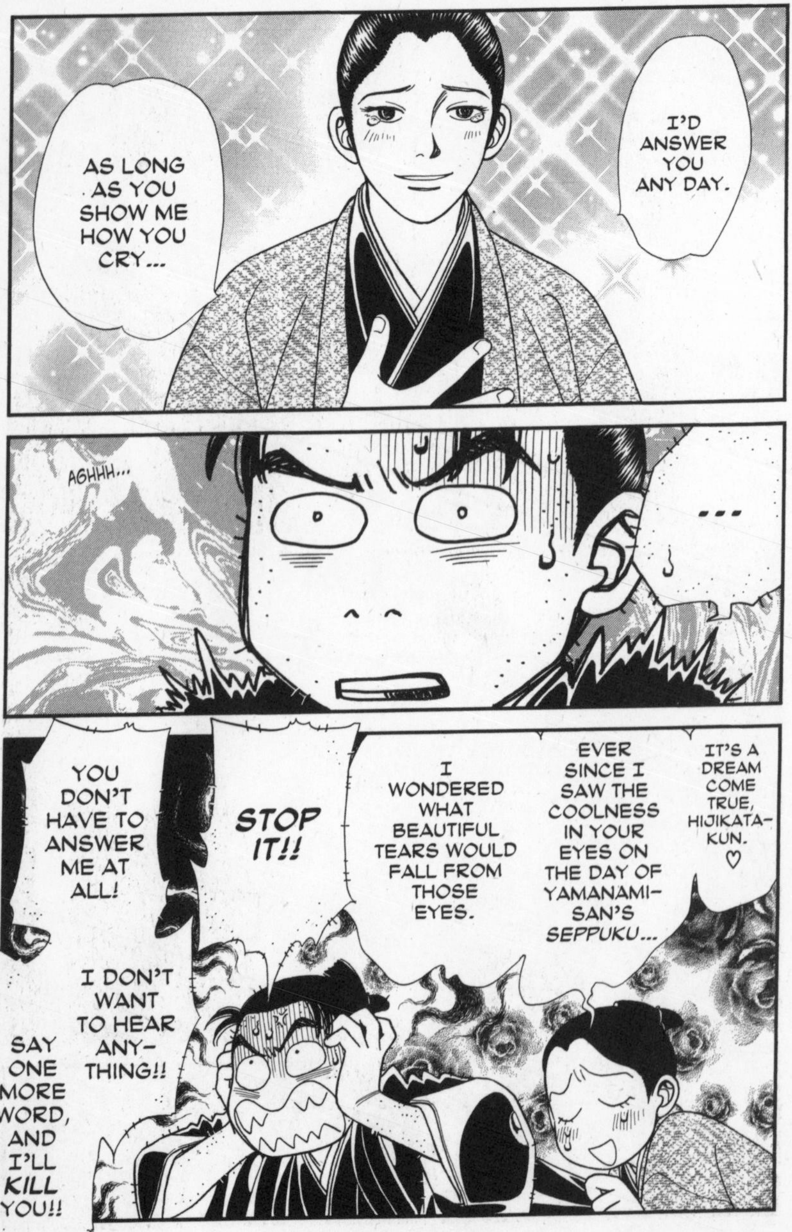
I'D ANSWER YOU ANY DAY.
AS LONG AS YOU SHOW ME HOW YOU CRY...
...
AGHHH...
IT'S A DREAM COME TRUE, HIJIKATA-KUN. ♡
EVER SINCE I SAW THE COOLNESS IN YOUR EYES ON THE DAY OF YAMANAMI-SAN'S *SEPPUKU*...
I WONDERED WHAT BEAUTIFUL TEARS WOULD FALL FROM THOSE EYES.
STOP IT!!
YOU DON'T HAVE TO ANSWER ME AT ALL!
I DON'T WANT TO HEAR ANY-THING!!
SAY ONE MORE WORD, AND I'LL *KILL* YOU!!

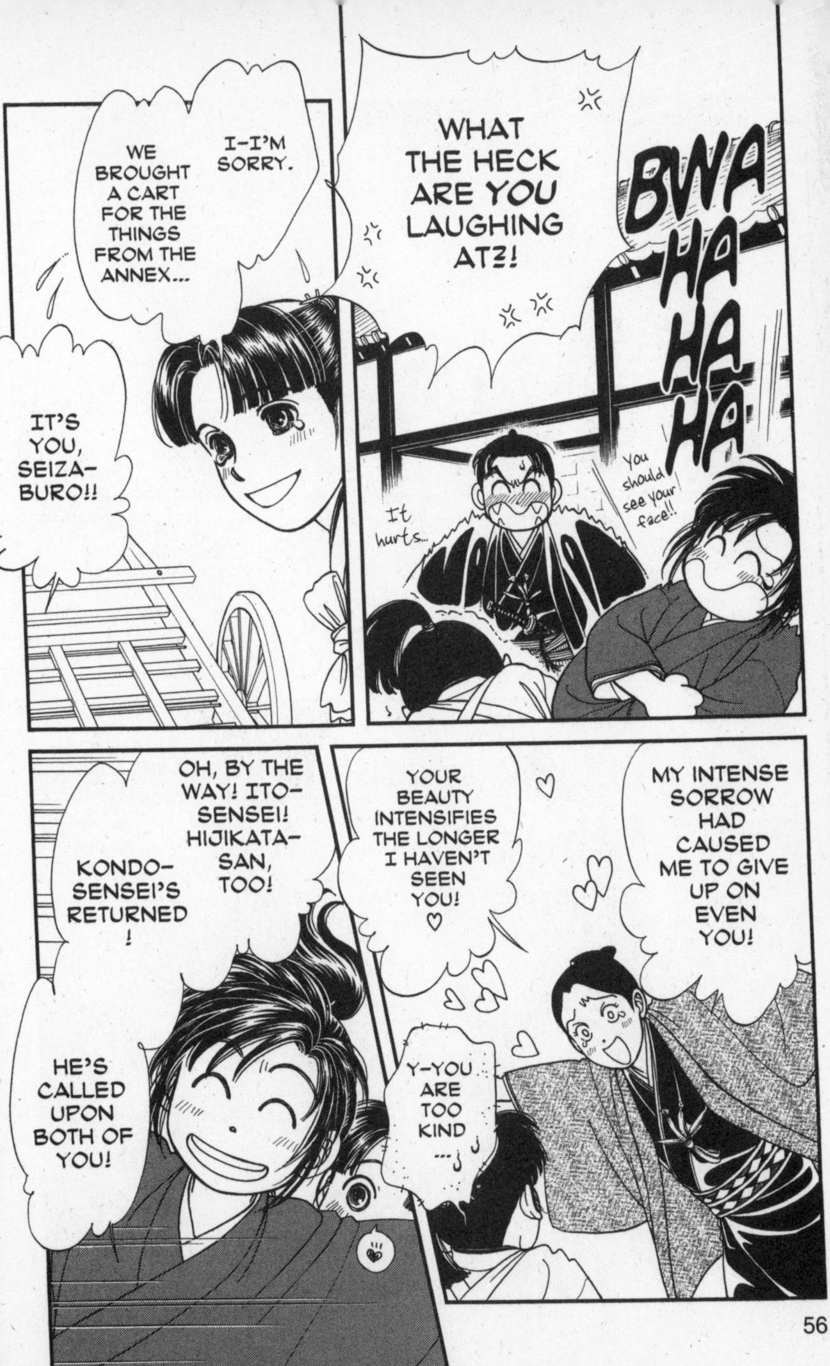
WHAT THE HECK ARE YOU LAUGHING AT?!
BWA HA HA HA HA
You should see your face!!
It hurts...
I-I'M SORRY.
WE BROUGHT A CART FOR THE THINGS FROM THE ANNEX...
IT'S YOU, SEIZA-BURO!!
MY INTENSE SORROW HAD CAUSED ME TO GIVE UP ON EVEN YOU!
YOUR BEAUTY INTENSIFIES THE LONGER I HAVEN'T SEEN YOU! ♡
Y-YOU ARE TOO KIND ...
OH, BY THE WAY! ITO-SENSEI! HIJIKATA-SAN, TOO!
KONDO-SENSEI'S RETURNED!
HE'S CALLED UPON BOTH OF YOU!

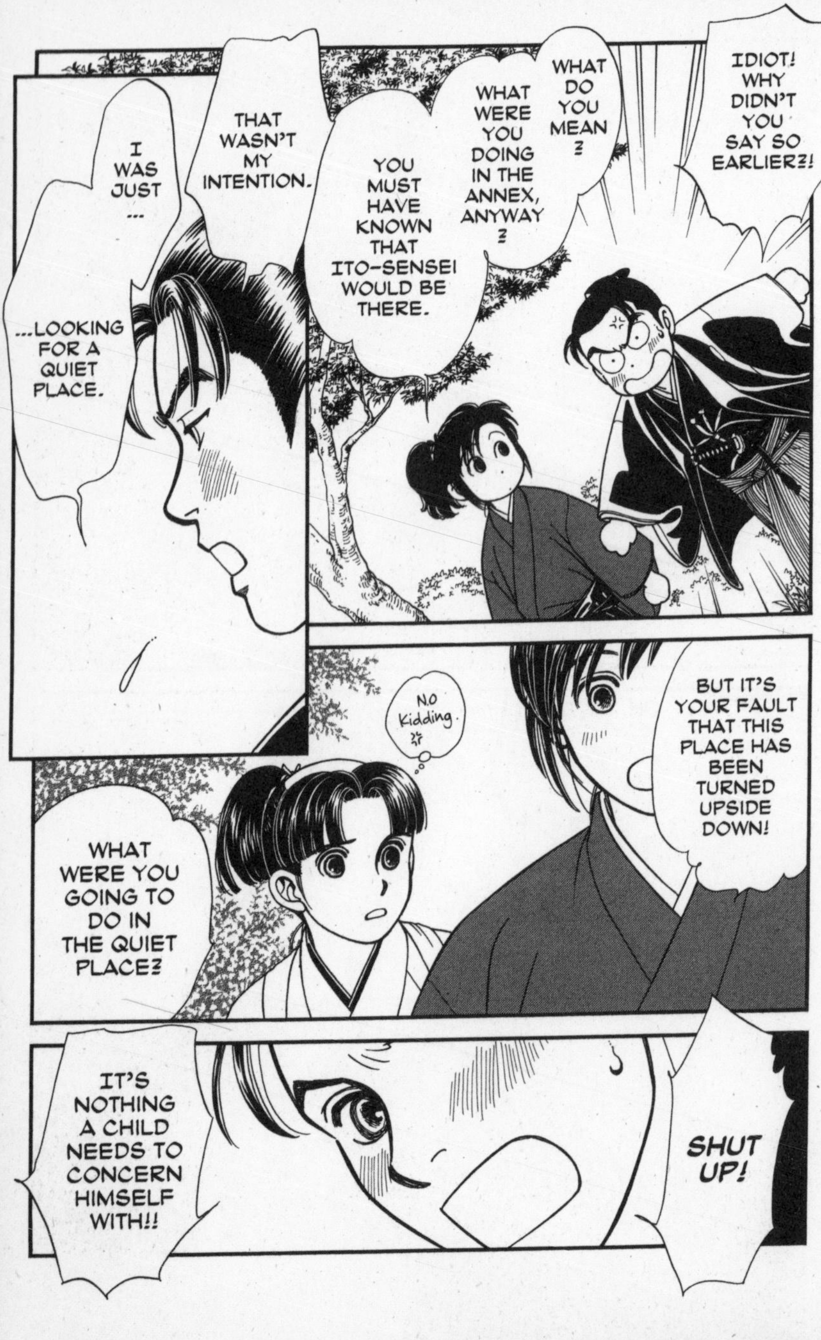
IDIOT! WHY DIDN'T YOU SAY SO EARLIER?!
WHAT DO YOU MEAN?
WHAT WERE YOU DOING IN THE ANNEX, ANYWAY?
YOU MUST HAVE KNOWN THAT ITO-SENSEI WOULD BE THERE.
THAT WASN'T MY INTENTION.
I WAS JUST ...
...LOOKING FOR A QUIET PLACE.
BUT IT'S YOUR FAULT THAT THIS PLACE HAS BEEN TURNED UPSIDE DOWN!
No kidding.
WHAT WERE YOU GOING TO DO IN THE QUIET PLACE?
SHUT UP!
IT'S NOTHING A CHILD NEEDS TO CONCERN HIMSELF WITH!!

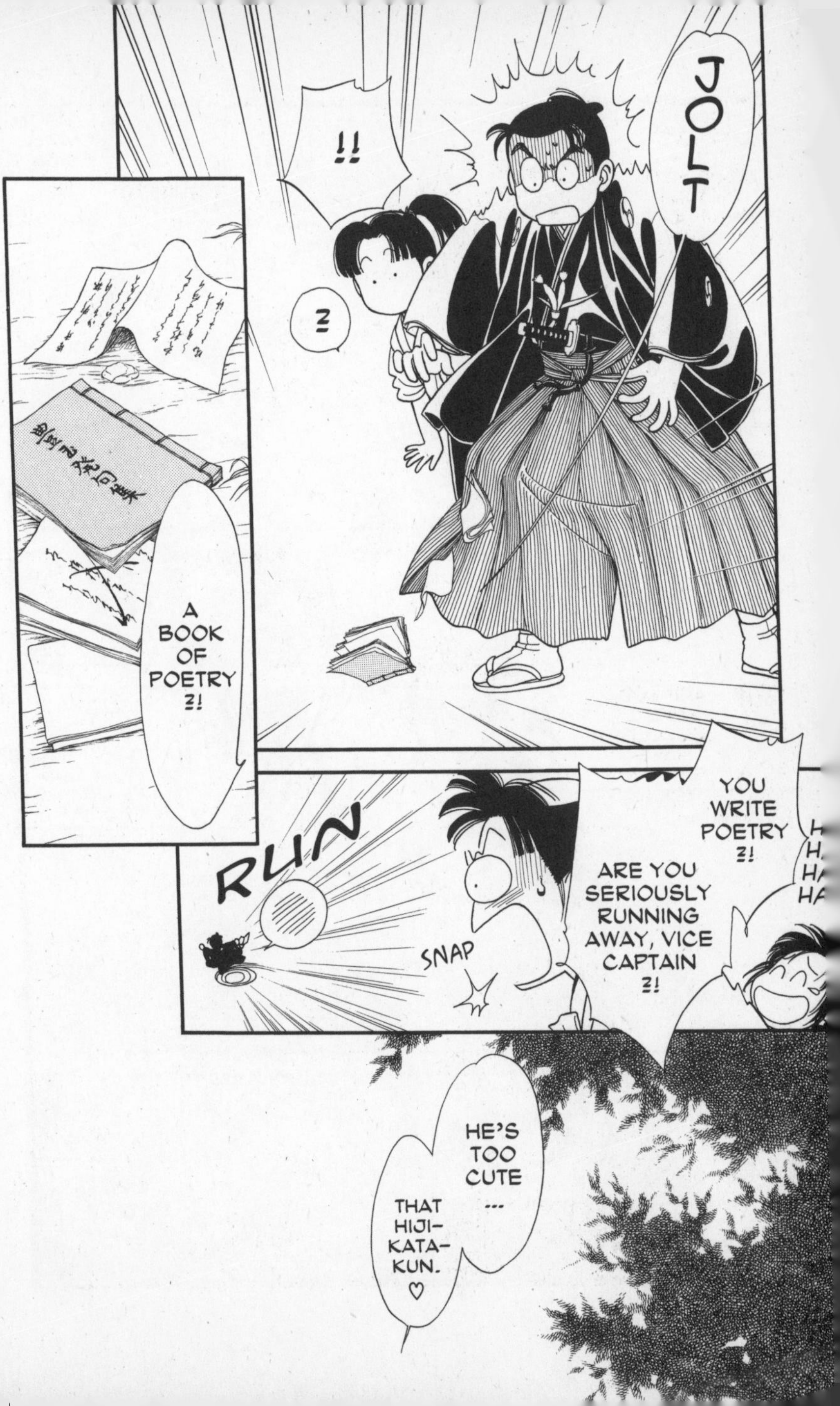
JOLT
!!
?
A BOOK OF POETRY ?!
YOU WRITE POETRY ?!
ARE YOU SERIOUSLY RUNNING AWAY, VICE CAPTAIN ?!
SNAP
RUN
HE'S TOO CUTE ...
THAT HIJI-KATA-KUN. ♡

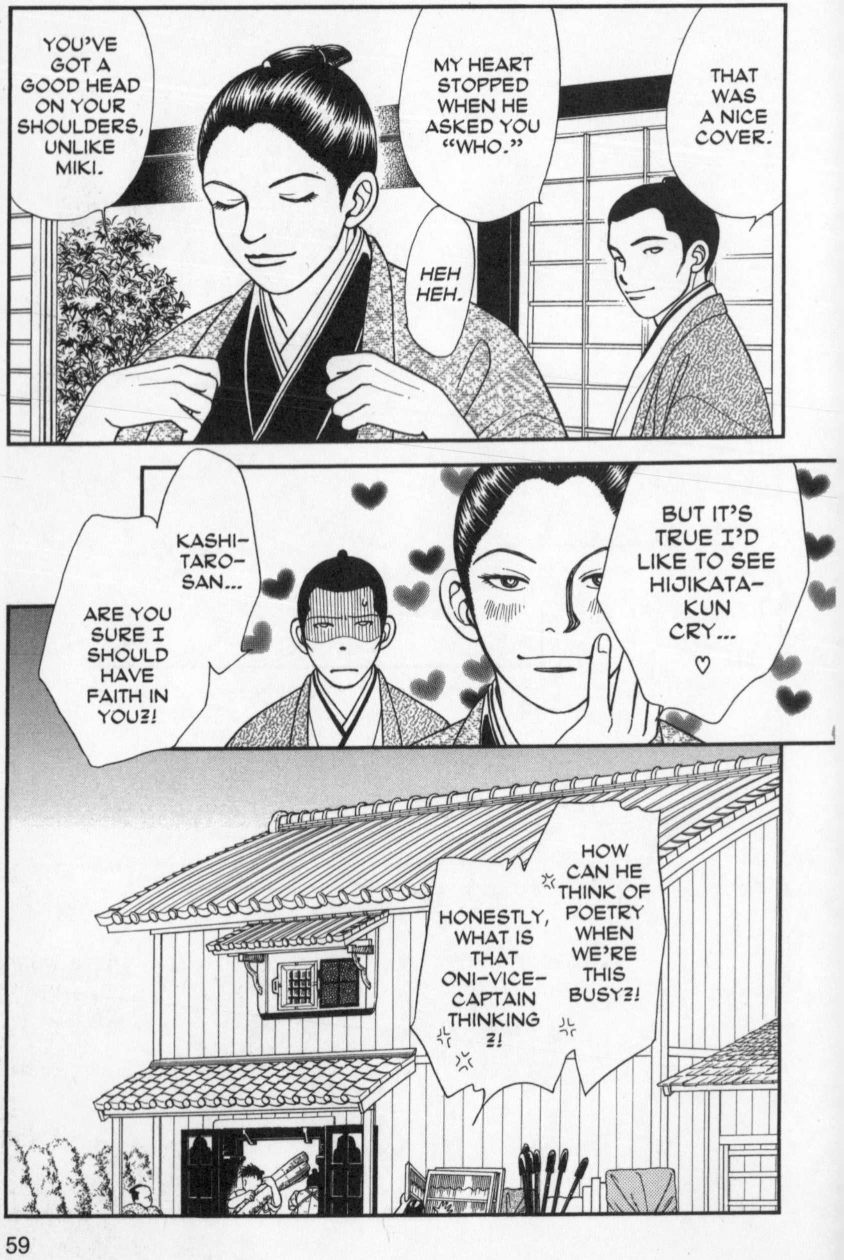
THAT WAS A NICE COVER.
MY HEART STOPPED WHEN HE ASKED YOU "WHO."
HEH HEH.
YOU'VE GOT A GOOD HEAD ON YOUR SHOULDERS, UNLIKE MIKI.
BUT IT'S TRUE I'D LIKE TO SEE HIJIKATA-KUN CRY... ♡
KASHI-TARO-SAN...
ARE YOU SURE I SHOULD HAVE FAITH IN YOU?!
HOW CAN HE THINK OF POETRY WHEN WE'RE THIS BUSY?!
HONESTLY, WHAT IS THAT ONI-VICE-CAPTAIN THINKING?!

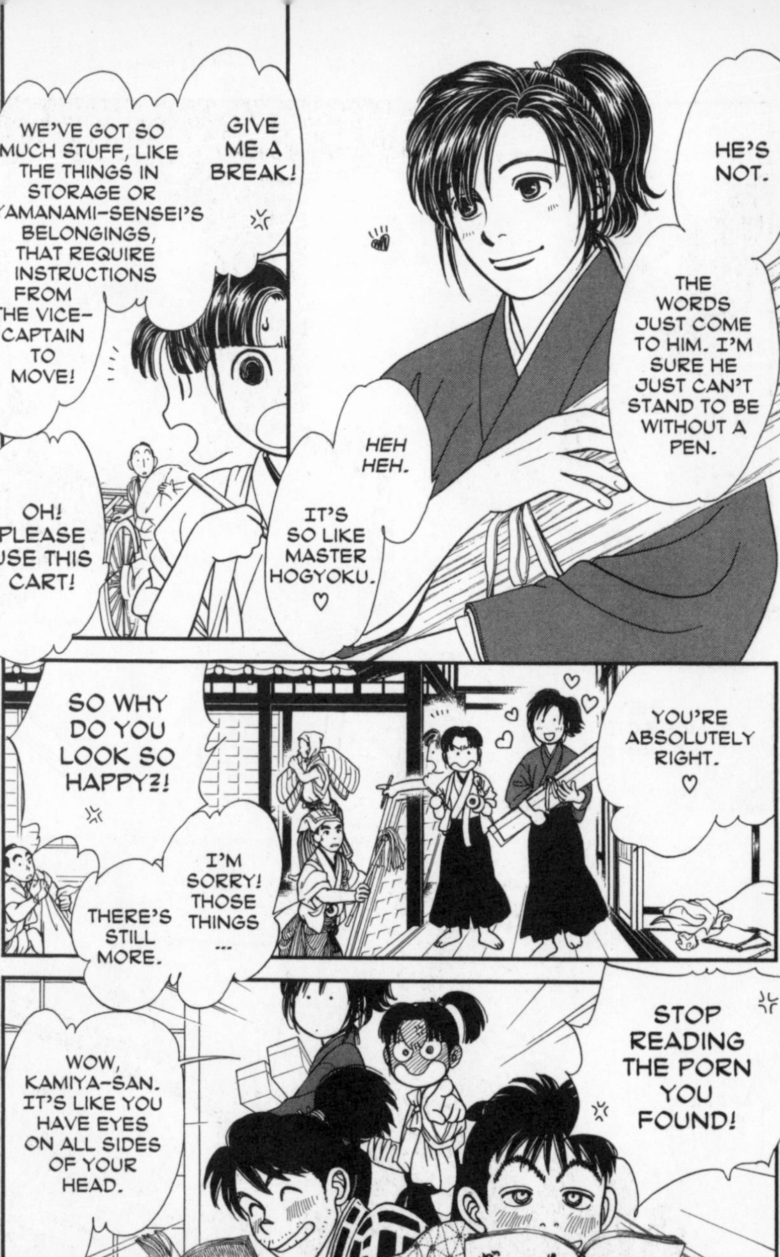
HE'S NOT.
THE WORDS JUST COME TO HIM. I'M SURE HE JUST CAN'T STAND TO BE WITHOUT A PEN.
HEH HEH.
IT'S SO LIKE MASTER HOGYOKU. ♡
GIVE ME A BREAK!
WE'VE GOT SO MUCH STUFF, LIKE THE THINGS IN STORAGE OR YAMANAMI-SENSEI'S BELONGINGS, THAT REQUIRE INSTRUCTIONS FROM THE VICE-CAPTAIN TO MOVE!
OH! PLEASE USE THIS CART!
YOU'RE ABSOLUTELY RIGHT. ♡
SO WHY DO YOU LOOK SO HAPPY?!
I'M SORRY! THOSE THINGS ...
THERE'S STILL MORE.
STOP READING THE PORN YOU FOUND!
WOW, KAMIYA-SAN. IT'S LIKE YOU HAVE EYES ON ALL SIDES OF YOUR HEAD.

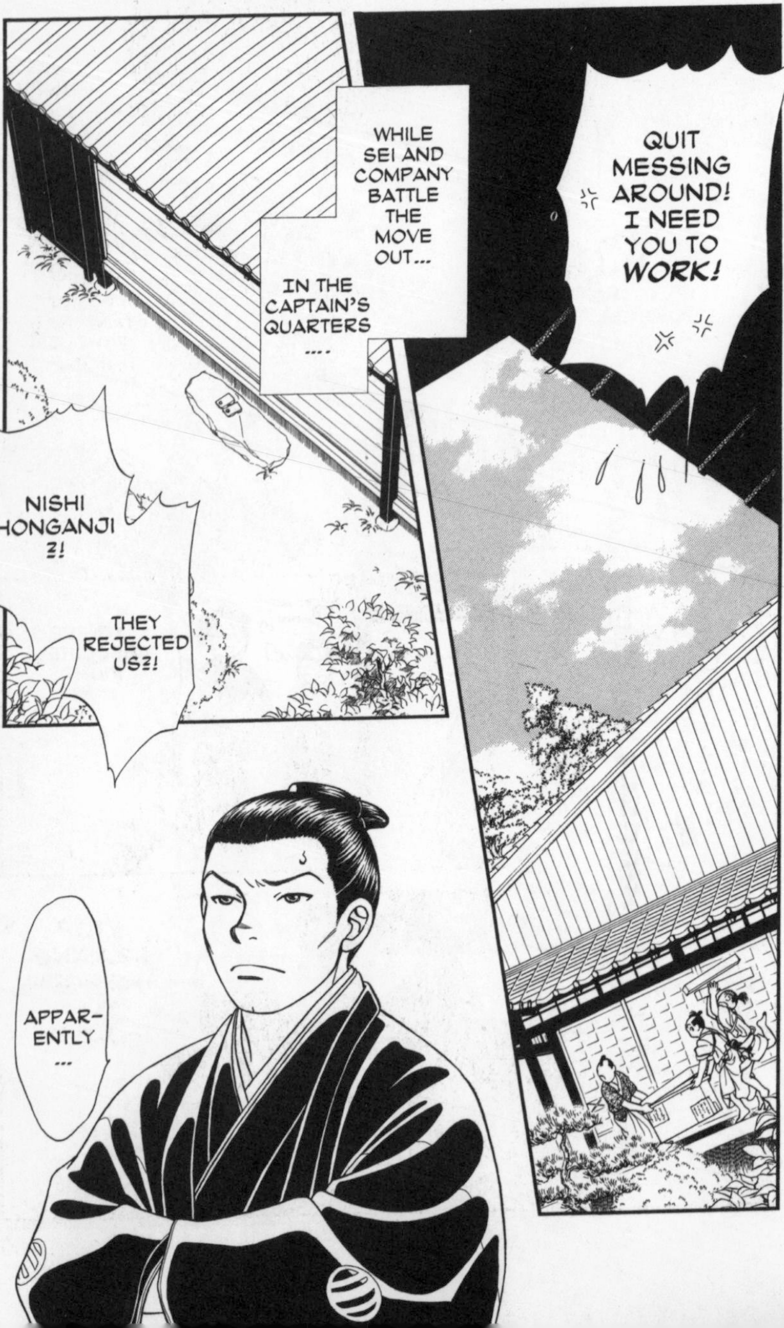
QUIT MESSING AROUND! I NEED YOU TO WORK!
WHILE SEI AND COMPANY BATTLE THE MOVE OUT...
IN THE CAPTAIN'S QUARTERS....
NISHI HONGANJI?!
THEY REJECTED US?!
APPAR-ENTLY...

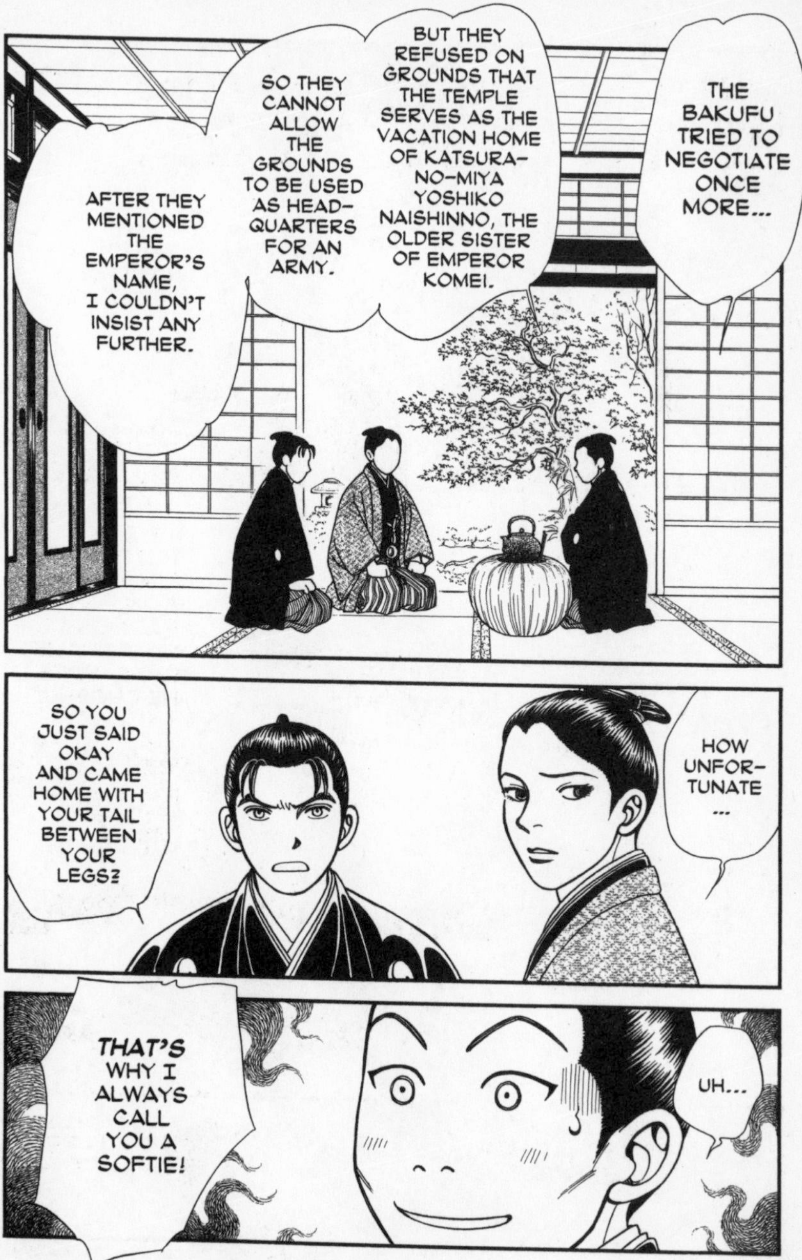
THE BAKUFU TRIED TO NEGOTIATE ONCE MORE...
BUT THEY REFUSED ON GROUNDS THAT THE TEMPLE SERVES AS THE VACATION HOME OF KATSURA-NO-MIYA YOSHIKO NAISHINNO, THE OLDER SISTER OF EMPEROR KOMEI.
SO THEY CANNOT ALLOW THE GROUNDS TO BE USED AS HEAD-QUARTERS FOR AN ARMY.
AFTER THEY MENTIONED THE EMPEROR'S NAME, I COULDN'T INSIST ANY FURTHER.
HOW UNFOR-TUNATE ...
SO YOU JUST SAID OKAY AND CAME HOME WITH YOUR TAIL BETWEEN YOUR LEGS?
UH...
THAT'S WHY I ALWAYS CALL YOU A SOFTIE!

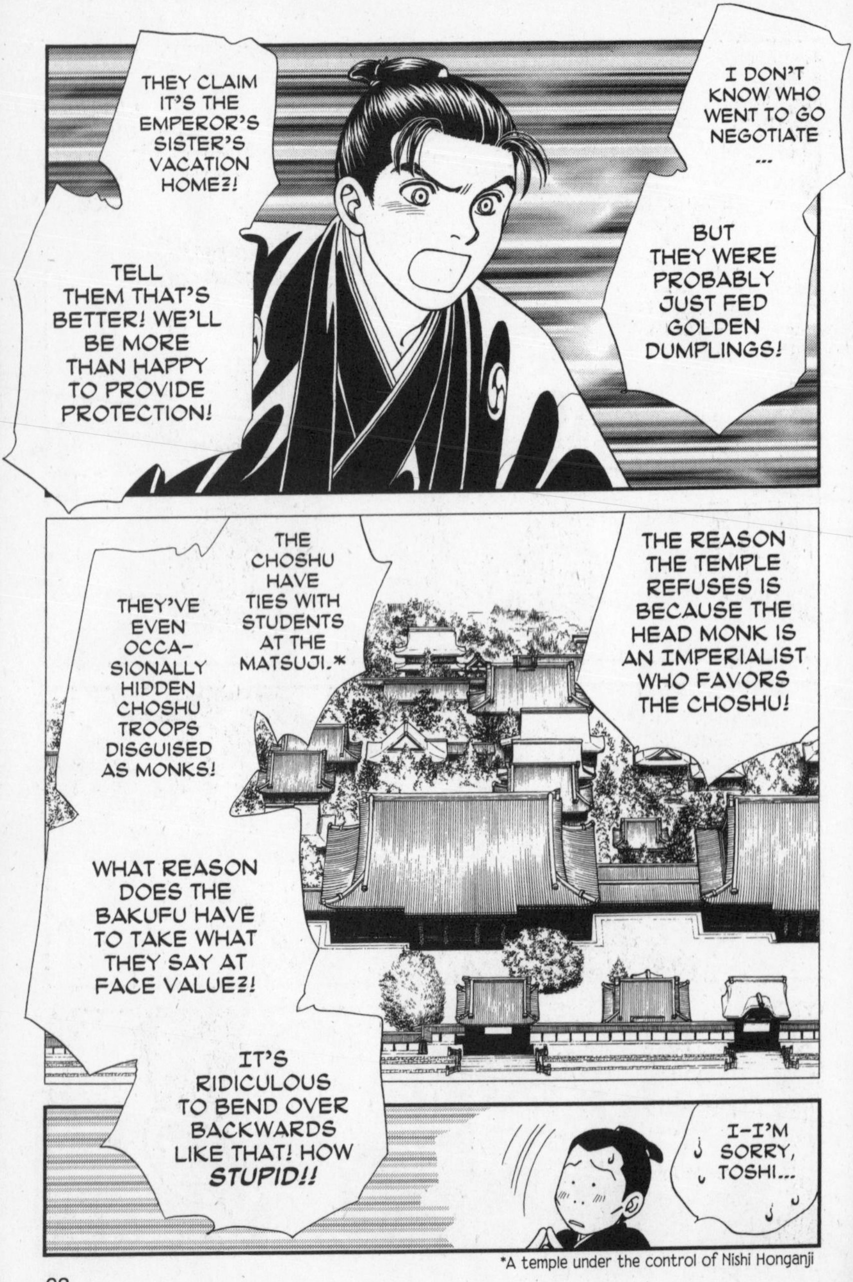
I DON'T KNOW WHO WENT TO GO NEGOTIATE ...
BUT THEY WERE PROBABLY JUST FED GOLDEN DUMPLINGS!
THEY CLAIM IT'S THE EMPEROR'S SISTER'S VACATION HOME?!
TELL THEM THAT'S BETTER! WE'LL BE MORE THAN HAPPY TO PROVIDE PROTECTION!
THE REASON THE TEMPLE REFUSES IS BECAUSE THE HEAD MONK IS AN IMPERIALIST WHO FAVORS THE CHOSHU!
THE CHOSHU HAVE TIES WITH STUDENTS AT THE MATSUJI.*
THEY'VE EVEN OCCA-SIONALLY HIDDEN CHOSHU TROOPS DISGUISED AS MONKS!
WHAT REASON DOES THE BAKUFU HAVE TO TAKE WHAT THEY SAY AT FACE VALUE?!
IT'S RIDICULOUS TO BEND OVER BACKWARDS LIKE THAT! HOW *STUPID!!*
I-I'M SORRY, TOSHI...

*A temple under the control of Nishi Honganji

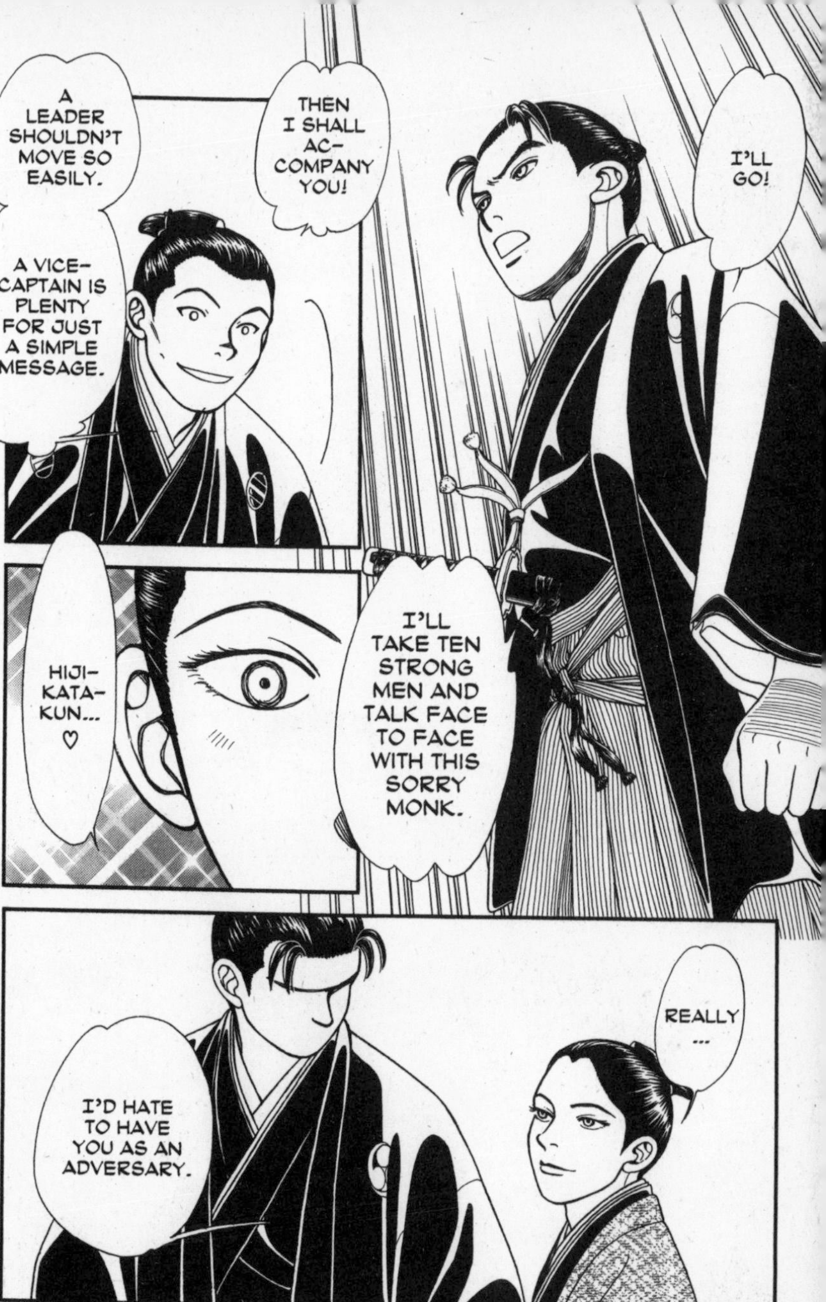
I'LL GO!
I'LL TAKE TEN STRONG MEN AND TALK FACE TO FACE WITH THIS SORRY MONK.
THEN I SHALL AC-COMPANY YOU!
A LEADER SHOULDN'T MOVE SO EASILY.
A VICE-CAPTAIN IS PLENTY FOR JUST A SIMPLE MESSAGE.
HIJI-KATA-KUN... ♡
REALLY...
I'D HATE TO HAVE YOU AS AN ADVERSARY.

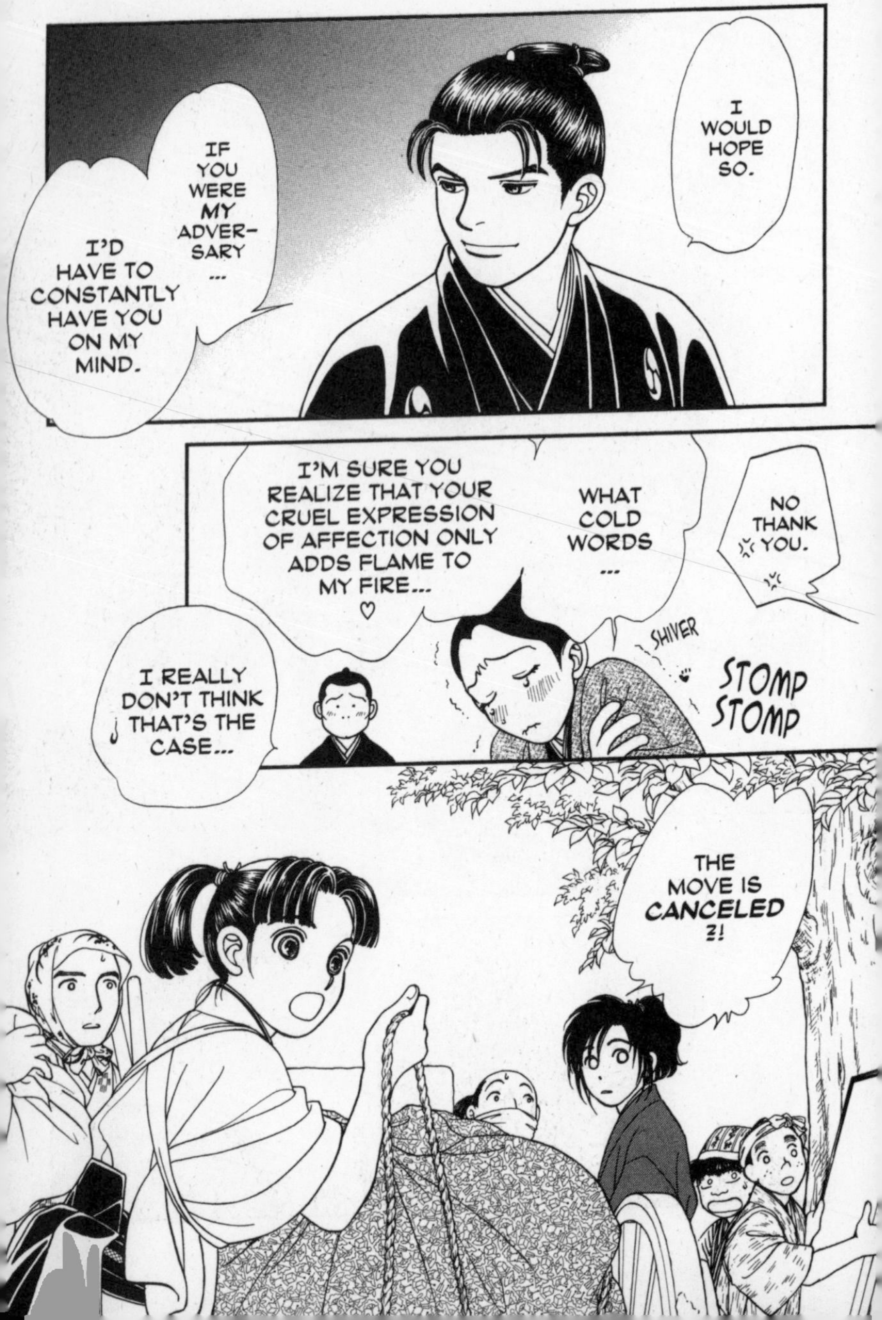
I WOULD HOPE SO.
IF YOU WERE MY ADVERSARY...
I'D HAVE TO CONSTANTLY HAVE YOU ON MY MIND.
NO THANK YOU.
WHAT COLD WORDS...
I'M SURE YOU REALIZE THAT YOUR CRUEL EXPRESSION OF AFFECTION ONLY ADDS FLAME TO MY FIRE... ♡
STOMP STOMP
SHIVER
I REALLY DON'T THINK THAT'S THE CASE...
THE MOVE IS CANCELED?!

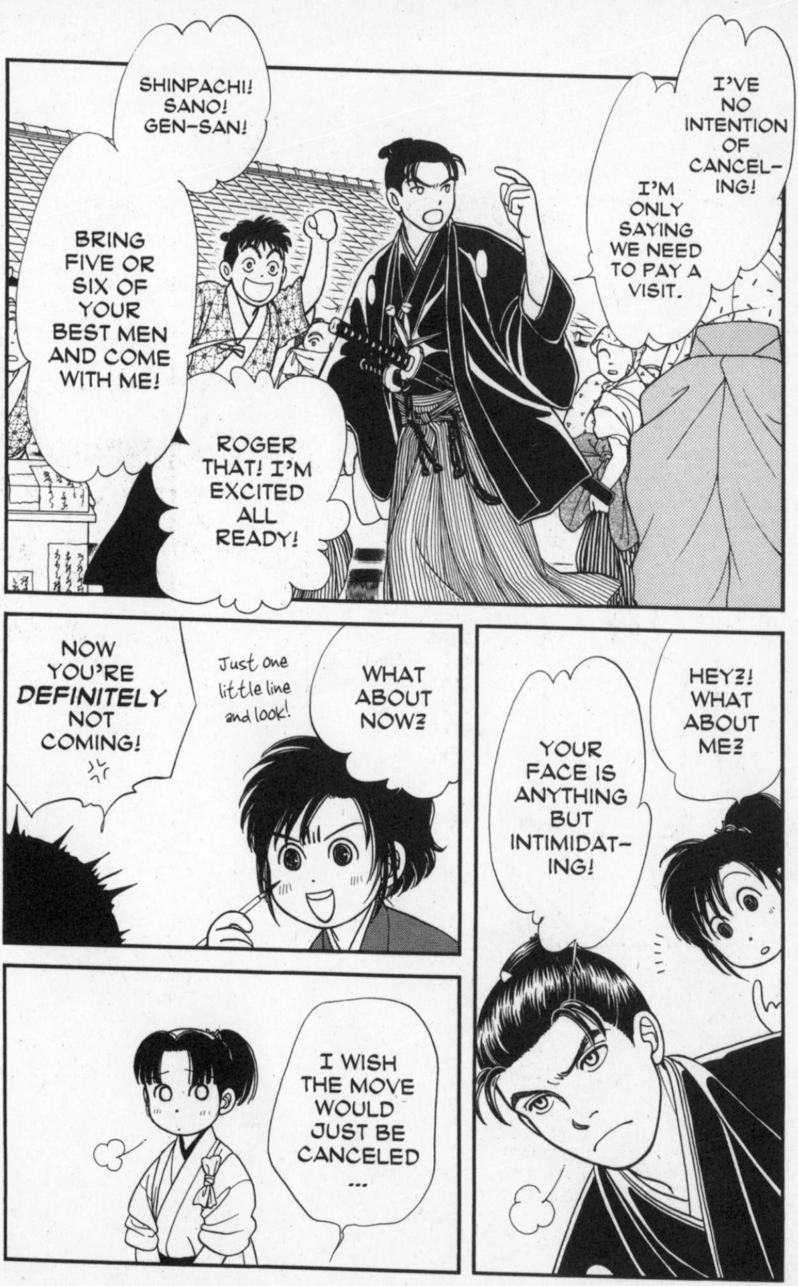
I'VE NO INTENTION OF CANCEL-ING!
I'M ONLY SAYING WE NEED TO PAY A VISIT.
SHINPACHI! SANO! GEN-SAN!
BRING FIVE OR SIX OF YOUR BEST MEN AND COME WITH ME!
ROGER THAT! I'M EXCITED ALL READY!
HEY?! WHAT ABOUT ME?
YOUR FACE IS ANYTHING BUT INTIMIDAT-ING!
WHAT ABOUT NOW?
Just one little line and look!
NOW YOU'RE ***DEFINITELY*** NOT COMING!
I WISH THE MOVE WOULD JUST BE CANCELED ...

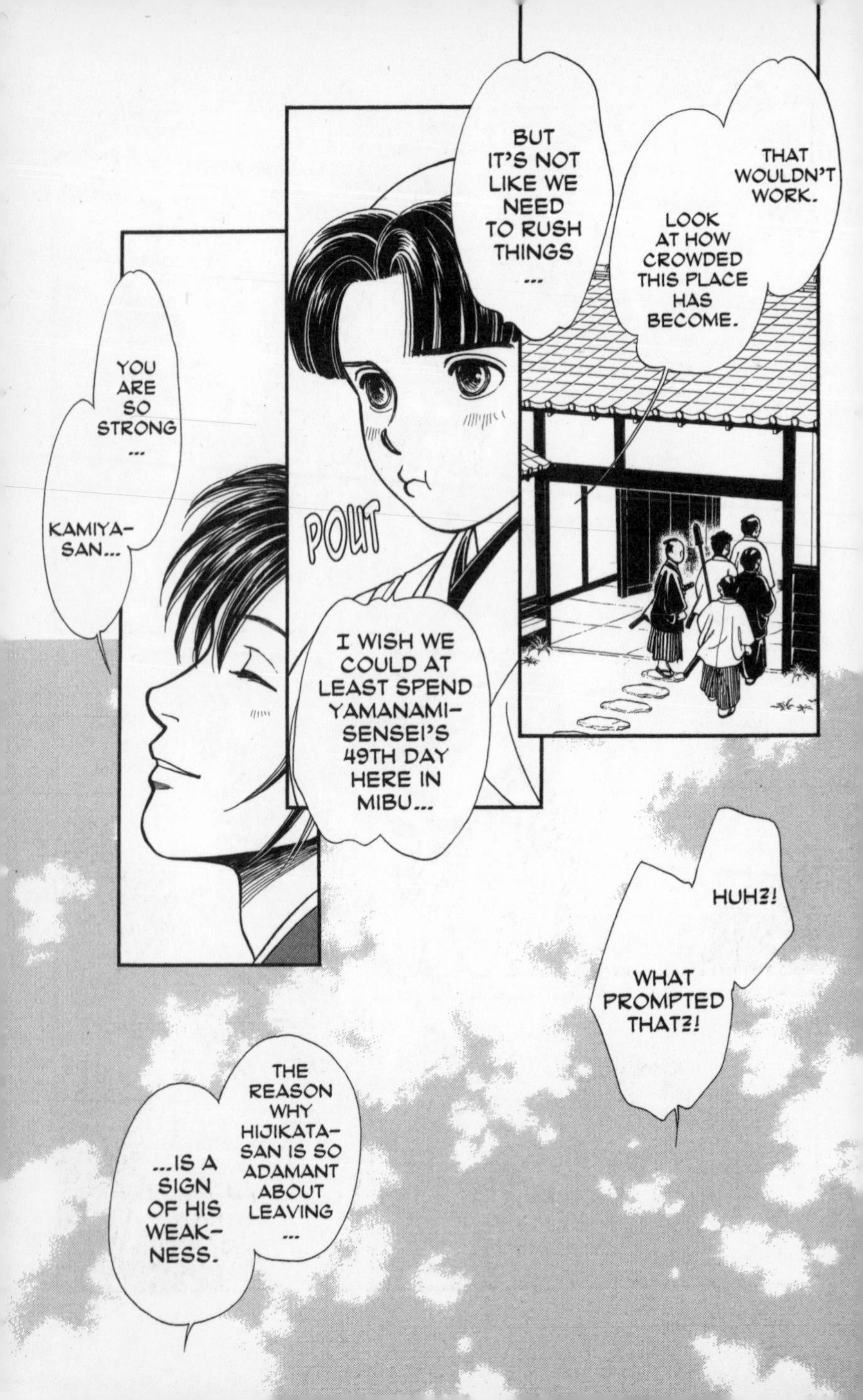

THAT WOULDN'T WORK.
LOOK AT HOW CROWDED THIS PLACE HAS BECOME.
BUT IT'S NOT LIKE WE NEED TO RUSH THINGS ...
POUT
I WISH WE COULD AT LEAST SPEND YAMANAMI-SENSEI'S 49TH DAY HERE IN MIBU...
YOU ARE SO STRONG ...
KAMIYA-SAN...
HUH?!
WHAT PROMPTED THAT?!
THE REASON WHY HIJIKATA-SAN IS SO ADAMANT ABOUT LEAVING ...
...IS A SIGN OF HIS WEAKNESS.

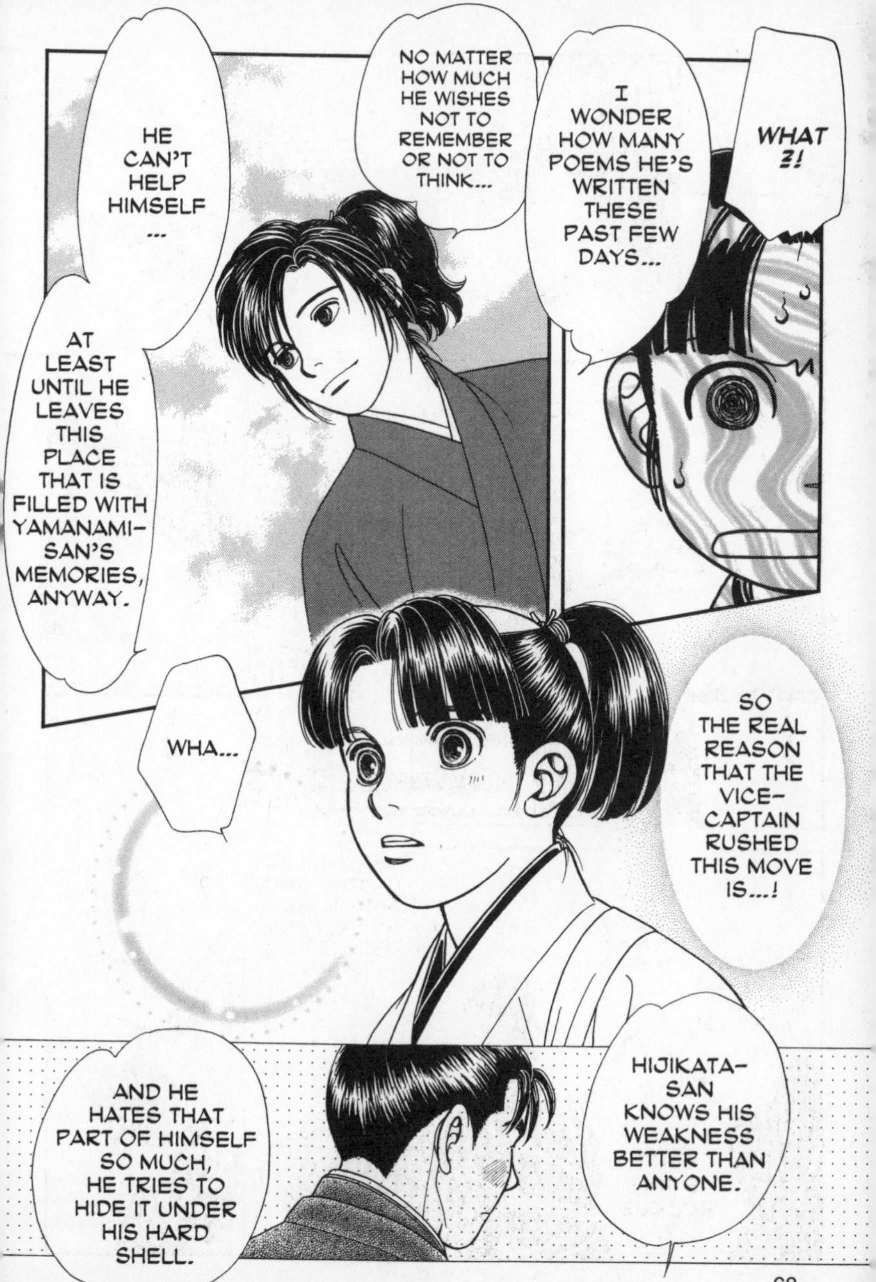

WHAT ?!
I WONDER HOW MANY POEMS HE'S WRITTEN THESE PAST FEW DAYS...
NO MATTER HOW MUCH HE WISHES NOT TO REMEMBER OR NOT TO THINK...
HE CAN'T HELP HIMSELF...
AT LEAST UNTIL HE LEAVES THIS PLACE THAT IS FILLED WITH YAMANAMI-SAN'S MEMORIES, ANYWAY.
SO THE REAL REASON THAT THE VICE-CAPTAIN RUSHED THIS MOVE IS...!
WHA...
HIJIKATA-SAN KNOWS HIS WEAKNESS BETTER THAN ANYONE.
AND HE HATES THAT PART OF HIMSELF SO MUCH, HE TRIES TO HIDE IT UNDER HIS HARD SHELL.

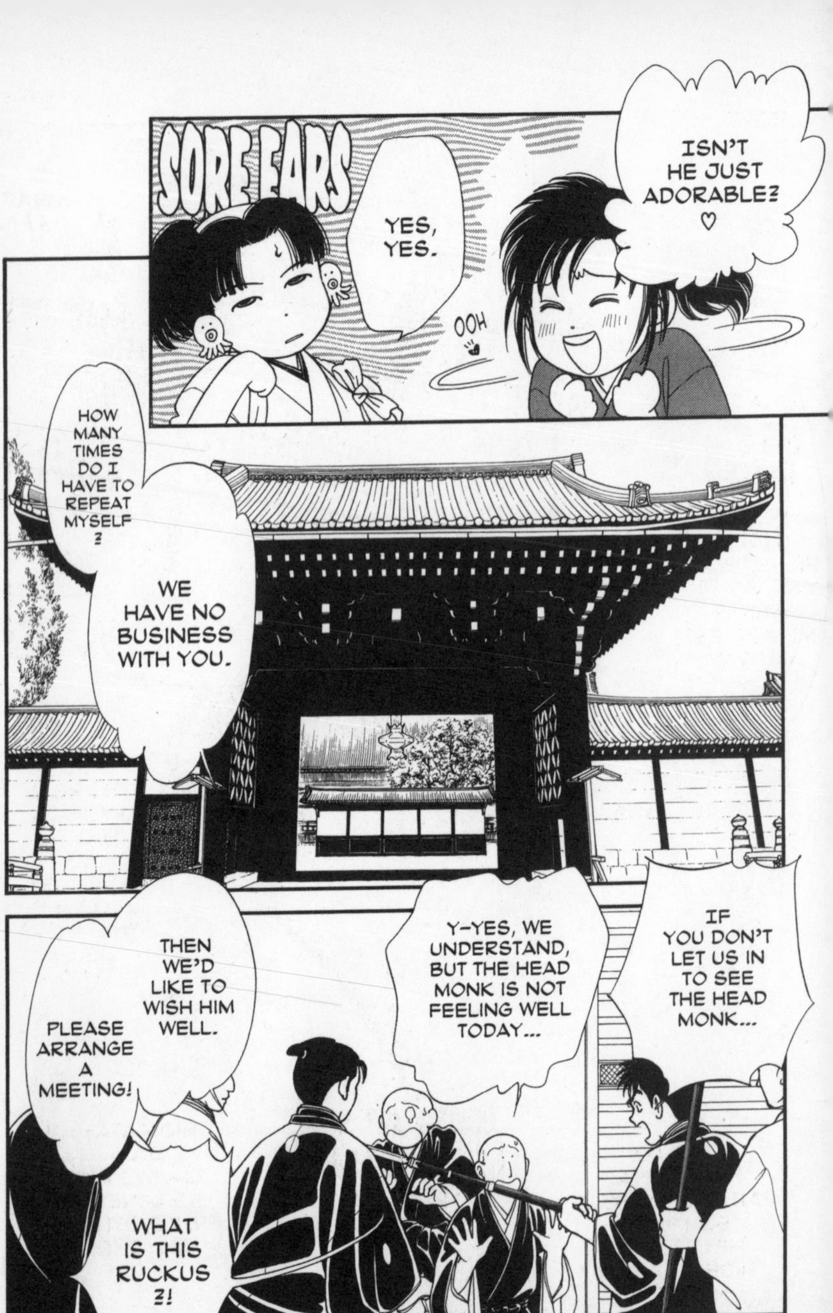

ISN'T HE JUST ADORABLE? ♡
OOH
YES, YES.
SORE EARS
HOW MANY TIMES DO I HAVE TO REPEAT MYSELF?
WE HAVE NO BUSINESS WITH YOU.
IF YOU DON'T LET US IN TO SEE THE HEAD MONK...
Y-YES, WE UNDERSTAND, BUT THE HEAD MONK IS NOT FEELING WELL TODAY...
THEN WE'D LIKE TO WISH HIM WELL.
PLEASE ARRANGE A MEETING!
WHAT IS THIS RUCKUS?!

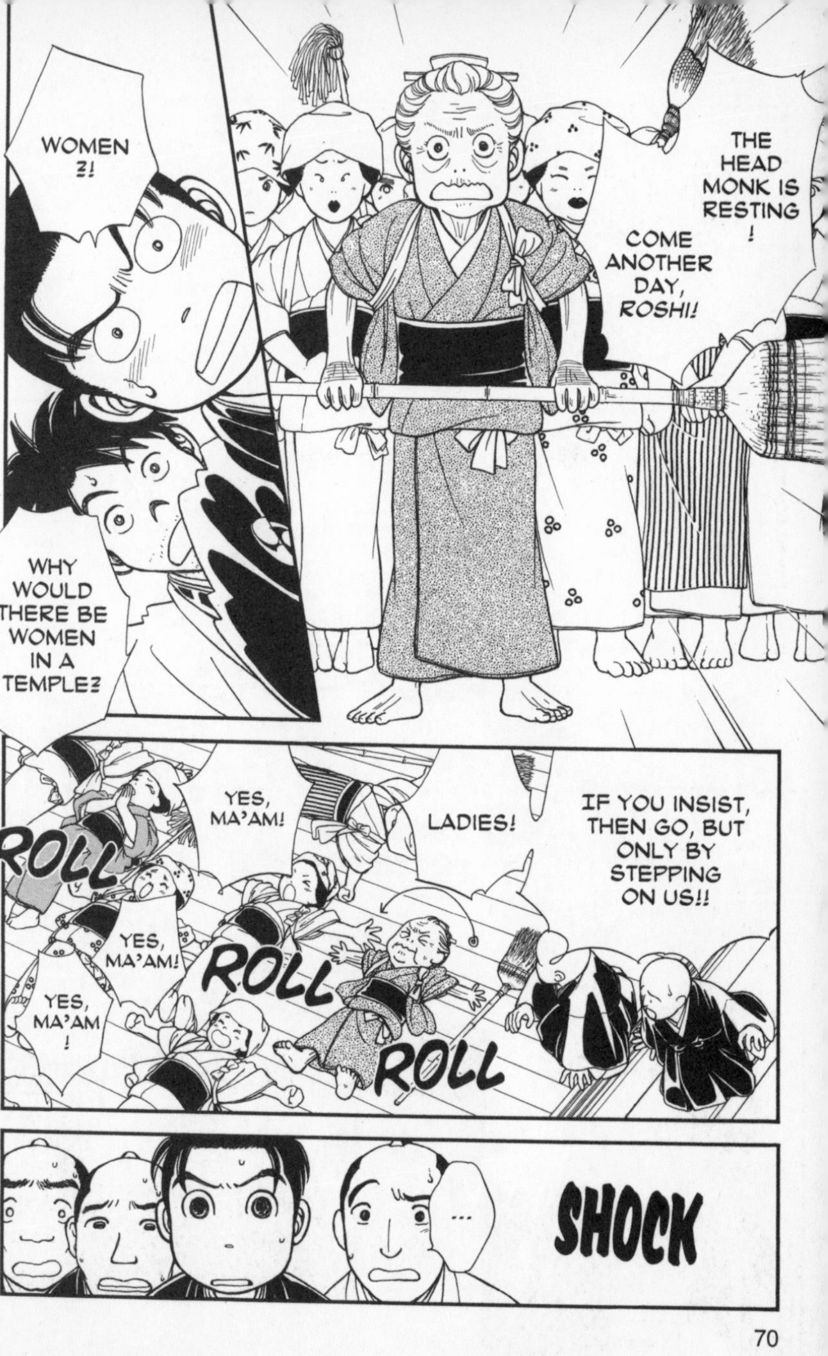
THE HEAD MONK IS RESTING!
COME ANOTHER DAY, ROSHI!
WOMEN?!
WHY WOULD THERE BE WOMEN IN A TEMPLE?
IF YOU INSIST, THEN GO, BUT ONLY BY STEPPING ON US!!
LADIES!
YES, MA'AM!
ROLL
YES, MA'AM!
ROLL
YES, MA'AM!
ROLL
SHOCK
...

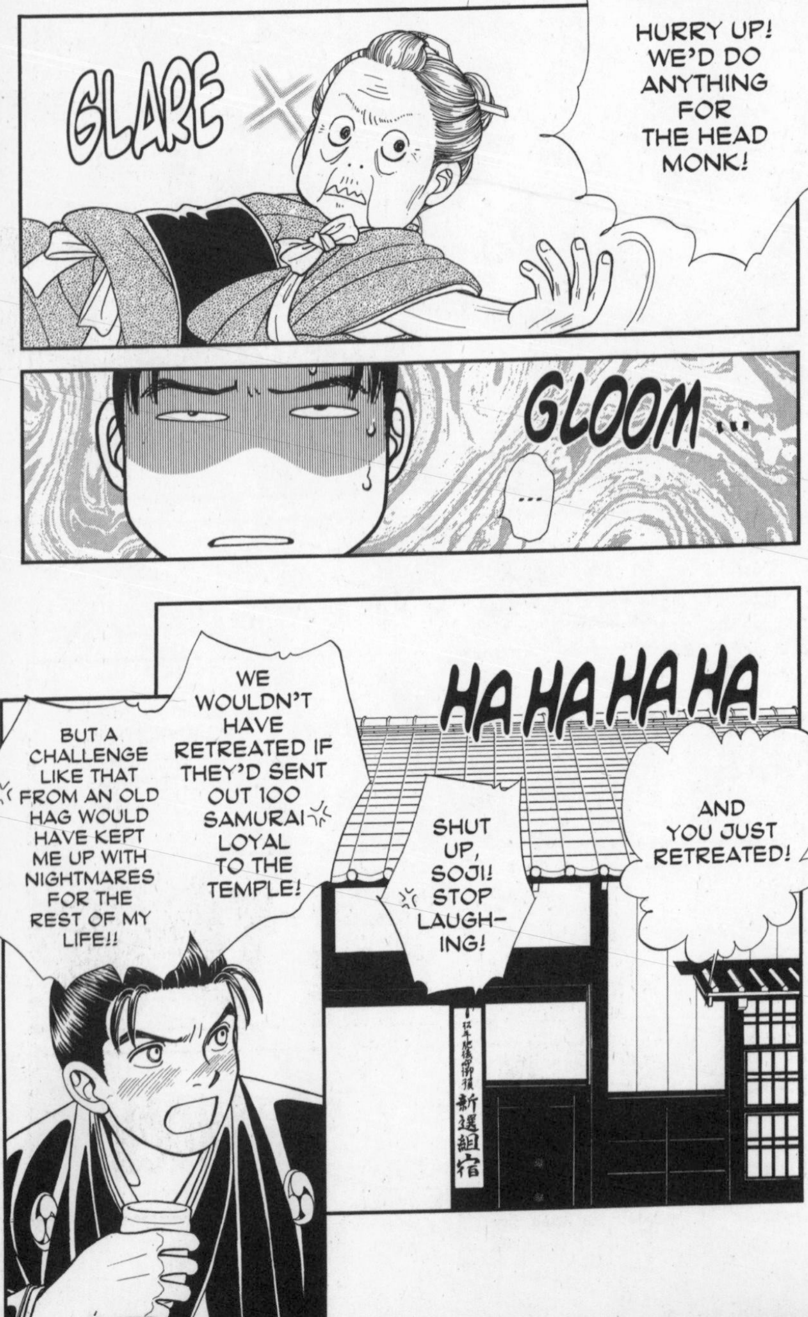
HURRY UP! WE'D DO ANYTHING FOR THE HEAD MONK!
GLARE
GLOOM...
...
HA HA HA HA HA
AND YOU JUST RETREATED!
SHUT UP, SOJI! STOP LAUGH-ING!
WE WOULDN'T HAVE RETREATED IF THEY'D SENT OUT 100 SAMURAI LOYAL TO THE TEMPLE!
BUT A CHALLENGE LIKE THAT FROM AN OLD HAG WOULD HAVE KEPT ME UP WITH NIGHTMARES FOR THE REST OF MY LIFE!!
新選組宿

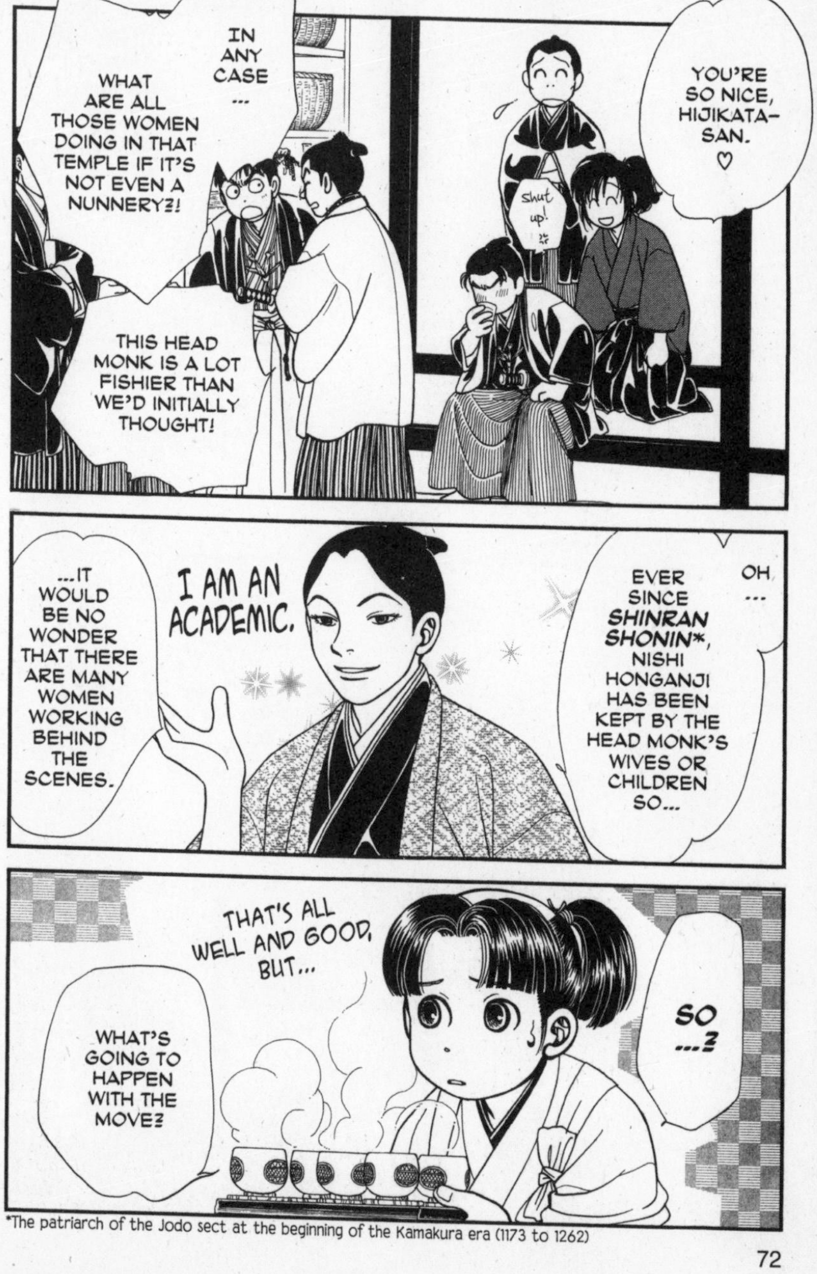

YOU'RE SO NICE, HIJIKATA-SAN. ♡
shut up!
IN ANY CASE ...
WHAT ARE ALL THOSE WOMEN DOING IN THAT TEMPLE IF IT'S NOT EVEN A NUNNERY?!
THIS HEAD MONK IS A LOT FISHIER THAN WE'D INITIALLY THOUGHT!
OH ...
EVER SINCE SHINRAN SHONIN*, NISHI HONGANJI HAS BEEN KEPT BY THE HEAD MONK'S WIVES OR CHILDREN SO...
I AM AN ACADEMIC.
...IT WOULD BE NO WONDER THAT THERE ARE MANY WOMEN WORKING BEHIND THE SCENES.
SO ...?
THAT'S ALL WELL AND GOOD, BUT...
WHAT'S GOING TO HAPPEN WITH THE MOVE?

*The patriarch of the Jodo sect at the beginning of the Kamakura era (1173 to 1262)

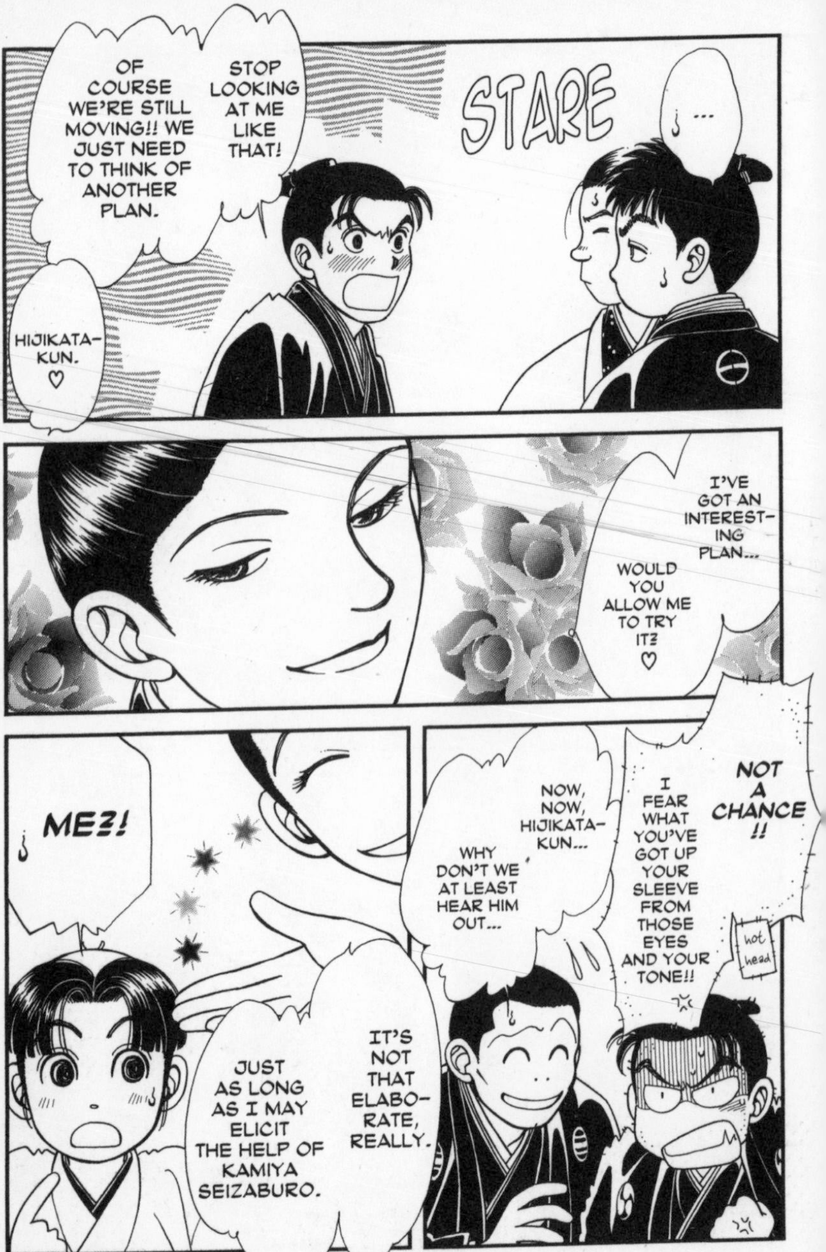
...
STARE
STOP LOOKING AT ME LIKE THAT!
OF COURSE WE'RE STILL MOVING!! WE JUST NEED TO THINK OF ANOTHER PLAN.
HIJIKATA-KUN. ♡
I'VE GOT AN INTERESTING PLAN...
WOULD YOU ALLOW ME TO TRY IT? ♡
NOT A CHANCE!!
I FEAR WHAT YOU'VE GOT UP YOUR SLEEVE FROM THOSE EYES AND YOUR TONE!!
hot head
NOW, NOW, HIJIKATA-KUN...
WHY DON'T WE AT LEAST HEAR HIM OUT...
ME?!
IT'S NOT THAT ELABORATE, REALLY.
JUST AS LONG AS I MAY ELICIT THE HELP OF KAMIYA SEIZABURO.

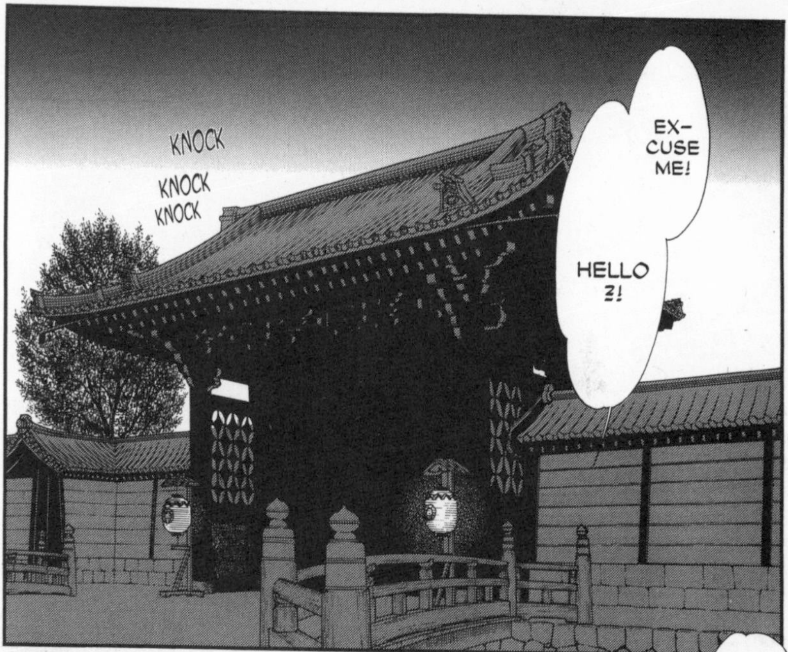
EX-CUSE ME!
HELLO?!
KNOCK
KNOCK KNOCK

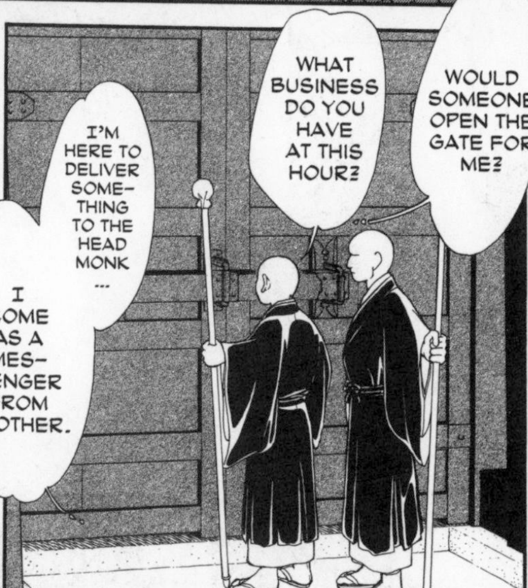
WOULD SOMEONE OPEN THE GATE FOR ME?
WHAT BUSINESS DO YOU HAVE AT THIS HOUR?
I'M HERE TO DELIVER SOME-THING TO THE HEAD MONK...
I COME AS A MES-SENGER FROM ANOTHER.

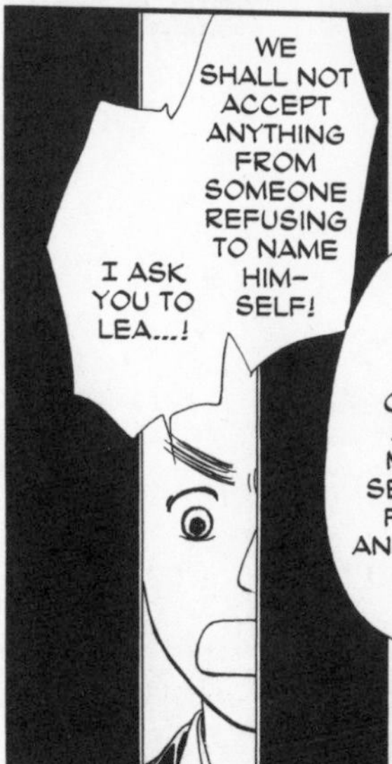
WE SHALL NOT ACCEPT ANYTHING FROM SOMEONE REFUSING TO NAME HIM-SELF!
I ASK YOU TO LEA...!

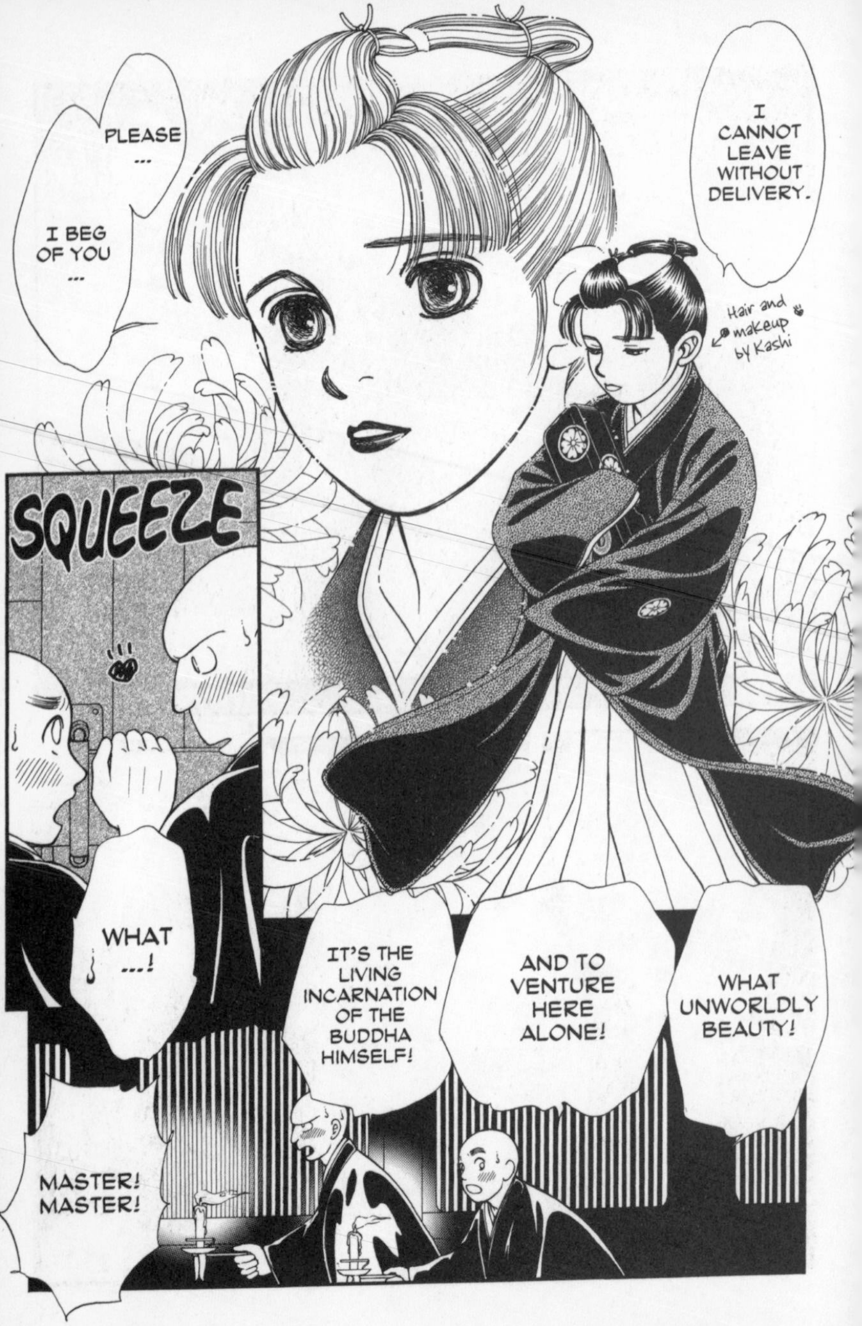
I CANNOT LEAVE WITHOUT DELIVERY.
Hair and makeup by Kashi
PLEASE ...
I BEG OF YOU ...
SQUEEZE
WHAT ...!
WHAT UNWORLDLY BEAUTY!
AND TO VENTURE HERE ALONE!
IT'S THE LIVING INCARNATION OF THE BUDDHA HIMSELF!
MASTER! MASTER!

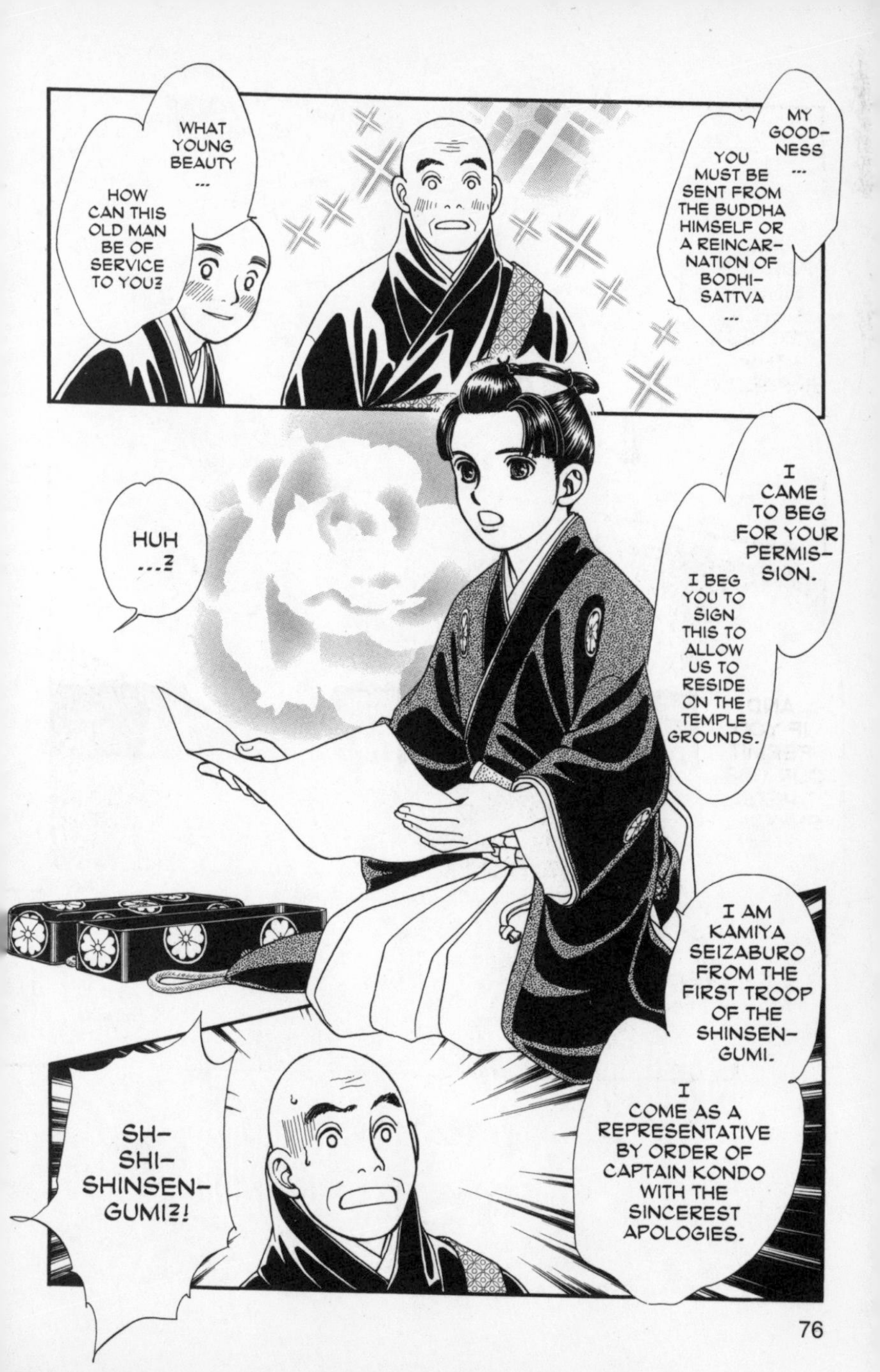
MY GOODNESS ...
YOU MUST BE SENT FROM THE BUDDHA HIMSELF OR A REINCARNATION OF BODHISATTVA ...
WHAT YOUNG BEAUTY ...
HOW CAN THIS OLD MAN BE OF SERVICE TO YOU?
I CAME TO BEG FOR YOUR PERMISSION.
I BEG YOU TO SIGN THIS TO ALLOW US TO RESIDE ON THE TEMPLE GROUNDS.
HUH ...?
I AM KAMIYA SEIZABURO FROM THE FIRST TROOP OF THE SHINSENGUMI.
I COME AS A REPRESENTATIVE BY ORDER OF CAPTAIN KONDO WITH THE SINCEREST APOLOGIES.
SH-SHI-SHINSENGUMI?!

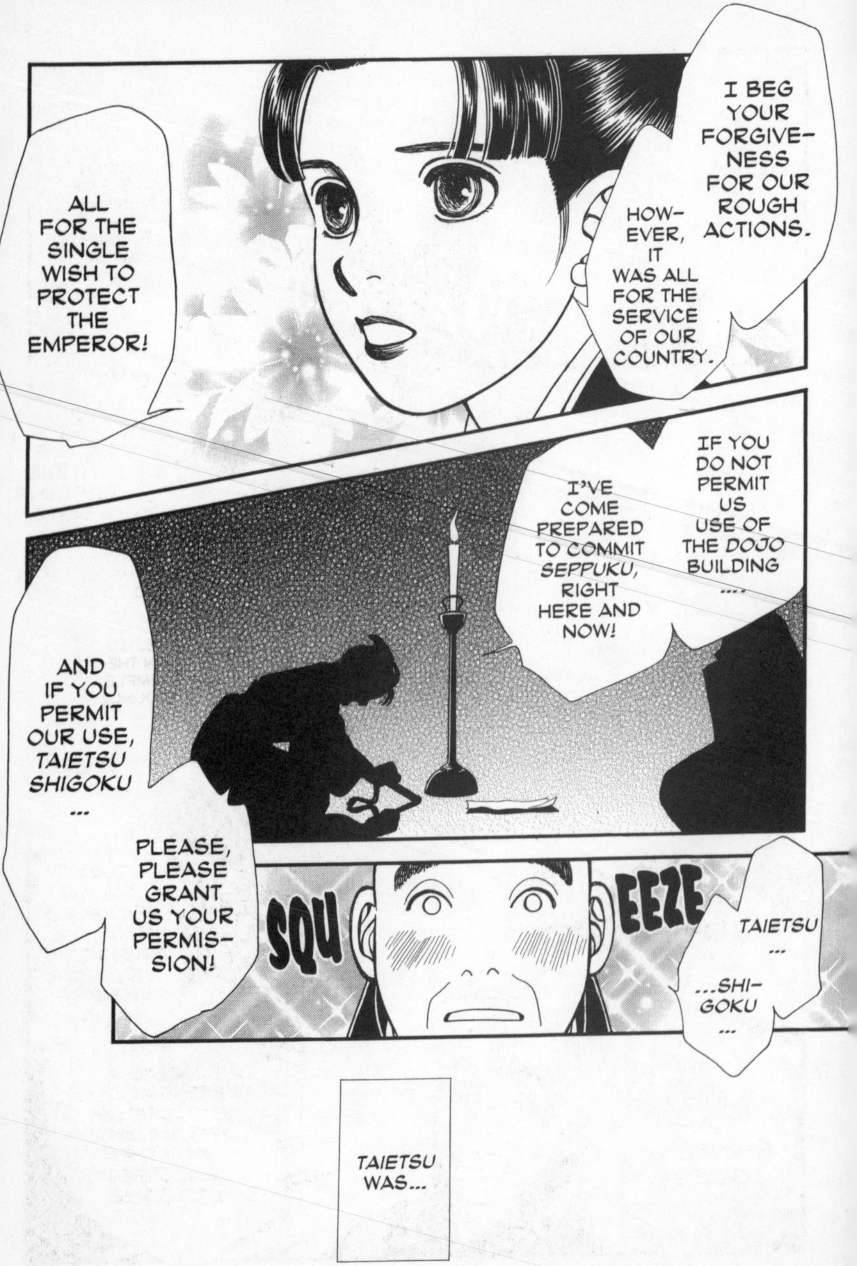

I BEG YOUR FORGIVENESS FOR OUR ROUGH ACTIONS.
HOWEVER, IT WAS ALL FOR THE SERVICE OF OUR COUNTRY.
ALL FOR THE SINGLE WISH TO PROTECT THE EMPEROR!
IF YOU DO NOT PERMIT US USE OF THE *DOJO* BUILDING...
I'VE COME PREPARED TO COMMIT *SEPPUKU*, RIGHT HERE AND NOW!
AND IF YOU PERMIT OUR USE, *TAIETSU SHIGOKU*...
PLEASE, PLEASE GRANT US YOUR PERMISSION!
TAIETSU... ...*SHIGOKU*...
SQUEEZE
TAIETSU WAS...

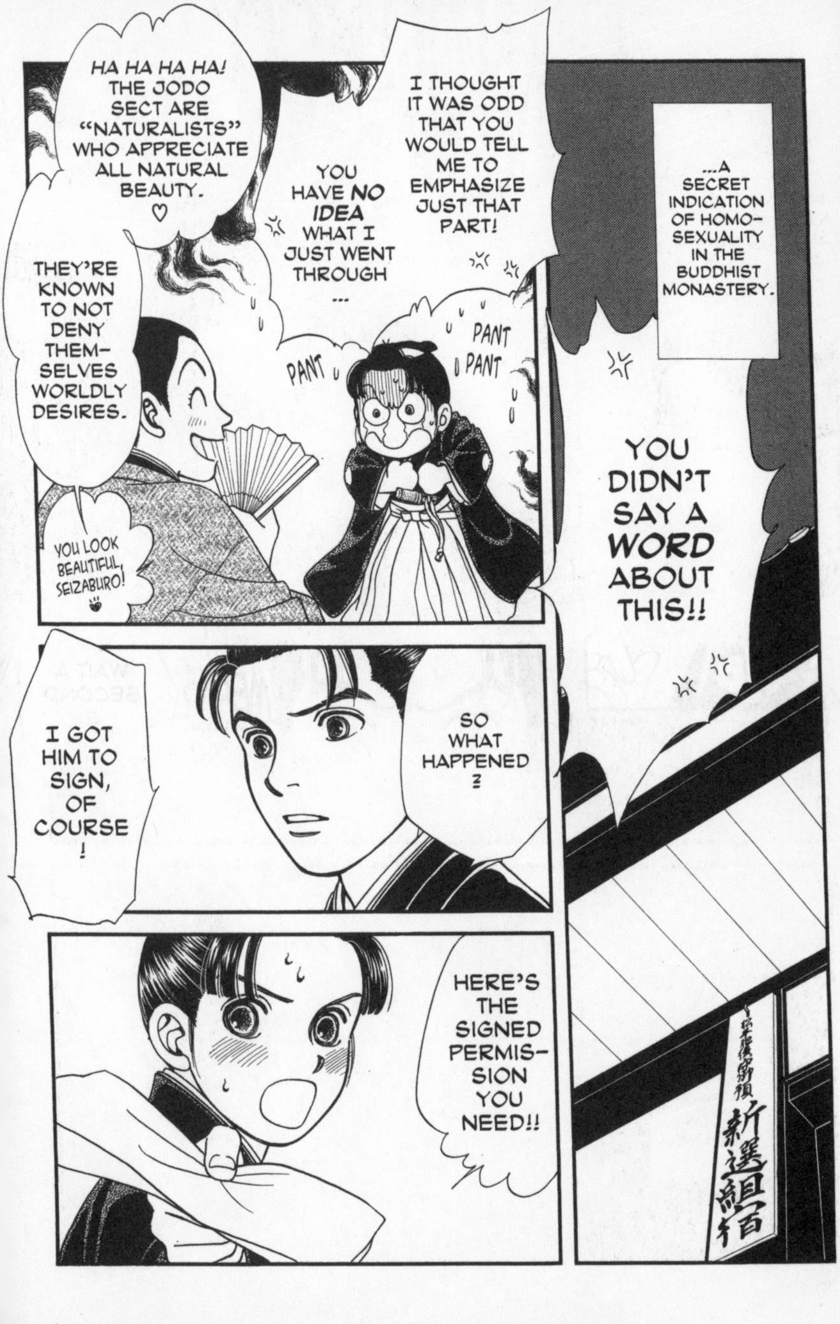
...A SECRET INDICATION OF HOMOSEXUALITY IN THE BUDDHIST MONASTERY.
YOU DIDN'T SAY A *WORD* ABOUT THIS!!
新選組宿
I THOUGHT IT WAS ODD THAT YOU WOULD TELL ME TO EMPHASIZE JUST THAT PART!
YOU HAVE *NO IDEA* WHAT I JUST WENT THROUGH ...
PANT PANT
PANT
HA HA HA HA! THE JODO SECT ARE "NATURALISTS" WHO APPRECIATE ALL NATURAL BEAUTY. ♡
THEY'RE KNOWN TO NOT DENY THEMSELVES WORLDLY DESIRES.
YOU LOOK BEAUTIFUL, SEIZABURO!
SO WHAT HAPPENED?
I GOT HIM TO SIGN, OF COURSE!
HERE'S THE SIGNED PERMISSION YOU NEED!!

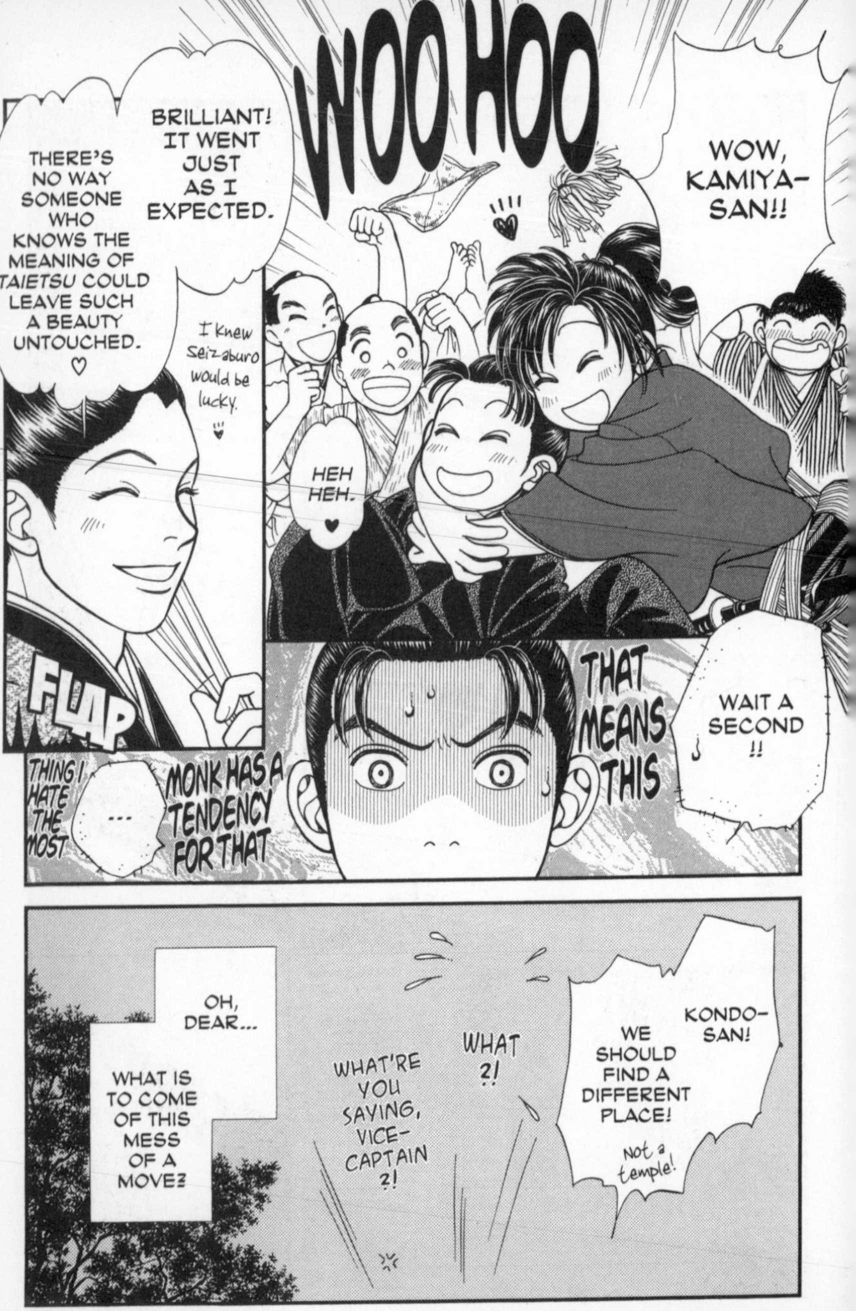
WOW, KAMIYA-SAN!!
WOO HOO
I knew Seizaburo would be lucky.
HEH HEH.
BRILLIANT! IT WENT JUST AS I EXPECTED.
THERE'S NO WAY SOMEONE WHO KNOWS THE MEANING OF *TAIETSU* COULD LEAVE SUCH A BEAUTY UNTOUCHED. ♡
FLAP
WAIT A SECOND!!
THAT MEANS THIS
MONK HAS A TENDENCY FOR THAT
...
THING I HATE THE MOST
KONDO-SAN! WE SHOULD FIND A DIFFERENT PLACE!
Not a temple!
WHAT?!
WHAT'RE YOU SAYING, VICE-CAPTAIN?!
OH, DEAR...
WHAT IS TO COME OF THIS MESS OF A MOVE?

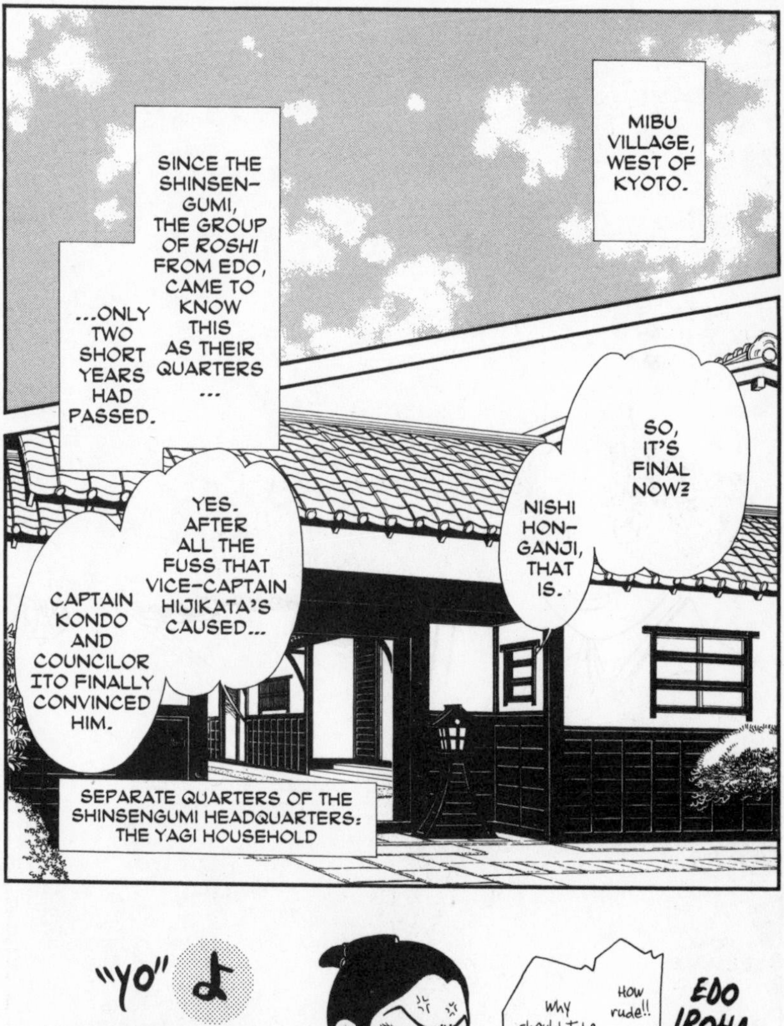
MIBU VILLAGE, WEST OF KYOTO.
SINCE THE SHINSEN-GUMI, THE GROUP OF *ROSHI* FROM EDO, CAME TO KNOW THIS AS THEIR QUARTERS...
...ONLY TWO SHORT YEARS HAD PASSED.
SO, IT'S FINAL NOW?
NISHI HON-GANJI, THAT IS.
YES. AFTER ALL THE FUSS THAT VICE-CAPTAIN HIJIKATA'S CAUSED...
CAPTAIN KONDO AND COUNCILOR ITO FINALLY CONVINCED HIM.
SEPARATE QUARTERS OF THE SHINSENGUMI HEADQUARTERS: THE YAGI HOUSEHOLD

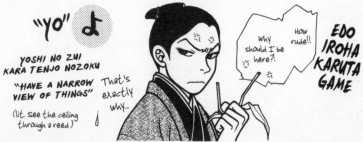

EDO IROHA KARUTA GAME

"YO" よ

YOSHI NO ZUI KARA TENJO NOZOKU

"HAVE A NARROW VIEW OF THINGS"

(lit. see the ceiling through a reed)

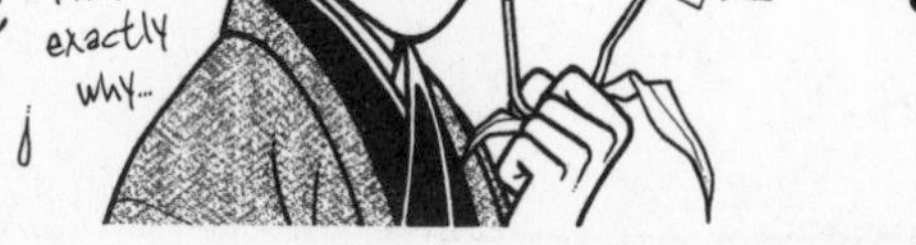
How rude!!
Why should I be here?!
That's exactly why...

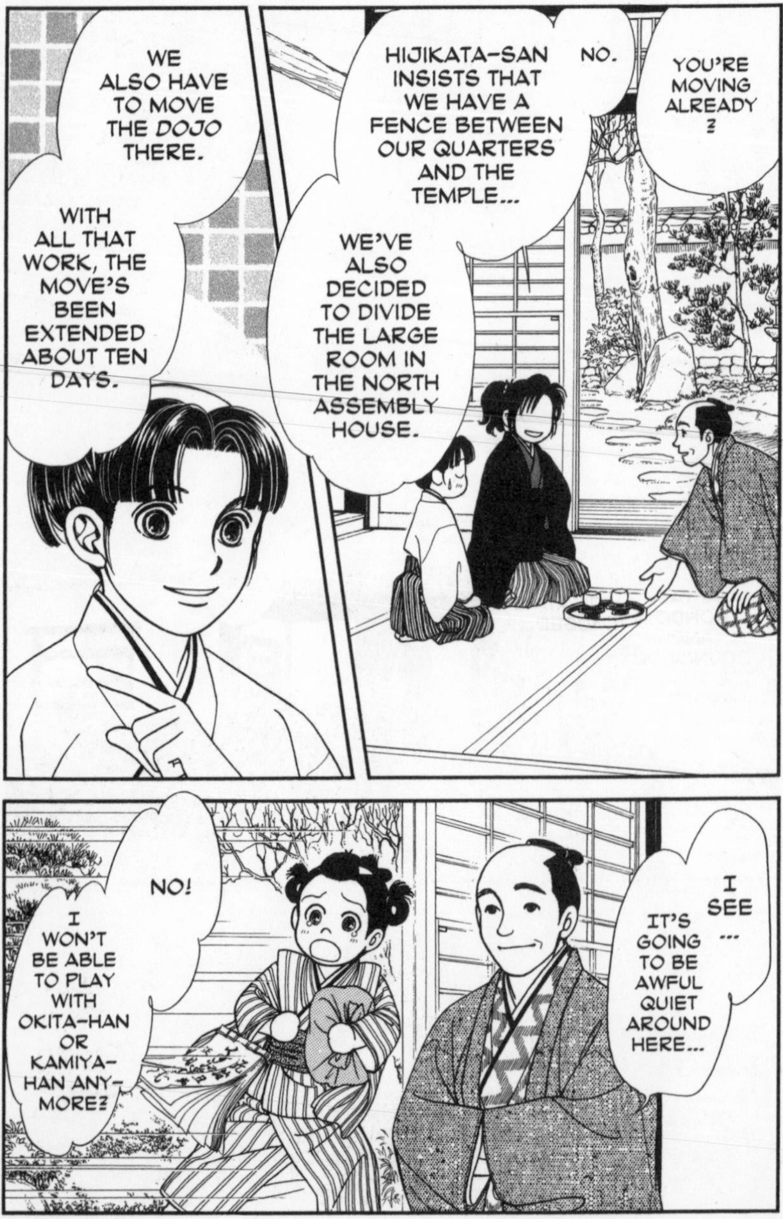
YOU'RE MOVING ALREADY?
NO.
HIJIKATA-SAN INSISTS THAT WE HAVE A FENCE BETWEEN OUR QUARTERS AND THE TEMPLE...
WE'VE ALSO DECIDED TO DIVIDE THE LARGE ROOM IN THE NORTH ASSEMBLY HOUSE.
WE ALSO HAVE TO MOVE THE *DOJO* THERE.
WITH ALL THAT WORK, THE MOVE'S BEEN EXTENDED ABOUT TEN DAYS.
I SEE...
IT'S GOING TO BE AWFUL QUIET AROUND HERE...
NO!
I WON'T BE ABLE TO PLAY WITH OKITA-HAN OR KAMIYA-HAN ANYMORE?

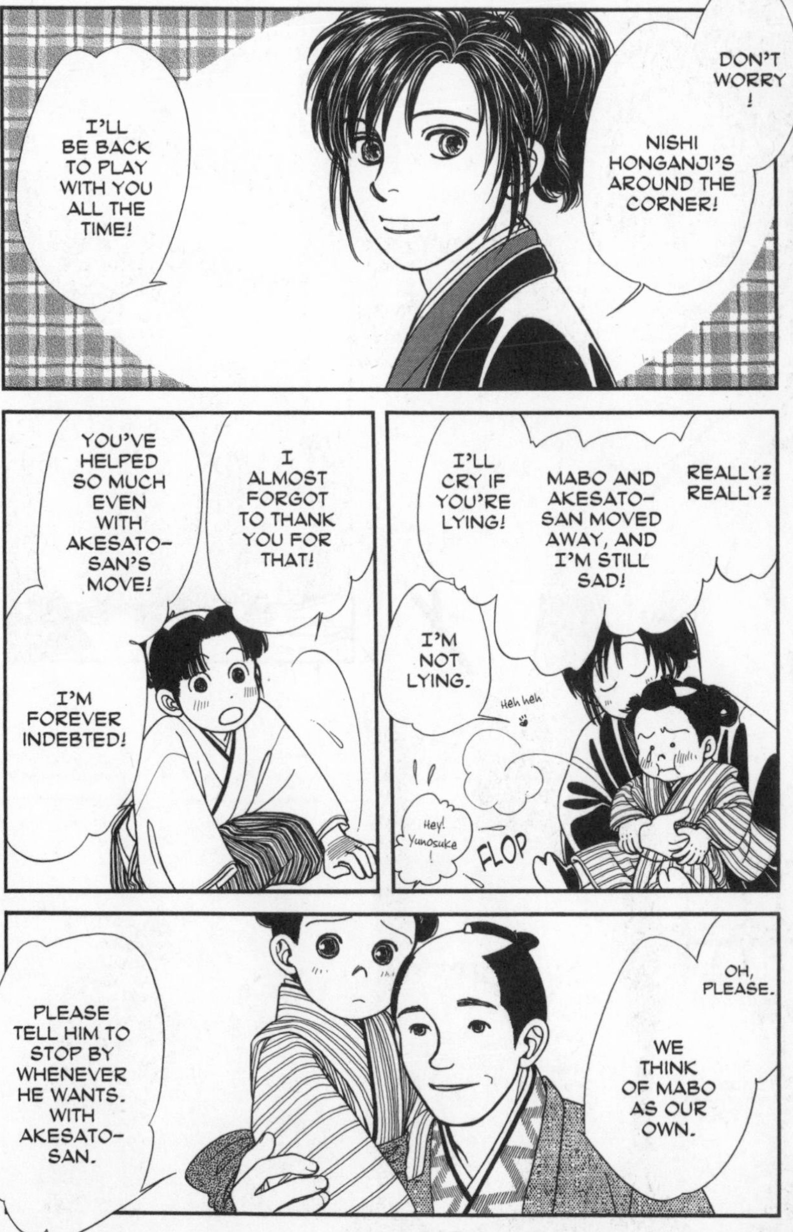
DON'T WORRY!
NISHI HONGANJI'S AROUND THE CORNER!
I'LL BE BACK TO PLAY WITH YOU ALL THE TIME!
REALLY? REALLY?
MABO AND AKESATO-SAN MOVED AWAY, AND I'M STILL SAD!
I'LL CRY IF YOU'RE LYING!
I'M NOT LYING.
Heh heh
FLOP
Hey! Yunosuke!
I ALMOST FORGOT TO THANK YOU FOR THAT!
YOU'VE HELPED SO MUCH EVEN WITH AKESATO-SAN'S MOVE!
I'M FOREVER INDEBTED!
OH, PLEASE.
WE THINK OF MABO AS OUR OWN.
PLEASE TELL HIM TO STOP BY WHENEVER HE WANTS. WITH AKESATO-SAN.

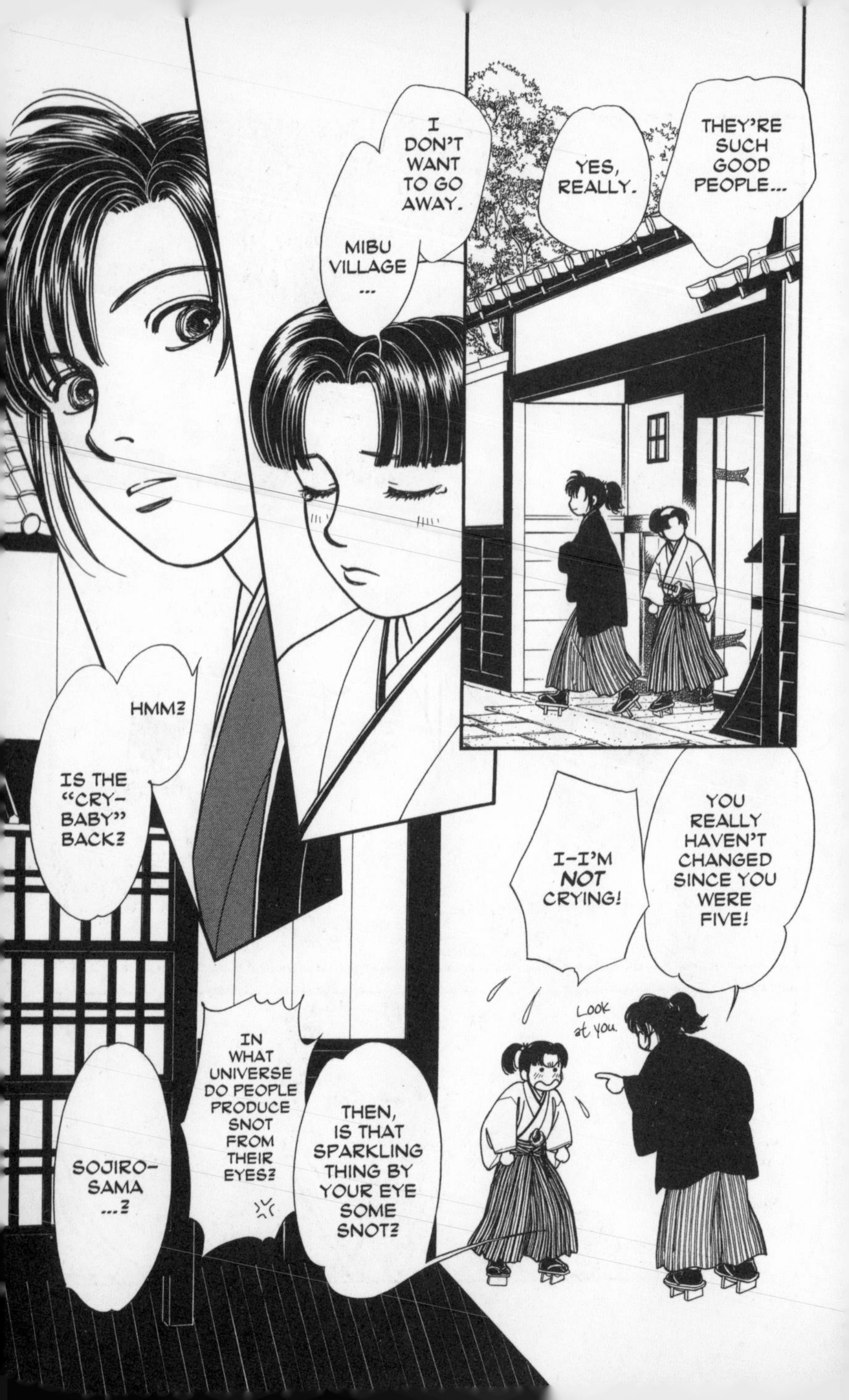
THEY'RE SUCH GOOD PEOPLE...
YES, REALLY.
YOU REALLY HAVEN'T CHANGED SINCE YOU WERE FIVE!
I-I'M NOT CRYING!
Look at you.
THEN, IS THAT SPARKLING THING BY YOUR EYE SOME SNOT?
IN WHAT UNIVERSE DO PEOPLE PRODUCE SNOT FROM THEIR EYES?
I DON'T WANT TO GO AWAY.
MIBU VILLAGE ...
HMM?
IS THE "CRY-BABY" BACK?
SOJIRO-SAMA ...?

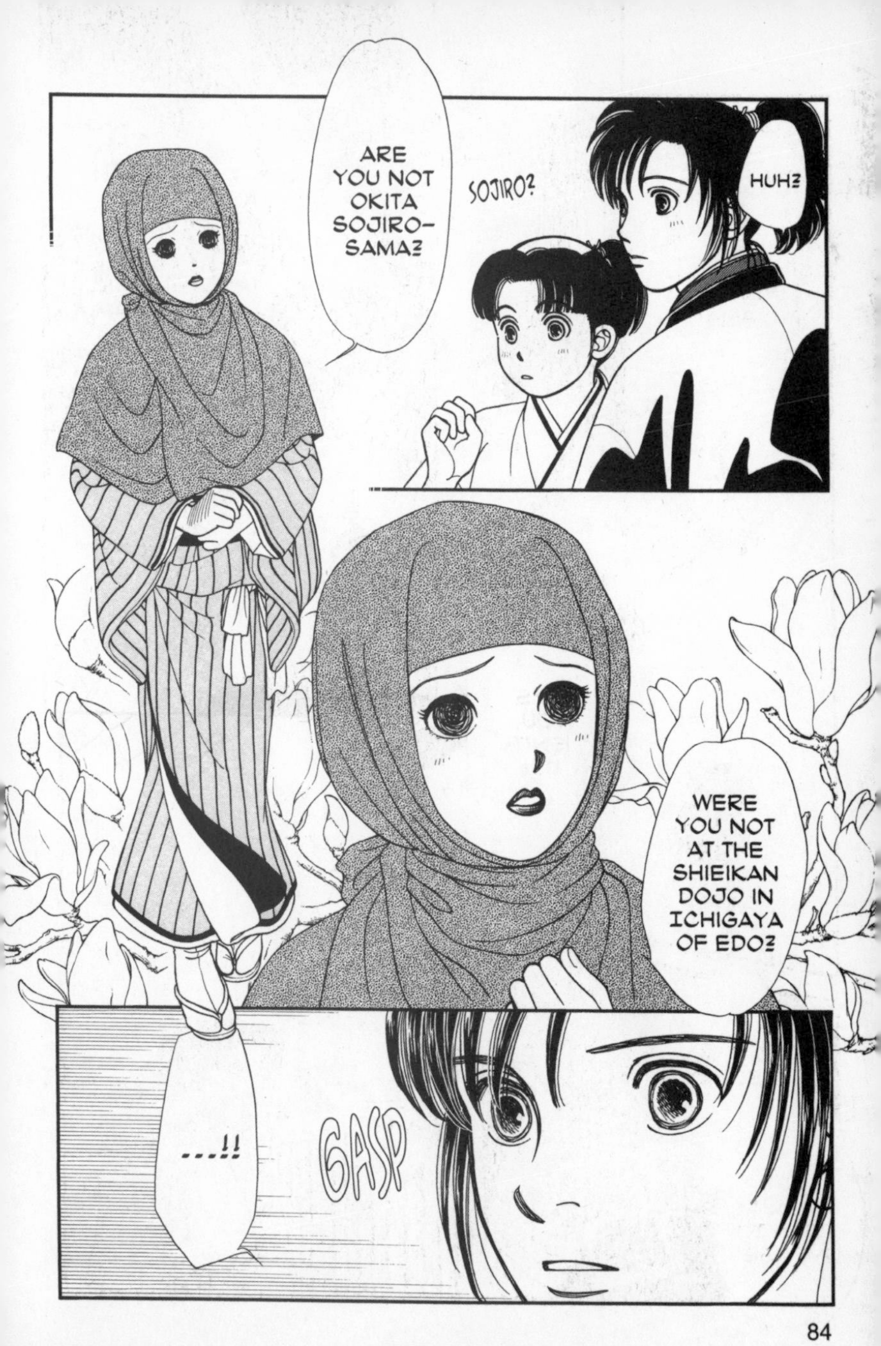
HUH?
SOJIRO?
ARE YOU NOT OKITA SOJIRO-SAMA?
WERE YOU NOT AT THE SHIEIKAN DOJO IN ICHIGAYA OF EDO?
GASP
...!!

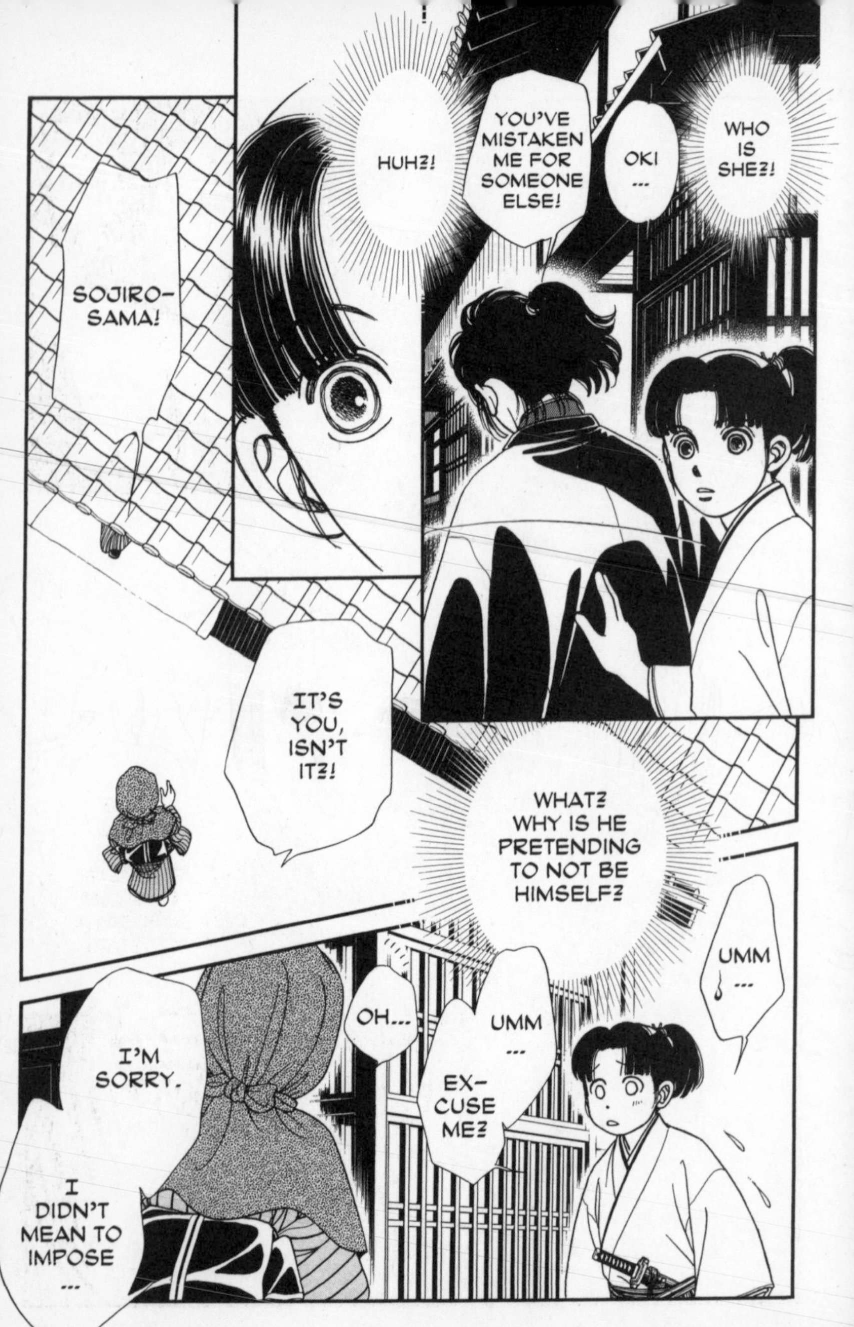
WHO IS SHE?!
OKI ...
YOU'VE MISTAKEN ME FOR SOMEONE ELSE!
HUH?!
SOJIRO-SAMA!
IT'S YOU, ISN'T IT?!
WHAT? WHY IS HE PRETENDING TO NOT BE HIMSELF?
UMM ...
UMM ...
EX-CUSE ME?
OH...
I'M SORRY.
I DIDN'T MEAN TO IMPOSE ...

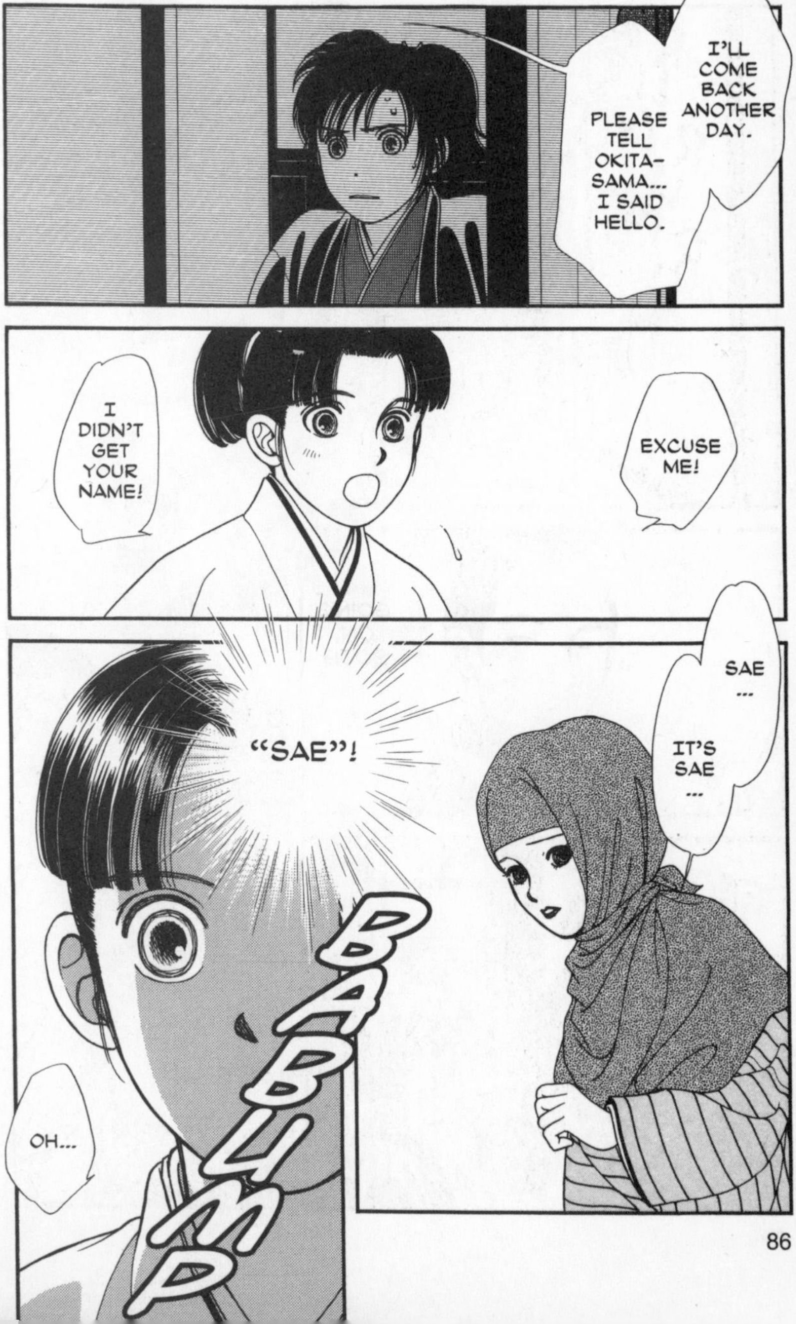
I'LL COME BACK ANOTHER DAY.
PLEASE TELL OKITA-SAMA... I SAID HELLO.
EXCUSE ME!
I DIDN'T GET YOUR NAME!
SAE ...
IT'S SAE ...
"SAE"!
BABUMP
OH...

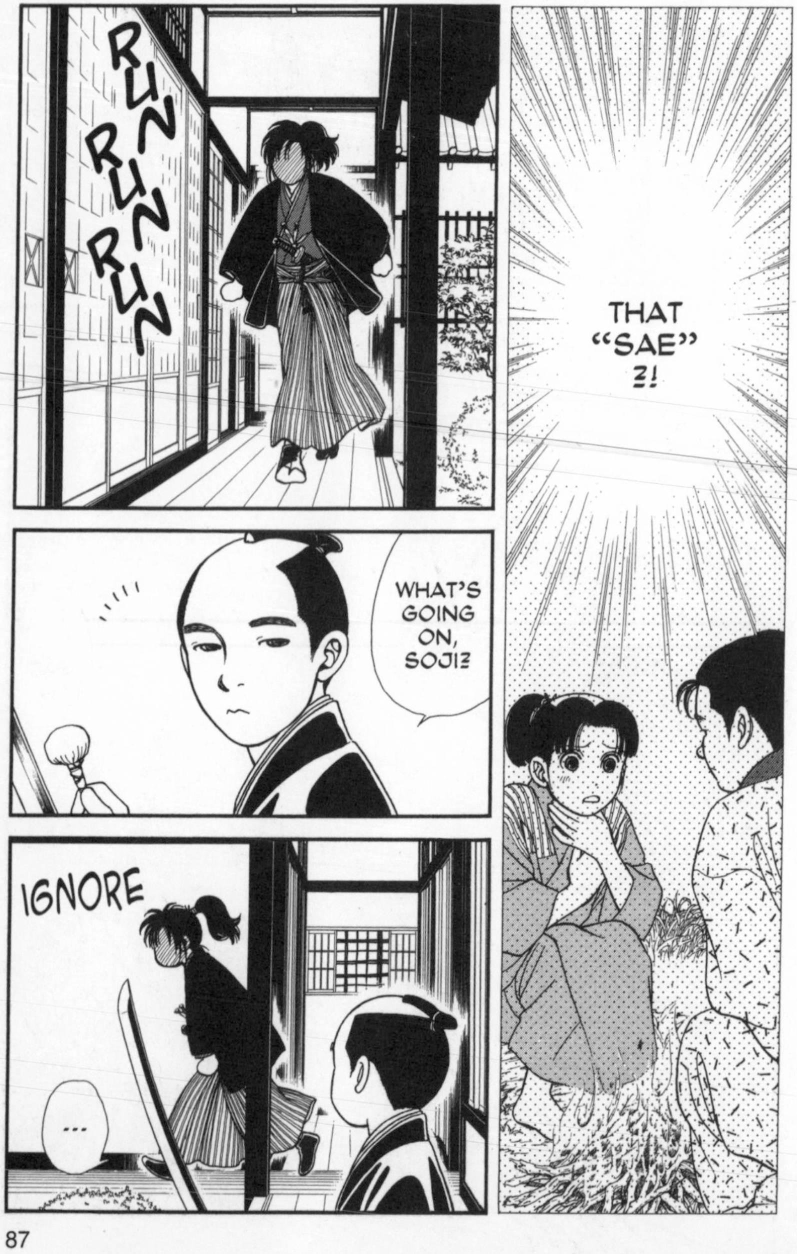
THAT "SAE" ?!
RUN RUN RUN RUN
...
WHAT'S GOING ON, SOJI?
IGNORE
...

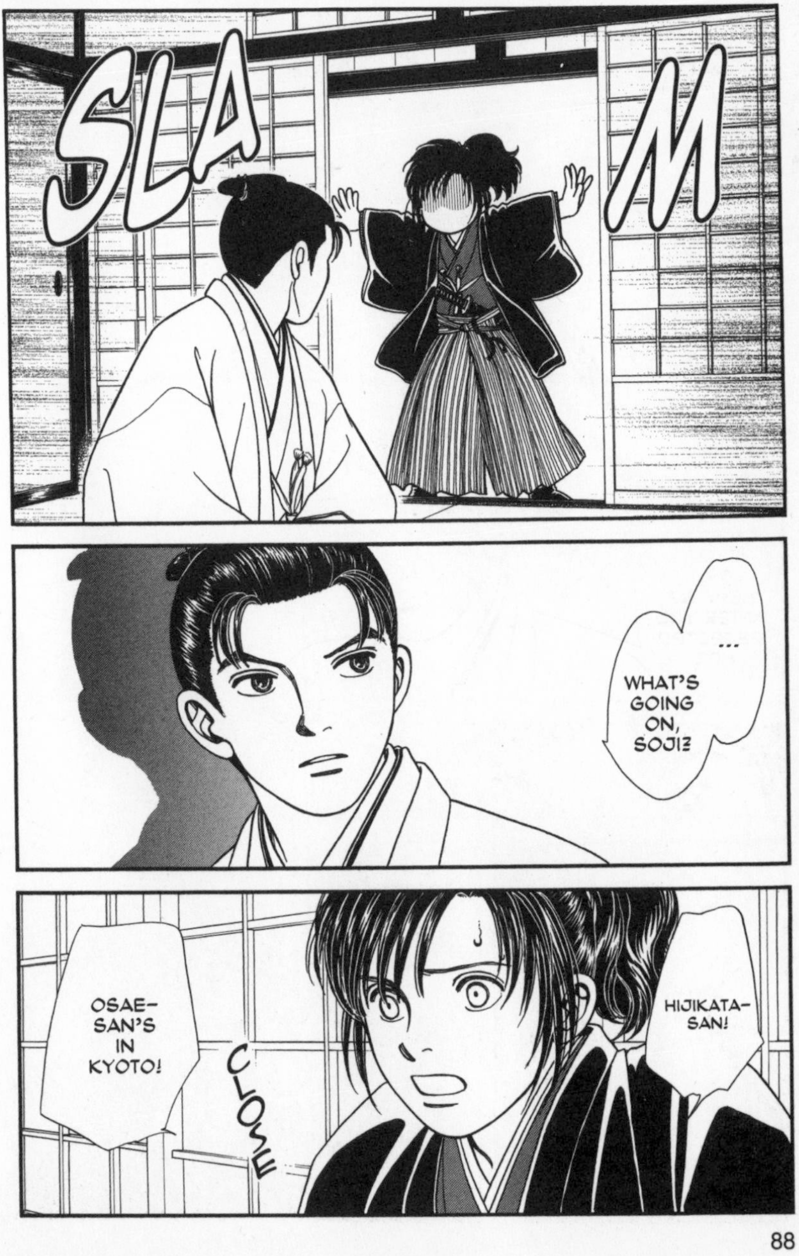
SLAM
...
WHAT'S GOING ON, SOJI!?
HIJIKATA-SAN!
OSAE-SAN'S IN KYOTO!
CLOSE

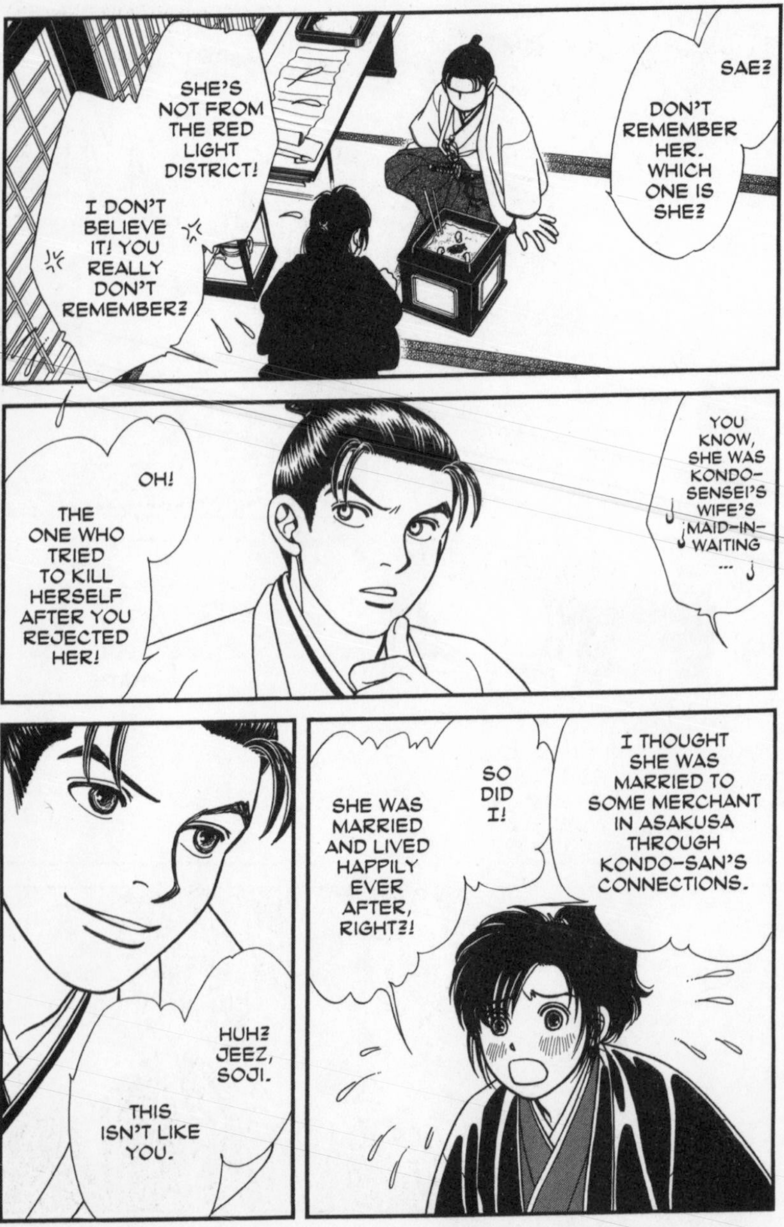
SAE?
DON'T REMEMBER HER. WHICH ONE IS SHE?
SHE'S NOT FROM THE RED LIGHT DISTRICT!
I DON'T BELIEVE IT! YOU REALLY DON'T REMEMBER?
YOU KNOW, SHE WAS KONDO-SENSEI'S WIFE'S MAID-IN-WAITING...
OH!
THE ONE WHO TRIED TO KILL HERSELF AFTER YOU REJECTED HER!
I THOUGHT SHE WAS MARRIED TO SOME MERCHANT IN ASAKUSA THROUGH KONDO-SAN'S CONNECTIONS.
SO DID I!
SHE WAS MARRIED AND LIVED HAPPILY EVER AFTER, RIGHT?!
HUH? JEEZ, SOJI.
THIS ISN'T LIKE YOU.

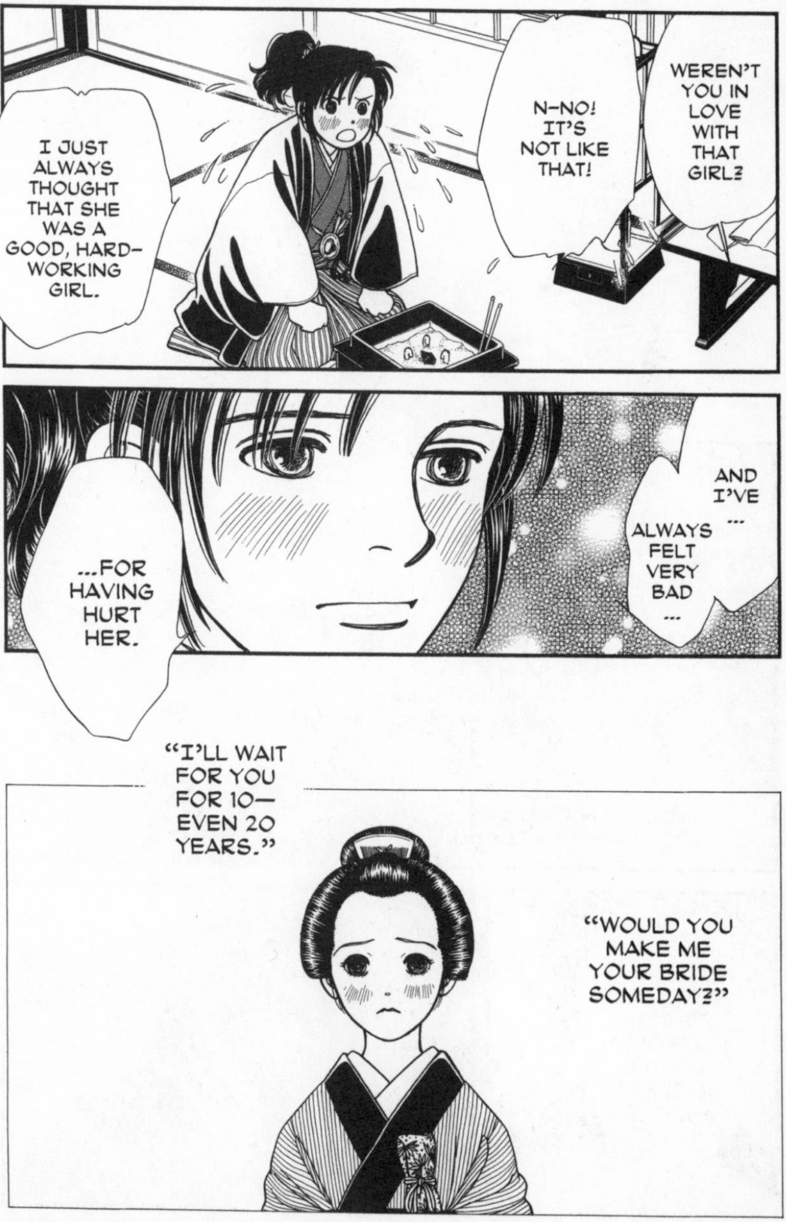
WEREN'T YOU IN LOVE WITH THAT GIRL?
N-NO! IT'S NOT LIKE THAT!
I JUST ALWAYS THOUGHT THAT SHE WAS A GOOD, HARD-WORKING GIRL.
AND I'VE ... ALWAYS FELT VERY BAD ...
...FOR HAVING HURT HER.
"WOULD YOU MAKE ME YOUR BRIDE SOMEDAY?"
"I'LL WAIT FOR YOU FOR 10— EVEN 20 YEARS."

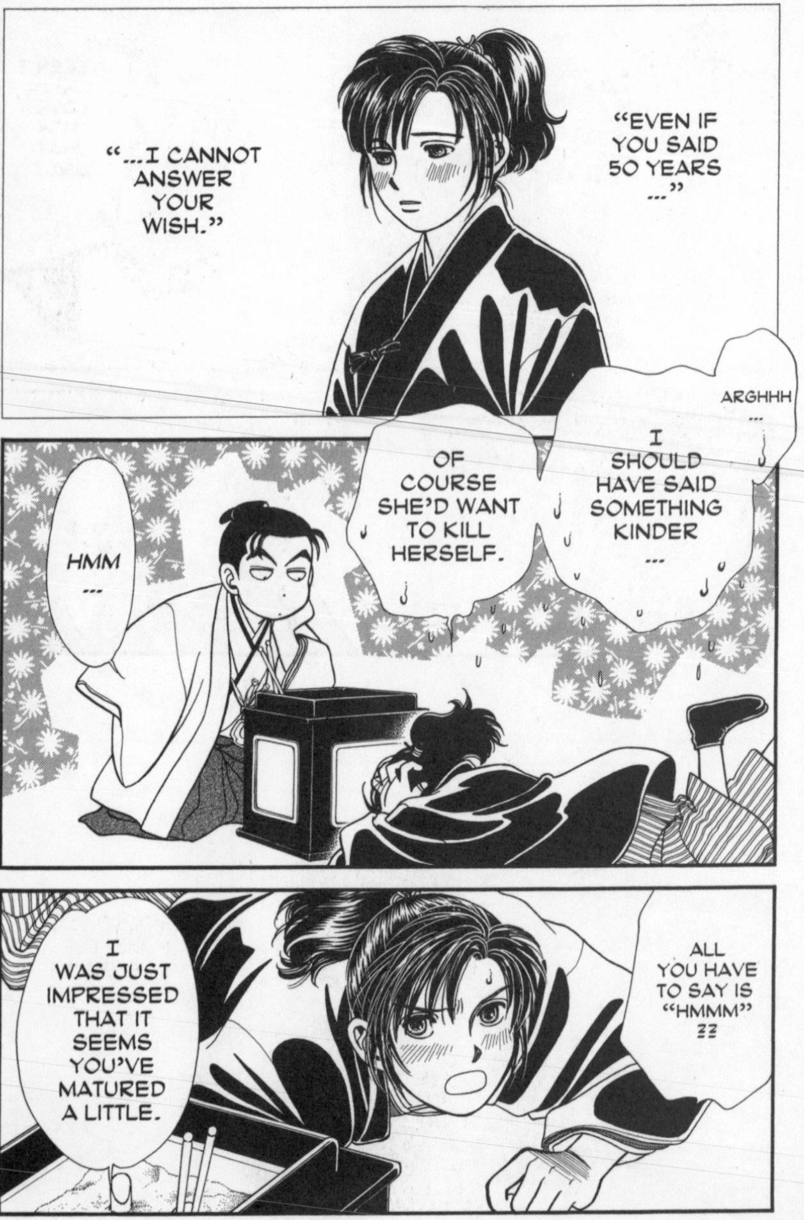
"EVEN IF YOU SAID 50 YEARS ..."
"...I CANNOT ANSWER YOUR WISH."
ARGHHH ...
I SHOULD HAVE SAID SOMETHING KINDER ...
OF COURSE SHE'D WANT TO KILL HERSELF.
HMM ...
ALL YOU HAVE TO SAY IS "HMMM"??
I WAS JUST IMPRESSED THAT IT SEEMS YOU'VE MATURED A LITTLE.

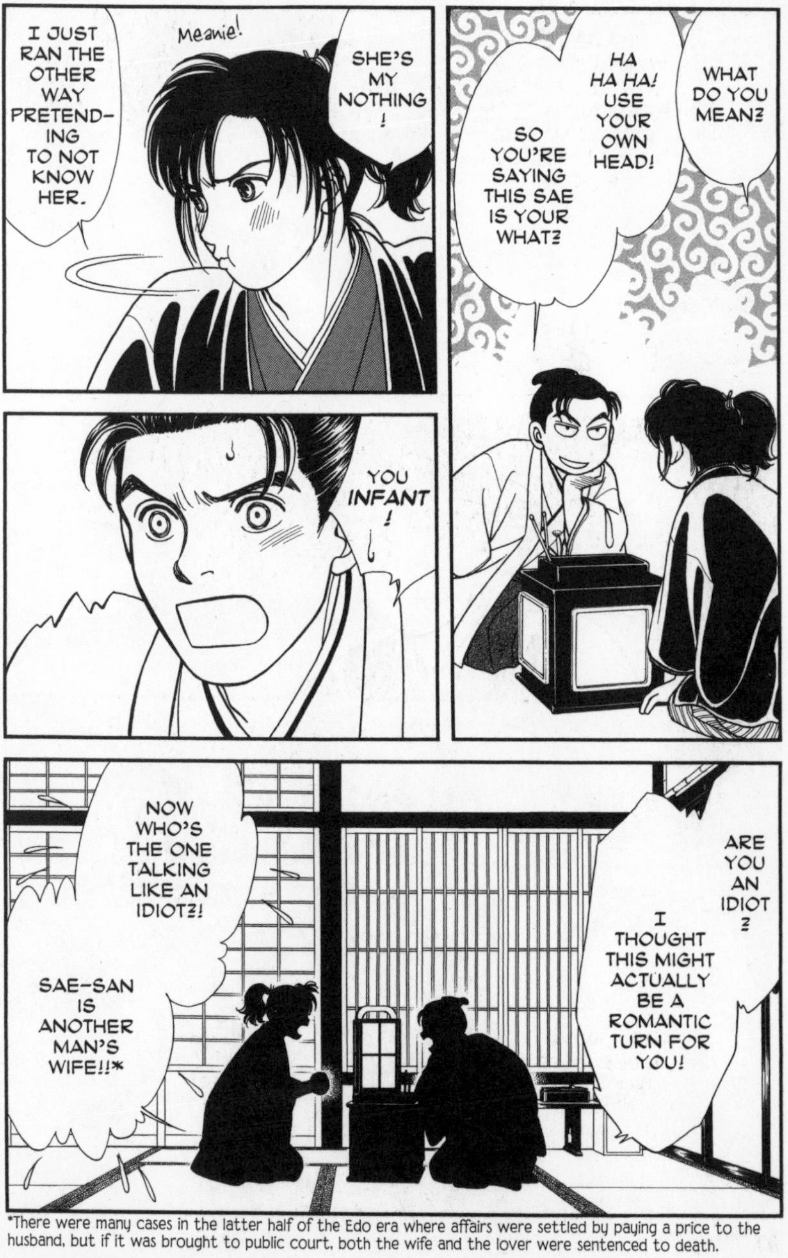
WHAT DO YOU MEAN?
HA HA HA! USE YOUR OWN HEAD!
SO YOU'RE SAYING THIS SAE IS YOUR WHAT?
SHE'S MY NOTHING!
Meanie!
I JUST RAN THE OTHER WAY PRETENDING TO NOT KNOW HER.
YOU **INFANT**!
ARE YOU AN IDIOT?
I THOUGHT THIS MIGHT ACTUALLY BE A ROMANTIC TURN FOR YOU!
NOW WHO'S THE ONE TALKING LIKE AN IDIOT?!
SAE-SAN IS ANOTHER MAN'S WIFE!!*

*There were many cases in the latter half of the Edo era where affairs were settled by paying a price to the husband, but if it was brought to public court, both the wife and the lover were sentenced to death.

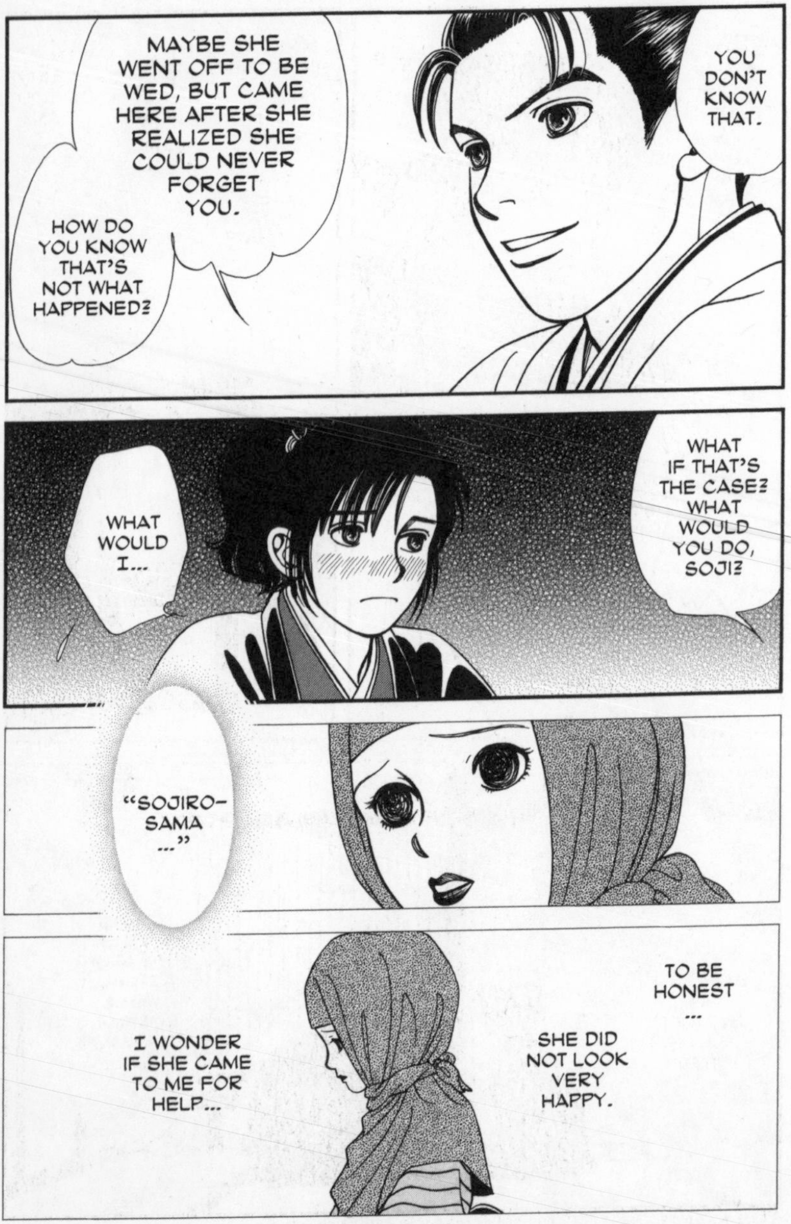
YOU DON'T KNOW THAT.
MAYBE SHE WENT OFF TO BE WED, BUT CAME HERE AFTER SHE REALIZED SHE COULD NEVER FORGET YOU.
HOW DO YOU KNOW THAT'S NOT WHAT HAPPENED?
WHAT IF THAT'S THE CASE? WHAT WOULD YOU DO, SOJI?
WHAT WOULD I...
"SOJIRO-SAMA..."
TO BE HONEST...
SHE DID NOT LOOK VERY HAPPY.
I WONDER IF SHE CAME TO ME FOR HELP...

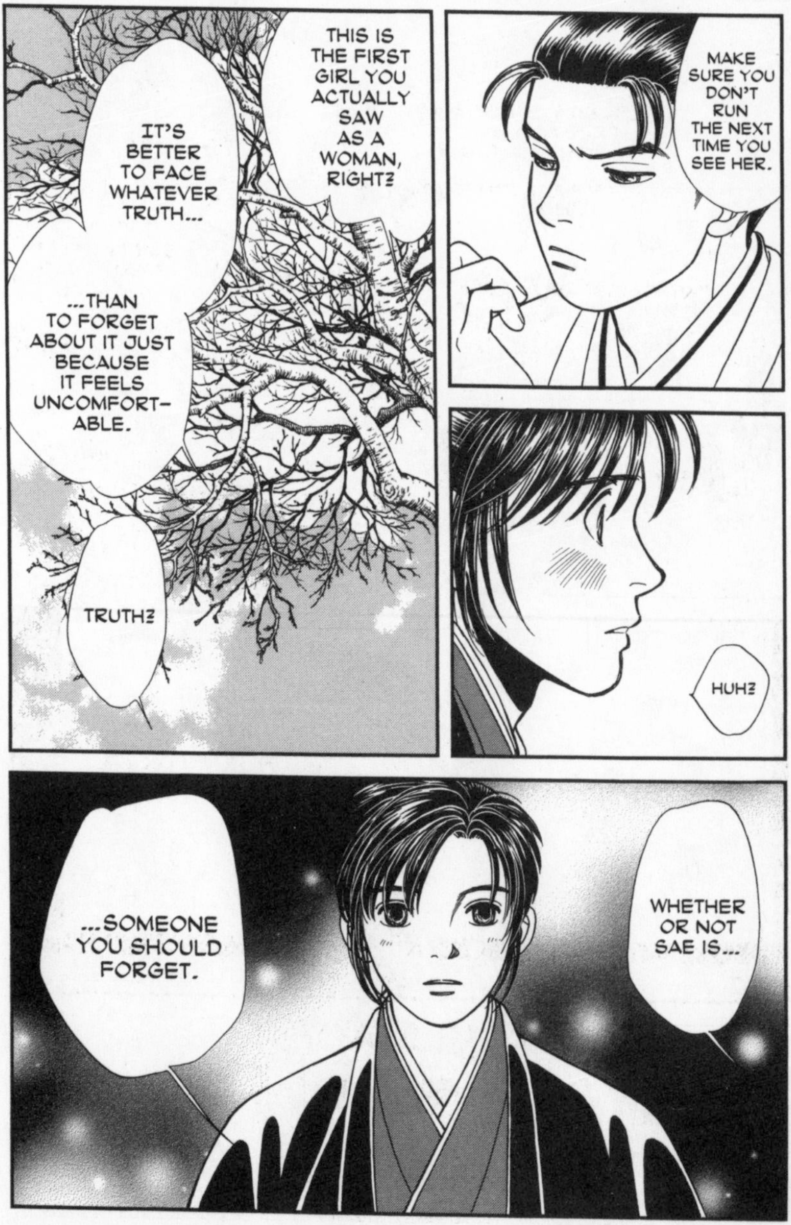
MAKE SURE YOU DON'T RUN THE NEXT TIME YOU SEE HER.
HUH?
THIS IS THE FIRST GIRL YOU ACTUALLY SAW AS A WOMAN, RIGHT?
IT'S BETTER TO FACE WHATEVER TRUTH...
...THAN TO FORGET ABOUT IT JUST BECAUSE IT FEELS UNCOMFORT-ABLE.
TRUTH?
WHETHER OR NOT SAE IS...
...SOMEONE YOU SHOULD FORGET.

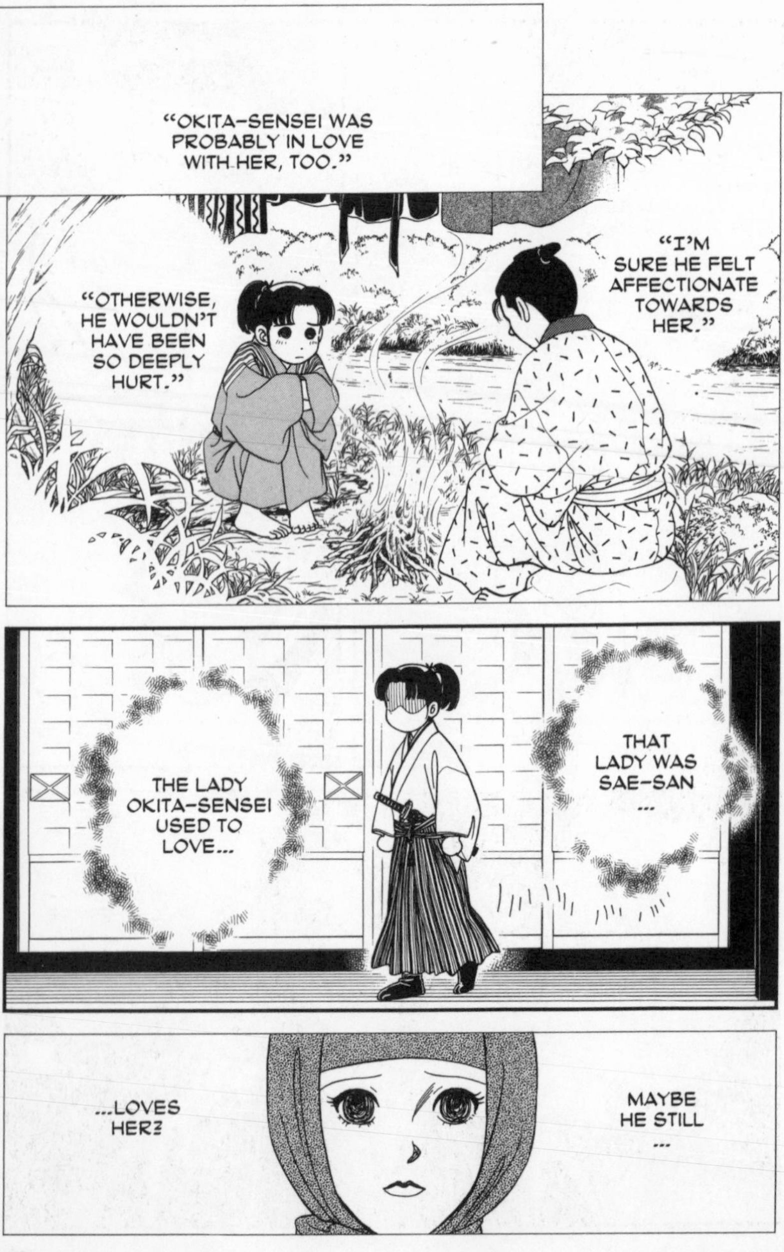
"OKITA-SENSEI WAS PROBABLY IN LOVE WITH HER, TOO."
"I'M SURE HE FELT AFFECTIONATE TOWARDS HER."
"OTHERWISE, HE WOULDN'T HAVE BEEN SO DEEPLY HURT."
THAT LADY WAS SAE-SAN ...
THE LADY OKITA-SENSEI USED TO LOVE...
MAYBE HE STILL ...
...LOVES HER?

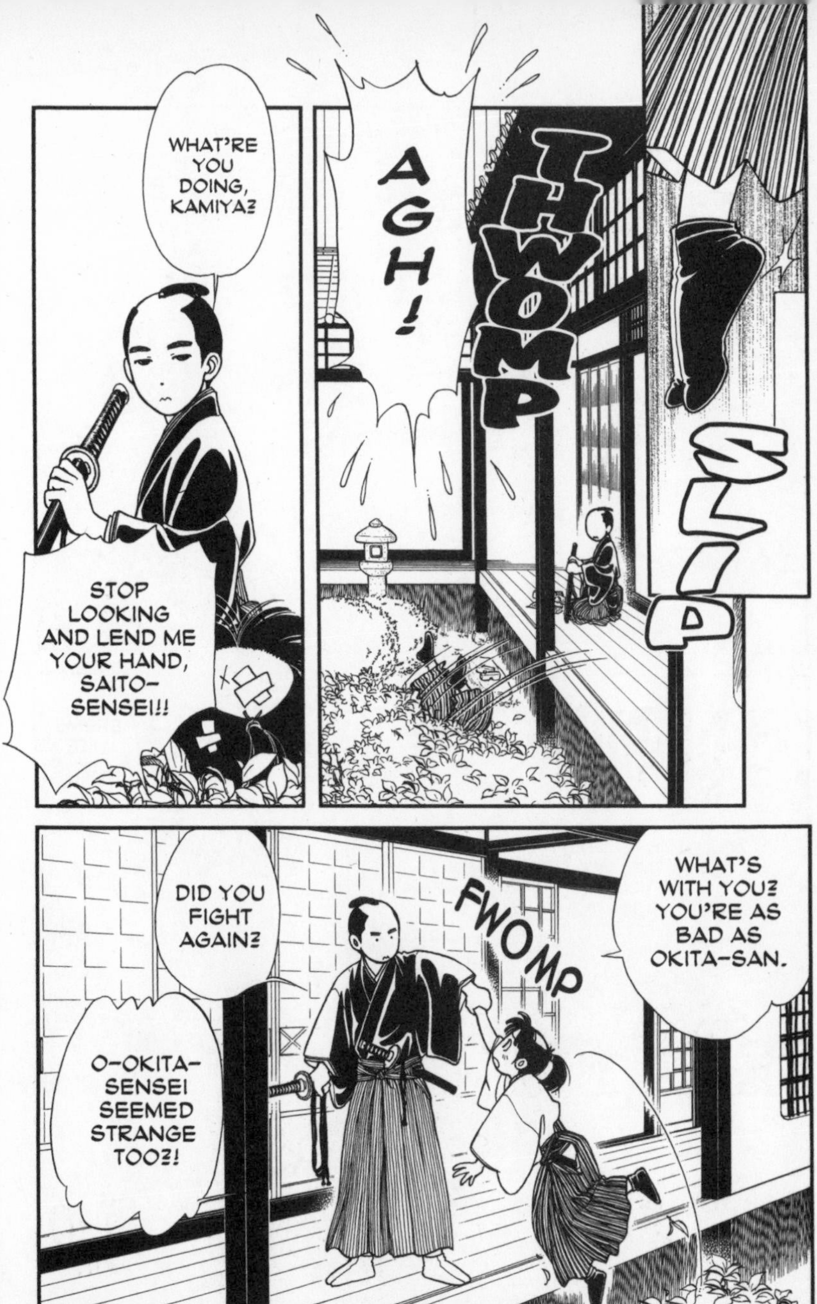
SLIP
THWOMP
AGH!
WHAT'RE YOU DOING, KAMIYA?
STOP LOOKING AND LEND ME YOUR HAND, SAITO-SENSEI!!
WHAT'S WITH YOU? YOU'RE AS BAD AS OKITA-SAN.
FWOMP
DID YOU FIGHT AGAIN?
O-OKITA-SENSEI SEEMED STRANGE TOO?!

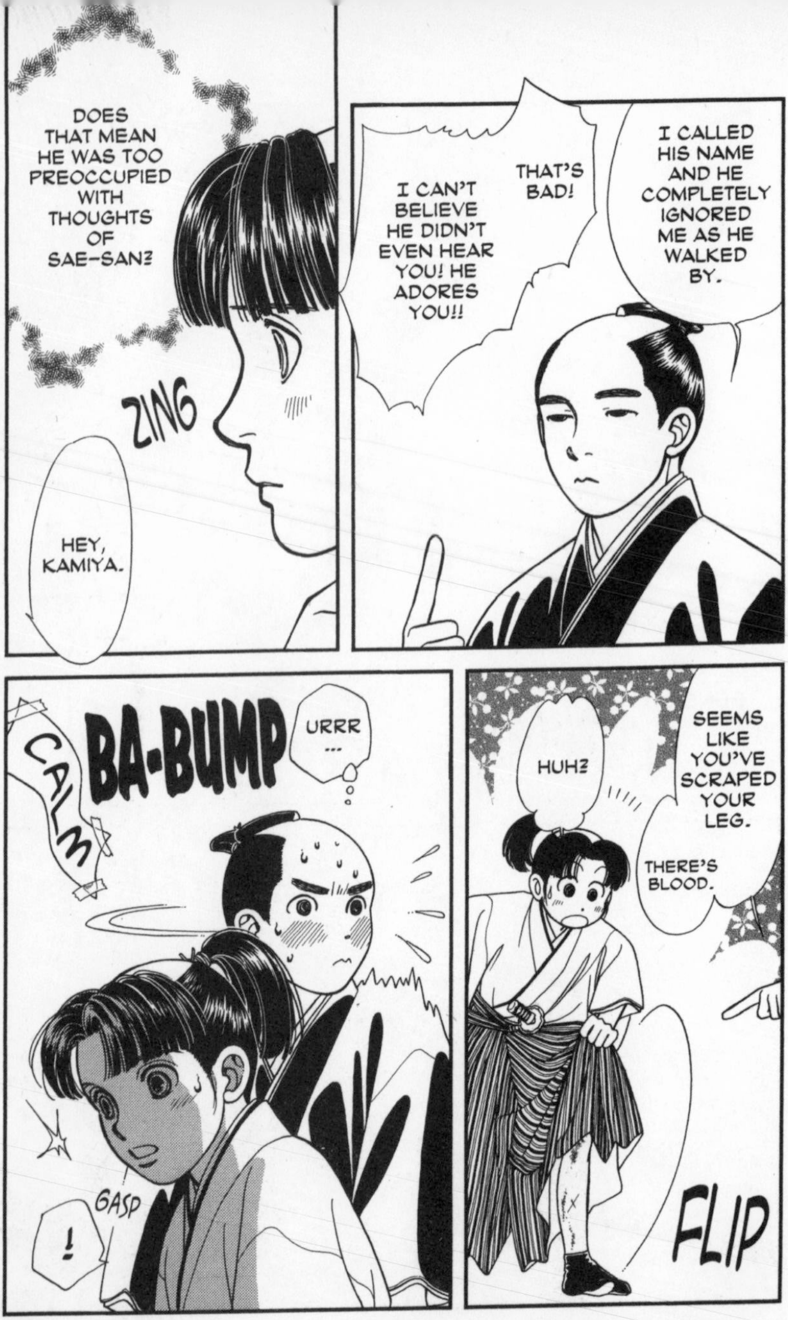
I CALLED HIS NAME AND HE COMPLETELY IGNORED ME AS HE WALKED BY.
THAT'S BAD!
I CAN'T BELIEVE HE DIDN'T EVEN HEAR YOU! HE ADORES YOU!!
DOES THAT MEAN HE WAS TOO PREOCCUPIED WITH THOUGHTS OF SAE-SAN?
ZING
HEY, KAMIYA.
SEEMS LIKE YOU'VE SCRAPED YOUR LEG.
THERE'S BLOOD.
HUH?
FLIP
URRR ...
BA-BUMP
CALM
GASP
!

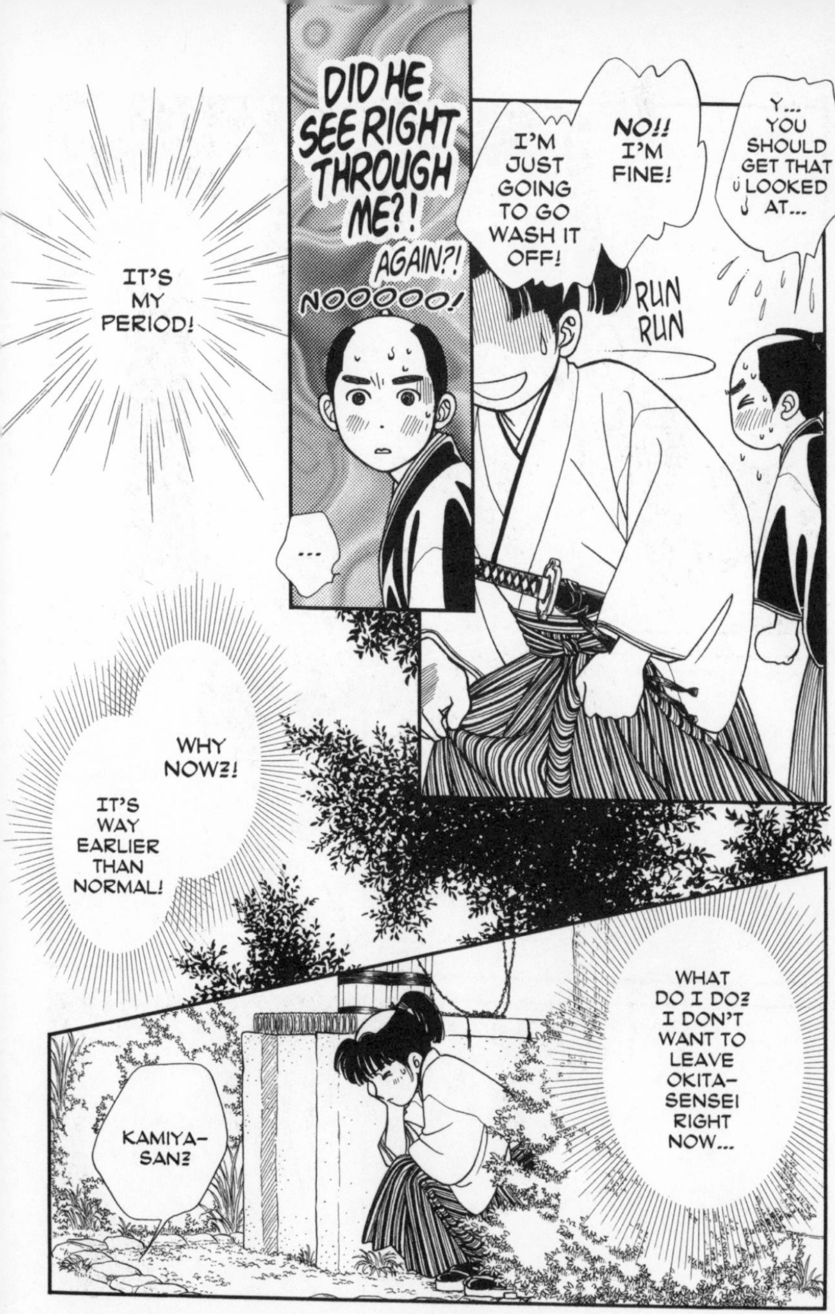
Y... YOU SHOULD GET THAT LOOKED AT...
NO!! I'M FINE!
I'M JUST GOING TO GO WASH IT OFF!
RUN RUN
DID HE SEE RIGHT THROUGH ME?!
AGAIN?!
NOOOOO!
...
IT'S MY PERIOD!
WHY NOW?!
IT'S WAY EARLIER THAN NORMAL!
WHAT DO I DO? I DON'T WANT TO LEAVE OKITA-SENSEI RIGHT NOW...
KAMIYA-SAN?

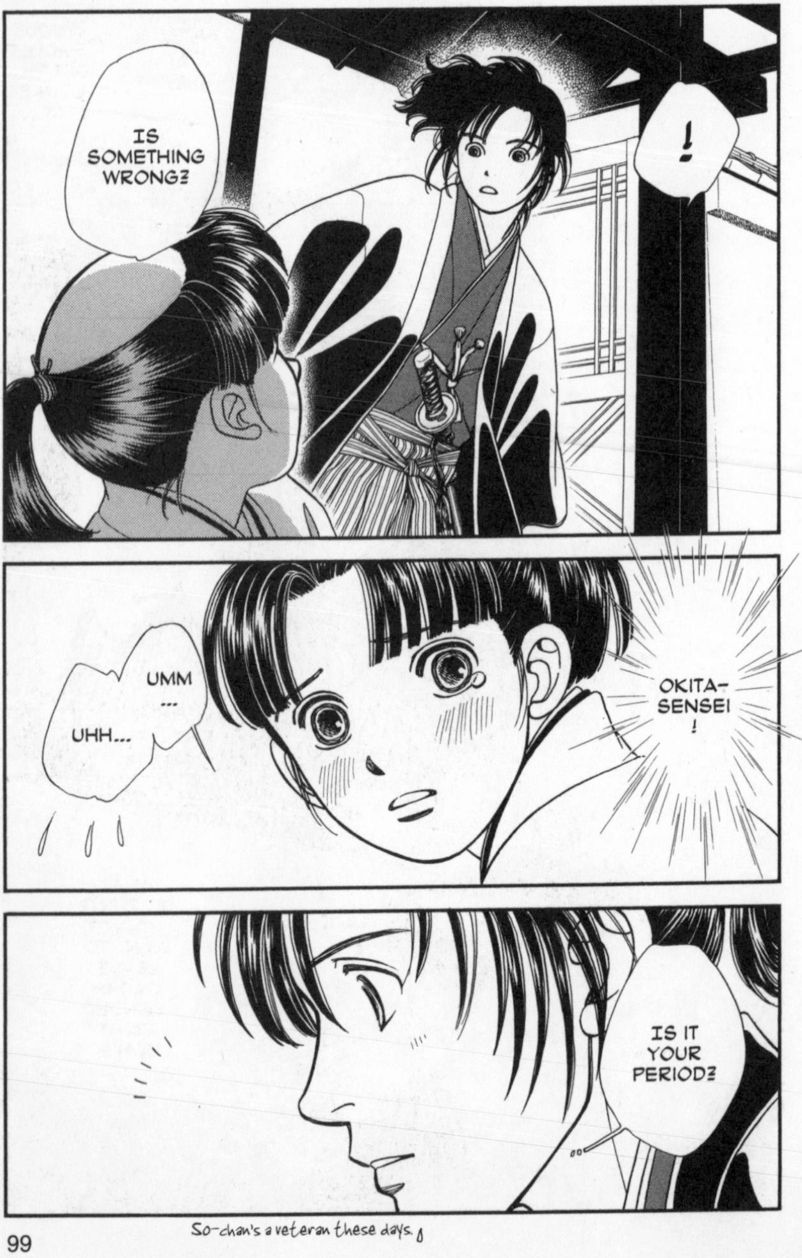
!
IS SOMETHING WRONG?
OKITA-SENSEI!
UMM... UHH...
IS IT YOUR PERIOD?

So-chan's a veteran these days.

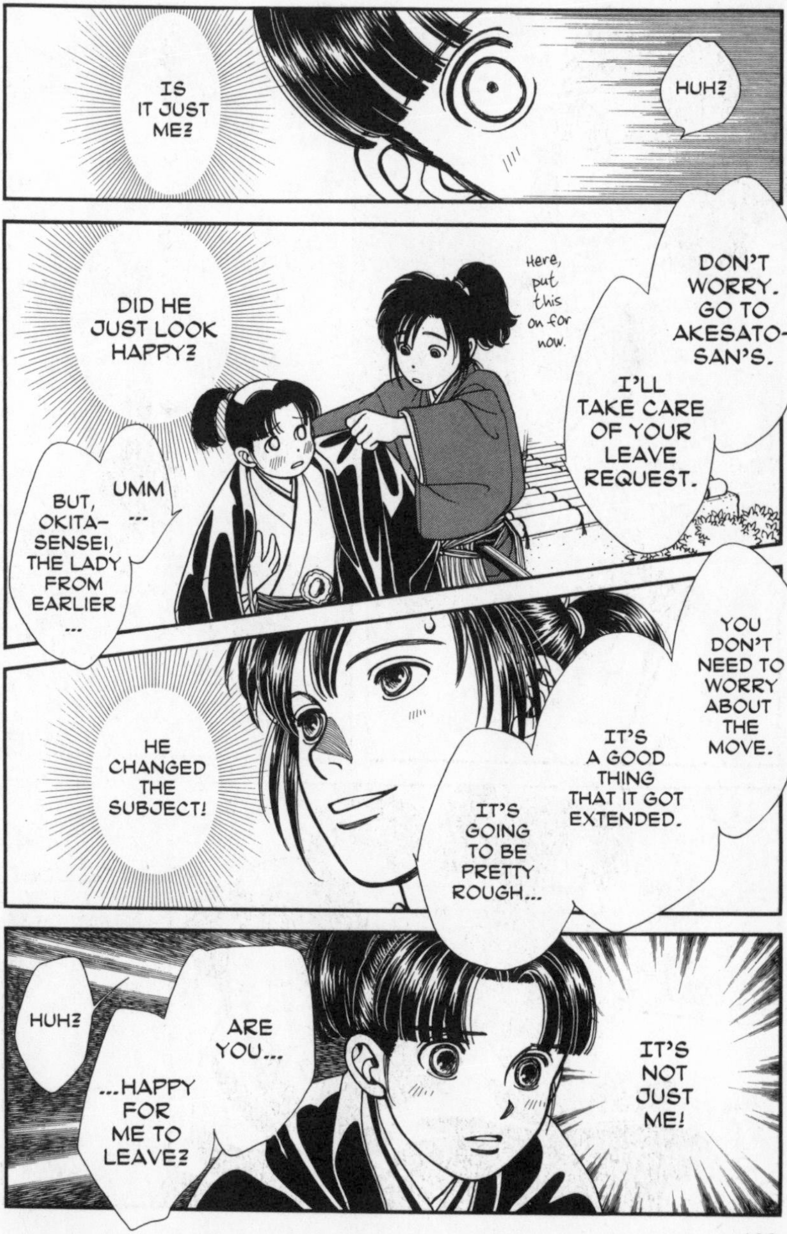
HUH?
IS IT JUST ME?
Here, put this on for now.
UMM...
BUT, OKITA-SENSEI, THE LADY FROM EARLIER...
DON'T WORRY. GO TO AKESATO-SAN'S.
I'LL TAKE CARE OF YOUR LEAVE REQUEST.
DID HE JUST LOOK HAPPY?
YOU DON'T NEED TO WORRY ABOUT THE MOVE.
IT'S A GOOD THING THAT IT GOT EXTENDED.
IT'S GOING TO BE PRETTY ROUGH...
HE CHANGED THE SUBJECT!
IT'S NOT JUST ME!
ARE YOU...
...HAPPY FOR ME TO LEAVE?
HUH?

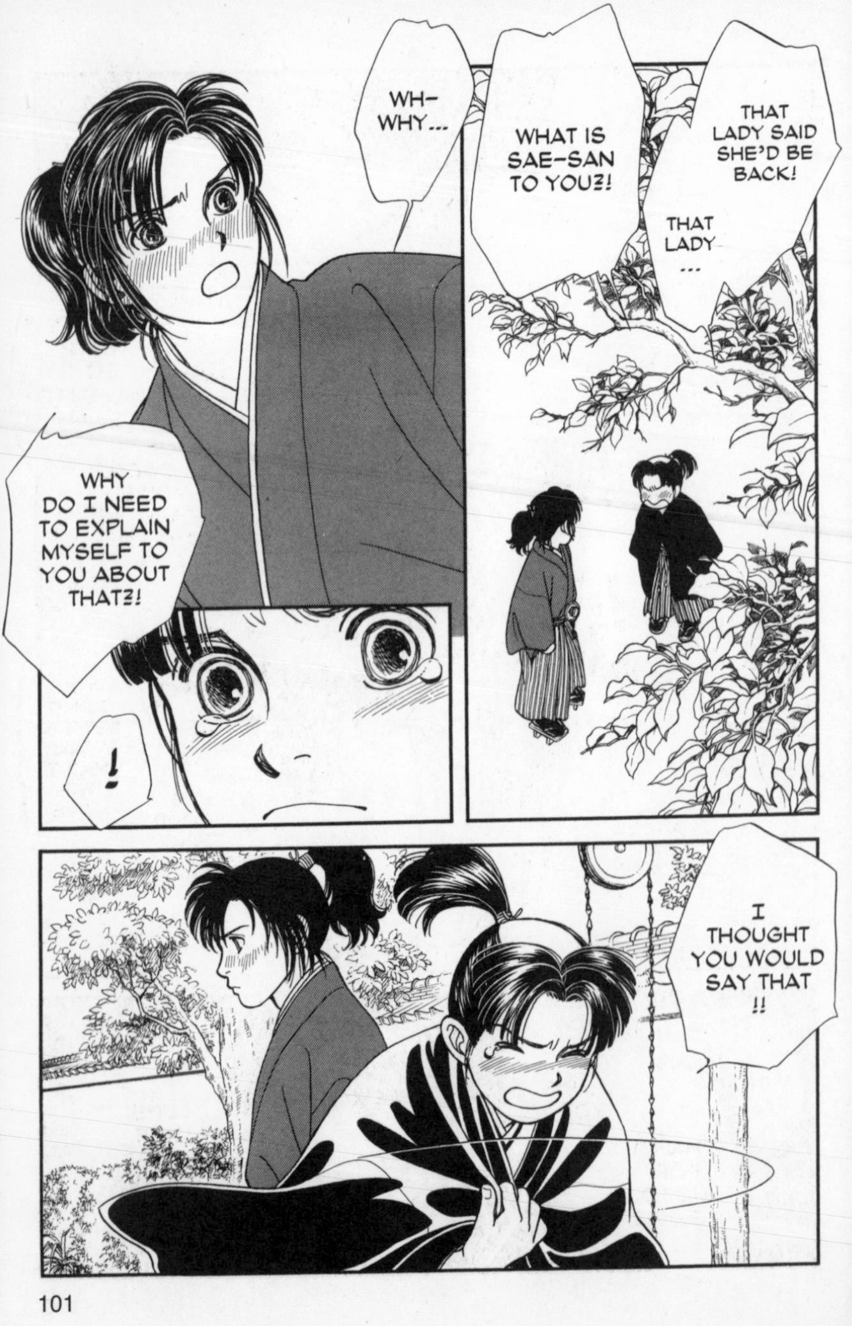
THAT LADY SAID SHE'D BE BACK!
THAT LADY...
WHAT IS SAE-SAN TO YOU?!
WH-WHY...
WHY DO I NEED TO EXPLAIN MYSELF TO YOU ABOUT THAT?!
!
I THOUGHT YOU WOULD SAY THAT!!

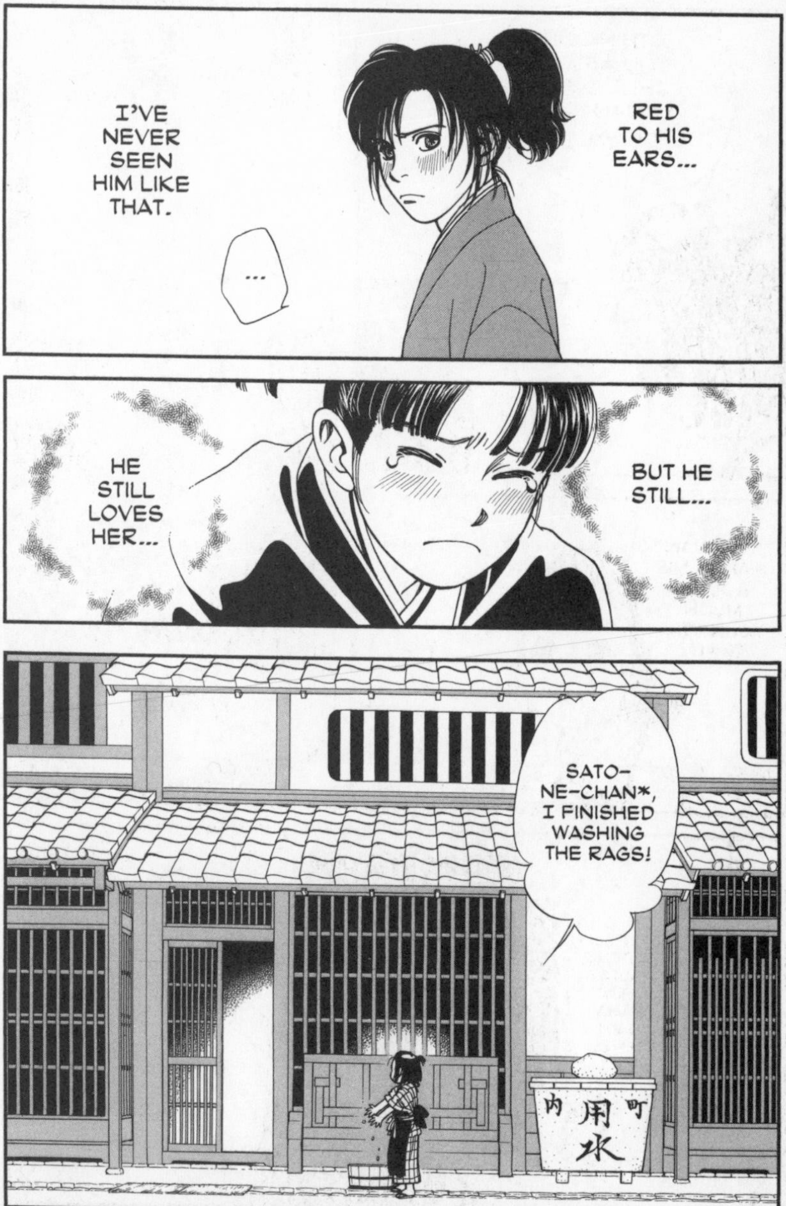
RED TO HIS EARS...
I'VE NEVER SEEN HIM LIKE THAT.
...
BUT HE STILL...
HE STILL LOVES HER...
SATO-NE-CHAN*, I FINISHED WASHING THE RAGS!
町内用水

*A term of endearment, usually referring to an older sister

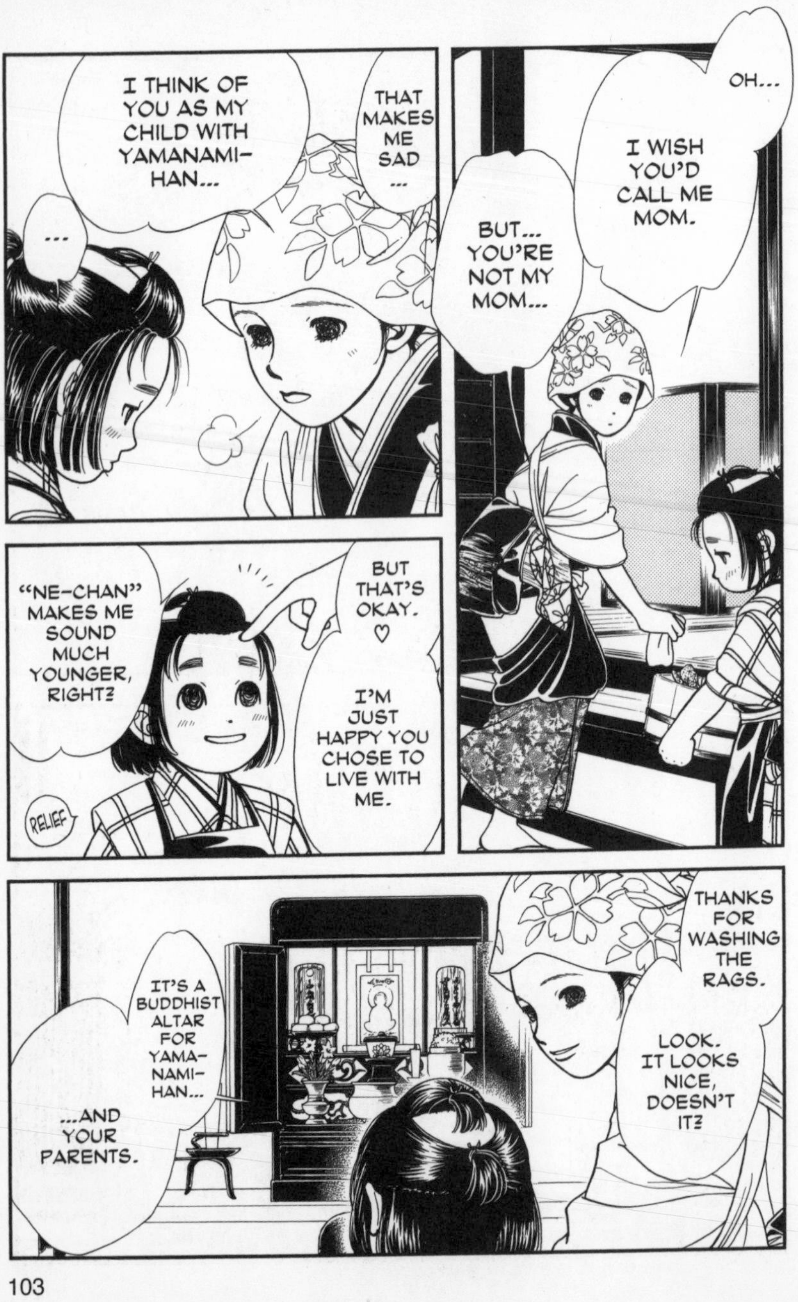
OH...
I WISH YOU'D CALL ME MOM.
BUT... YOU'RE NOT MY MOM...
THAT MAKES ME SAD ...
I THINK OF YOU AS MY CHILD WITH YAMANAMI-HAN...
...
BUT THAT'S OKAY. ♡
I'M JUST HAPPY YOU CHOSE TO LIVE WITH ME.
"NE-CHAN" MAKES ME SOUND MUCH YOUNGER, RIGHT?
RELIEF
THANKS FOR WASHING THE RAGS.
LOOK. IT LOOKS NICE, DOESN'T IT?
IT'S A BUDDHIST ALTAR FOR YAMANAMI-HAN...
...AND YOUR PARENTS.

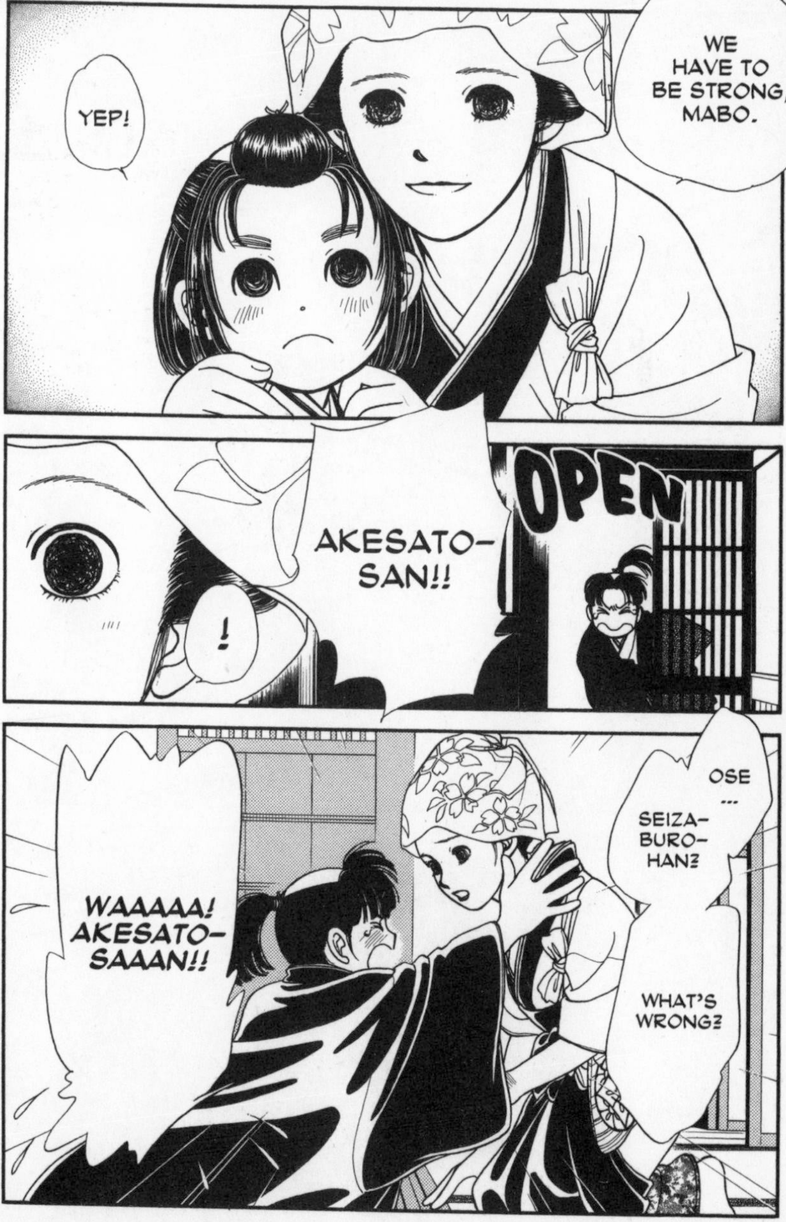
WE HAVE TO BE STRONG, MABO.
YEP!
OPEN
AKESATO-SAN!!
!
OSE ... SEIZABURO-HAN?
WHAT'S WRONG?
WAAAAA! AKESATO-SAAAN!!

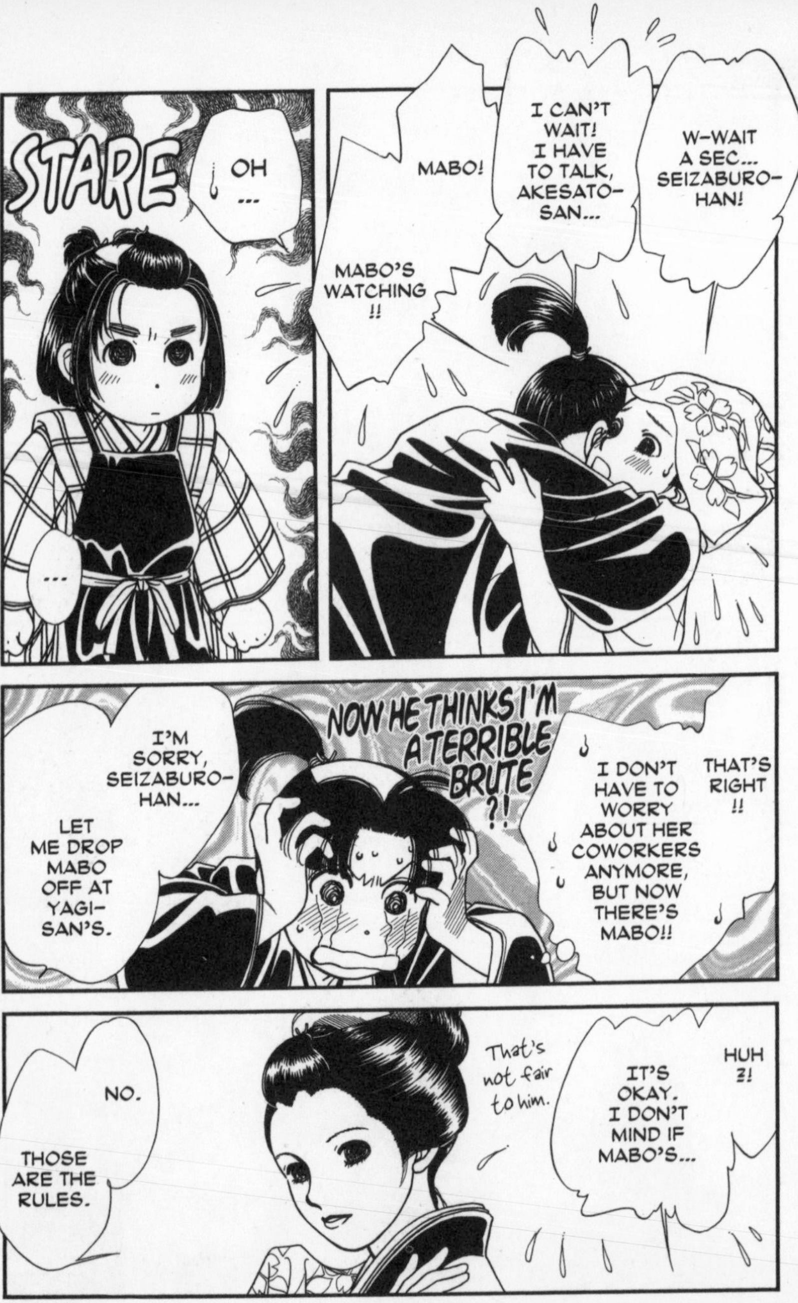
W-WAIT A SEC... SEIZABURO-HAN!
I CAN'T WAIT! I HAVE TO TALK, AKESATO-SAN...
MABO!
MABO'S WATCHING !!
STARE
OH ...
...
THAT'S RIGHT !!
I DON'T HAVE TO WORRY ABOUT HER COWORKERS ANYMORE, BUT NOW THERE'S MABO!!
NOW HE THINKS I'M A TERRIBLE BRUTE ?!
I'M SORRY, SEIZABURO-HAN...
LET ME DROP MABO OFF AT YAGI-SAN'S.
HUH ?!
IT'S OKAY. I DON'T MIND IF MABO'S...
That's not fair to him.
NO.
THOSE ARE THE RULES.

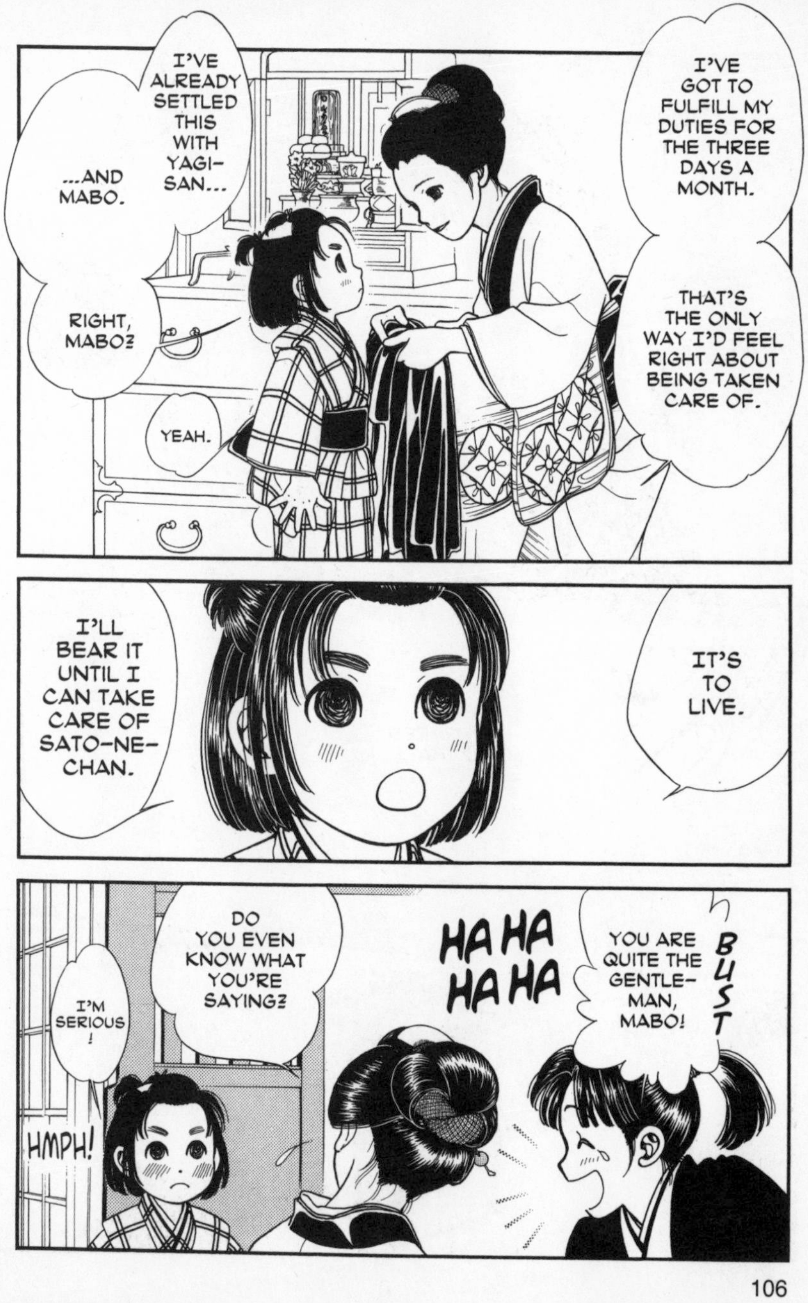
I'VE GOT TO FULFILL MY DUTIES FOR THE THREE DAYS A MONTH.
THAT'S THE ONLY WAY I'D FEEL RIGHT ABOUT BEING TAKEN CARE OF.
I'VE ALREADY SETTLED THIS WITH YAGI-SAN...
...AND MABO.
RIGHT, MABO?
YEAH.
IT'S TO LIVE.
I'LL BEAR IT UNTIL I CAN TAKE CARE OF SATO-NE-CHAN.
BUST
YOU ARE QUITE THE GENTLEMAN, MABO!
HA HA HA HA
DO YOU EVEN KNOW WHAT YOU'RE SAYING?
I'M SERIOUS!
HMPH!

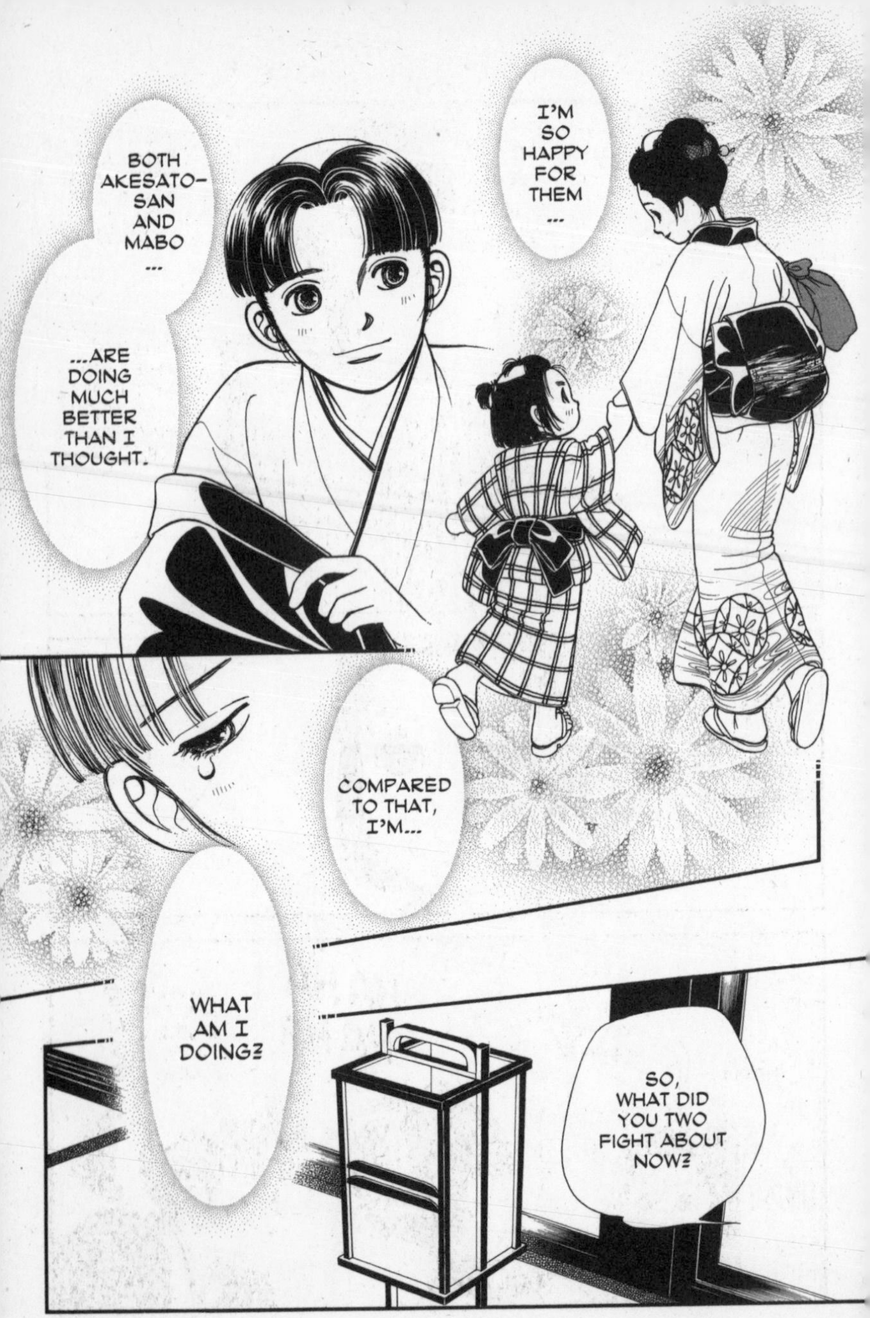
I'M SO HAPPY FOR THEM...
BOTH AKESATO-SAN AND MABO...
...ARE DOING MUCH BETTER THAN I THOUGHT.
COMPARED TO THAT, I'M...
WHAT AM I DOING?
SO, WHAT DID YOU TWO FIGHT ABOUT NOW?

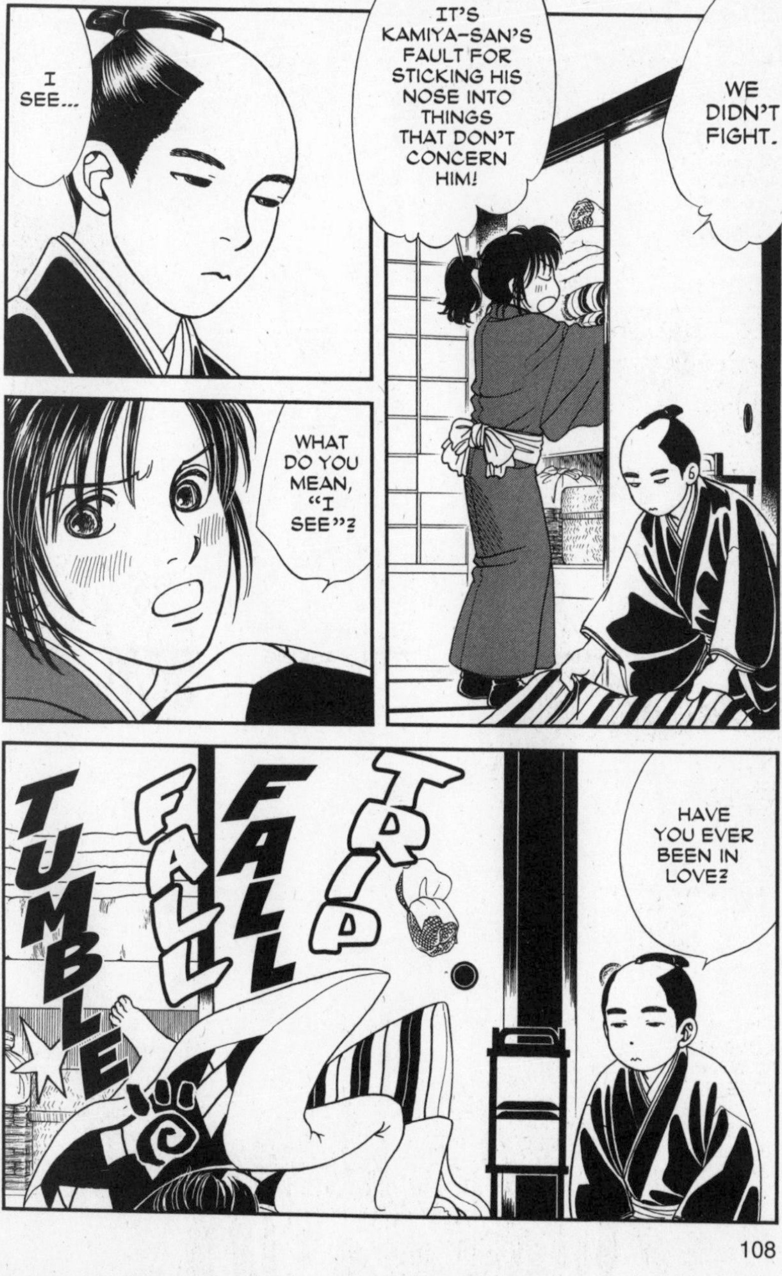
WE DIDN'T FIGHT.
IT'S KAMIYA-SAN'S FAULT FOR STICKING HIS NOSE INTO THINGS THAT DON'T CONCERN HIM!
I SEE...
WHAT DO YOU MEAN, "I SEE"?
HAVE YOU EVER BEEN IN LOVE?
TRIP
FALL
FALL
TUMBLE

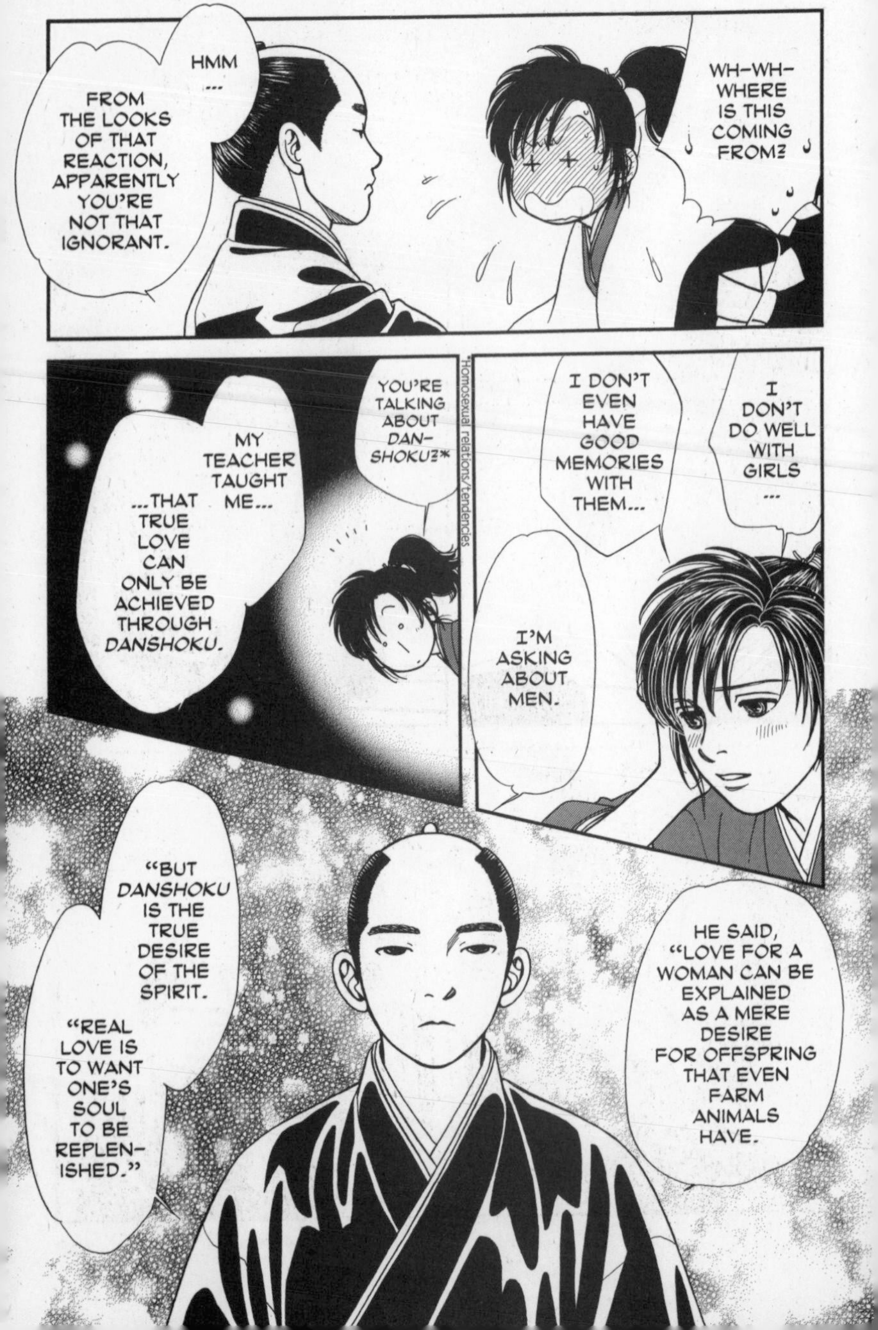
WH-WH-WHERE IS THIS COMING FROM?
HMM...
FROM THE LOOKS OF THAT REACTION, APPARENTLY YOU'RE NOT THAT IGNORANT.
I DON'T DO WELL WITH GIRLS...
I DON'T EVEN HAVE GOOD MEMORIES WITH THEM...
I'M ASKING ABOUT MEN.
YOU'RE TALKING ABOUT *DANSHOKU*?*
*Homosexual relations/tendencies
MY TEACHER TAUGHT ME...
...THAT TRUE LOVE CAN ONLY BE ACHIEVED THROUGH *DANSHOKU*.
HE SAID, "LOVE FOR A WOMAN CAN BE EXPLAINED AS A MERE DESIRE FOR OFFSPRING THAT EVEN FARM ANIMALS HAVE.
"BUT *DANSHOKU* IS THE TRUE DESIRE OF THE SPIRIT.
"REAL LOVE IS TO WANT ONE'S SOUL TO BE REPLENISHED."

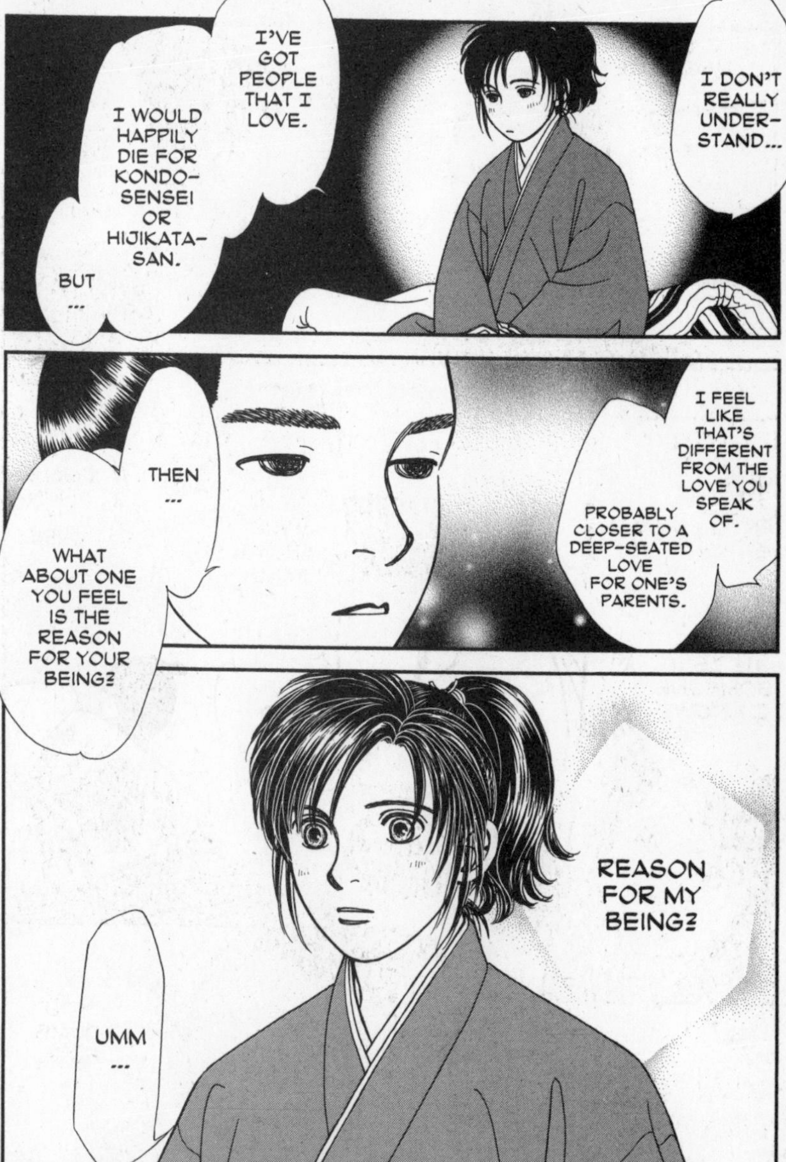
I DON'T REALLY UNDER-STAND...
I'VE GOT PEOPLE THAT I LOVE.
I WOULD HAPPILY DIE FOR KONDO-SENSEI OR HIJIKATA-SAN.
BUT ...
I FEEL LIKE THAT'S DIFFERENT FROM THE LOVE YOU SPEAK OF.
PROBABLY CLOSER TO A DEEP-SEATED LOVE FOR ONE'S PARENTS.
THEN ...
WHAT ABOUT ONE YOU FEEL IS THE REASON FOR YOUR BEING?
REASON FOR MY BEING?
UMM ...

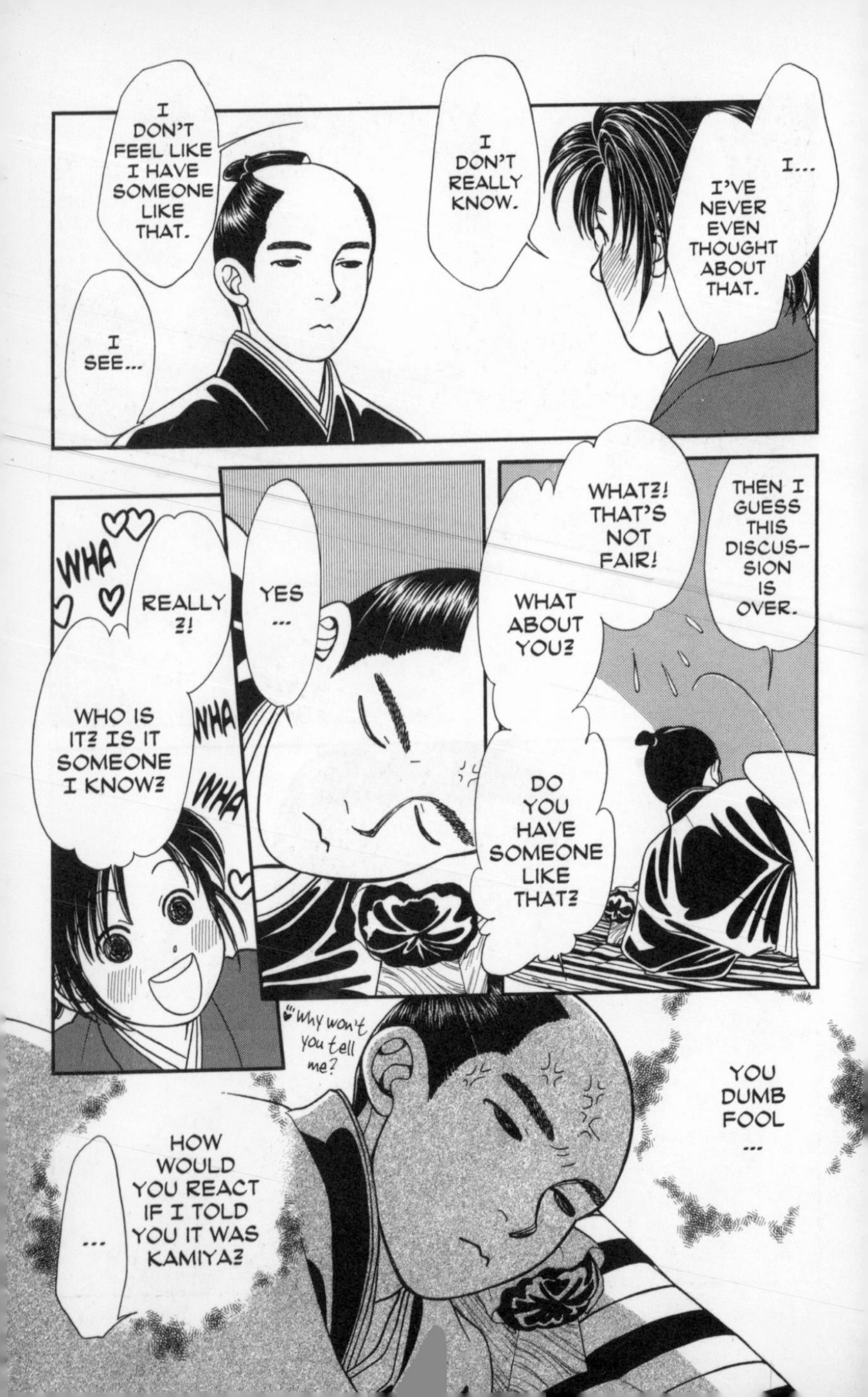
I...
I'VE NEVER EVEN THOUGHT ABOUT THAT.
I DON'T REALLY KNOW.
I DON'T FEEL LIKE I HAVE SOMEONE LIKE THAT.
I SEE...
THEN I GUESS THIS DISCUSSION IS OVER.
WHAT?! THAT'S NOT FAIR!
WHAT ABOUT YOU?
DO YOU HAVE SOMEONE LIKE THAT?
YES...
REALLY?!
WHA
WHO IS IT? IS IT SOMEONE I KNOW?
WHA
WHA
Why won't you tell me?
YOU DUMB FOOL...
HOW WOULD YOU REACT IF I TOLD YOU IT WAS KAMIYA?
...

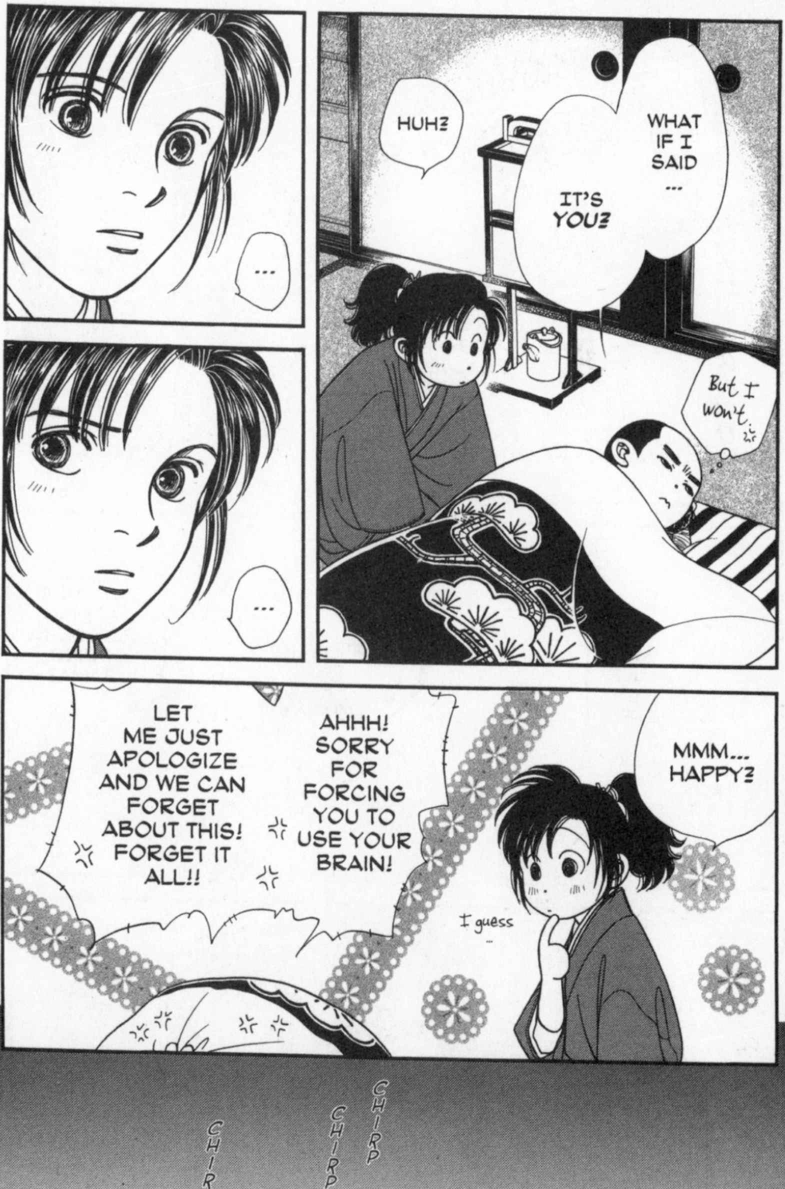
WHAT IF I SAID ... IT'S YOU?
HUH?
But I won't.
...
...
MMM... HAPPY?
I guess ...
AHHH! SORRY FOR FORCING YOU TO USE YOUR BRAIN!
LET ME JUST APOLOGIZE AND WE CAN FORGET ABOUT THIS! FORGET IT ALL!!
CHIRP
CHIRP
CHIRP

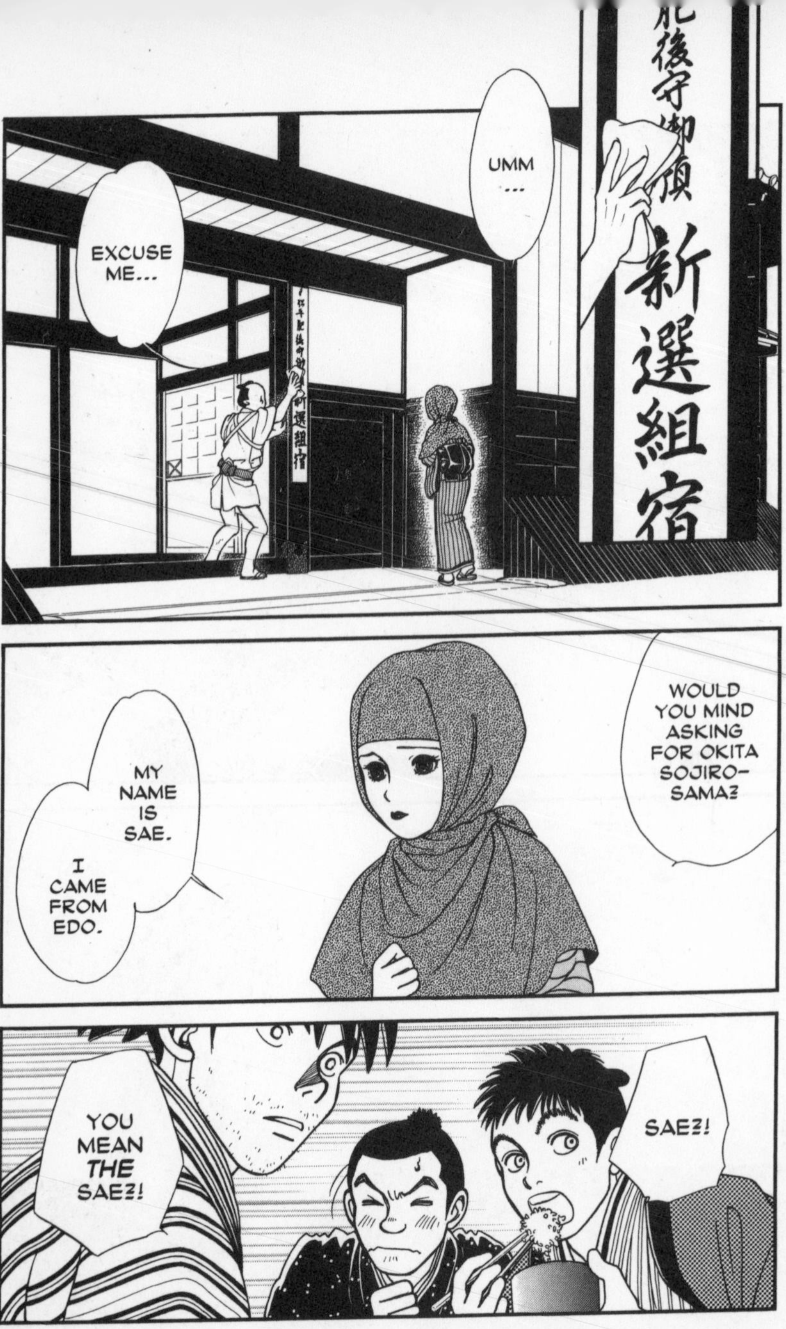
新選組宿
UMM...
EXCUSE ME...
WOULD YOU MIND ASKING FOR OKITA SOJIRO-SAMA?
MY NAME IS SAE.
I CAME FROM EDO.
SAE?!
YOU MEAN THE SAE?!

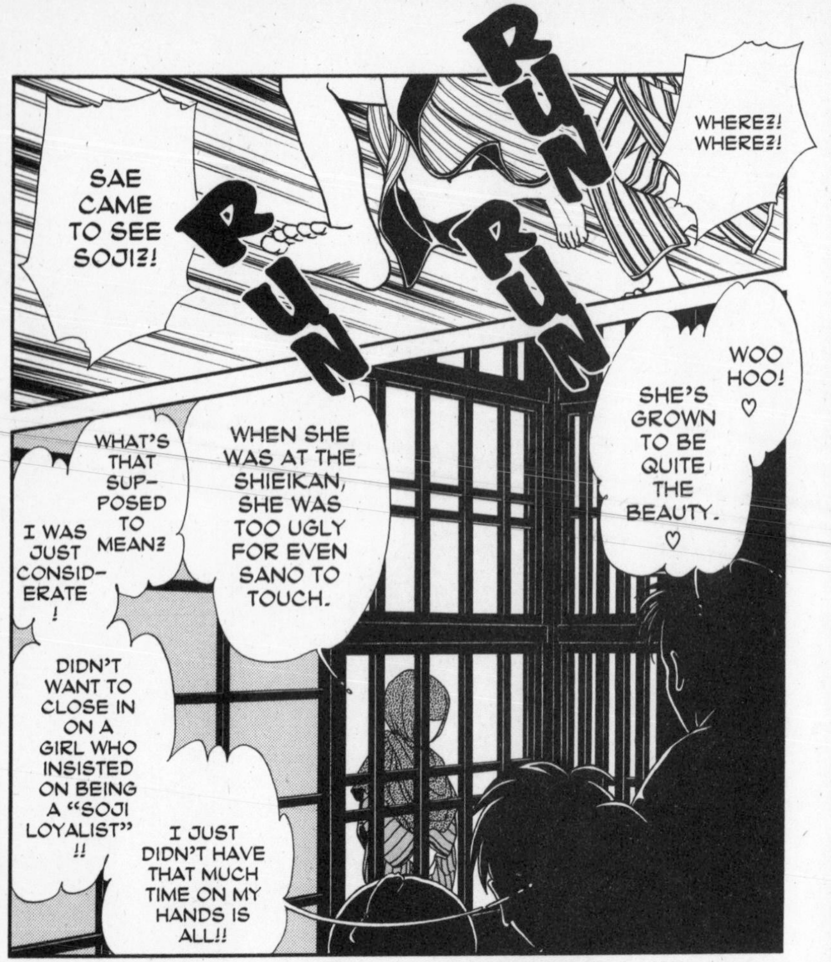
WHERE?! WHERE?!
RUN RUN
RUN RUN
SAE CAME TO SEE SOJI?!
WOO HOO! ♡
SHE'S GROWN TO BE QUITE THE BEAUTY. ♡
WHEN SHE WAS AT THE SHIEIKAN, SHE WAS TOO UGLY FOR EVEN SANO TO TOUCH.
WHAT'S THAT SUP-POSED TO MEAN?
I WAS JUST CONSID-ERATE!
DIDN'T WANT TO CLOSE IN ON A GIRL WHO INSISTED ON BEING A "SOJI LOYALIST"!!
I JUST DIDN'T HAVE THAT MUCH TIME ON MY HANDS IS ALL!!

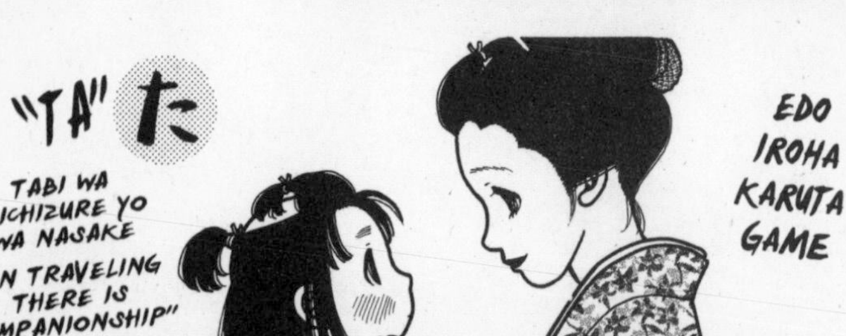
EDO IROHA KARUTA GAME
"TA" た
TABI WA MICHIZURE YO WA NASAKE
"IN TRAVELING THERE IS COMPANIONSHIP"
(lit. Travel together, compassion)

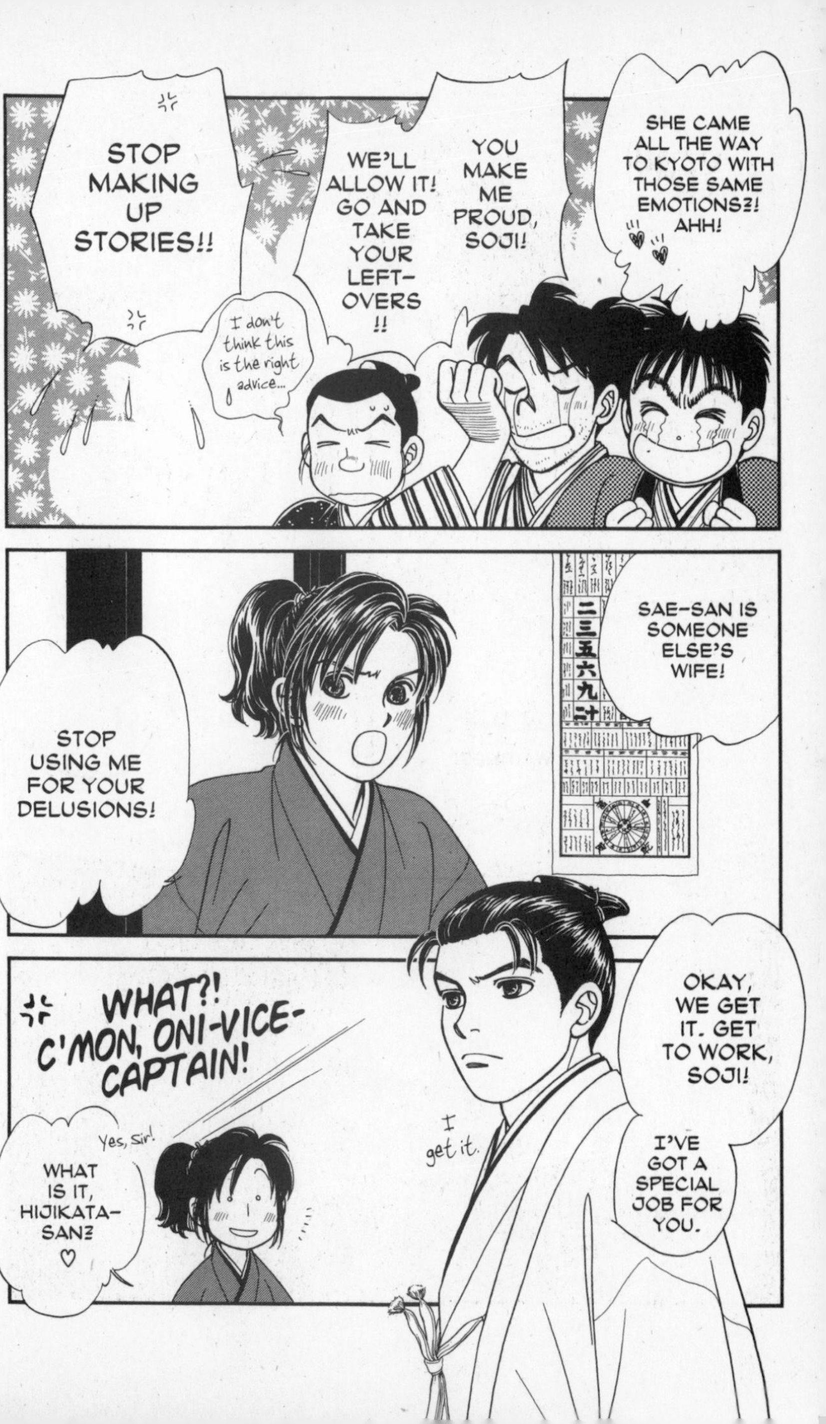

SHE CAME ALL THE WAY TO KYOTO WITH THOSE SAME EMOTIONS?! AHH!
YOU MAKE ME PROUD, SOJI!
WE'LL ALLOW IT! GO AND TAKE YOUR LEFT-OVERS!!
I don't think this is the right advice...
STOP MAKING UP STORIES!!
SAE-SAN IS SOMEONE ELSE'S WIFE!
STOP USING ME FOR YOUR DELUSIONS!
OKAY, WE GET IT. GET TO WORK, SOJI!
I'VE GOT A SPECIAL JOB FOR YOU.
I get it.
WHAT?! C'MON, ONI-VICE-CAPTAIN!
Yes, Sir!
WHAT IS IT, HIJIKATA-SAN? ♡

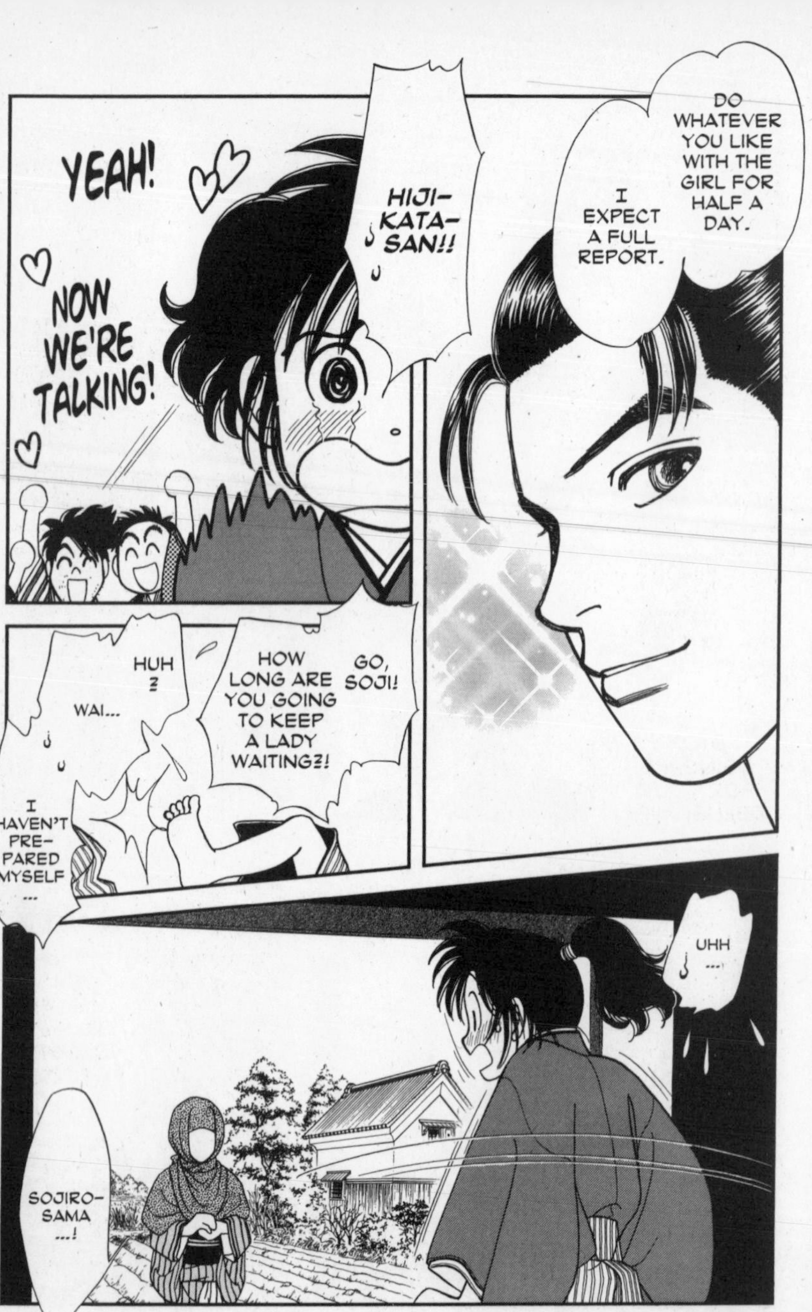
DO WHATEVER YOU LIKE WITH THE GIRL FOR HALF A DAY.
I EXPECT A FULL REPORT.
HIJI-KATA-SAN!!
YEAH!
NOW WE'RE TALKING!
GO, SOJI!
HOW LONG ARE YOU GOING TO KEEP A LADY WAITING?!
HUH?
WAI...
I HAVEN'T PRE-PARED MYSELF...
UHH...
SOJIRO-SAMA...!

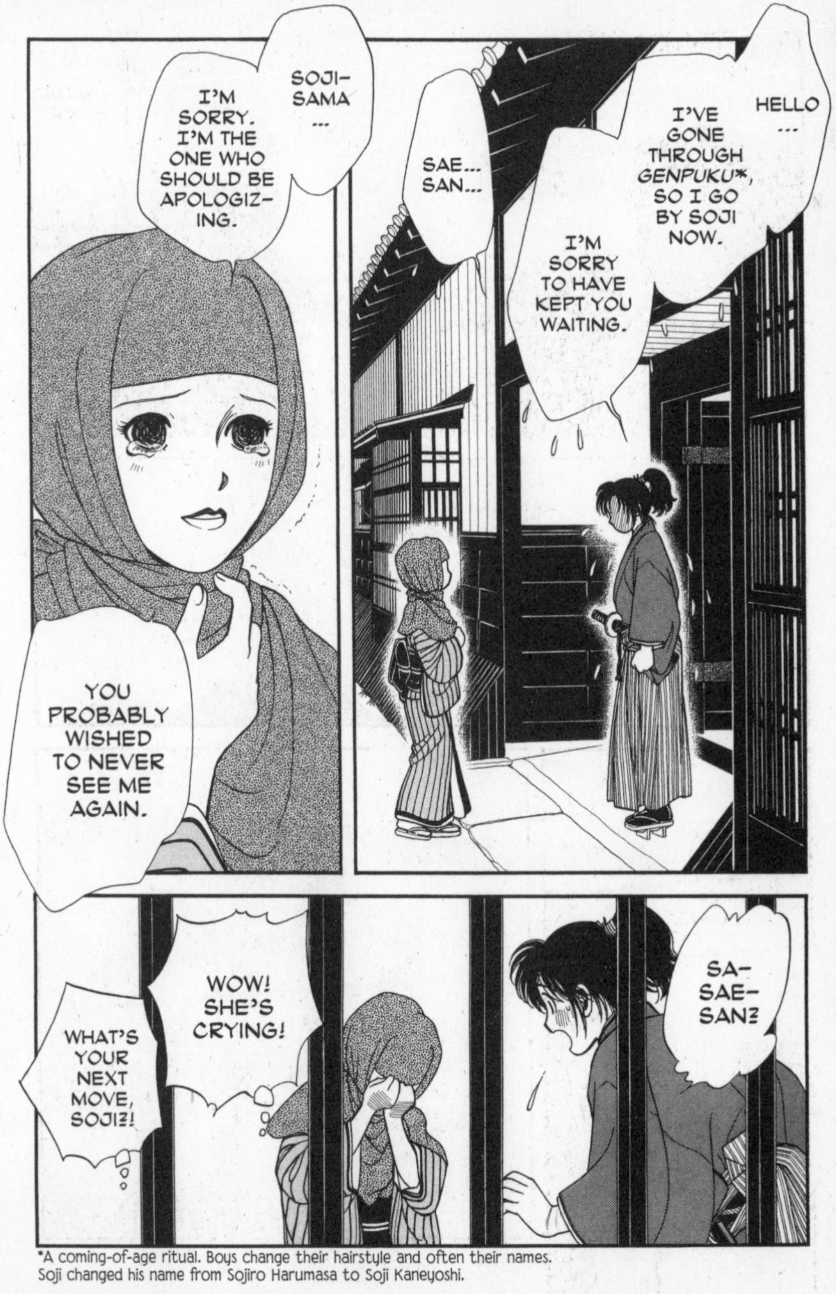
HELLO...
I'VE GONE THROUGH GENPUKU*, SO I GO BY SOJI NOW.
I'M SORRY TO HAVE KEPT YOU WAITING.
SAE... SAN...
SOJI-SAMA...
I'M SORRY. I'M THE ONE WHO SHOULD BE APOLOGIZING.
YOU PROBABLY WISHED TO NEVER SEE ME AGAIN.
SA-SAE-SAN?
WOW! SHE'S CRYING!
WHAT'S YOUR NEXT MOVE, SOJI?!

*A coming-of-age ritual. Boys change their hairstyle and often their names. Soji changed his name from Sojiro Harumasa to Soji Kaneyoshi.

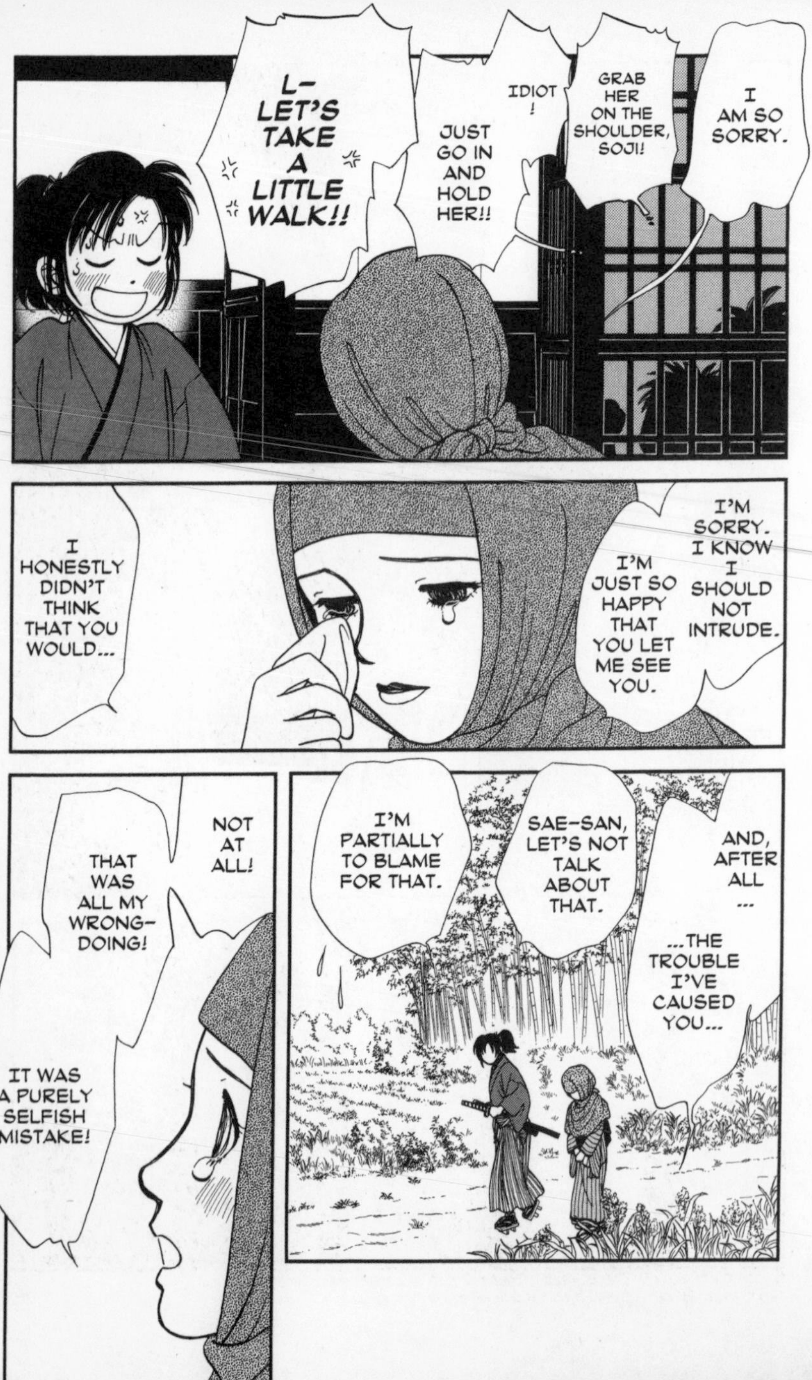
I AM SO SORRY.
GRAB HER ON THE SHOULDER, SOJI!
IDIOT!
JUST GO IN AND HOLD HER!!
L-LET'S TAKE A LITTLE WALK!!
I'M SORRY. I KNOW I SHOULD NOT INTRUDE.
I'M JUST SO HAPPY THAT YOU LET ME SEE YOU.
I HONESTLY DIDN'T THINK THAT YOU WOULD...
AND, AFTER ALL...
...THE TROUBLE I'VE CAUSED YOU...
SAE-SAN, LET'S NOT TALK ABOUT THAT.
I'M PARTIALLY TO BLAME FOR THAT.
NOT AT ALL!
THAT WAS ALL MY WRONG-DOING!
IT WAS A PURELY SELFISH MISTAKE!

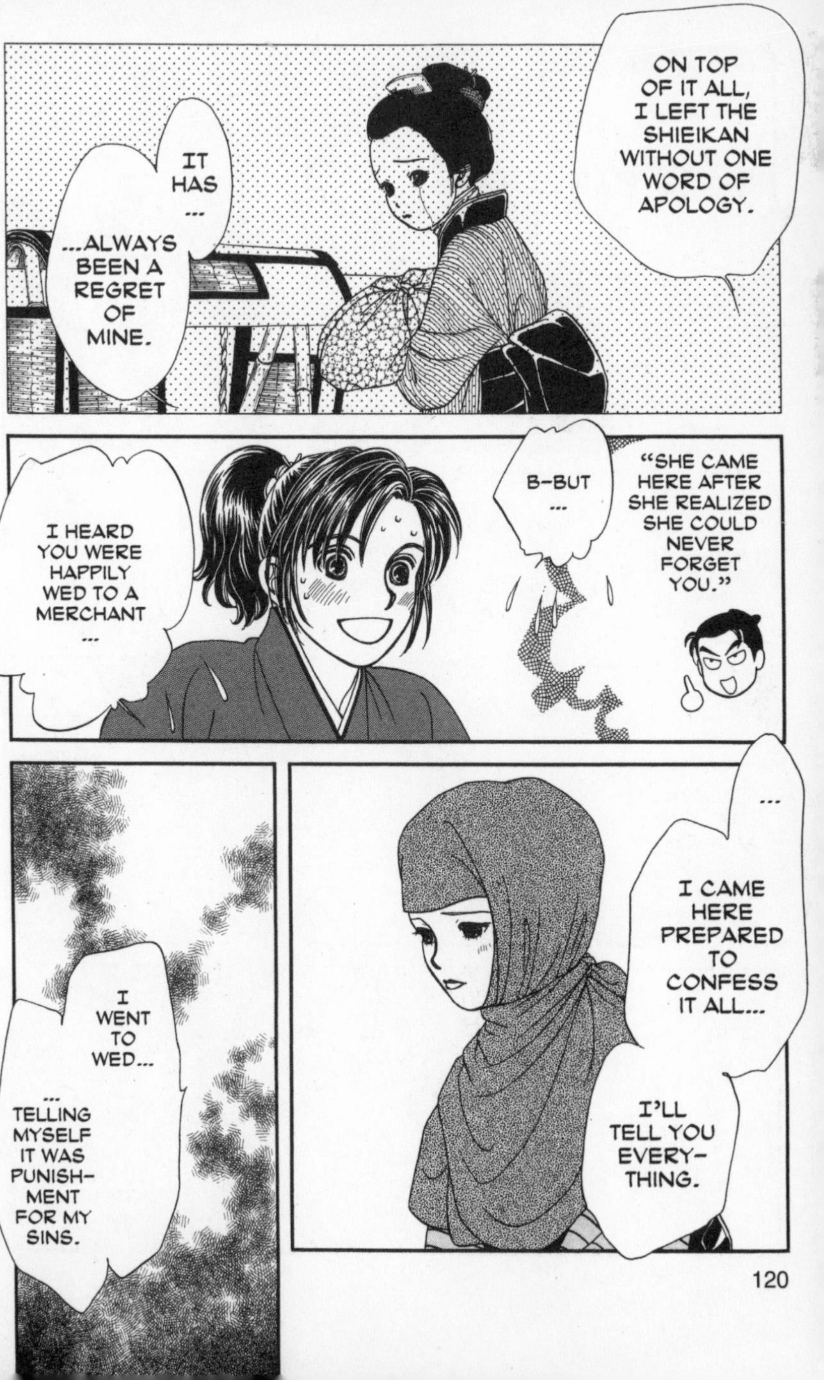
ON TOP OF IT ALL, I LEFT THE SHIEIKAN WITHOUT ONE WORD OF APOLOGY.
IT HAS ...
...ALWAYS BEEN A REGRET OF MINE.
"SHE CAME HERE AFTER SHE REALIZED SHE COULD NEVER FORGET YOU."
B-BUT ...
I HEARD YOU WERE HAPPILY WED TO A MERCHANT ...
...
I CAME HERE PREPARED TO CONFESS IT ALL...
I'LL TELL YOU EVERY-THING.
I WENT TO WED...
... TELLING MYSELF IT WAS PUNISH-MENT FOR MY SINS.

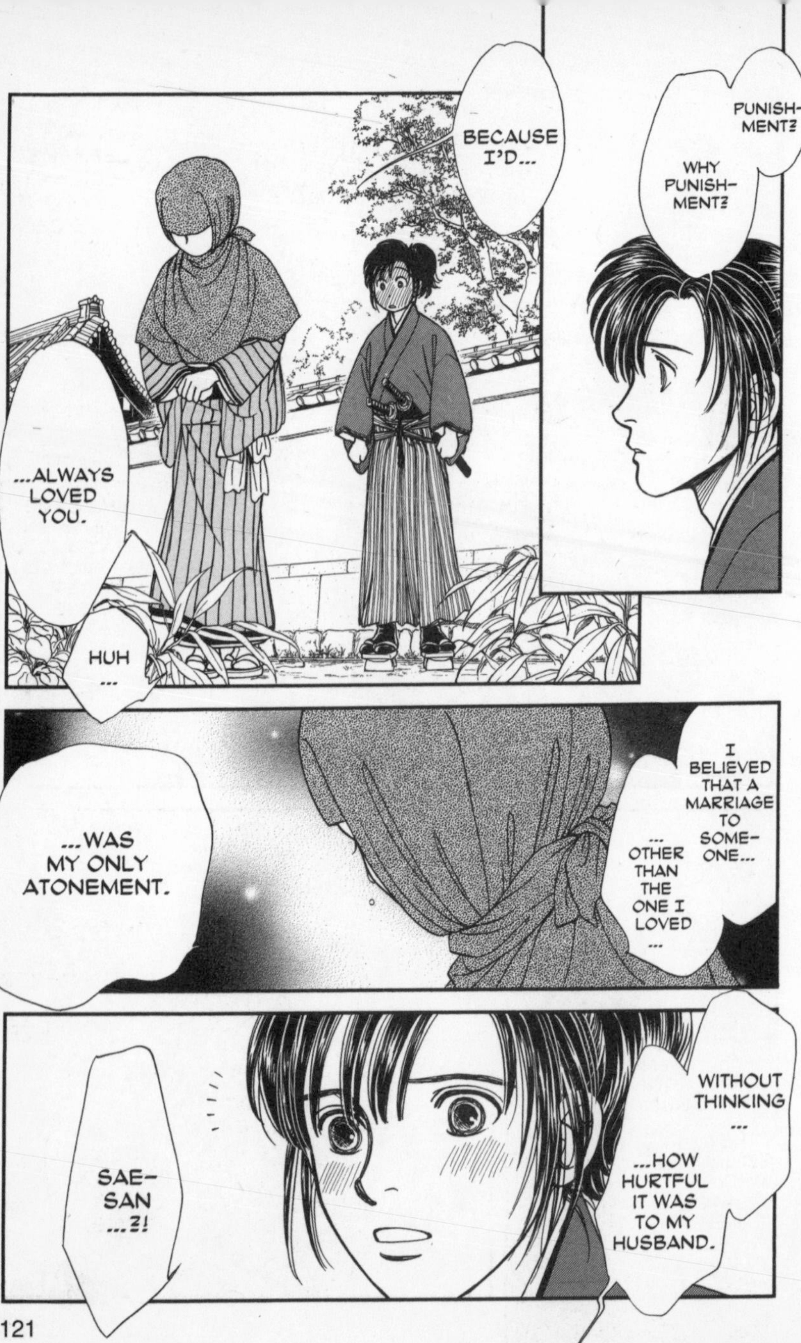
PUNISHMENT? WHY PUNISHMENT?
BECAUSE I'D...
...ALWAYS LOVED YOU.
HUH ...
I BELIEVED THAT A MARRIAGE TO SOMEONE...
...OTHER THAN THE ONE I LOVED ...
...WAS MY ONLY ATONEMENT.
WITHOUT THINKING ...
...HOW HURTFUL IT WAS TO MY HUSBAND.
SAE-SAN ...?!

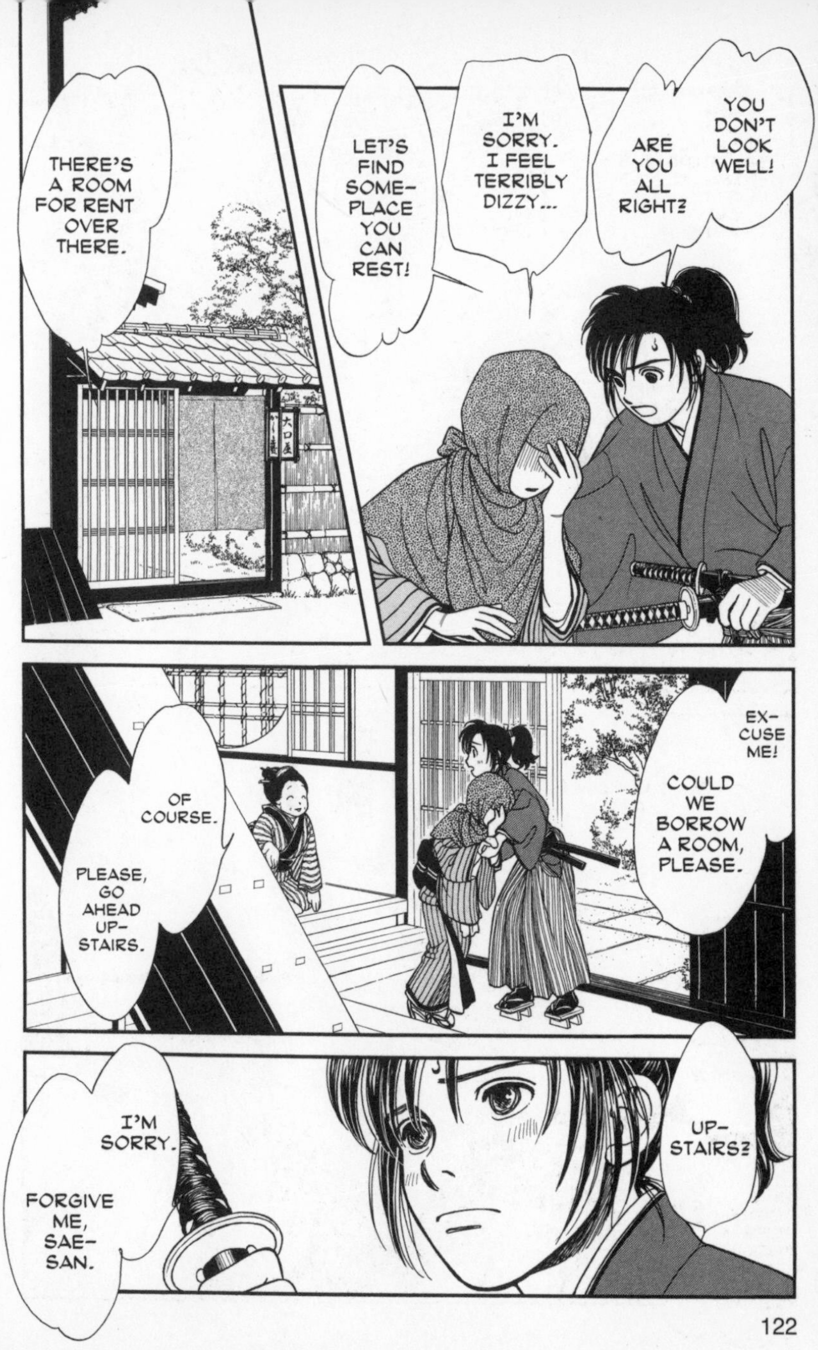
YOU DON'T LOOK WELL!
ARE YOU ALL RIGHT?
I'M SORRY. I FEEL TERRIBLY DIZZY...
LET'S FIND SOME-PLACE YOU CAN REST!
THERE'S A ROOM FOR RENT OVER THERE.
EX-CUSE ME!
COULD WE BORROW A ROOM, PLEASE.
OF COURSE.
PLEASE, GO AHEAD UP-STAIRS.
UP-STAIRS?
I'M SORRY.
FORGIVE ME, SAE-SAN.

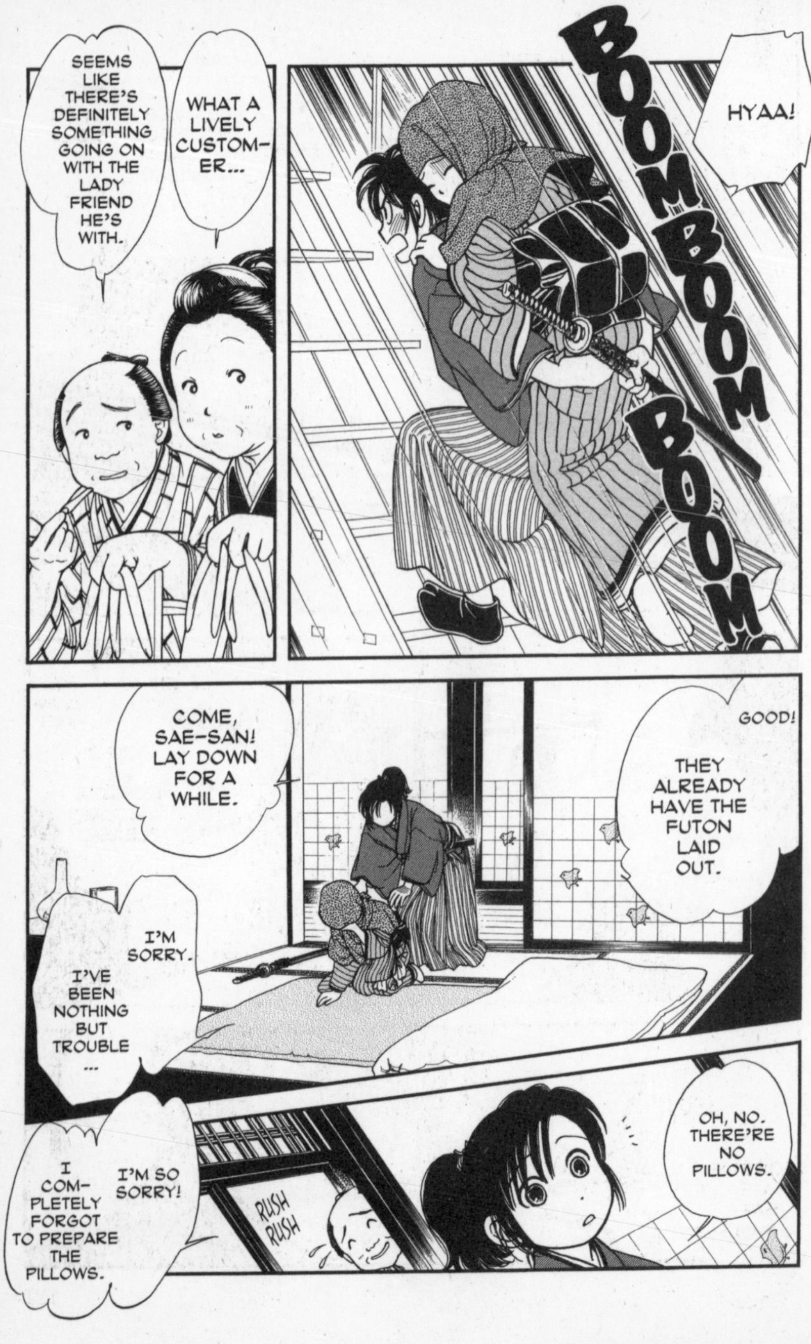
HYAA!
BOOM BOOM BOOM
WHAT A LIVELY CUSTOMER...
SEEMS LIKE THERE'S DEFINITELY SOMETHING GOING ON WITH THE LADY FRIEND HE'S WITH.
GOOD!
THEY ALREADY HAVE THE FUTON LAID OUT.
COME, SAE-SAN! LAY DOWN FOR A WHILE.
I'M SORRY.
I'VE BEEN NOTHING BUT TROUBLE...
OH, NO. THERE'RE NO PILLOWS.
RUSH RUSH
I'M SO SORRY!
I COMPLETELY FORGOT TO PREPARE THE PILLOWS.

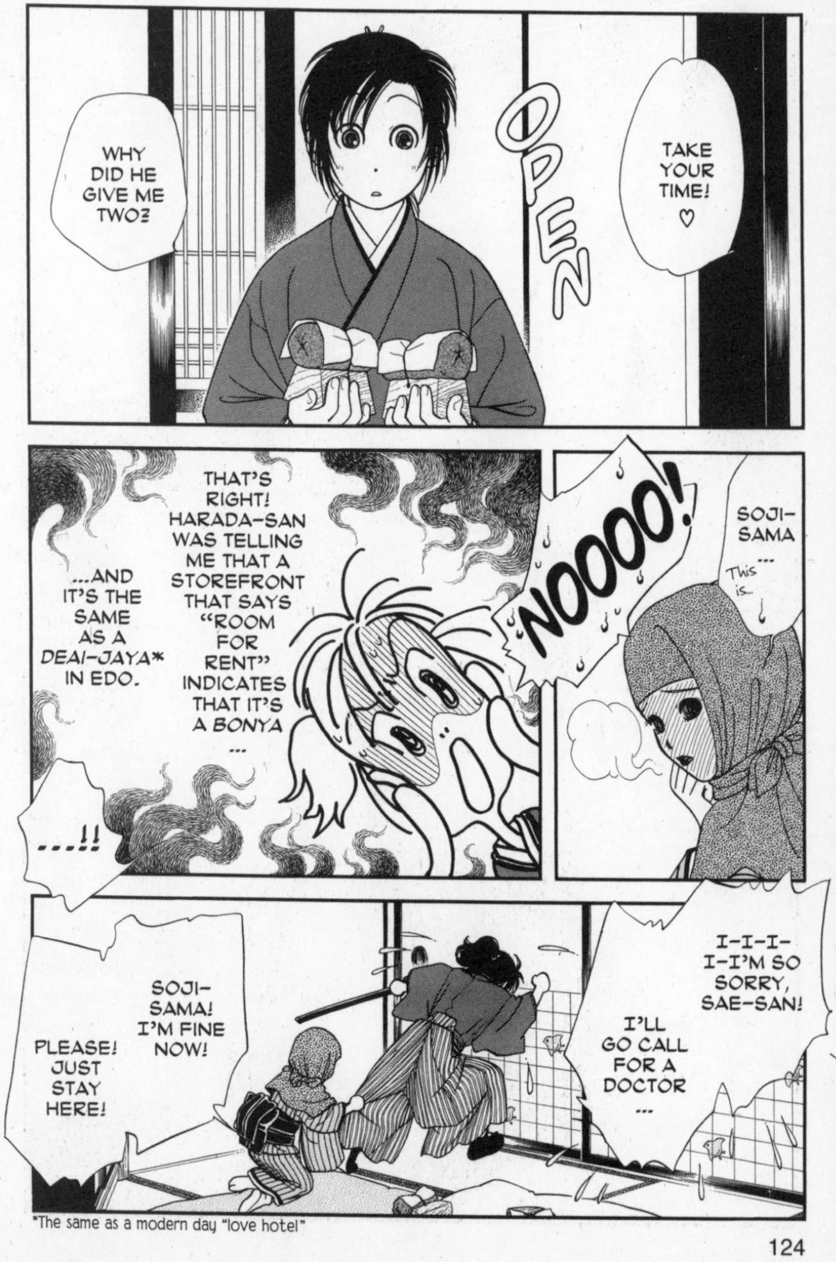
TAKE YOUR TIME! ♡
OPEN
WHY DID HE GIVE ME TWO?
SOJI-SAMA ...
This is..
NOOOO!
THAT'S RIGHT! HARADA-SAN WAS TELLING ME THAT A STOREFRONT THAT SAYS "ROOM FOR RENT" INDICATES THAT IT'S A *BONYA* ...
...AND IT'S THE SAME AS A *DEAI-JAYA** IN EDO.
...!!
I-I-I-I-I'M SO SORRY, SAE-SAN!
I'LL GO CALL FOR A DOCTOR ...
SOJI-SAMA! I'M FINE NOW!
PLEASE! JUST STAY HERE!

*The same as a modern day "love hotel"

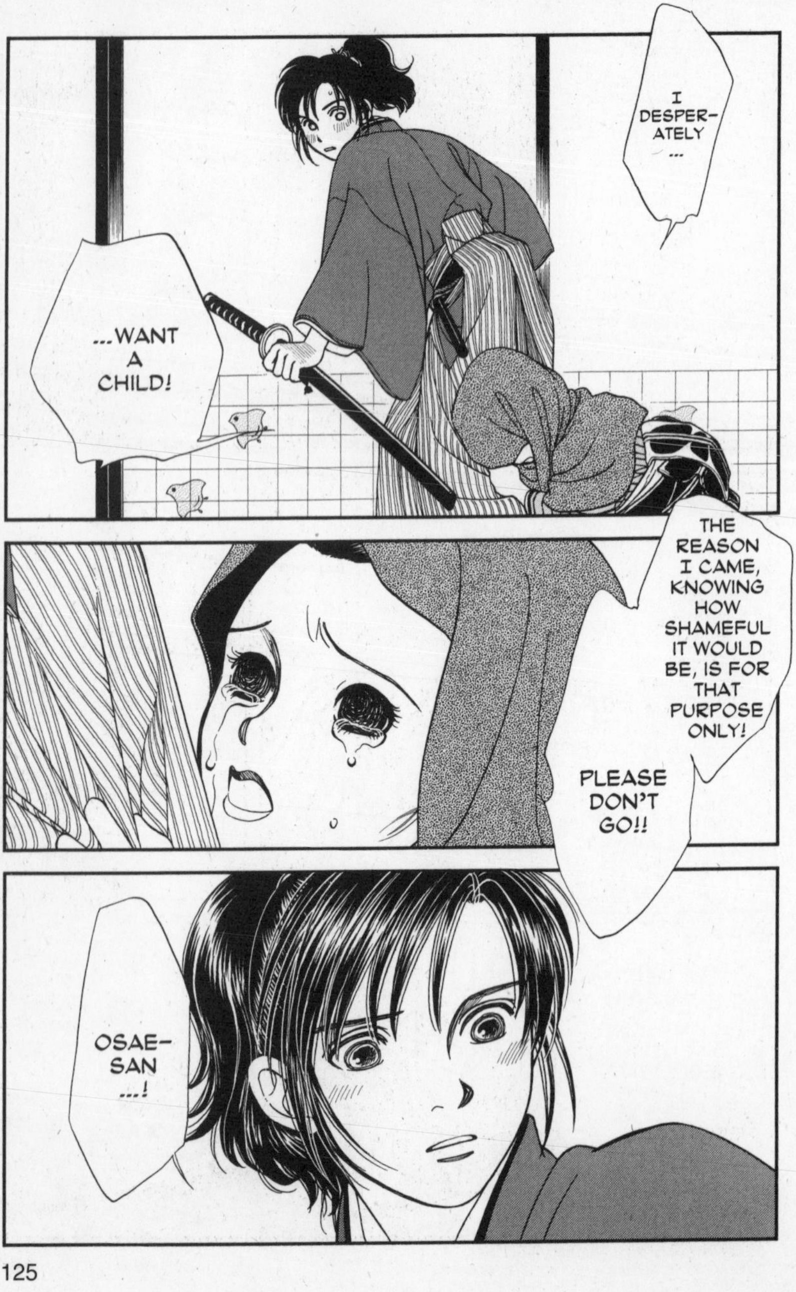
I DESPERATELY...
...WANT A CHILD!
THE REASON I CAME, KNOWING HOW SHAMEFUL IT WOULD BE, IS FOR THAT PURPOSE ONLY!
PLEASE DON'T GO!!
OSAE-SAN...!

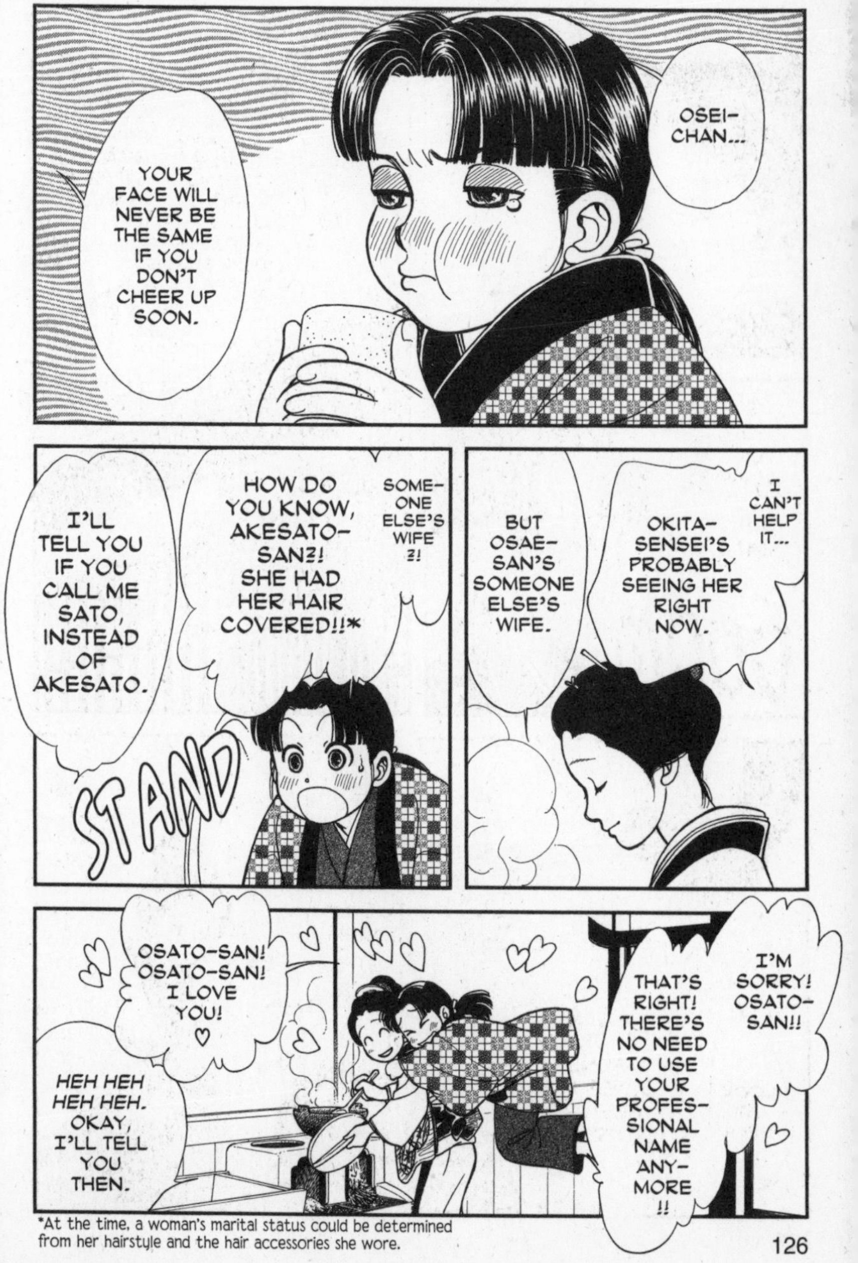
OSEI-CHAN...
YOUR FACE WILL NEVER BE THE SAME IF YOU DON'T CHEER UP SOON.
I CAN'T HELP IT...
OKITA-SENSEI'S PROBABLY SEEING HER RIGHT NOW.
BUT OSAE-SAN'S SOMEONE ELSE'S WIFE.
SOMEONE ELSE'S WIFE?!
HOW DO YOU KNOW, AKESATO-SAN?! SHE HAD HER HAIR COVERED!!*
STAND
I'LL TELL YOU IF YOU CALL ME SATO, INSTEAD OF AKESATO.
I'M SORRY! OSATO-SAN!!
THAT'S RIGHT! THERE'S NO NEED TO USE YOUR PROFESSIONAL NAME ANYMORE!!
OSATO-SAN! OSATO-SAN! I LOVE YOU! ♡
HEH HEH HEH HEH. OKAY, I'LL TELL YOU THEN.

*At the time, a woman's marital status could be determined from her hairstyle and the hair accessories she wore.

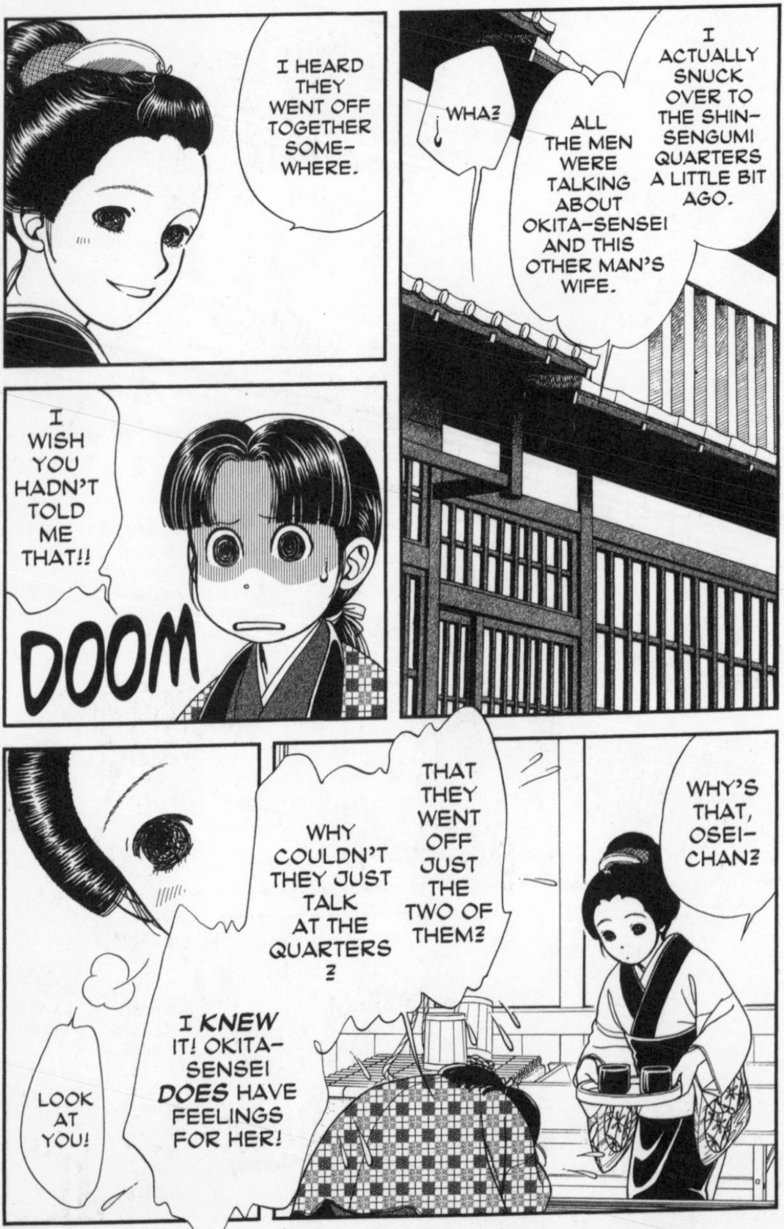
I ACTUALLY SNUCK OVER TO THE SHIN-SENGUMI QUARTERS A LITTLE BIT AGO.
ALL THE MEN WERE TALKING ABOUT OKITA-SENSEI AND THIS OTHER MAN'S WIFE.
WHA?
I HEARD THEY WENT OFF TOGETHER SOME-WHERE.
I WISH YOU HADN'T TOLD ME THAT!!
DOOM
WHY'S THAT, OSEI-CHAN?
THAT THEY WENT OFF JUST THE TWO OF THEM?
WHY COULDN'T THEY JUST TALK AT THE QUARTERS?
I *KNEW* IT! OKITA-SENSEI *DOES* HAVE FEELINGS FOR HER!
LOOK AT YOU!

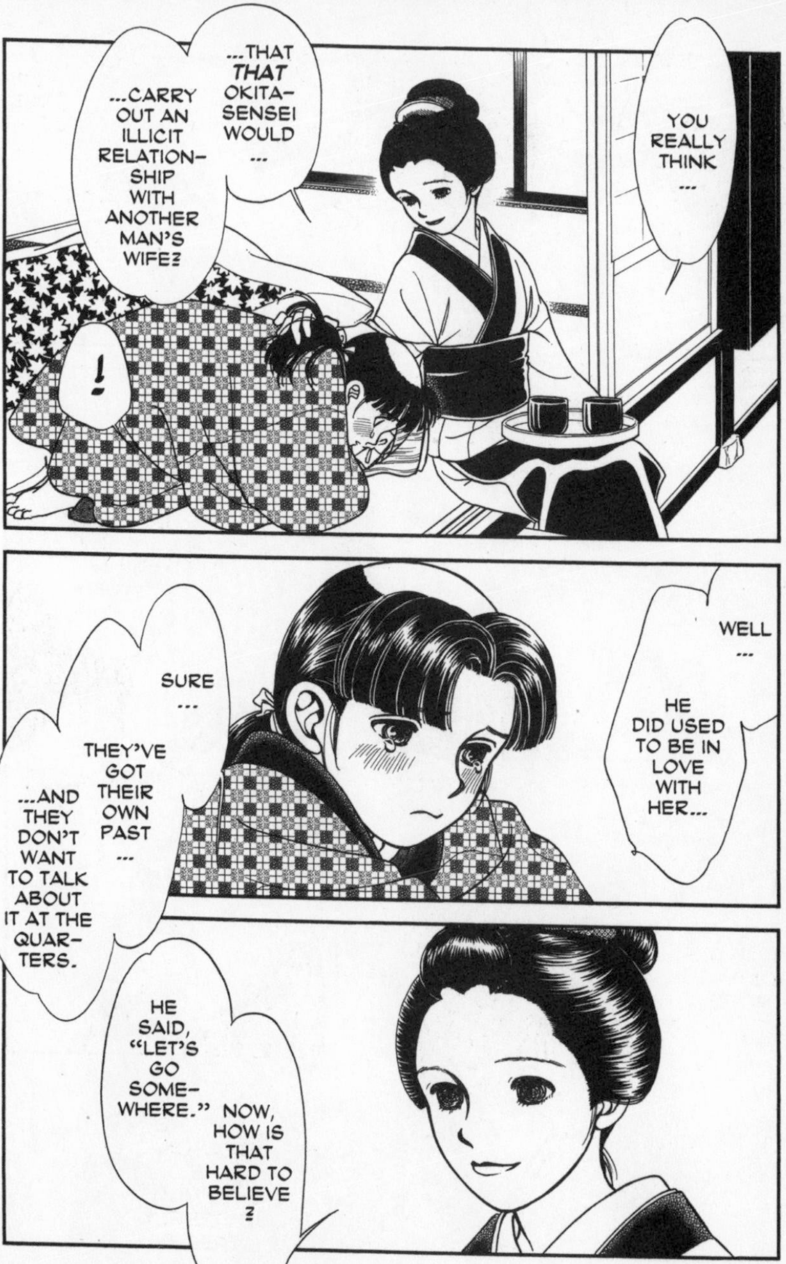
YOU REALLY THINK ...
...THAT *THAT* OKITA-SENSEI WOULD ...
...CARRY OUT AN ILLICIT RELATIONSHIP WITH ANOTHER MAN'S WIFE?
!
WELL ... HE DID USED TO BE IN LOVE WITH HER...
SURE ... THEY'VE GOT THEIR OWN PAST ...
...AND THEY DON'T WANT TO TALK ABOUT IT AT THE QUARTERS.
HE SAID, "LET'S GO SOMEWHERE." NOW, HOW IS THAT HARD TO BELIEVE?

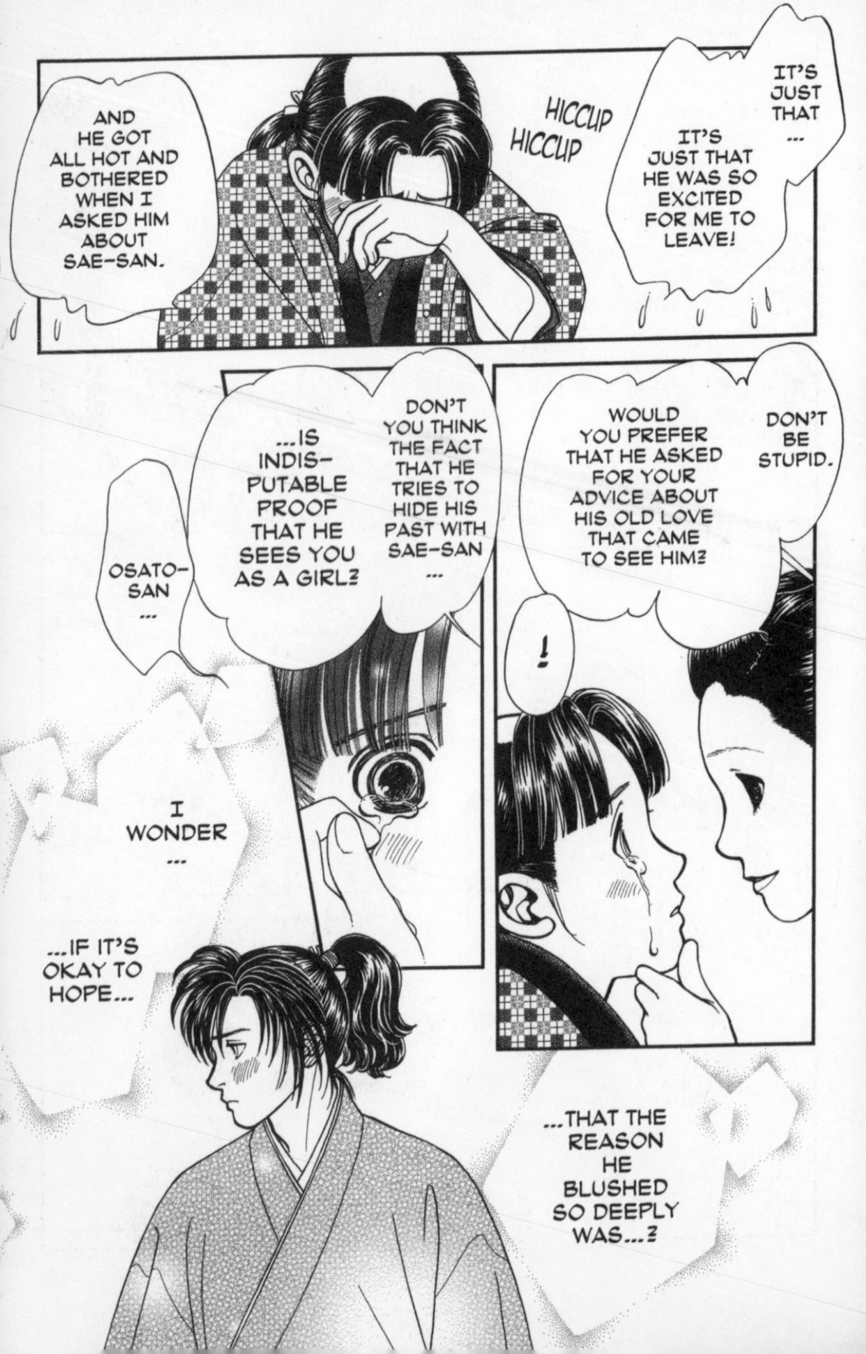
IT'S JUST THAT ...
IT'S JUST THAT HE WAS SO EXCITED FOR ME TO LEAVE!
HICCUP HICCUP
AND HE GOT ALL HOT AND BOTHERED WHEN I ASKED HIM ABOUT SAE-SAN.
DON'T BE STUPID.
WOULD YOU PREFER THAT HE ASKED FOR YOUR ADVICE ABOUT HIS OLD LOVE THAT CAME TO SEE HIM?
!
DON'T YOU THINK THE FACT THAT HE TRIES TO HIDE HIS PAST WITH SAE-SAN ...
...IS INDIS-PUTABLE PROOF THAT HE SEES YOU AS A GIRL?
OSATO-SAN ...
I WONDER ...
...IF IT'S OKAY TO HOPE...
...THAT THE REASON HE BLUSHED SO DEEPLY WAS...?

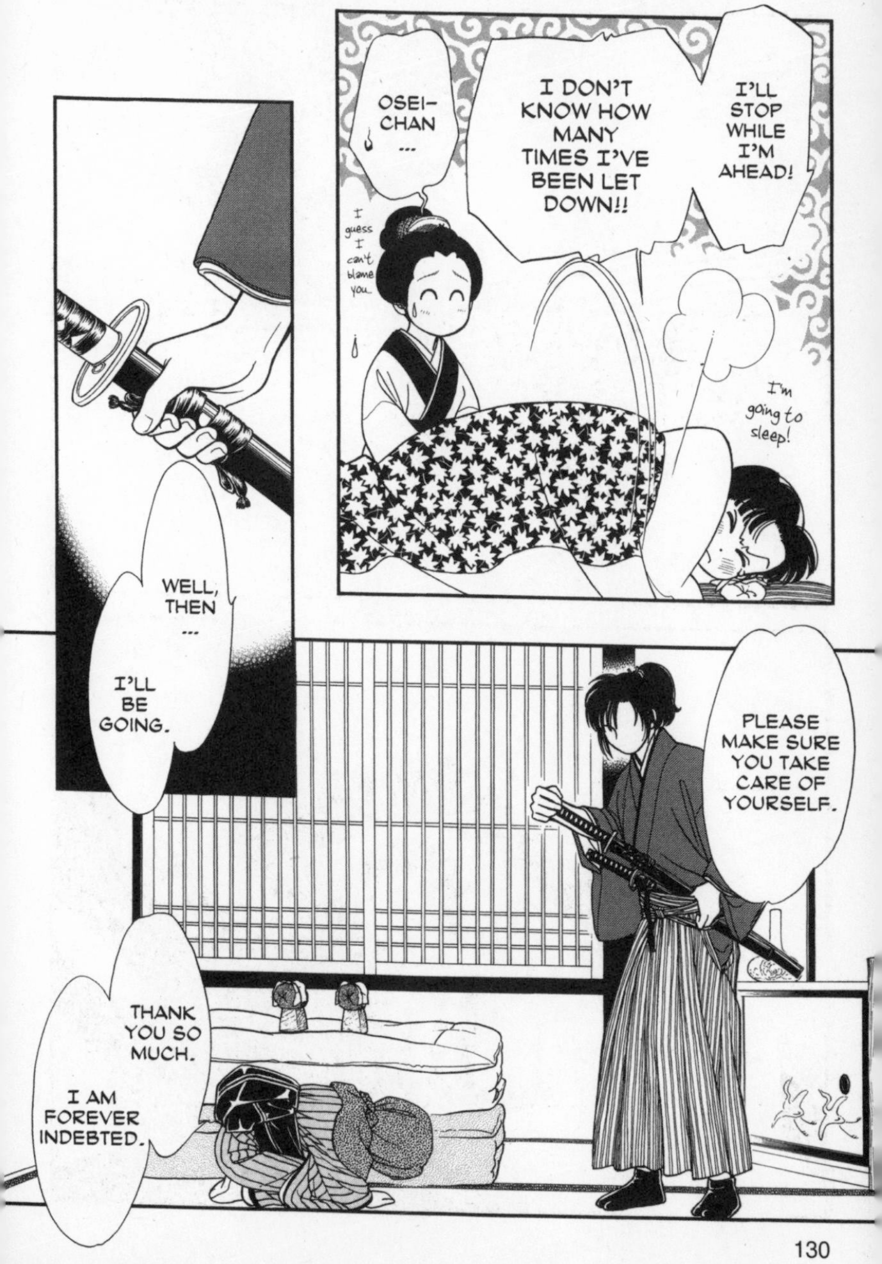
I'LL STOP WHILE I'M AHEAD!
I DON'T KNOW HOW MANY TIMES I'VE BEEN LET DOWN!!
OSEI-CHAN ...
I'm going to sleep!
I guess I can't blame you.
WELL, THEN ...
I'LL BE GOING.
PLEASE MAKE SURE YOU TAKE CARE OF YOURSELF.
THANK YOU SO MUCH.
I AM FOREVER INDEBTED.

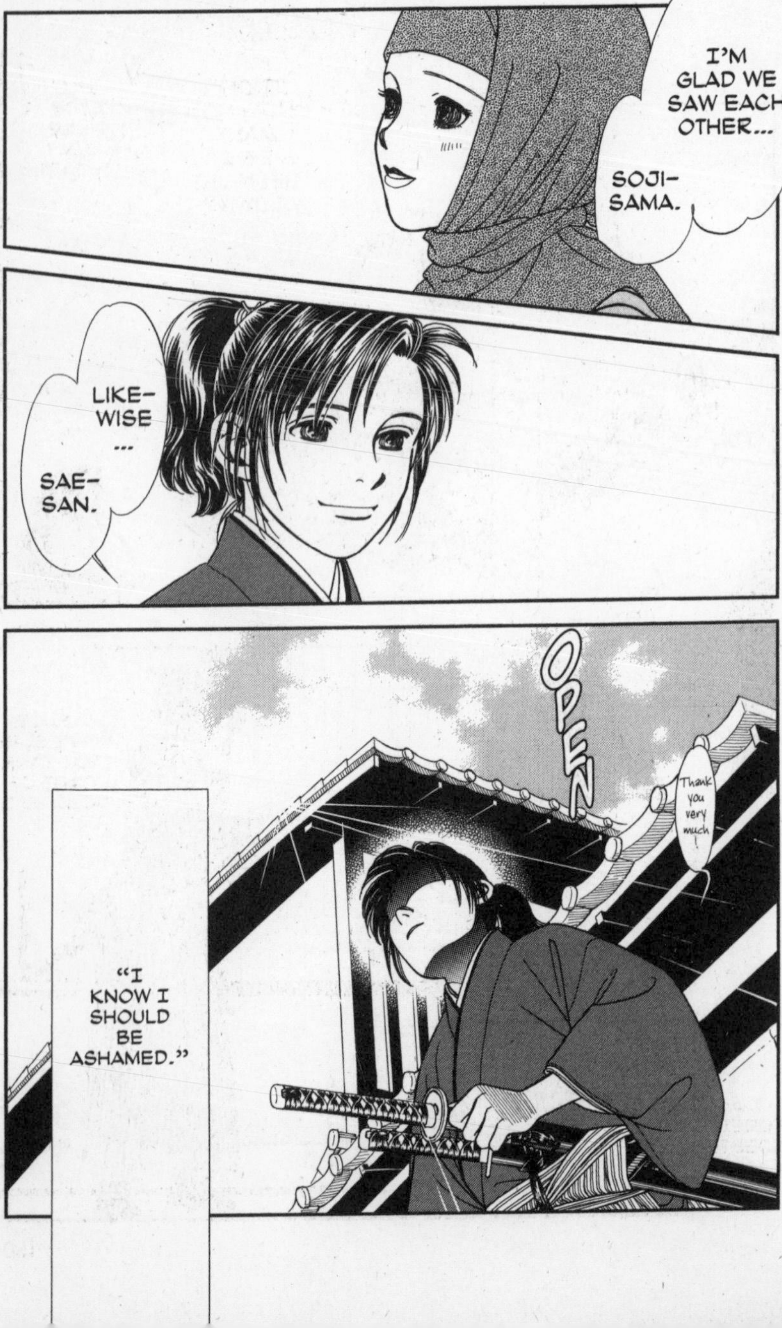
I'M GLAD WE SAW EACH OTHER...
SOJI-SAMA.
LIKE-WISE ...
SAE-SAN.
OPEN
Thank you very much!
"I KNOW I SHOULD BE ASHAMED."

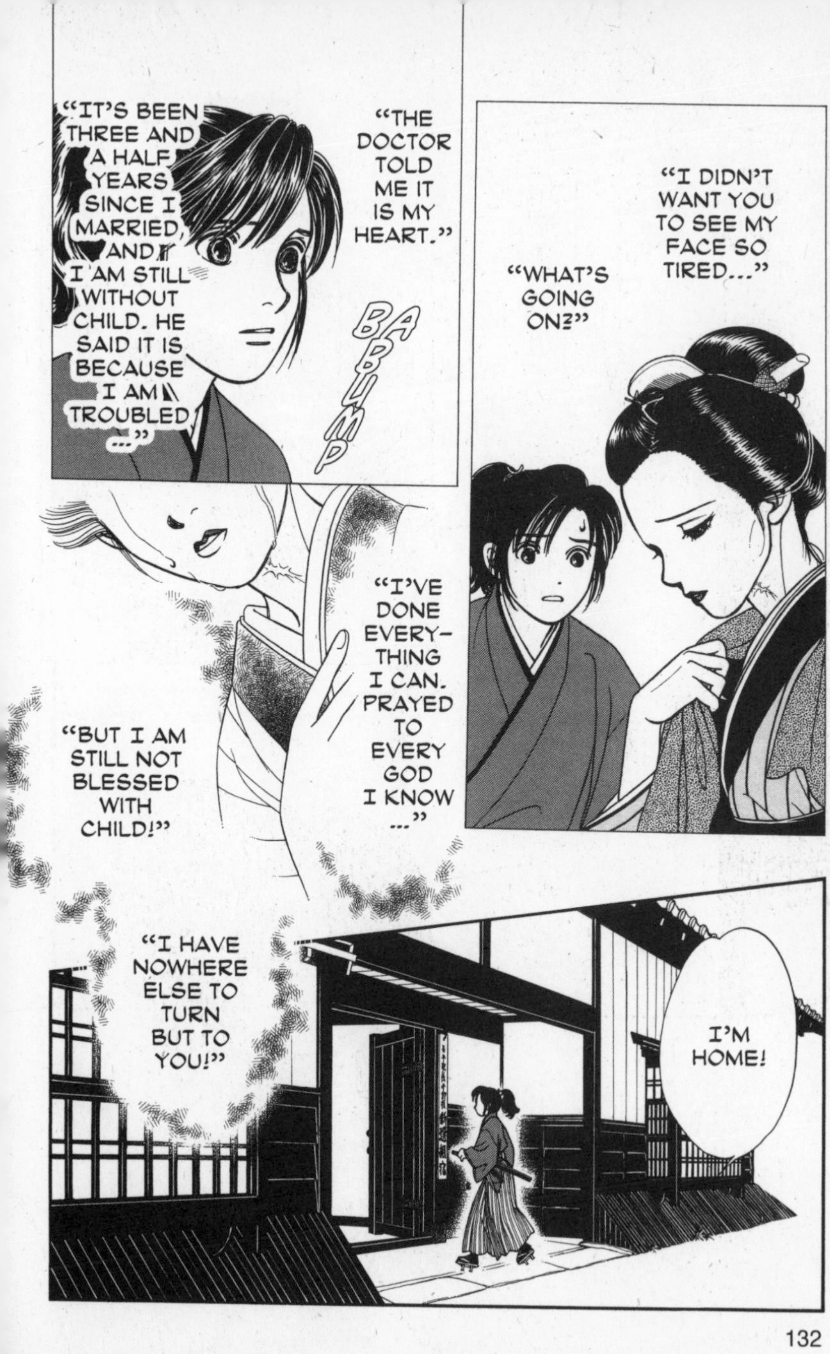
"I DIDN'T WANT YOU TO SEE MY FACE SO TIRED..."
"WHAT'S GOING ON?"
"THE DOCTOR TOLD ME IT IS MY HEART."
"IT'S BEEN THREE AND A HALF YEARS SINCE I MARRIED, AND I AM STILL WITHOUT CHILD. HE SAID IT IS BECAUSE I AM TROUBLED..."
BABUMP
"I'VE DONE EVERY-THING I CAN. PRAYED TO EVERY GOD I KNOW..."
"BUT I AM STILL NOT BLESSED WITH CHILD!"
I'M HOME!
"I HAVE NOWHERE ELSE TO TURN BUT TO YOU!"

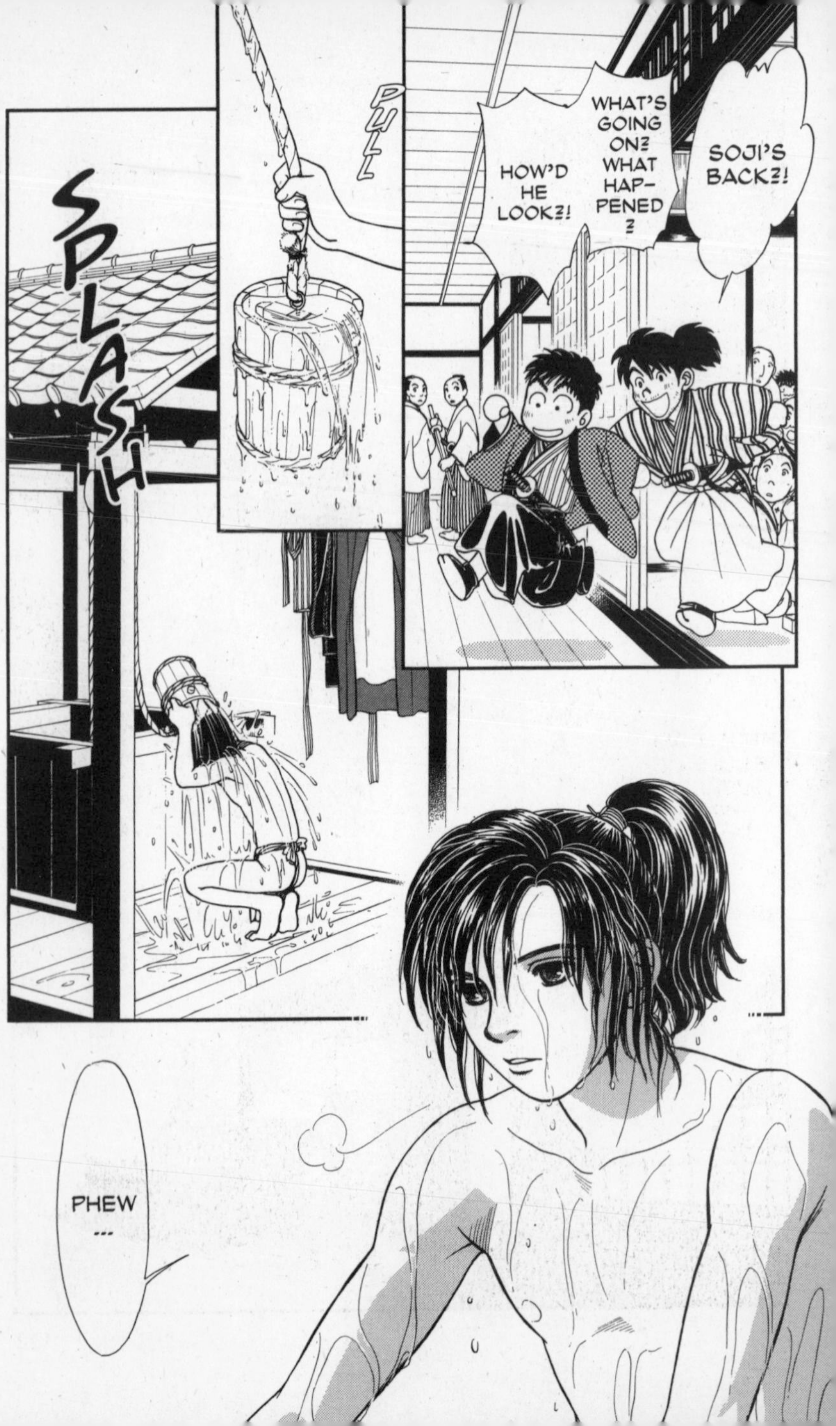
SOJI'S BACK?!
WHAT'S GOING ON? WHAT HAPPENED?
HOW'D HE LOOK?!
PULL
SPLASH
PHEW ...

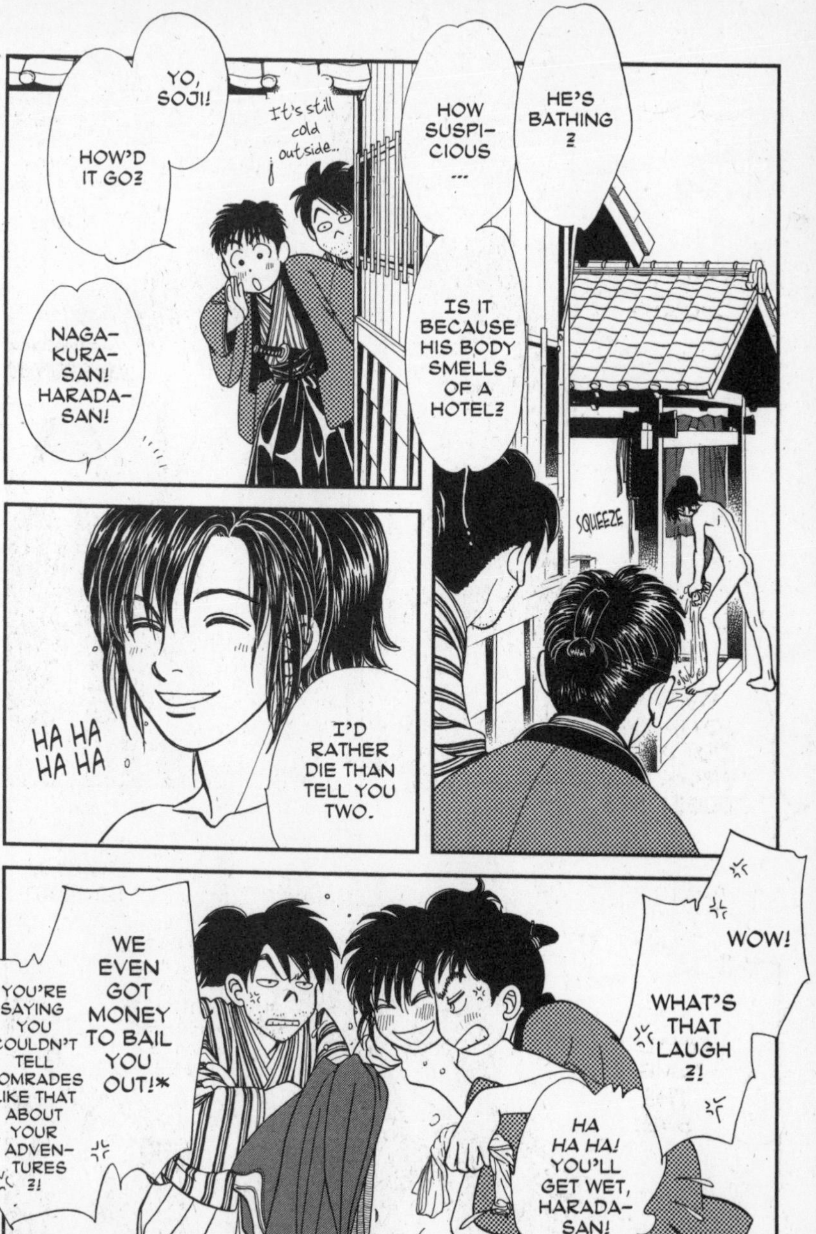
HE'S BATHING?
HOW SUSPICIOUS...
IS IT BECAUSE HIS BODY SMELLS OF A HOTEL?
SQUEEZE
YO, SOJI! HOW'D IT GO?
It's still cold outside..
NAGAKURA-SAN! HARADA-SAN!
I'D RATHER DIE THAN TELL YOU TWO.
HA HA HA HA
WOW! WHAT'S THAT LAUGH?!
HA HA HA! YOU'LL GET WET, HARADA-SAN!
WE EVEN GOT MONEY TO BAIL YOU OUT!*
YOU'RE SAYING YOU COULDN'T TELL COMRADES LIKE THAT ABOUT YOUR ADVENTURES?!

*Money to pay off the husband to keep quiet

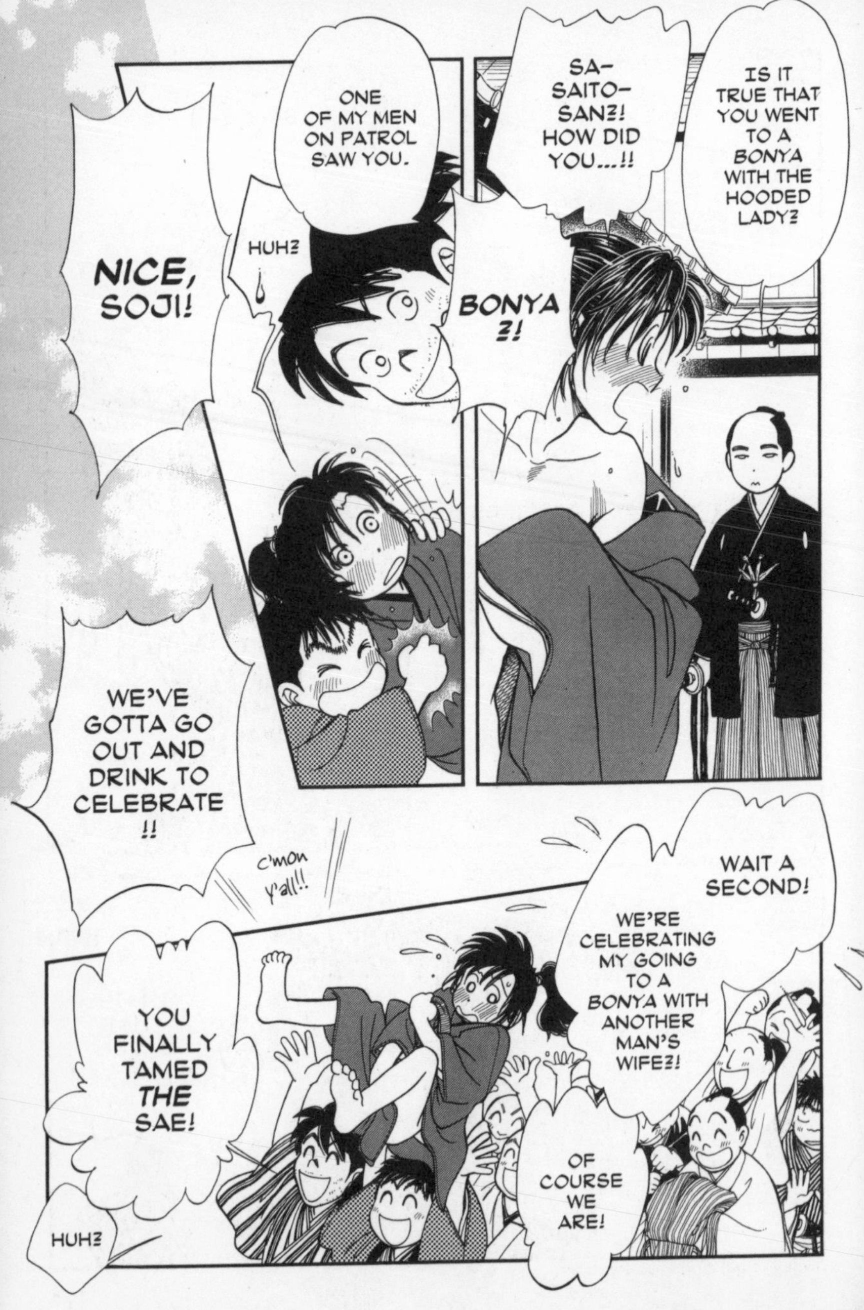
IS IT TRUE THAT YOU WENT TO A *BONYA* WITH THE HOODED LADY?
SA-SAITO-SAN?! HOW DID YOU...!!
ONE OF MY MEN ON PATROL SAW YOU.
BONYA?!
HUH?
NICE, SOJI!
WE'VE GOTTA GO OUT AND DRINK TO CELEBRATE!!
c'mon y'all!!
WAIT A SECOND!
WE'RE CELEBRATING MY GOING TO A *BONYA* WITH ANOTHER MAN'S WIFE?!
OF COURSE WE ARE!
YOU FINALLY TAMED *THE* SAE!
HUH?

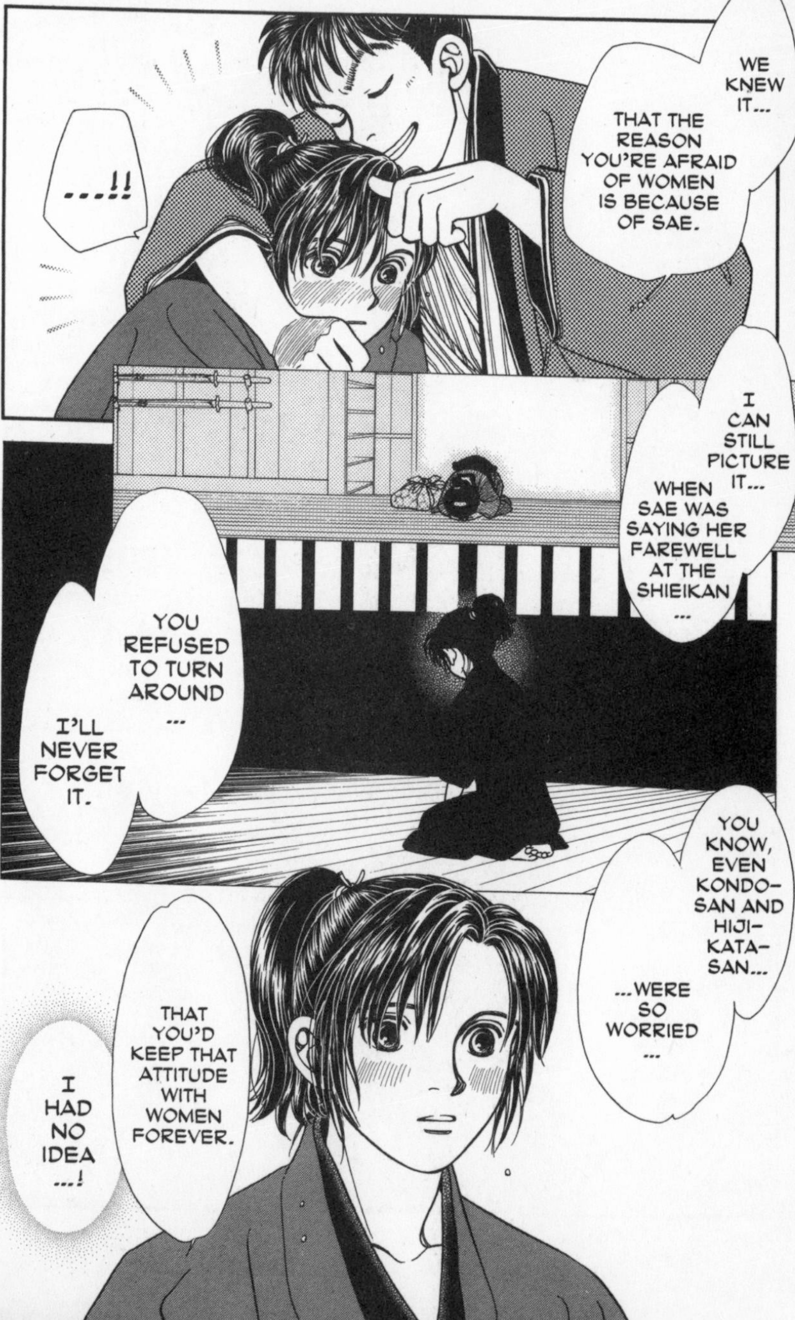
WE KNEW IT... THAT THE REASON YOU'RE AFRAID OF WOMEN IS BECAUSE OF SAE.
...!!
I CAN STILL PICTURE IT... WHEN SAE WAS SAYING HER FAREWELL AT THE SHIEIKAN...
YOU REFUSED TO TURN AROUND... I'LL NEVER FORGET IT.
YOU KNOW, EVEN KONDO-SAN AND HIJI-KATA-SAN... ...WERE SO WORRIED...
THAT YOU'D KEEP THAT ATTITUDE WITH WOMEN FOREVER.
I HAD NO IDEA...!

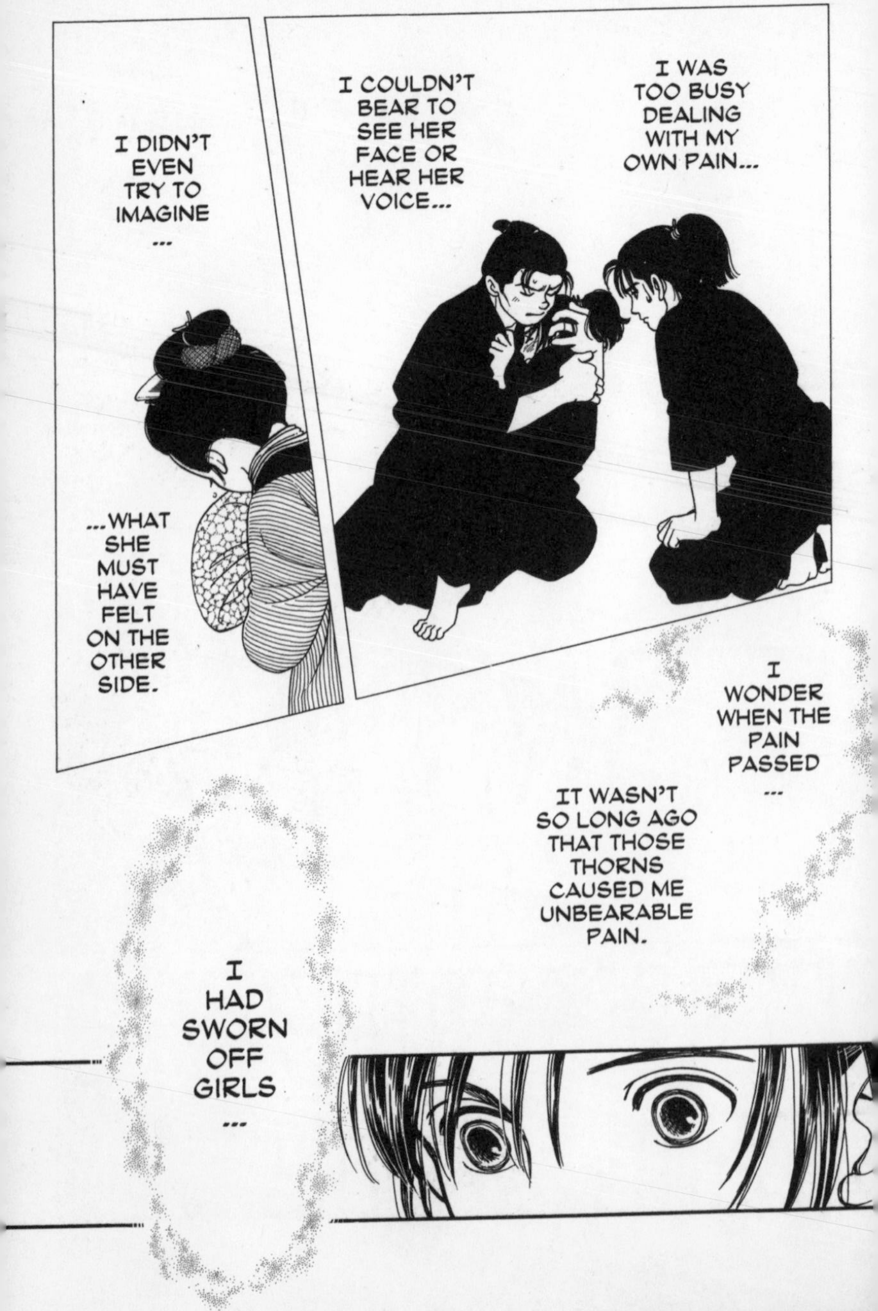
I WAS TOO BUSY DEALING WITH MY OWN PAIN...
I COULDN'T BEAR TO SEE HER FACE OR HEAR HER VOICE...
I DIDN'T EVEN TRY TO IMAGINE ...
...WHAT SHE MUST HAVE FELT ON THE OTHER SIDE.
I WONDER WHEN THE PAIN PASSED ...
IT WASN'T SO LONG AGO THAT THOSE THORNS CAUSED ME UNBEARABLE PAIN.
I HAD SWORN OFF GIRLS ...

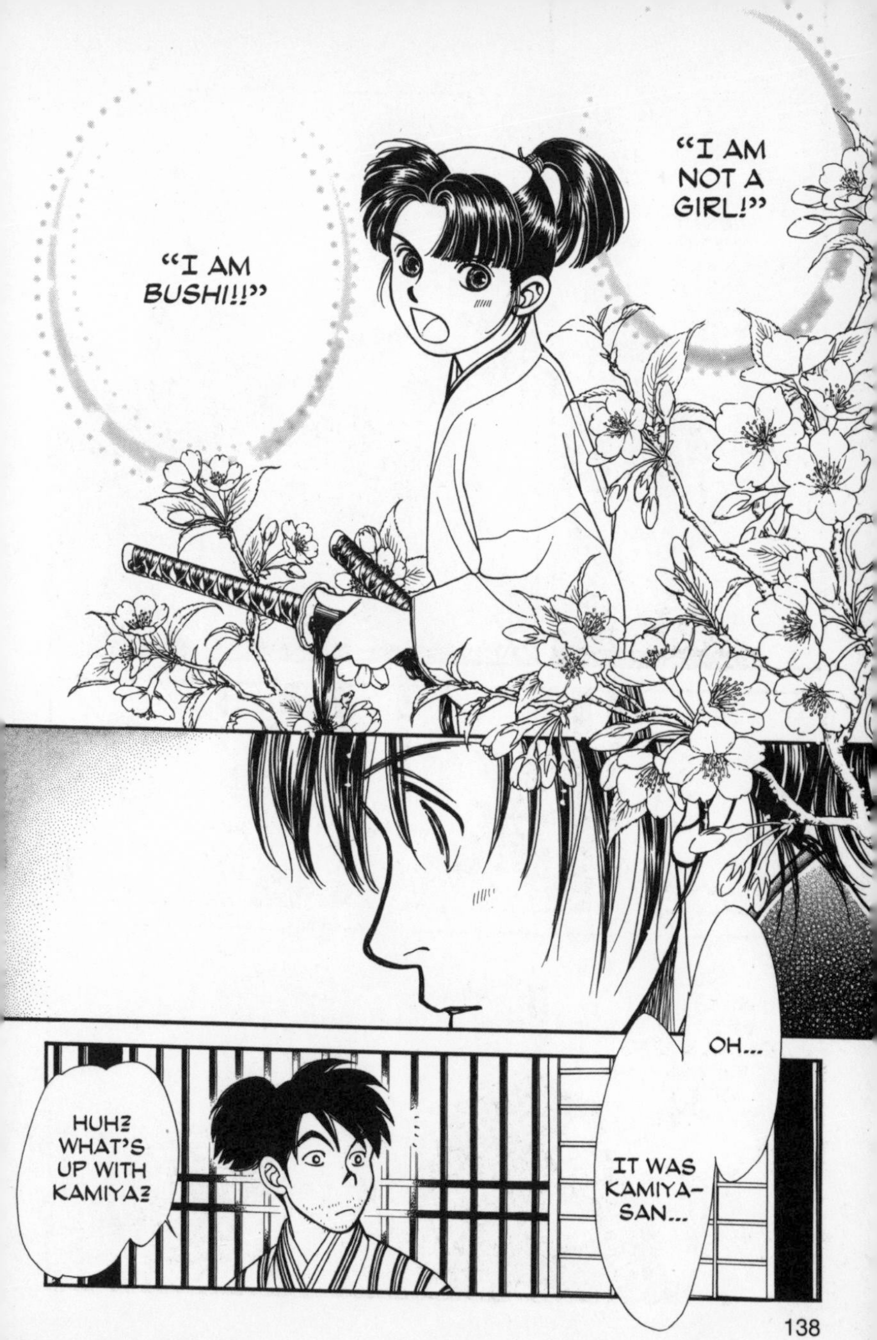
"I AM NOT A GIRL!"
"I AM BUSHI!!!"
OH...
IT WAS KAMIYA-SAN...
HUH? WHAT'S UP WITH KAMIYA?

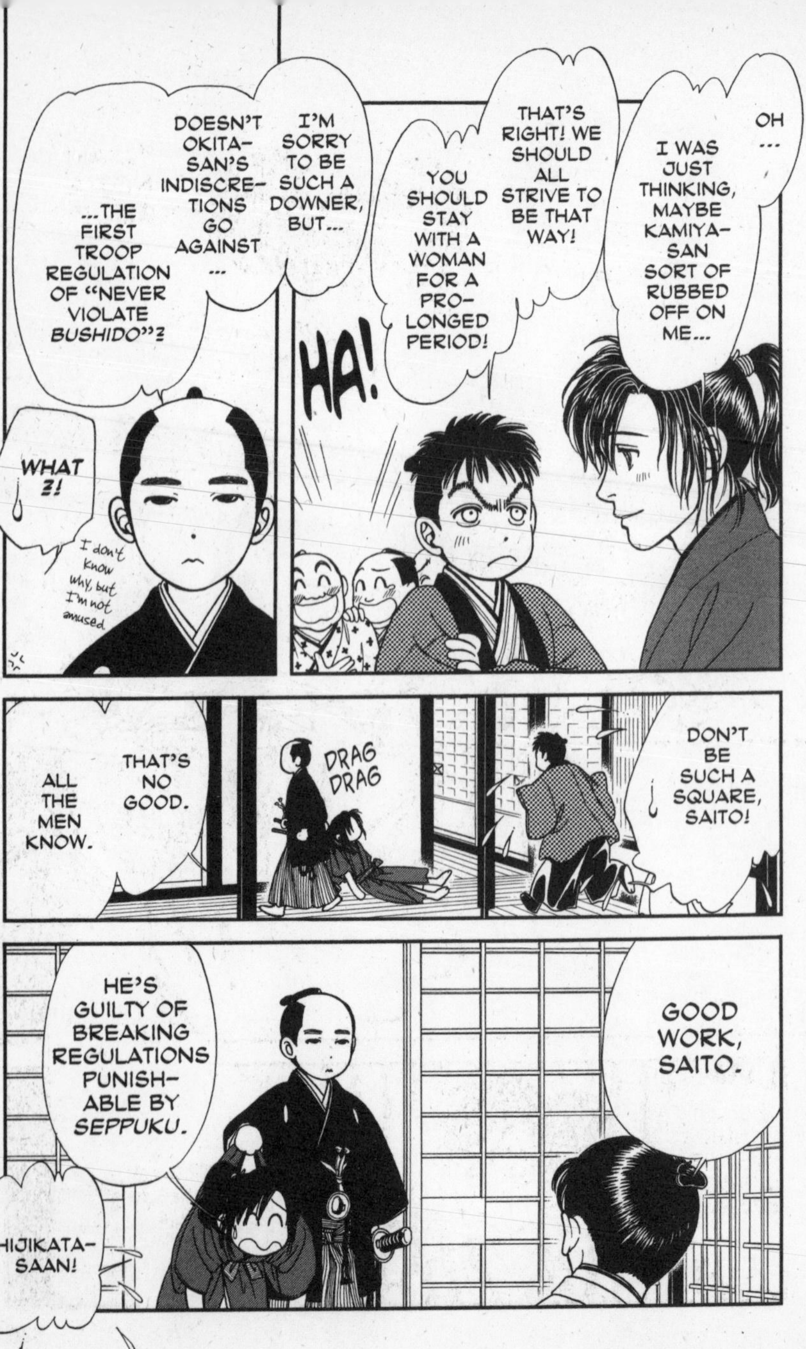
OH ... I WAS JUST THINKING, MAYBE KAMIYA-SAN SORT OF RUBBED OFF ON ME...
THAT'S RIGHT! WE SHOULD ALL STRIVE TO BE THAT WAY!
YOU SHOULD STAY WITH A WOMAN FOR A PRO-LONGED PERIOD!
HA!
I'M SORRY TO BE SUCH A DOWNER, BUT...
DOESN'T OKITA-SAN'S INDISCRE-TIONS GO AGAINST ...
...THE FIRST TROOP REGULATION OF "NEVER VIOLATE *BUSHIDO*"?
WHAT?!
I don't know why, but I'm not amused
DON'T BE SUCH A SQUARE, SAITO!
DRAG DRAG
THAT'S NO GOOD.
ALL THE MEN KNOW.
GOOD WORK, SAITO.
HE'S GUILTY OF BREAKING REGULATIONS PUNISH-ABLE BY *SEPPUKU*.
HIJIKATA-SAAN!

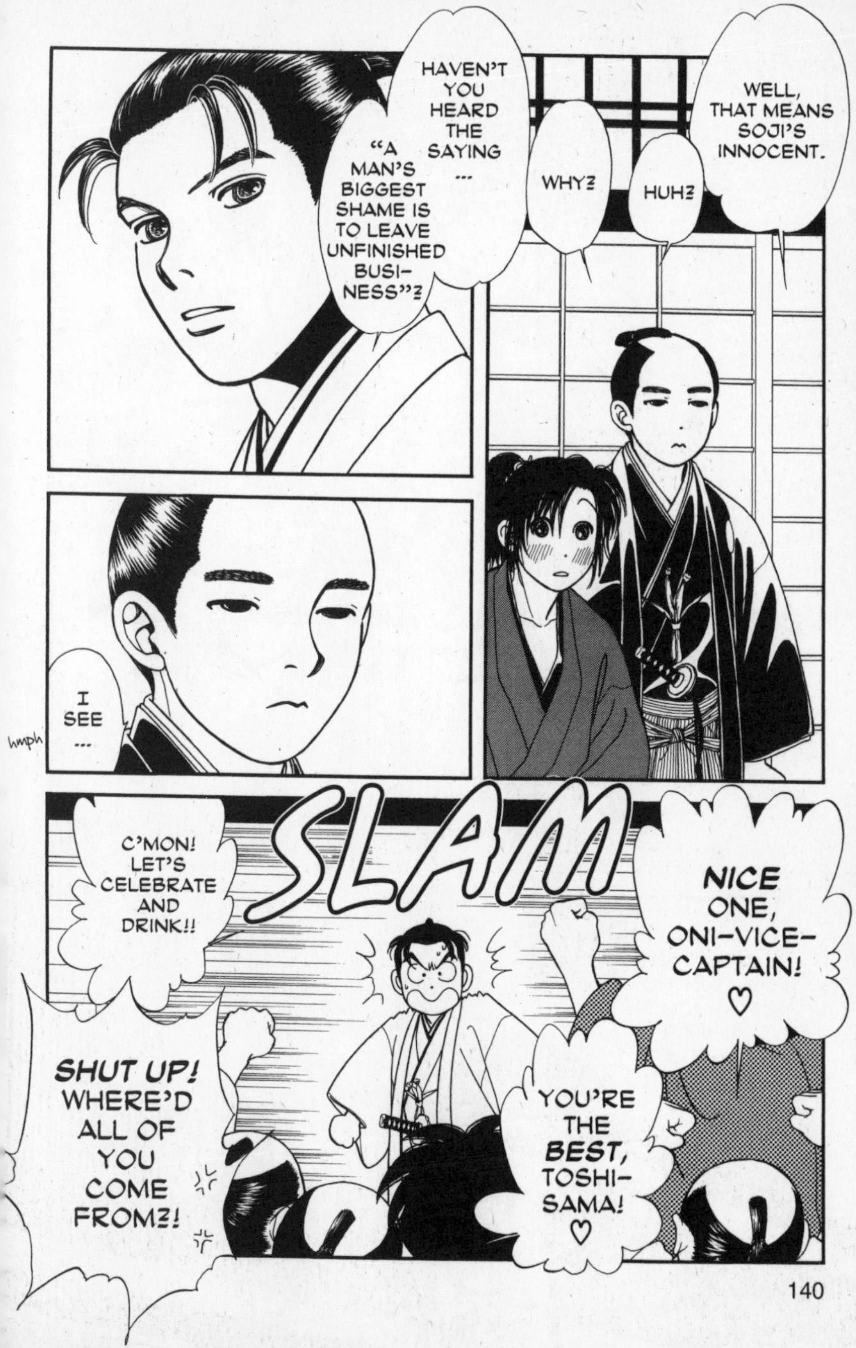
WELL, THAT MEANS SOJI'S INNOCENT.
HUH?
WHY?
HAVEN'T YOU HEARD THE SAYING...
"A MAN'S BIGGEST SHAME IS TO LEAVE UNFINISHED BUSI-NESS"?
I SEE...
hmph
SLAM
NICE ONE, ONI-VICE-CAPTAIN! ♡
C'MON! LET'S CELEBRATE AND DRINK!!
YOU'RE THE BEST, TOSHI-SAMA! ♡
SHUT UP! WHERE'D ALL OF YOU COME FROM?!

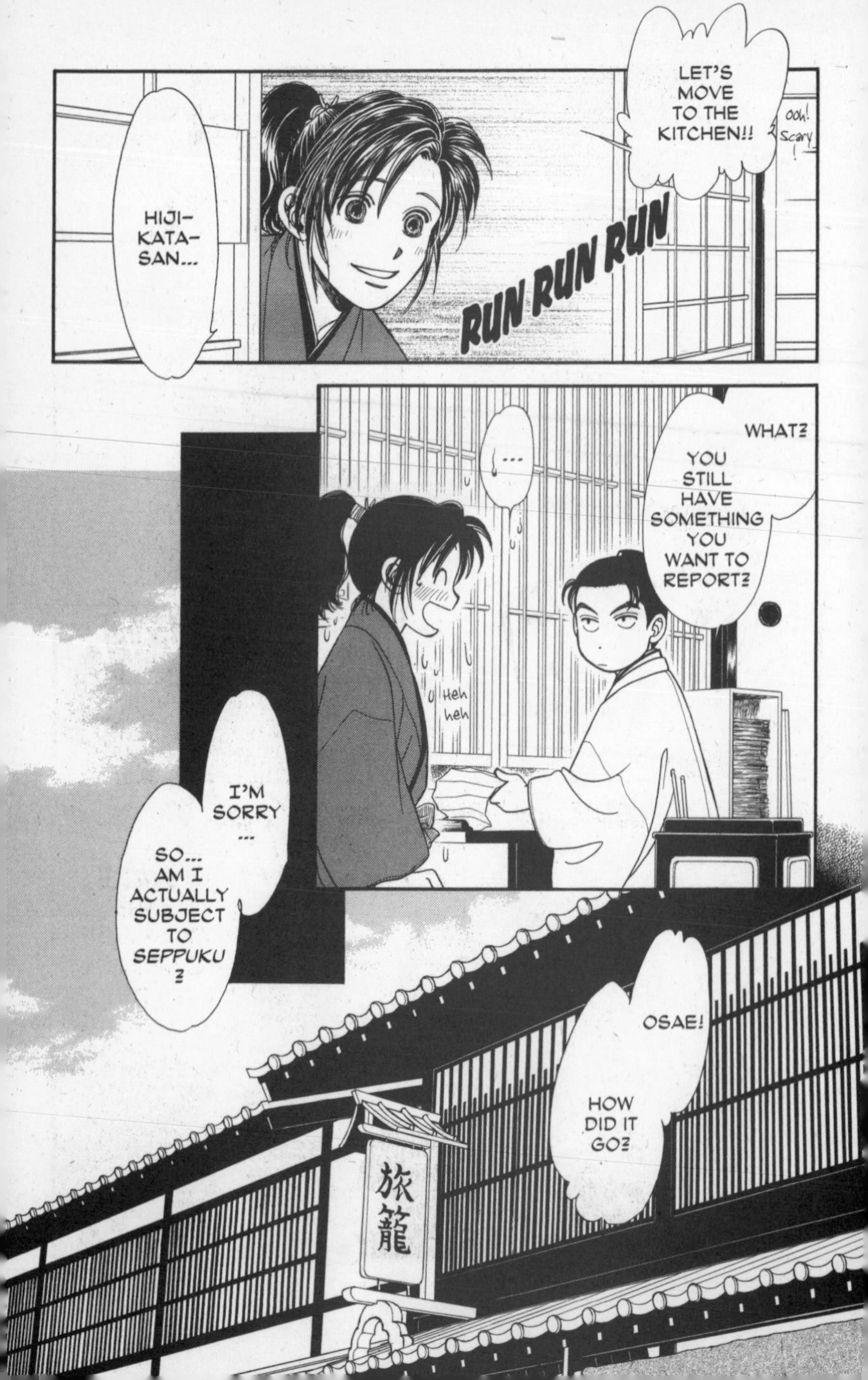
LET'S MOVE TO THE KITCHEN!!
Ooh! Scary!
RUN RUN RUN
HIJI-KATA-SAN...
WHAT?
YOU STILL HAVE SOMETHING YOU WANT TO REPORT?
...
Heh heh
I'M SORRY...
SO... AM I ACTUALLY SUBJECT TO SEPPUKU?
OSAE!
HOW DID IT GO?
旅籠

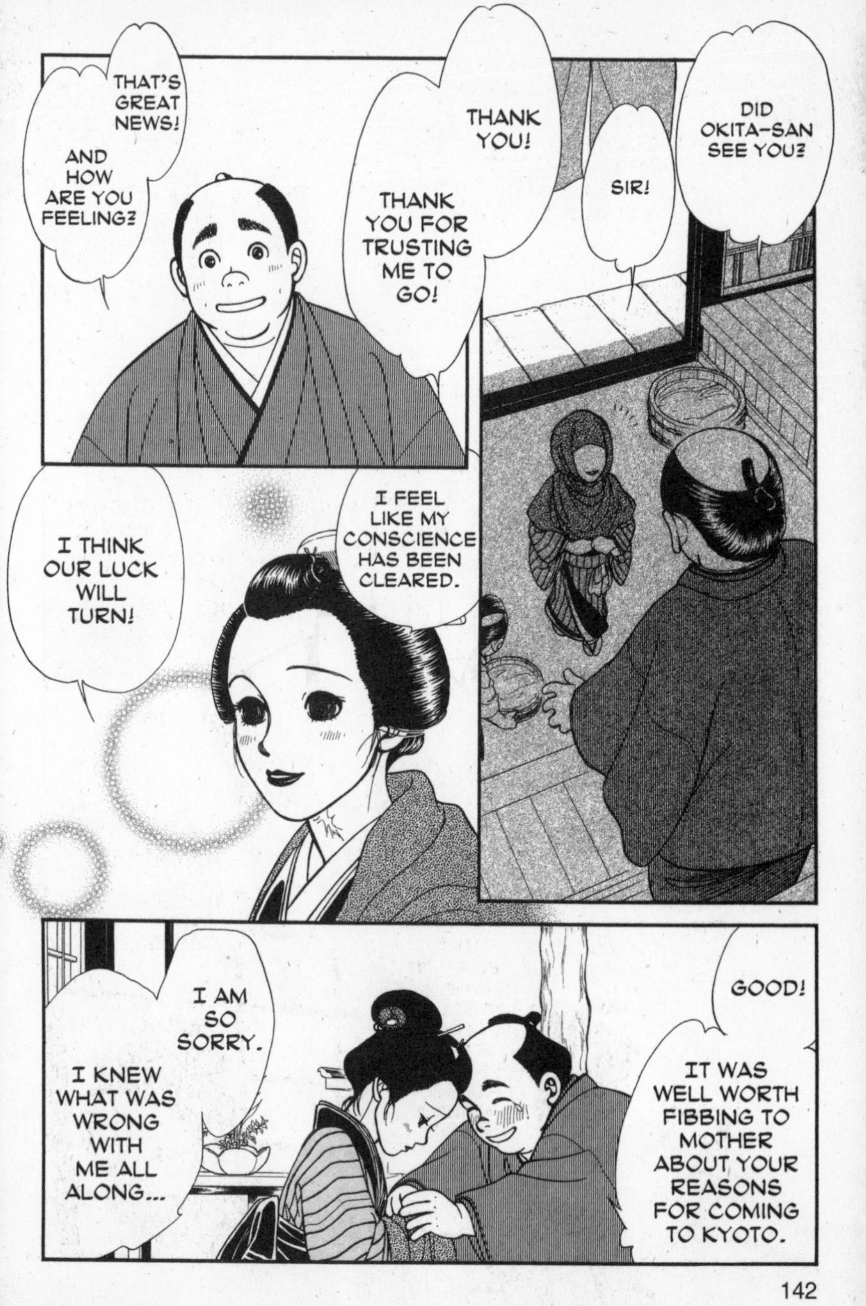
DID OKITA-SAN SEE YOU?
SIR!
THANK YOU!
THANK YOU FOR TRUSTING ME TO GO!
THAT'S GREAT NEWS!
AND HOW ARE YOU FEELING?
I FEEL LIKE MY CONSCIENCE HAS BEEN CLEARED.
I THINK OUR LUCK WILL TURN!
GOOD!
IT WAS WELL WORTH FIBBING TO MOTHER ABOUT YOUR REASONS FOR COMING TO KYOTO.
I AM SO SORRY.
I KNEW WHAT WAS WRONG WITH ME ALL ALONG...

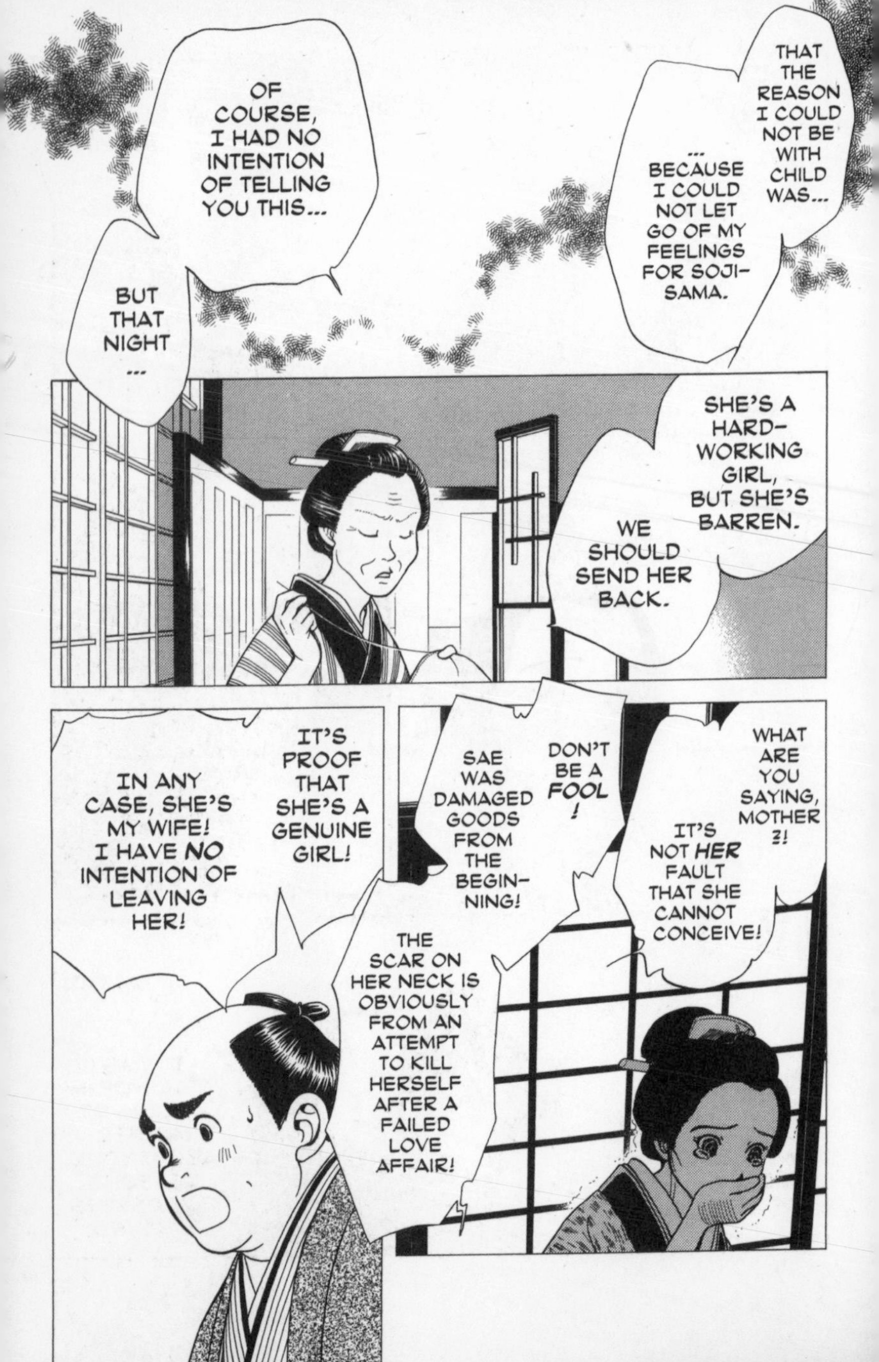
THAT THE REASON I COULD NOT BE WITH CHILD WAS...
...BECAUSE I COULD NOT LET GO OF MY FEELINGS FOR SOJI-SAMA.
OF COURSE, I HAD NO INTENTION OF TELLING YOU THIS...
BUT THAT NIGHT...
SHE'S A HARD-WORKING GIRL, BUT SHE'S BARREN.
WE SHOULD SEND HER BACK.
WHAT ARE YOU SAYING, MOTHER?!
IT'S NOT *HER* FAULT THAT SHE CANNOT CONCEIVE!
DON'T BE A *FOOL*!
SAE WAS DAMAGED GOODS FROM THE BEGIN-NING!
THE SCAR ON HER NECK IS OBVIOUSLY FROM AN ATTEMPT TO KILL HERSELF AFTER A FAILED LOVE AFFAIR!
IT'S PROOF THAT SHE'S A GENUINE GIRL!
IN ANY CASE, SHE'S MY WIFE! I HAVE *NO* INTENTION OF LEAVING HER!

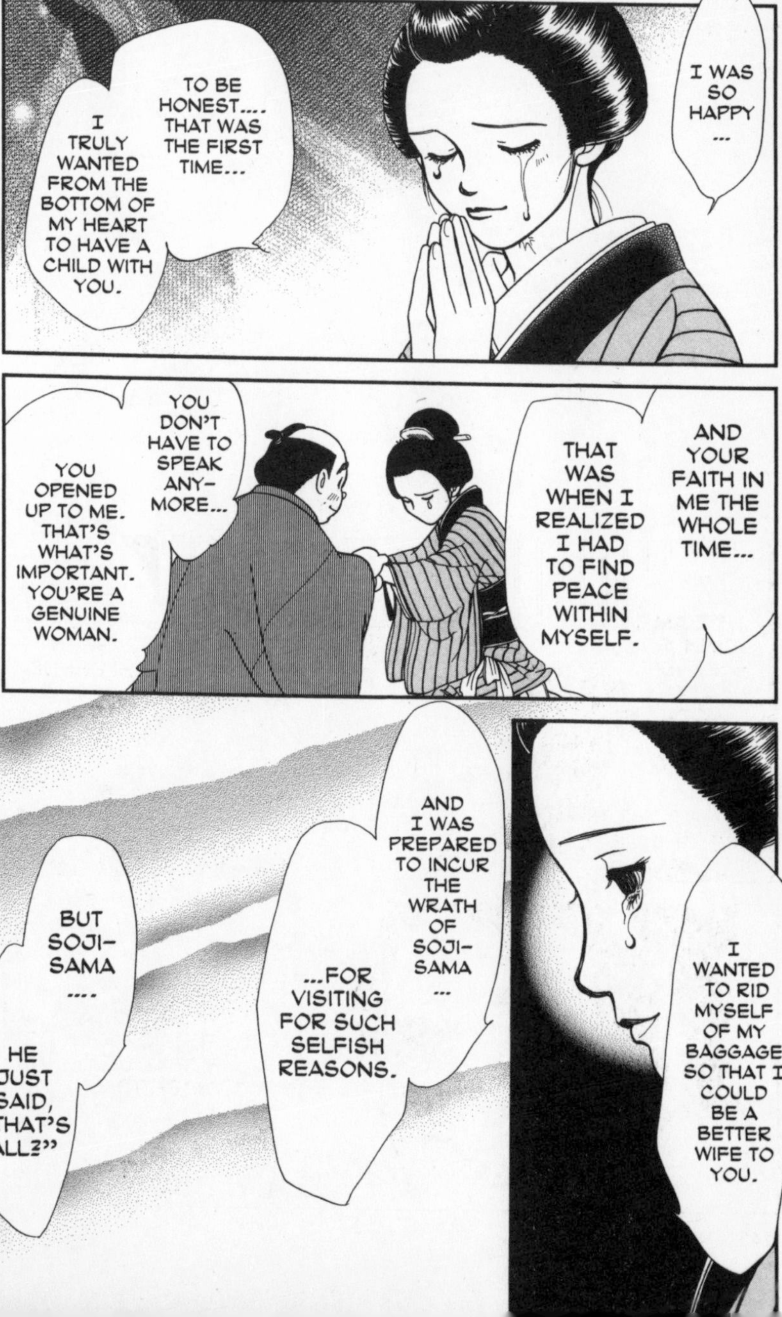
I WAS SO HAPPY...
TO BE HONEST.... THAT WAS THE FIRST TIME...
I TRULY WANTED FROM THE BOTTOM OF MY HEART TO HAVE A CHILD WITH YOU.
AND YOUR FAITH IN ME THE WHOLE TIME...
THAT WAS WHEN I REALIZED I HAD TO FIND PEACE WITHIN MYSELF.
YOU DON'T HAVE TO SPEAK ANYMORE...
YOU OPENED UP TO ME. THAT'S WHAT'S IMPORTANT. YOU'RE A GENUINE WOMAN.
I WANTED TO RID MYSELF OF MY BAGGAGE SO THAT I COULD BE A BETTER WIFE TO YOU.
AND I WAS PREPARED TO INCUR THE WRATH OF SOJI-SAMA...
...FOR VISITING FOR SUCH SELFISH REASONS.
BUT SOJI-SAMA....
HE JUST SAID, "THAT'S ALL?"

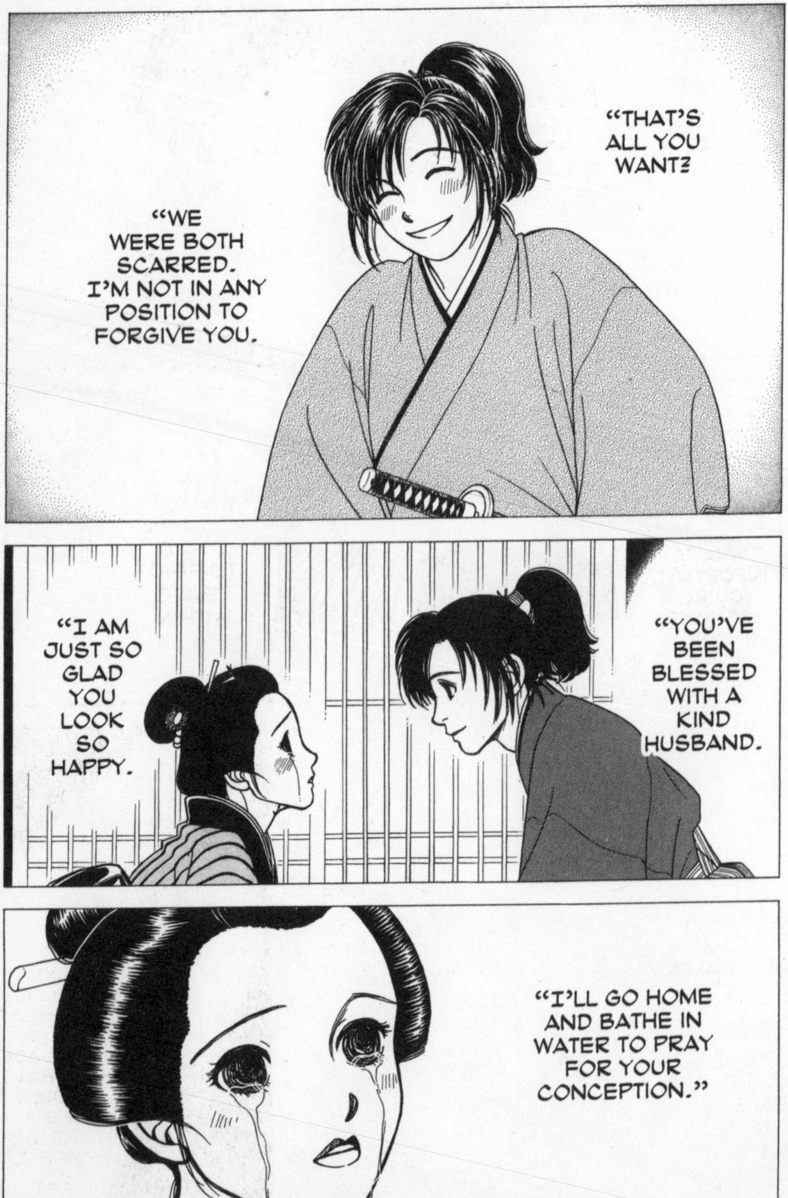
“THAT’S ALL YOU WANT?
“WE WERE BOTH SCARRED. I’M NOT IN ANY POSITION TO FORGIVE YOU.
“YOU’VE BEEN BLESSED WITH A KIND HUSBAND.
“I AM JUST SO GLAD YOU LOOK SO HAPPY.
“I’LL GO HOME AND BATHE IN WATER TO PRAY FOR YOUR CONCEPTION.”

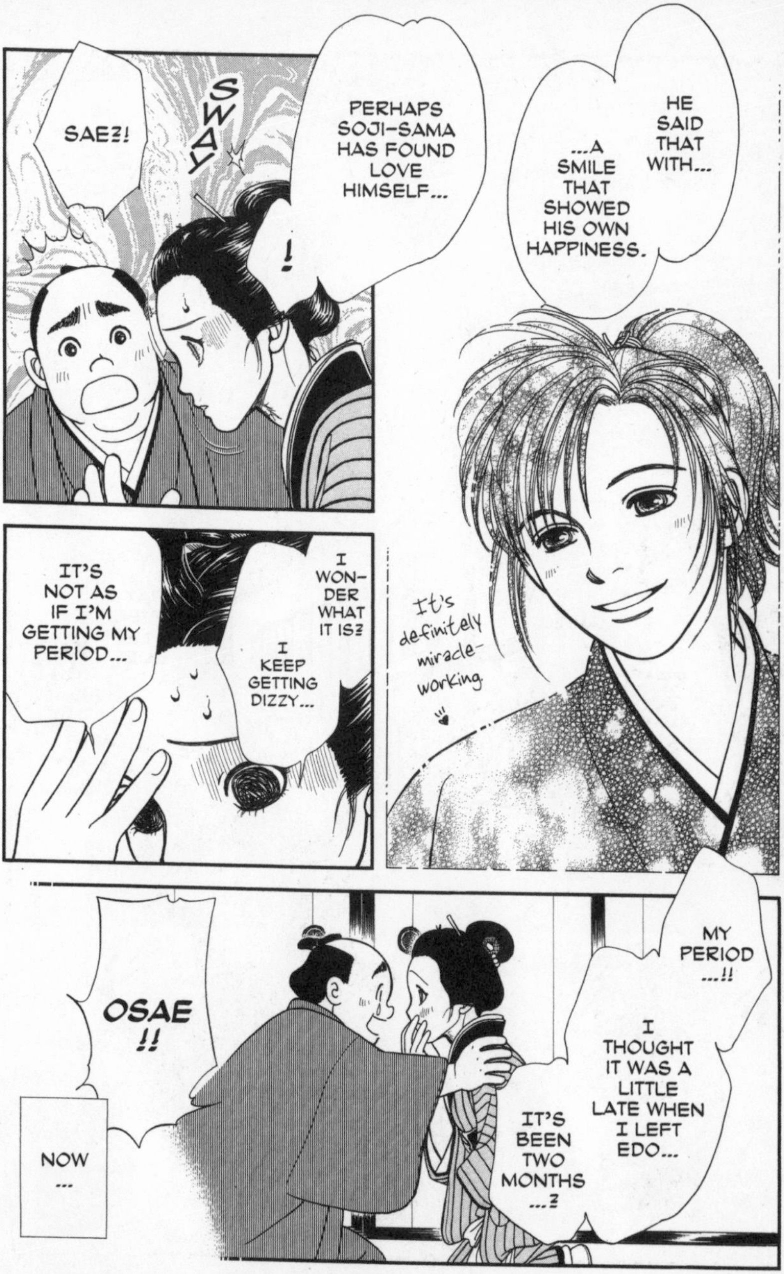
HE SAID THAT WITH...
...A SMILE THAT SHOWED HIS OWN HAPPINESS.
It's definitely miracle-working.
PERHAPS SOJI-SAMA HAS FOUND LOVE HIMSELF...
!
SWAY
SAE?!
I WONDER WHAT IT IS?
I KEEP GETTING DIZZY...
IT'S NOT AS IF I'M GETTING MY PERIOD...
MY PERIOD ...!!
I THOUGHT IT WAS A LITTLE LATE WHEN I LEFT EDO...
IT'S BEEN TWO MONTHS ...?
OSAE !!
NOW ...

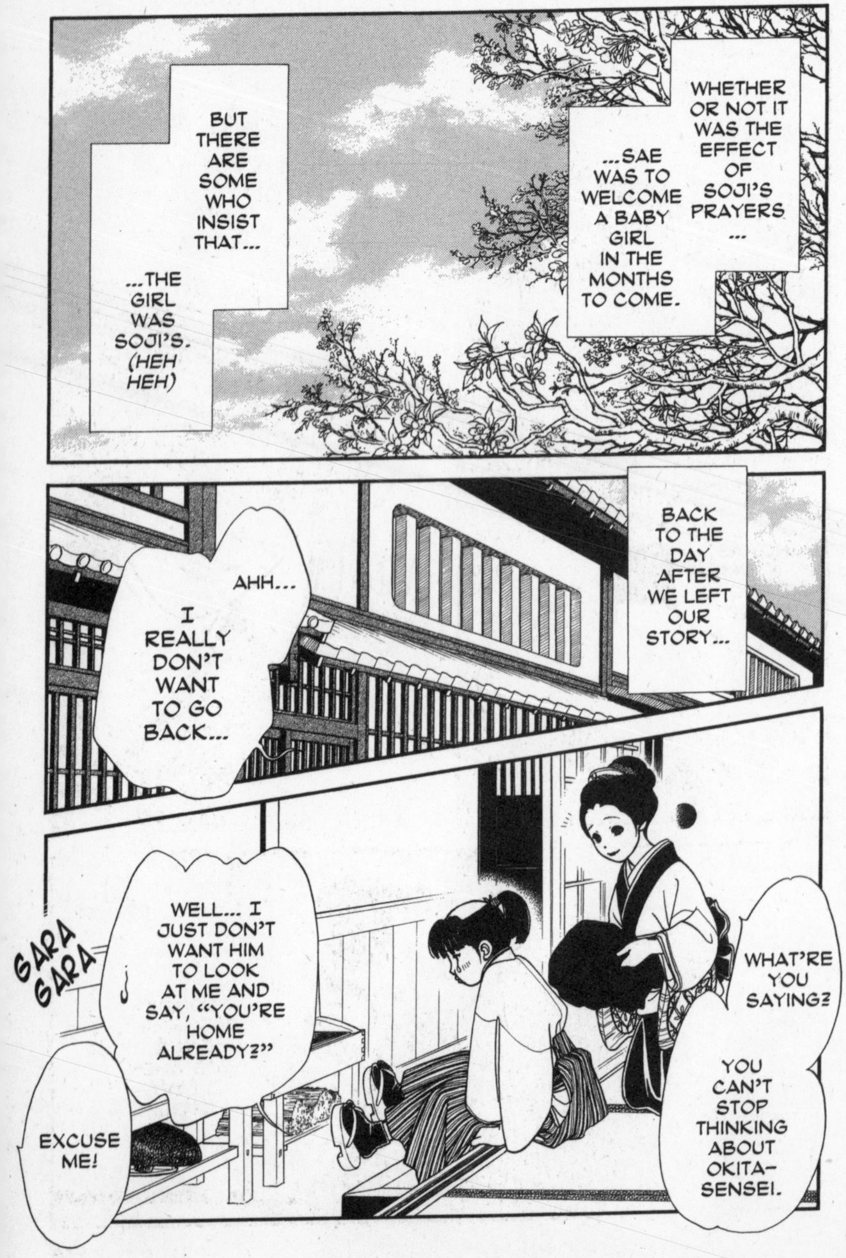
WHETHER OR NOT IT WAS THE EFFECT OF SOJI'S PRAYERS...
...SAE WAS TO WELCOME A BABY GIRL IN THE MONTHS TO COME.
BUT THERE ARE SOME WHO INSIST THAT...
...THE GIRL WAS SOJI'S. (HEH HEH)
BACK TO THE DAY AFTER WE LEFT OUR STORY...
AHH... I REALLY DON'T WANT TO GO BACK...
WHAT'RE YOU SAYING?
YOU CAN'T STOP THINKING ABOUT OKITA-SENSEI.
WELL... I JUST DON'T WANT HIM TO LOOK AT ME AND SAY, "YOU'RE HOME ALREADY?"
GARA GARA
EXCUSE ME!

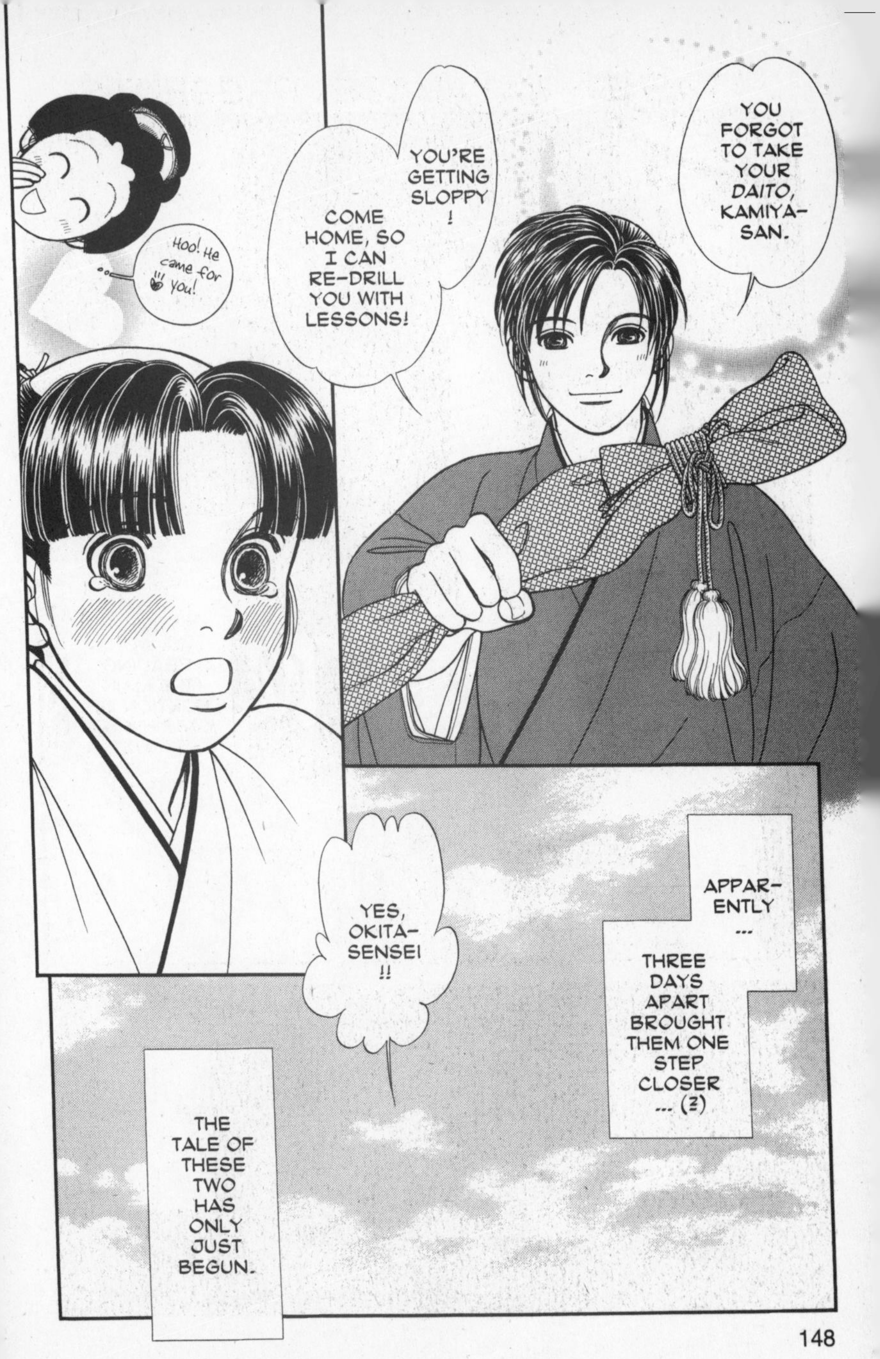
YOU FORGOT TO TAKE YOUR *DAITO*, KAMIYA-SAN.
YOU'RE GETTING SLOPPY!
COME HOME, SO I CAN RE-DRILL YOU WITH LESSONS!
YES, OKITA-SENSEI!!
Hoo! He came for you!
APPARENTLY... THREE DAYS APART BROUGHT THEM ONE STEP CLOSER... (2)
THE TALE OF THESE TWO HAS ONLY JUST BEGUN.

TAEKO WATANABE PRESENTS

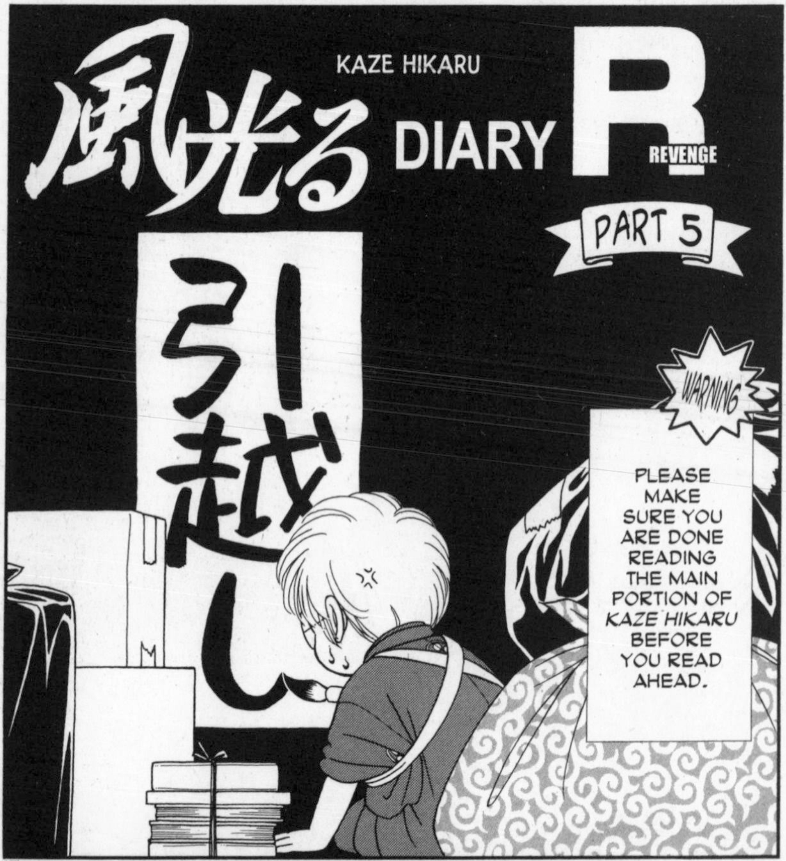
風光る
KAZE HIKARU
DIARY R REVENGE
PART 5
WARNING
PLEASE MAKE SURE YOU ARE DONE READING THE MAIN PORTION OF *KAZE HIKARU* BEFORE YOU READ AHEAD.
引越し

*The Move

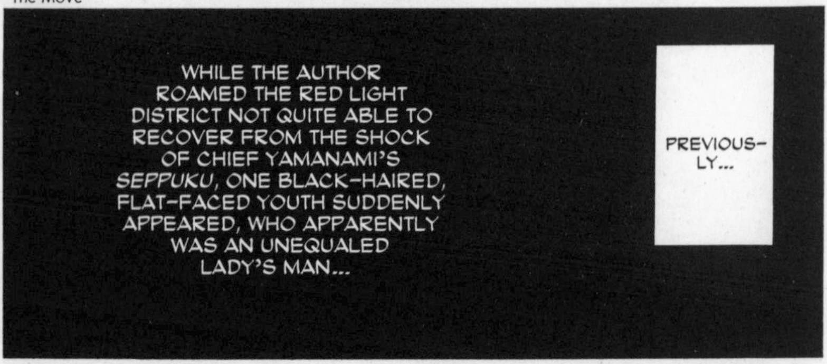
PREVIOUSLY...
WHILE THE AUTHOR ROAMED THE RED LIGHT DISTRICT NOT QUITE ABLE TO RECOVER FROM THE SHOCK OF CHIEF YAMANAMI'S *SEPPUKU*, ONE BLACK-HAIRED, FLAT-FACED YOUTH SUDDENLY APPEARED, WHO APPARENTLY WAS AN UNEQUALED LADY'S MAN...

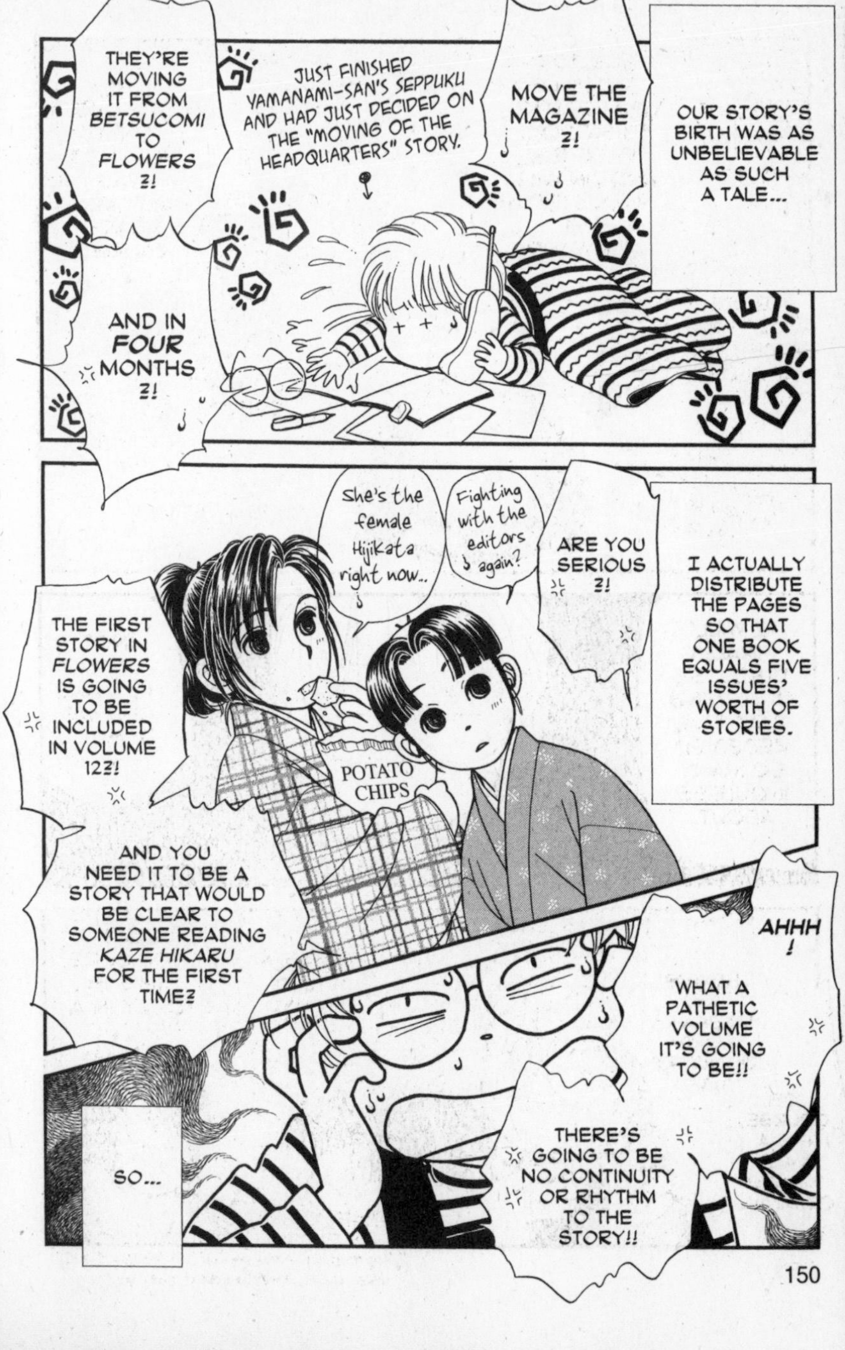
OUR STORY'S BIRTH WAS AS UNBELIEVABLE AS SUCH A TALE...
MOVE THE MAGAZINE ?!
JUST FINISHED YAMANAMI-SAN'S SEPPUKU AND HAD JUST DECIDED ON THE "MOVING OF THE HEADQUARTERS" STORY.
THEY'RE MOVING IT FROM *BETSUCOMI* TO *FLOWERS* ?!
AND IN **FOUR** MONTHS ?!
I ACTUALLY DISTRIBUTE THE PAGES SO THAT ONE BOOK EQUALS FIVE ISSUES' WORTH OF STORIES.
ARE YOU SERIOUS ?!
Fighting with the editors again?
She's the female Hijikata right now..
THE FIRST STORY IN *FLOWERS* IS GOING TO BE INCLUDED IN VOLUME 12?!
POTATO CHIPS
AND YOU NEED IT TO BE A STORY THAT WOULD BE CLEAR TO SOMEONE READING *KAZE HIKARU* FOR THE FIRST TIME?
AHHH !
WHAT A PATHETIC VOLUME IT'S GOING TO BE!!
THERE'S GOING TO BE NO CONTINUITY OR RHYTHM TO THE STORY!!
SO...

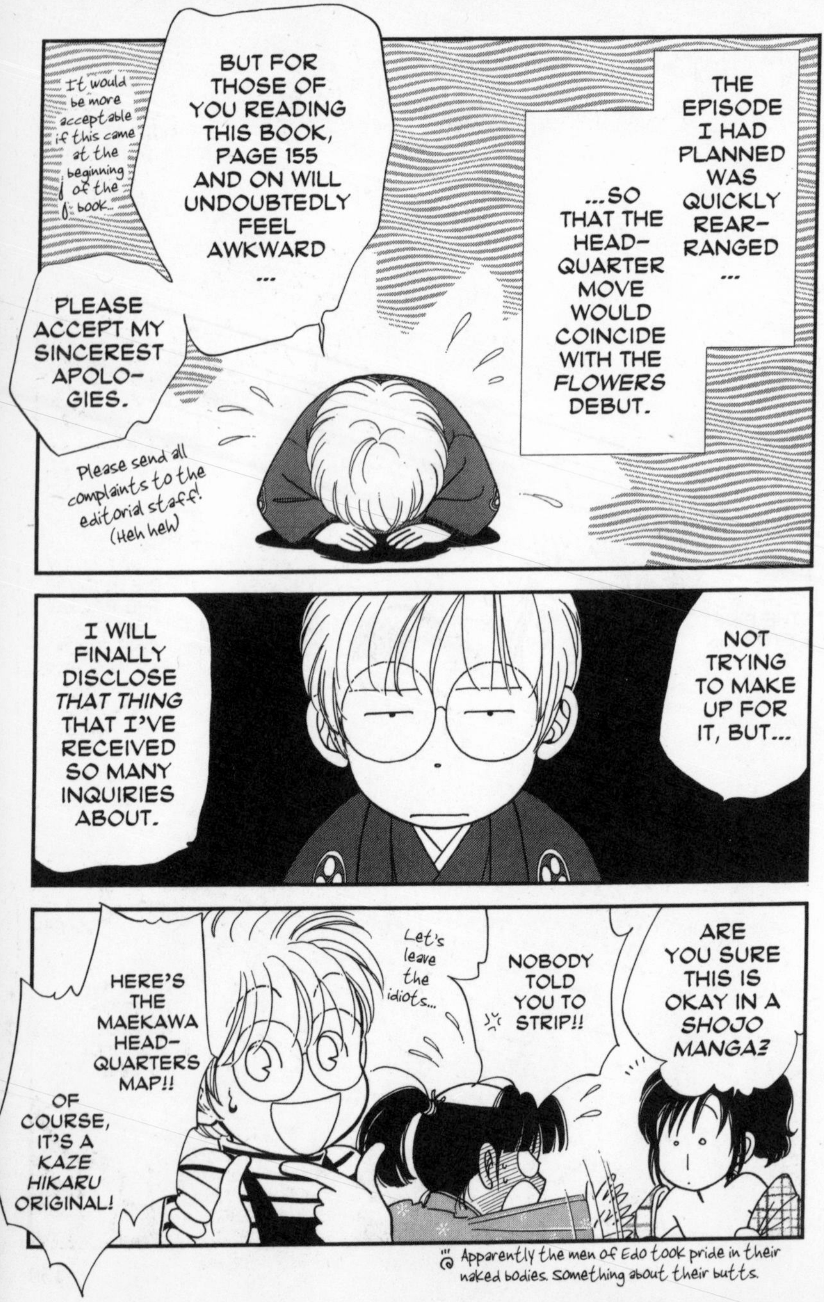
THE EPISODE I HAD PLANNED WAS QUICKLY REARRANGED...
...SO THAT THE HEADQUARTER MOVE WOULD COINCIDE WITH THE *FLOWERS* DEBUT.
BUT FOR THOSE OF YOU READING THIS BOOK, PAGE 155 AND ON WILL UNDOUBTEDLY FEEL AWKWARD...
It would be more acceptable if this came at the beginning of the book...
PLEASE ACCEPT MY SINCEREST APOLOGIES.
Please send all complaints to the editorial staff! (Heh heh)
NOT TRYING TO MAKE UP FOR IT, BUT...
I WILL FINALLY DISCLOSE *THAT THING* THAT I'VE RECEIVED SO MANY INQUIRIES ABOUT.
ARE YOU SURE THIS IS OKAY IN A *SHOJO MANGA*?
NOBODY TOLD YOU TO STRIP!!
Let's leave the idiots...
HERE'S THE MAEKAWA HEADQUARTERS MAP!!
OF COURSE, IT'S A KAZE HIKARU ORIGINAL!
Apparently the men of Edo took pride in their naked bodies. Something about their butts.

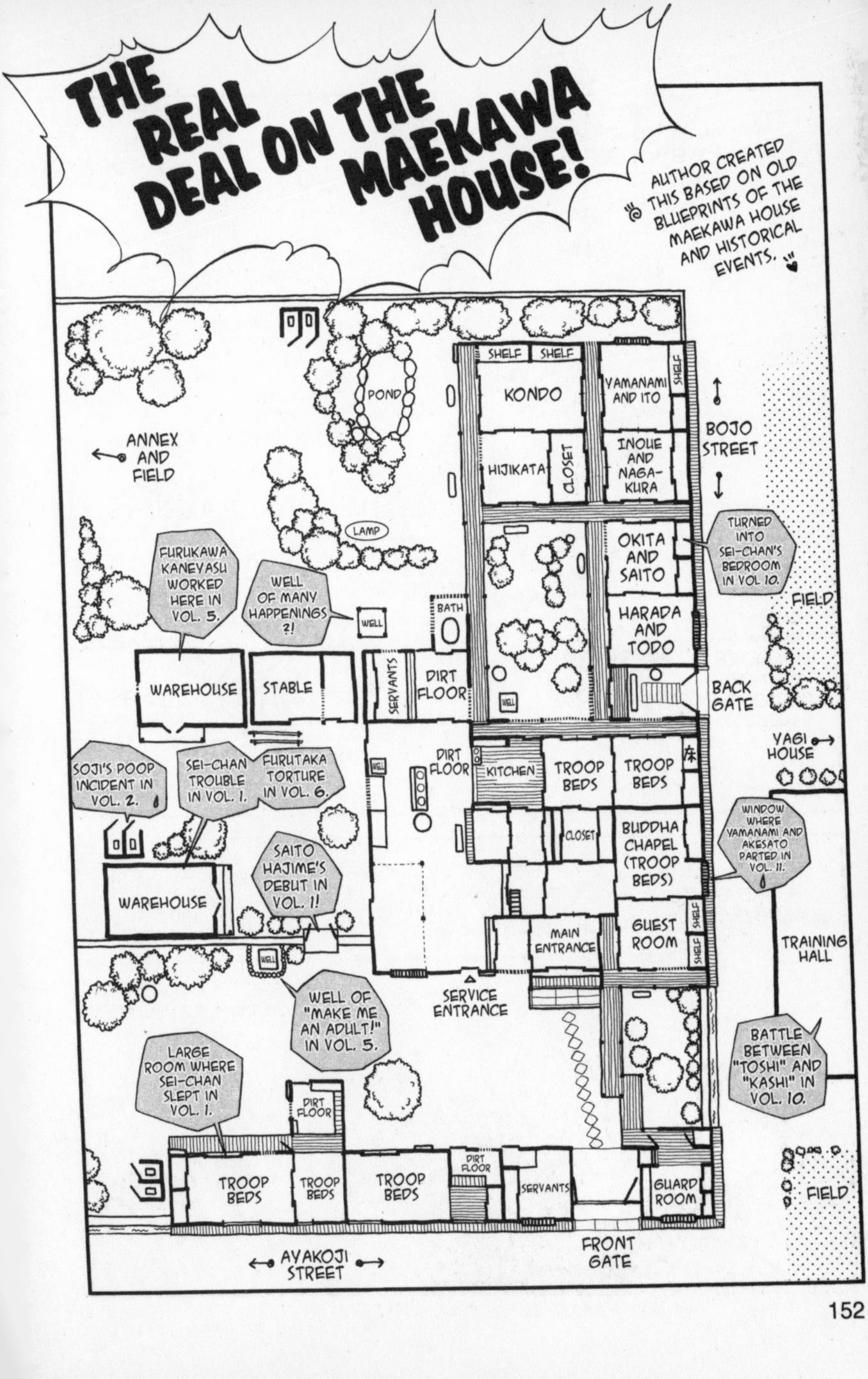
THE REAL DEAL ON THE MAEKAWA HOUSE!
AUTHOR CREATED THIS BASED ON OLD BLUEPRINTS OF THE MAEKAWA HOUSE AND HISTORICAL EVENTS.
SHELF
SHELF
KONDO
YAMANAMI AND ITO
SHELF
POND
BOJO STREET
ANNEX AND FIELD
HIJIKATA
CLOSET
INOUE AND NAGA-KURA
LAMP
OKITA AND SAITO
TURNED INTO SEI-CHAN'S BEDROOM IN VOL 10.
FURUKAWA KANEYASU WORKED HERE IN VOL. 5.
WELL OF MANY HAPPENINGS ?!
WELL
BATH
FIELD
HARADA AND TODO
WAREHOUSE
STABLE
SERVANTS
DIRT FLOOR
WELL
BACK GATE
YAGI HOUSE
SOJI'S POOP INCIDENT IN VOL. 2.
SEI-CHAN TROUBLE IN VOL. 1.
FURUTAKA TORTURE IN VOL. 6.
WELL
DIRT FLOOR
KITCHEN
TROOP BEDS
TROOP BEDS
CLOSET
BUDDHA CHAPEL (TROOP BEDS)
WINDOW WHERE YAMANAMI AND AKESATO PARTED IN VOL. 11.
SAITO HAJIME'S DEBUT IN VOL. 1!
WAREHOUSE
MAIN ENTRANCE
GUEST ROOM
SHELF
SHELF
TRAINING HALL
WELL
WELL OF "MAKE ME AN ADULT!" IN VOL. 5.
SERVICE ENTRANCE
LARGE ROOM WHERE SEI-CHAN SLEPT IN VOL. 1.
BATTLE BETWEEN "TOSHI" AND "KASHI" IN VOL. 10.
DIRT FLOOR
TROOP BEDS
TROOP BEDS
TROOP BEDS
DIRT FLOOR
SERVANTS
GUARD ROOM
FIELD
AYAKOJI STREET
FRONT GATE

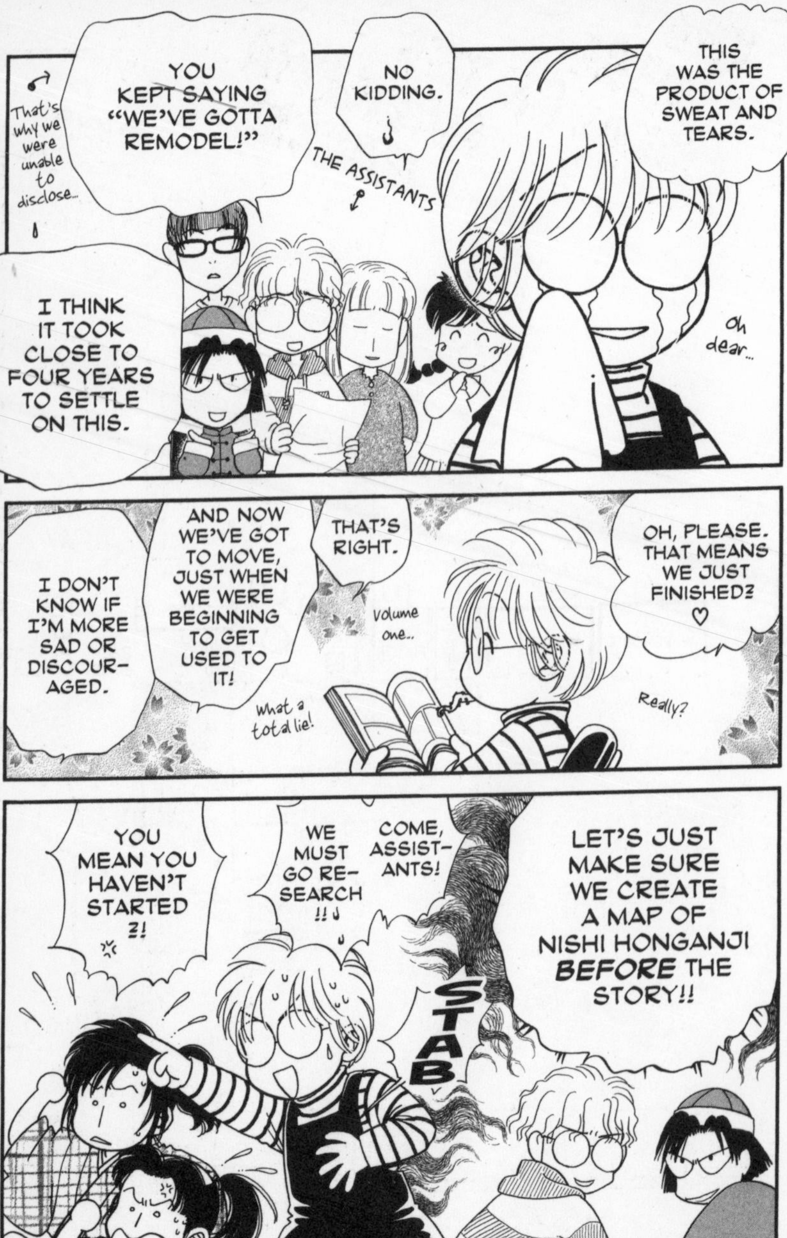
THIS WAS THE PRODUCT OF SWEAT AND TEARS.
Oh dear...
NO KIDDING.
THE ASSISTANTS
YOU KEPT SAYING "WE'VE GOTTA REMODEL!"
That's why we were unable to disclose...
I THINK IT TOOK CLOSE TO FOUR YEARS TO SETTLE ON THIS.
OH, PLEASE. THAT MEANS WE JUST FINISHED? ♡
Really?
THAT'S RIGHT.
Volume one..
AND NOW WE'VE GOT TO MOVE, JUST WHEN WE WERE BEGINNING TO GET USED TO IT!
What a total lie!
I DON'T KNOW IF I'M MORE SAD OR DISCOUR-AGED.
LET'S JUST MAKE SURE WE CREATE A MAP OF NISHI HONGANJI *BEFORE* THE STORY!!
STAB
COME, ASSIST-ANTS!
WE MUST GO RE-SEARCH!!
YOU MEAN YOU HAVEN'T STARTED ?!

KAZE HIKARU DIARY R: THE END

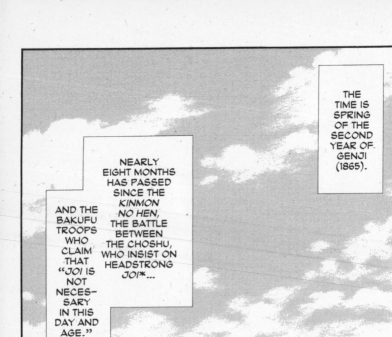

THE TIME IS SPRING OF THE SECOND YEAR OF GENJI (1865).

NEARLY EIGHT MONTHS HAS PASSED SINCE THE *KINMON NO HEN,* THE BATTLE BETWEEN THE CHOSHU, WHO INSIST ON HEADSTRONG *JOI**...

AND THE BAKUFU TROOPS WHO CLAIM THAT "*JOI* IS NOT NECESSARY IN THIS DAY AND AGE."

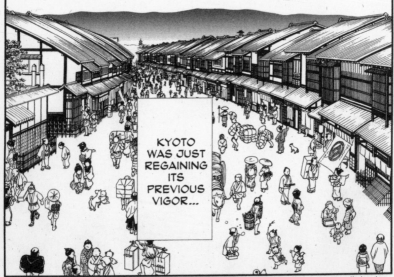

KYOTO WAS JUST REGAINING ITS PREVIOUS VIGOR...

*A school of belief that wanted to fend off those demanding that Japan open its borders

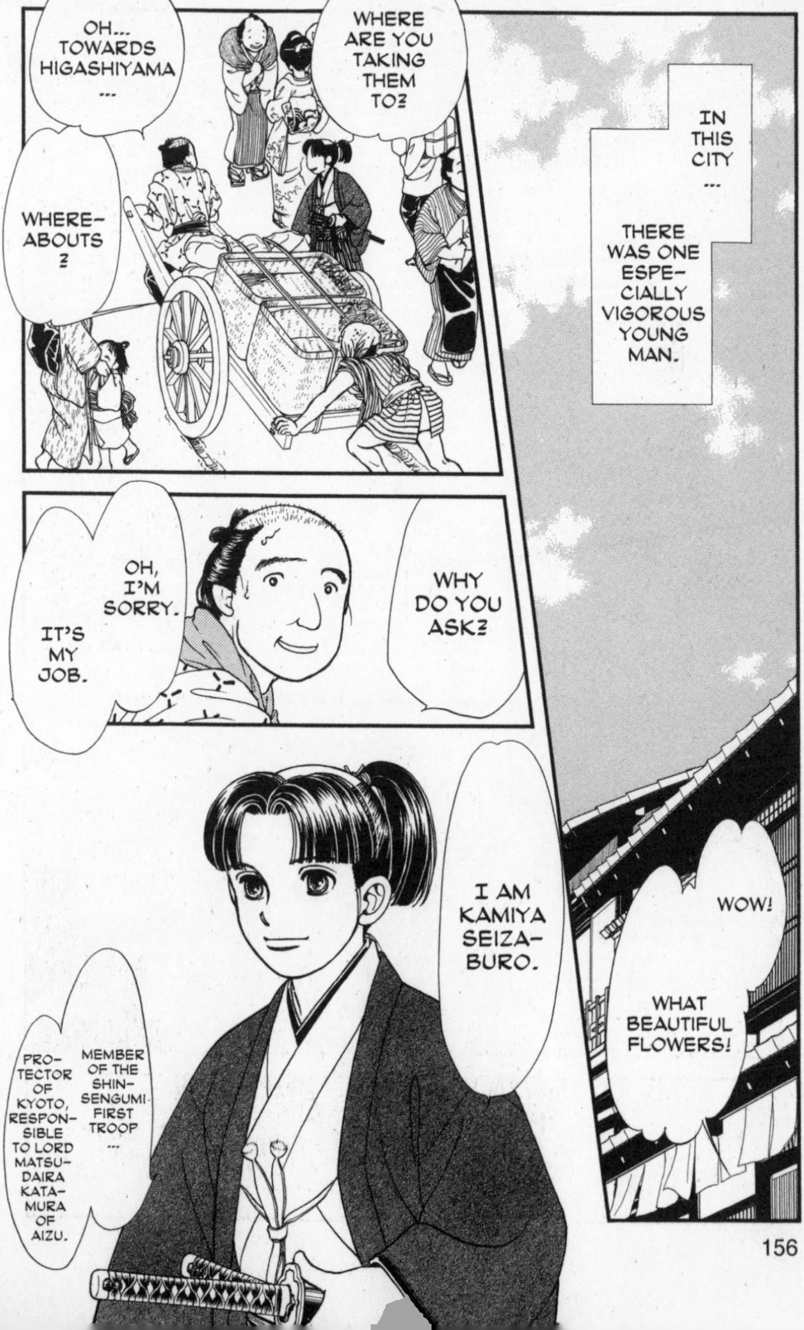
IN THIS CITY...
THERE WAS ONE ESPECIALLY VIGOROUS YOUNG MAN.
WOW!
WHAT BEAUTIFUL FLOWERS!
WHERE ARE YOU TAKING THEM TO?
OH... TOWARDS HIGASHIYAMA...
WHEREABOUTS?
WHY DO YOU ASK?
OH, I'M SORRY.
IT'S MY JOB.
I AM KAMIYA SEIZABURO.
MEMBER OF THE SHINSENGUMI FIRST TROOP...
PROTECTOR OF KYOTO, RESPONSIBLE TO LORD MATSUDAIRA KATAMURA OF AIZU.

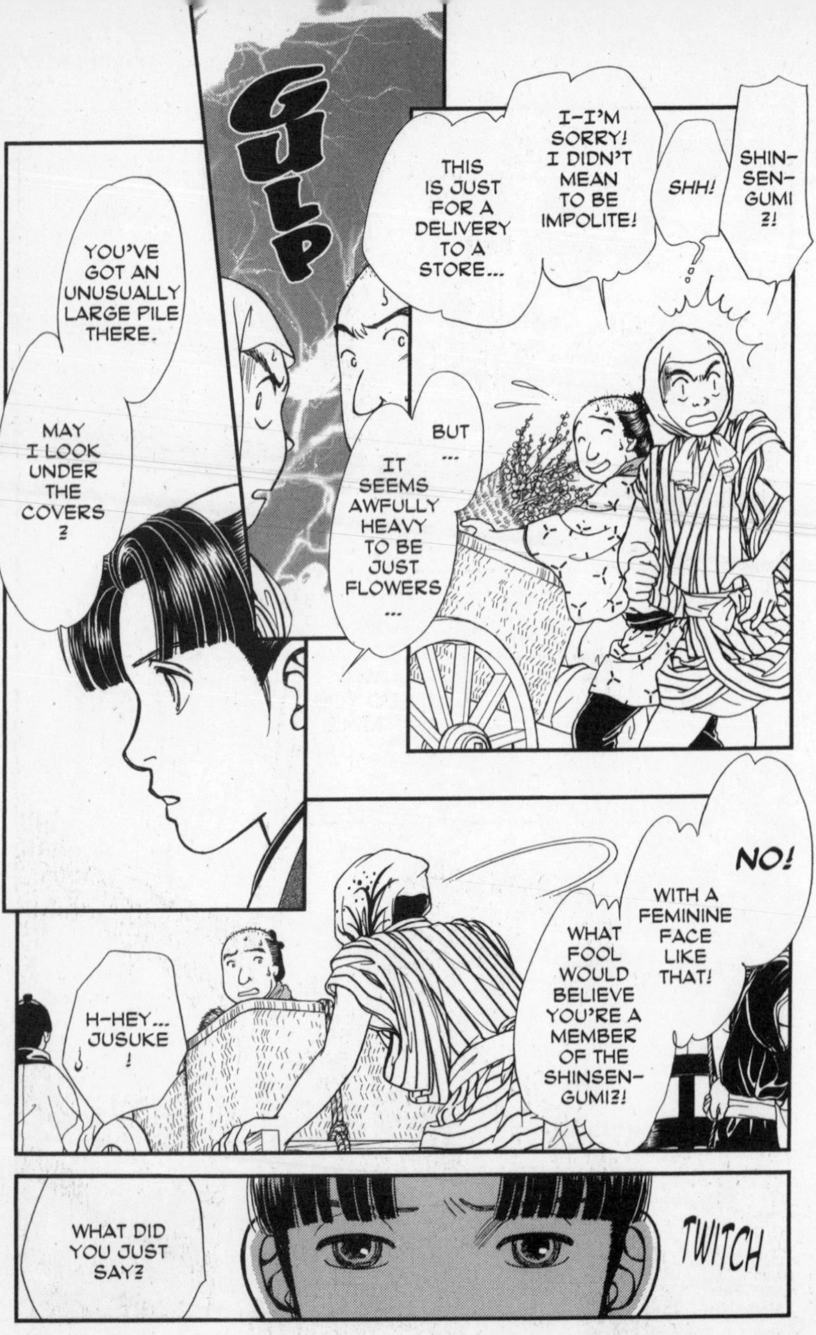
SHIN-SEN-GUMI?!
SHH!
I-I'M SORRY! I DIDN'T MEAN TO BE IMPOLITE!
THIS IS JUST FOR A DELIVERY TO A STORE...
BUT...
IT SEEMS AWFULLY HEAVY TO BE JUST FLOWERS...
GULP
YOU'VE GOT AN UNUSUALLY LARGE PILE THERE.
MAY I LOOK UNDER THE COVERS?
NO!
WITH A FEMININE FACE LIKE THAT!
WHAT FOOL WOULD BELIEVE YOU'RE A MEMBER OF THE SHINSEN-GUMI?!
H-HEY... JUSUKE!
TWITCH
WHAT DID YOU JUST SAY?

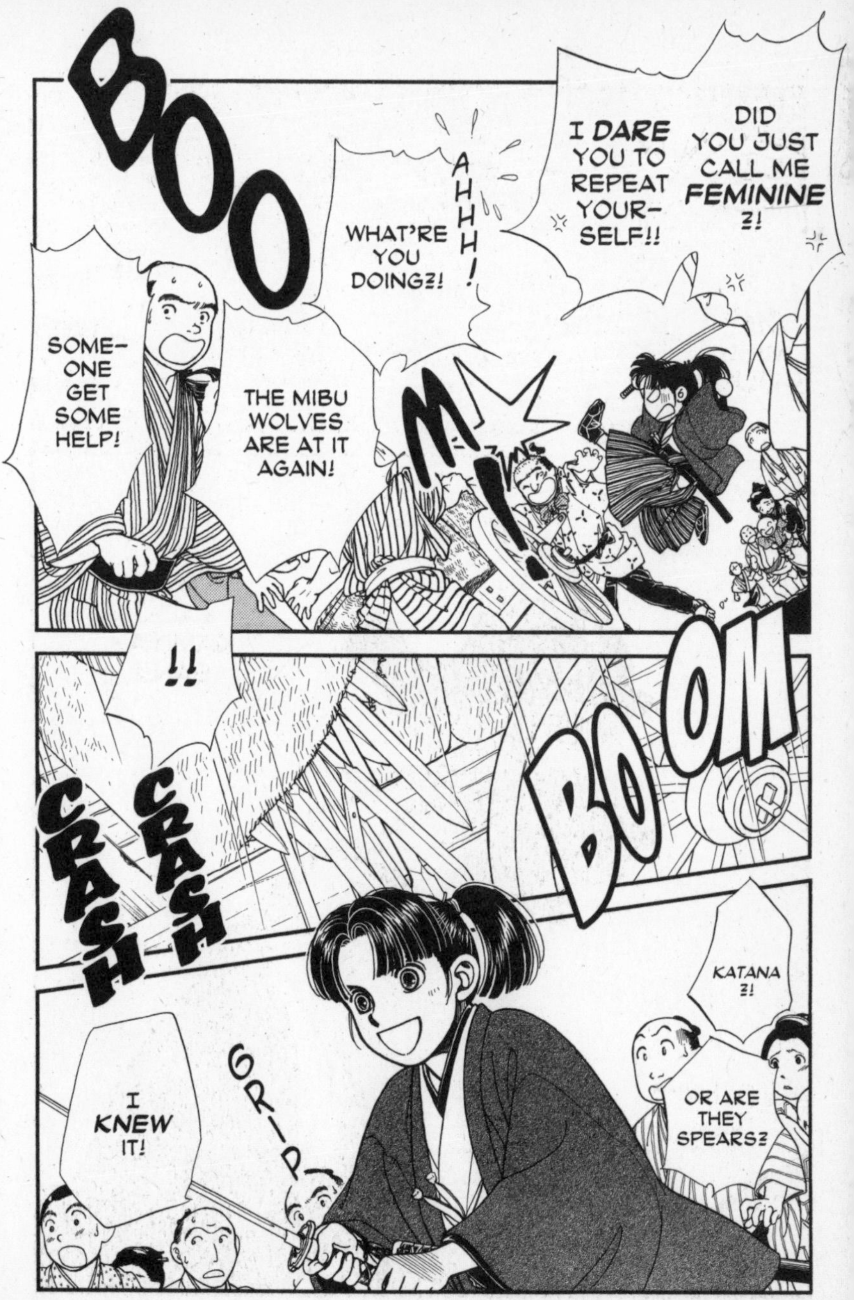
DID YOU JUST CALL ME FEMININE?!
I DARE YOU TO REPEAT YOUR-SELF!!
AHHHH!
WHAT'RE YOU DOING?!
BOO
M
THE MIBU WOLVES ARE AT IT AGAIN!
SOME-ONE GET SOME HELP!
BOOM
!!
CRASH
CRASH
KATANA?!
OR ARE THEY SPEARS?
GRIP
I KNEW IT!

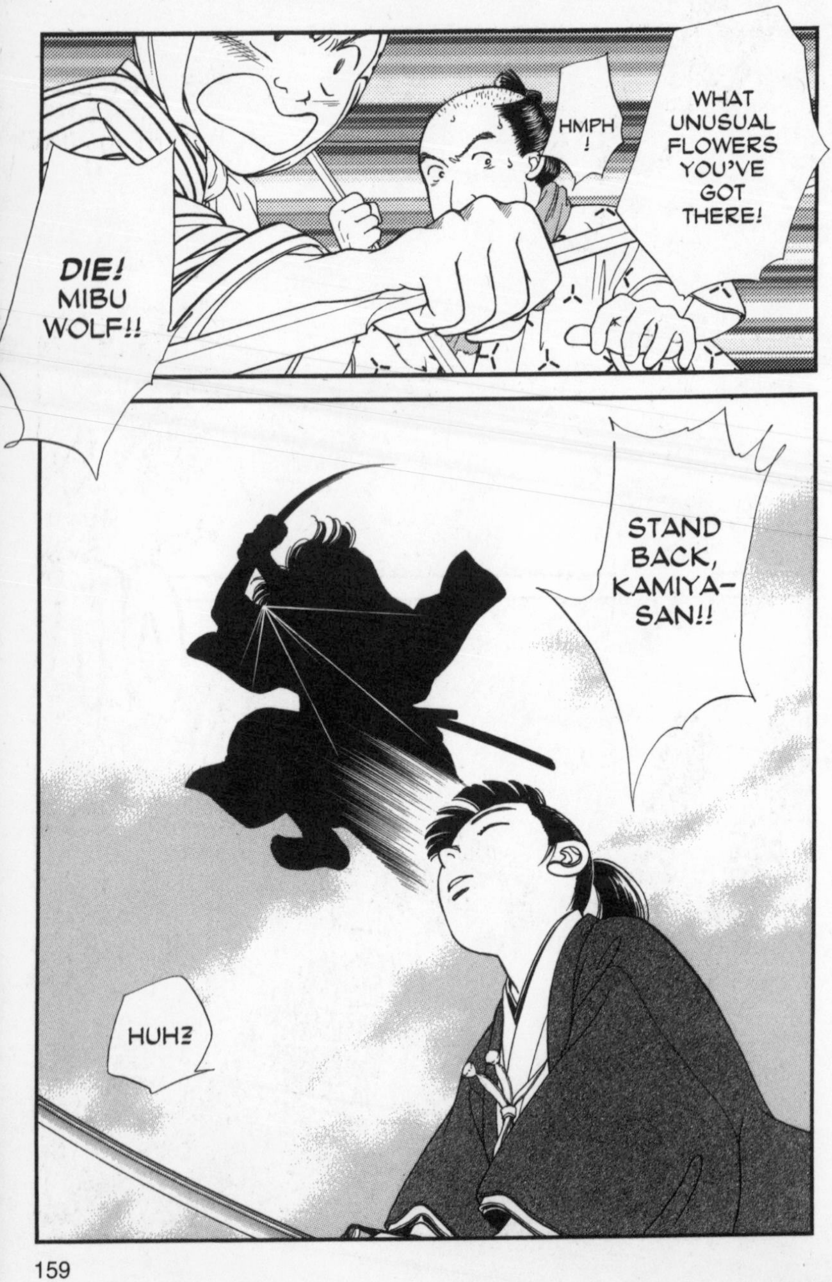
WHAT UNUSUAL FLOWERS YOU'VE GOT THERE!
HMPH!
DIE! MIBU WOLF!!
STAND BACK, KAMIYA-SAN!!
HUH?

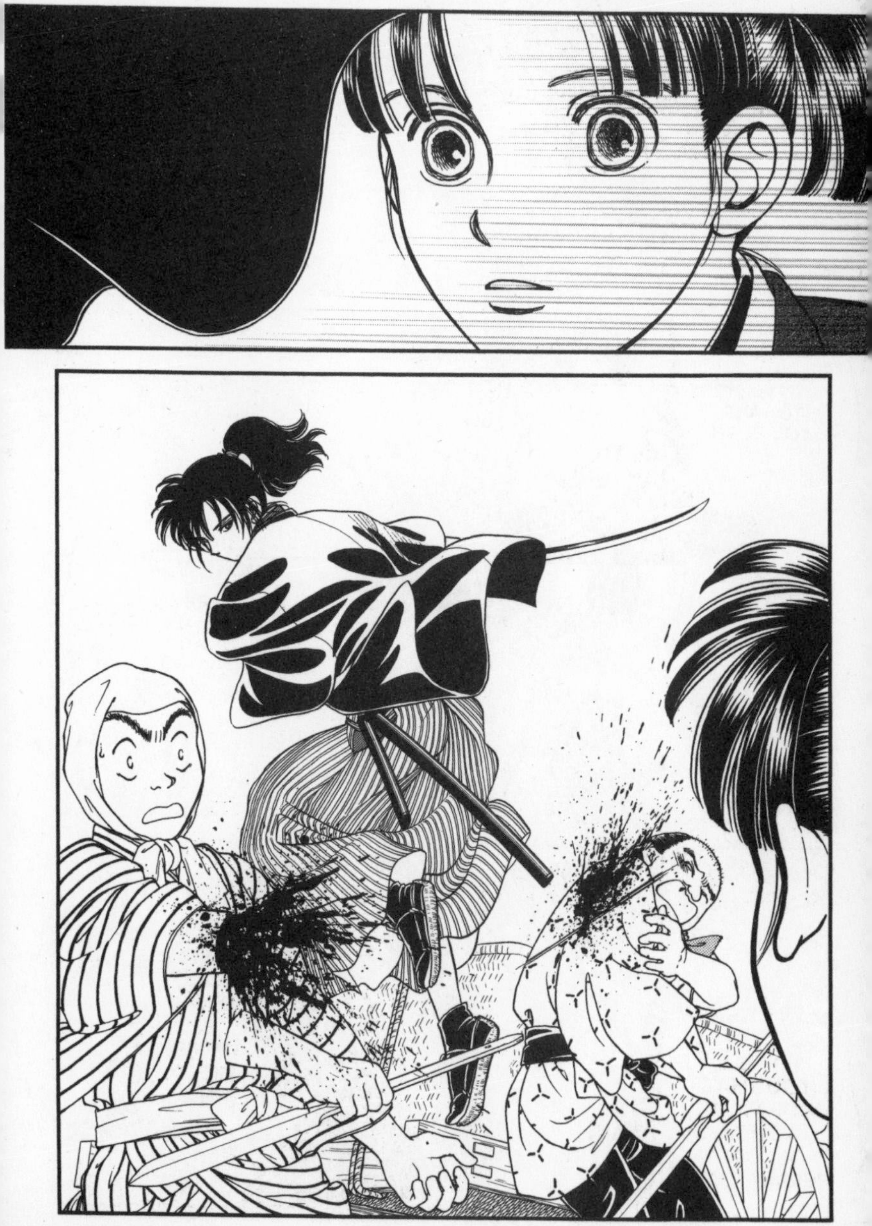

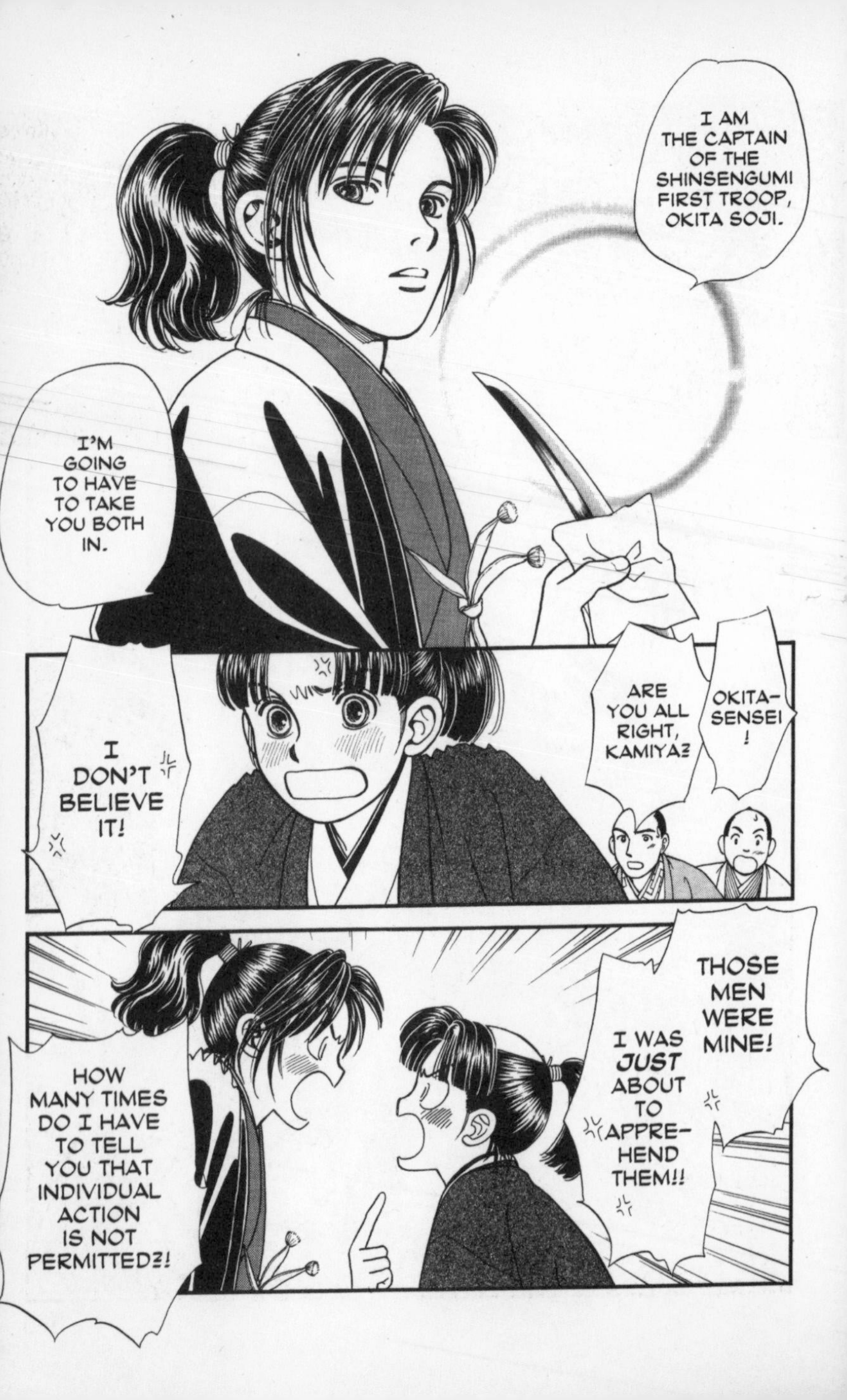
I AM THE CAPTAIN OF THE SHINSENGUMI FIRST TROOP, OKITA SOJI.
I'M GOING TO HAVE TO TAKE YOU BOTH IN.
OKITA-SENSEI!
ARE YOU ALL RIGHT, KAMIYA?
I DON'T BELIEVE IT!
THOSE MEN WERE MINE!
I WAS *JUST* ABOUT TO APPREHEND THEM!!
HOW MANY TIMES DO I HAVE TO TELL YOU THAT INDIVIDUAL ACTION IS NOT PERMITTED?!

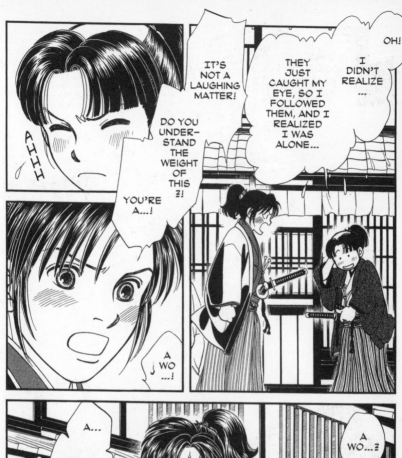

OH!
I DIDN'T REALIZE ...
THEY JUST CAUGHT MY EYE, SO I FOLLOWED THEM, AND I REALIZED I WAS ALONE...
IT'S NOT A LAUGHING MATTER!
DO YOU UNDER-STAND THE WEIGHT OF THIS ?!
AHHH
YOU'RE A...!
A WO ...!
A WO...?
A...
AN UN-WORTHY APPREN-TICE!
I'VE TOLD YOU BEFORE !!

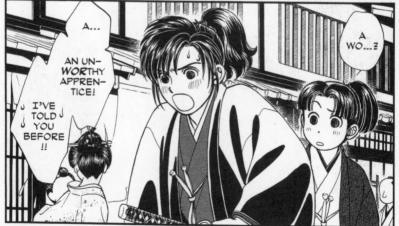

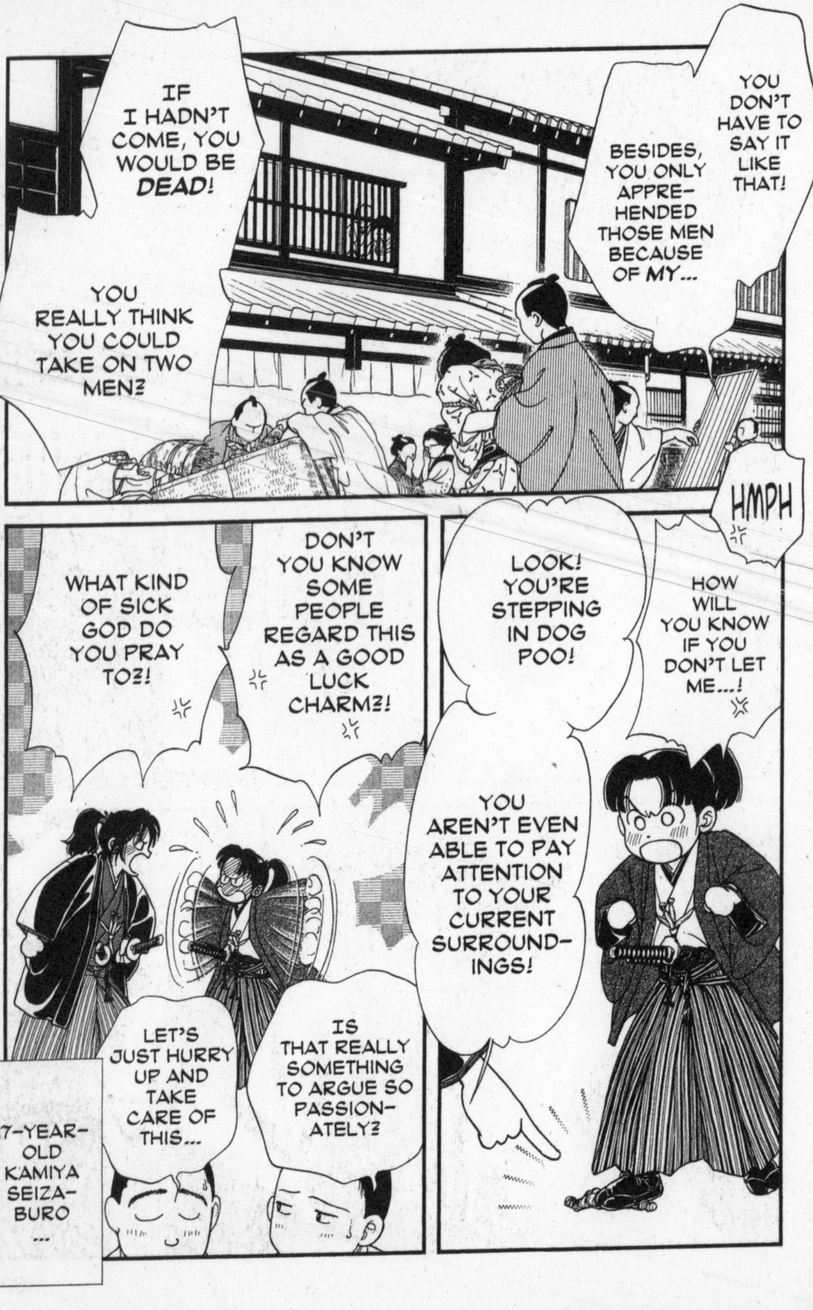

YOU DON'T HAVE TO SAY IT LIKE THAT!
BESIDES, YOU ONLY APPREHENDED THOSE MEN BECAUSE OF MY...
IF I HADN'T COME, YOU WOULD BE *DEAD*!
YOU REALLY THINK YOU COULD TAKE ON TWO MEN?
HMPH
HOW WILL YOU KNOW IF YOU DON'T LET ME...!
LOOK! YOU'RE STEPPING IN DOG POO!
YOU AREN'T EVEN ABLE TO PAY ATTENTION TO YOUR CURRENT SURROUNDINGS!
DON'T YOU KNOW SOME PEOPLE REGARD THIS AS A GOOD LUCK CHARM?!
WHAT KIND OF SICK GOD DO YOU PRAY TO?!
IS THAT REALLY SOMETHING TO ARGUE SO PASSIONATELY?
LET'S JUST HURRY UP AND TAKE CARE OF THIS...
17-YEAR-OLD KAMIYA SEIZABURO ...

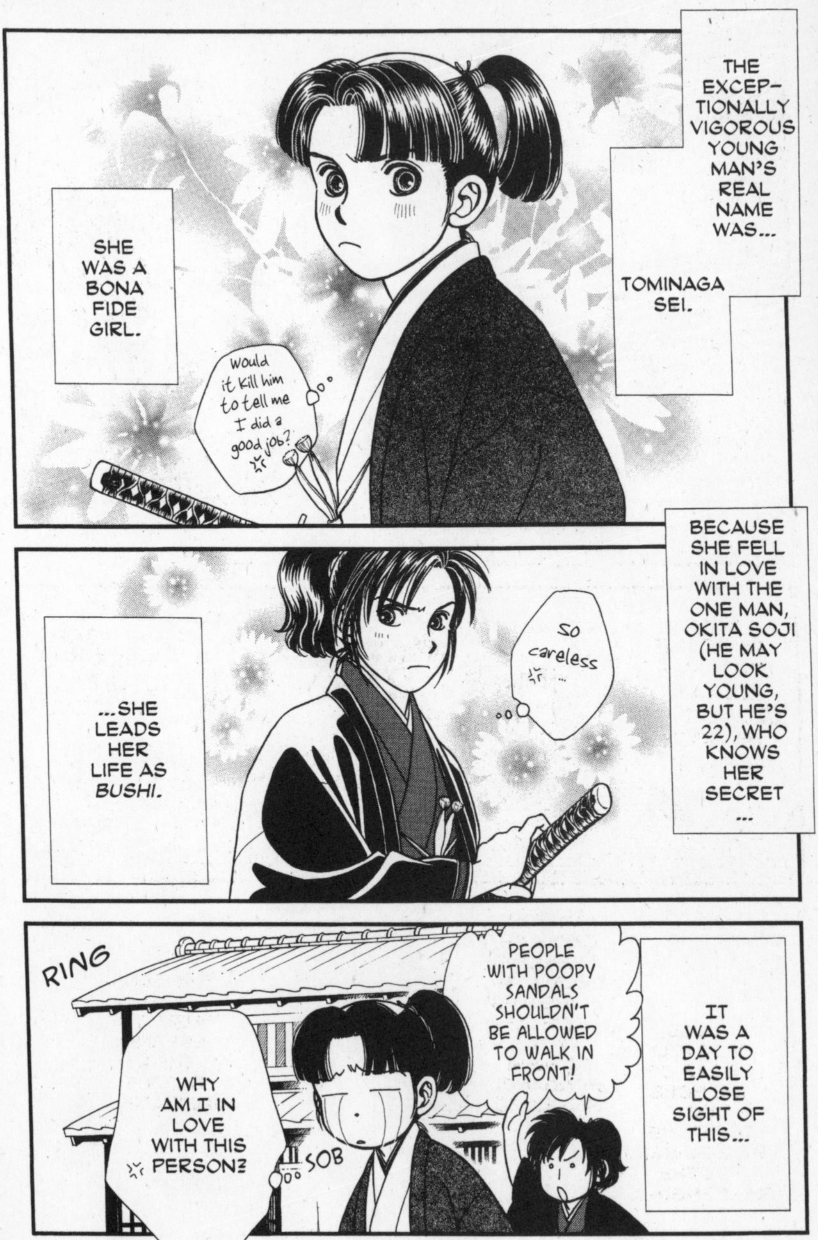
THE EXCEPTIONALLY VIGOROUS YOUNG MAN'S REAL NAME WAS...
TOMINAGA SEI.
Would it kill him to tell me I did a good job?
SHE WAS A BONA FIDE GIRL.
BECAUSE SHE FELL IN LOVE WITH THE ONE MAN, OKITA SOJI (HE MAY LOOK YOUNG, BUT HE'S 22), WHO KNOWS HER SECRET...
So careless...
...SHE LEADS HER LIFE AS *BUSHI*.
IT WAS A DAY TO EASILY LOSE SIGHT OF THIS...
PEOPLE WITH POOPY SANDALS SHOULDN'T BE ALLOWED TO WALK IN FRONT!
SOB
WHY AM I IN LOVE WITH THIS PERSON?
RING

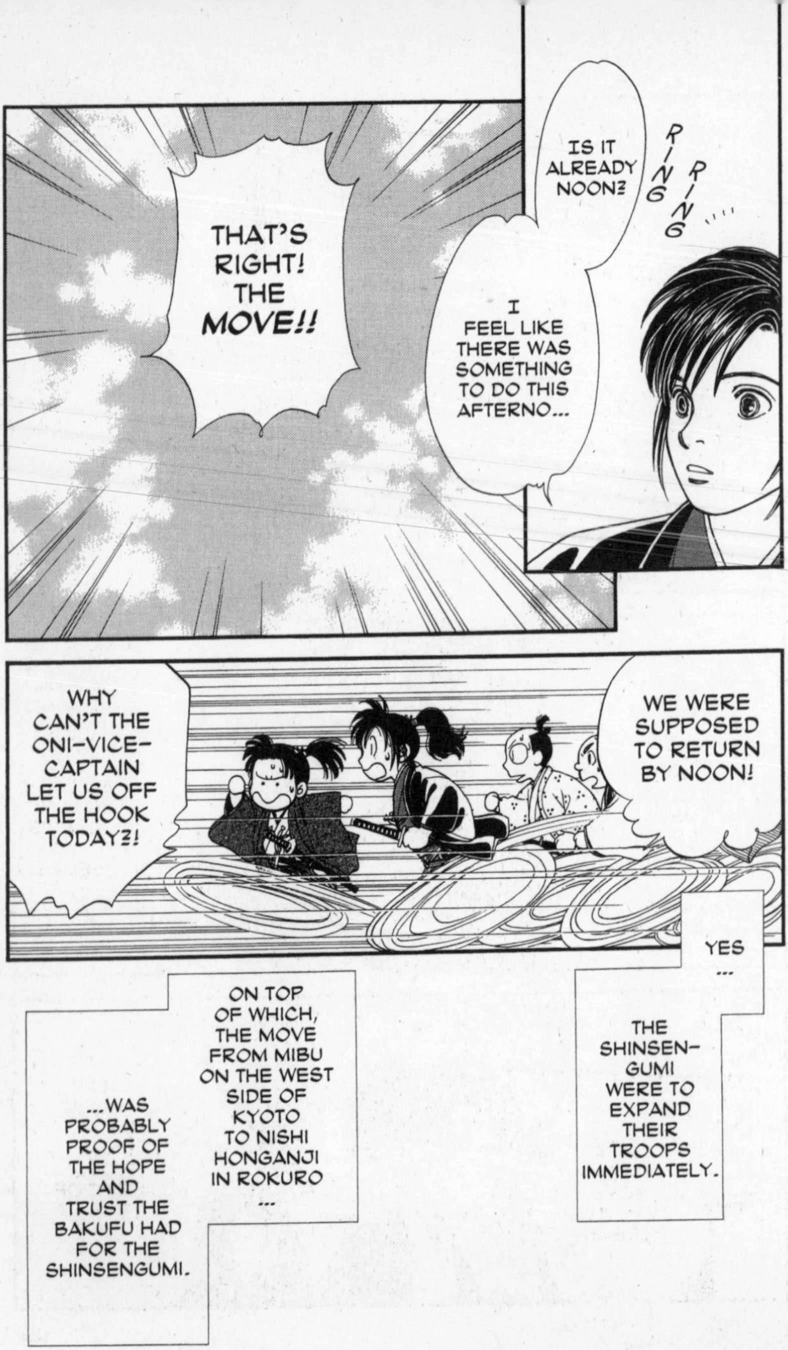
IS IT ALREADY NOON?
RING RING
I FEEL LIKE THERE WAS SOMETHING TO DO THIS AFTERNO...
THAT'S RIGHT! THE *MOVE!!*
WE WERE SUPPOSED TO RETURN BY NOON!
WHY CAN'T THE ONI-VICE-CAPTAIN LET US OFF THE HOOK TODAY?!
YES...
THE SHINSEN-GUMI WERE TO EXPAND THEIR TROOPS IMMEDIATELY.
ON TOP OF WHICH, THE MOVE FROM MIBU ON THE WEST SIDE OF KYOTO TO NISHI HONGANJI IN ROKURO...
...WAS PROBABLY PROOF OF THE HOPE AND TRUST THE BAKUFU HAD FOR THE SHINSENGUMI.

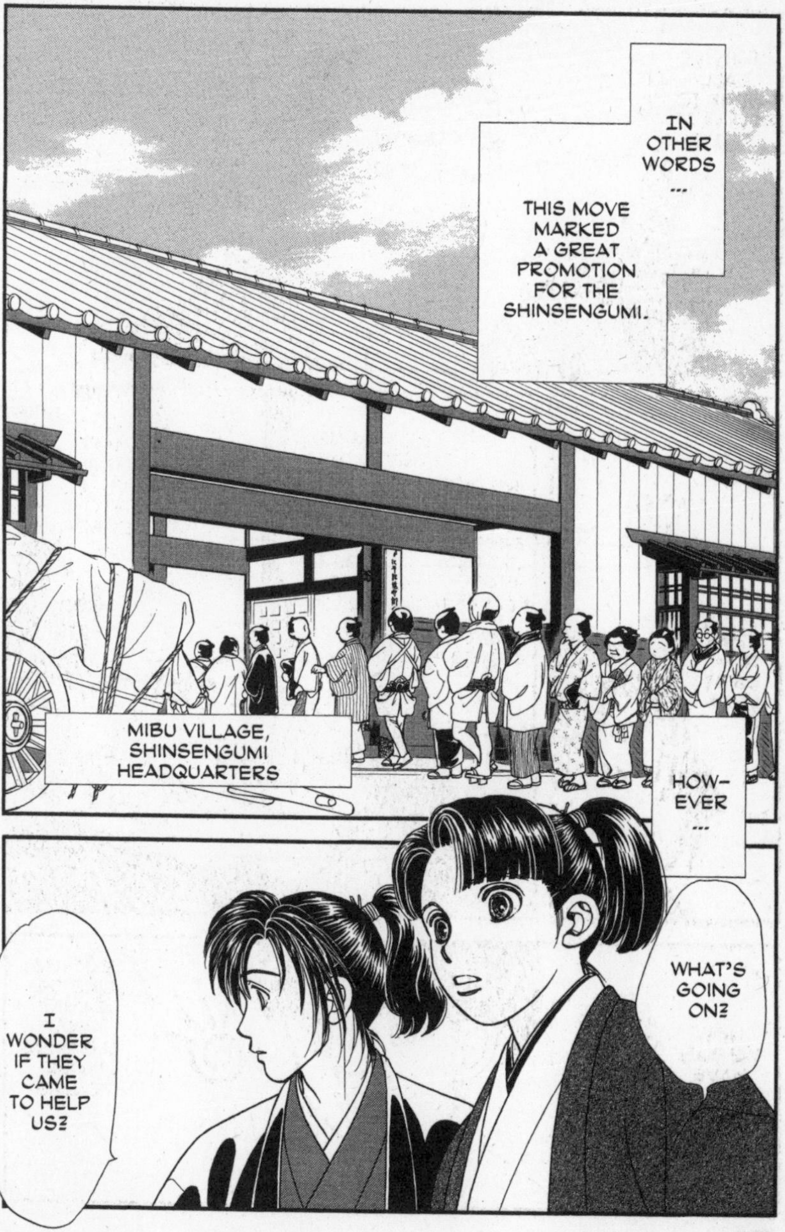
IN OTHER WORDS ...
THIS MOVE MARKED A GREAT PROMOTION FOR THE SHINSENGUMI.
MIBU VILLAGE, SHINSENGUMI HEADQUARTERS
HOW-EVER ...
WHAT'S GOING ON?
I WONDER IF THEY CAME TO HELP US?

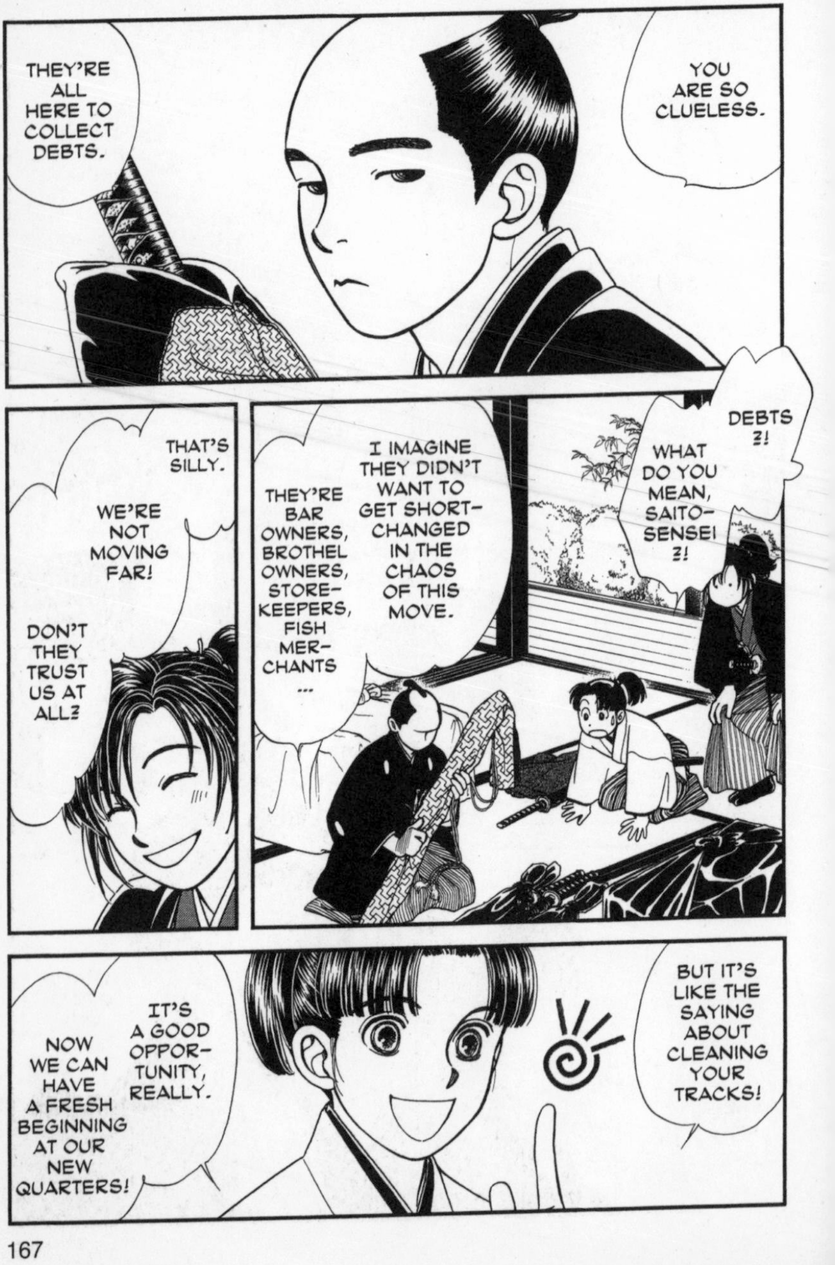
YOU ARE SO CLUELESS.
THEY'RE ALL HERE TO COLLECT DEBTS.
DEBTS?!
WHAT DO YOU MEAN, SAITO-SENSEI?!
I IMAGINE THEY DIDN'T WANT TO GET SHORT-CHANGED IN THE CHAOS OF THIS MOVE.
THEY'RE BAR OWNERS, BROTHEL OWNERS, STORE-KEEPERS, FISH MER-CHANTS...
THAT'S SILLY.
WE'RE NOT MOVING FAR!
DON'T THEY TRUST US AT ALL?
BUT IT'S LIKE THE SAYING ABOUT CLEANING YOUR TRACKS!
IT'S A GOOD OPPOR-TUNITY, REALLY.
NOW WE CAN HAVE A FRESH BEGINNING AT OUR NEW QUARTERS!

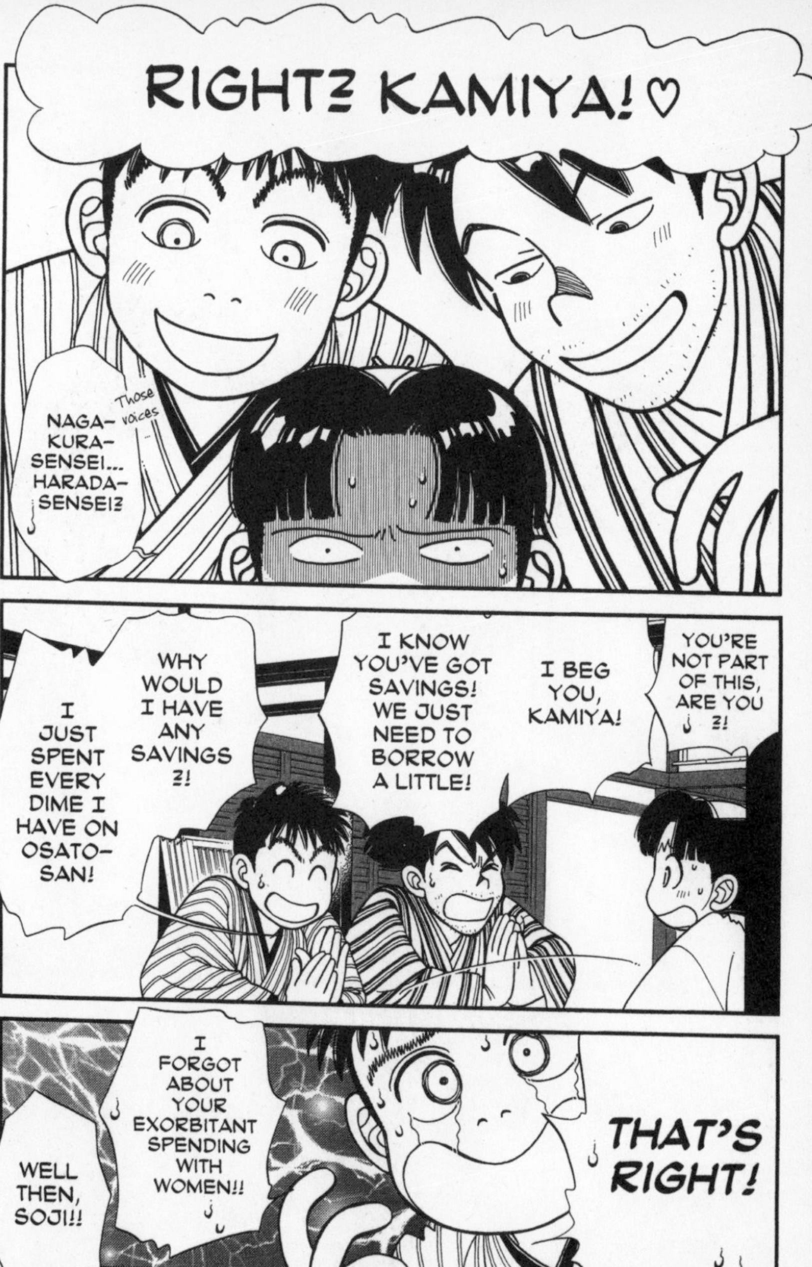
RIGHT?! KAMIYA! ♡
Those voices...
NAGAKURA-SENSEI... HARADA-SENSEI!?
YOU'RE NOT PART OF THIS, ARE YOU?!
I BEG YOU, KAMIYA!
I KNOW YOU'VE GOT SAVINGS! WE JUST NEED TO BORROW A LITTLE!
WHY WOULD I HAVE ANY SAVINGS?!
I JUST SPENT EVERY DIME I HAVE ON OSATO-SAN!
THAT'S RIGHT!
I FORGOT ABOUT YOUR EXORBITANT SPENDING WITH WOMEN!!
WELL THEN, SOJI!!

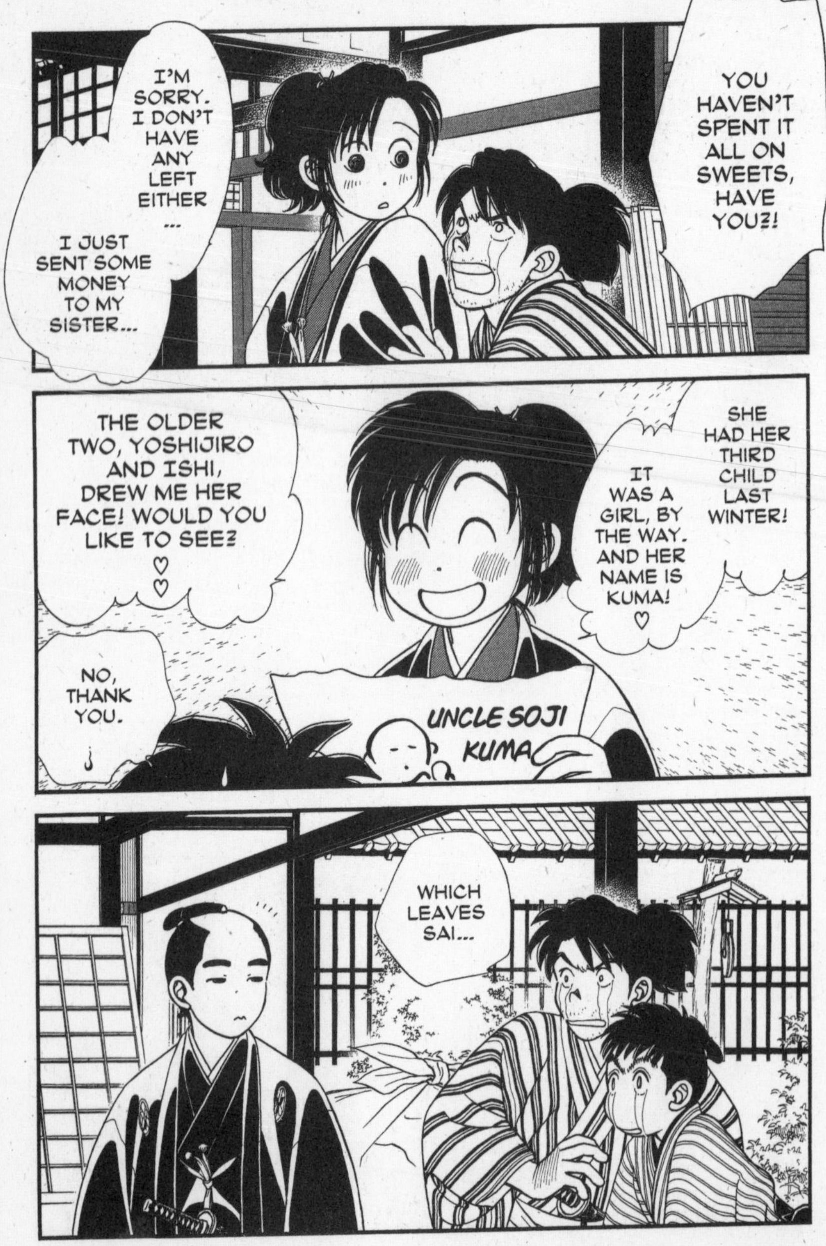
YOU HAVEN'T SPENT IT ALL ON SWEETS, HAVE YOU?!
I'M SORRY. I DON'T HAVE ANY LEFT EITHER ...
I JUST SENT SOME MONEY TO MY SISTER...
SHE HAD HER THIRD CHILD LAST WINTER!
IT WAS A GIRL, BY THE WAY. AND HER NAME IS KUMA! ♡
THE OLDER TWO, YOSHIJIRO AND ISHI, DREW ME HER FACE! WOULD YOU LIKE TO SEE? ♡ ♡
UNCLE SOJI
KUMA
NO, THANK YOU.
WHICH LEAVES SAI...

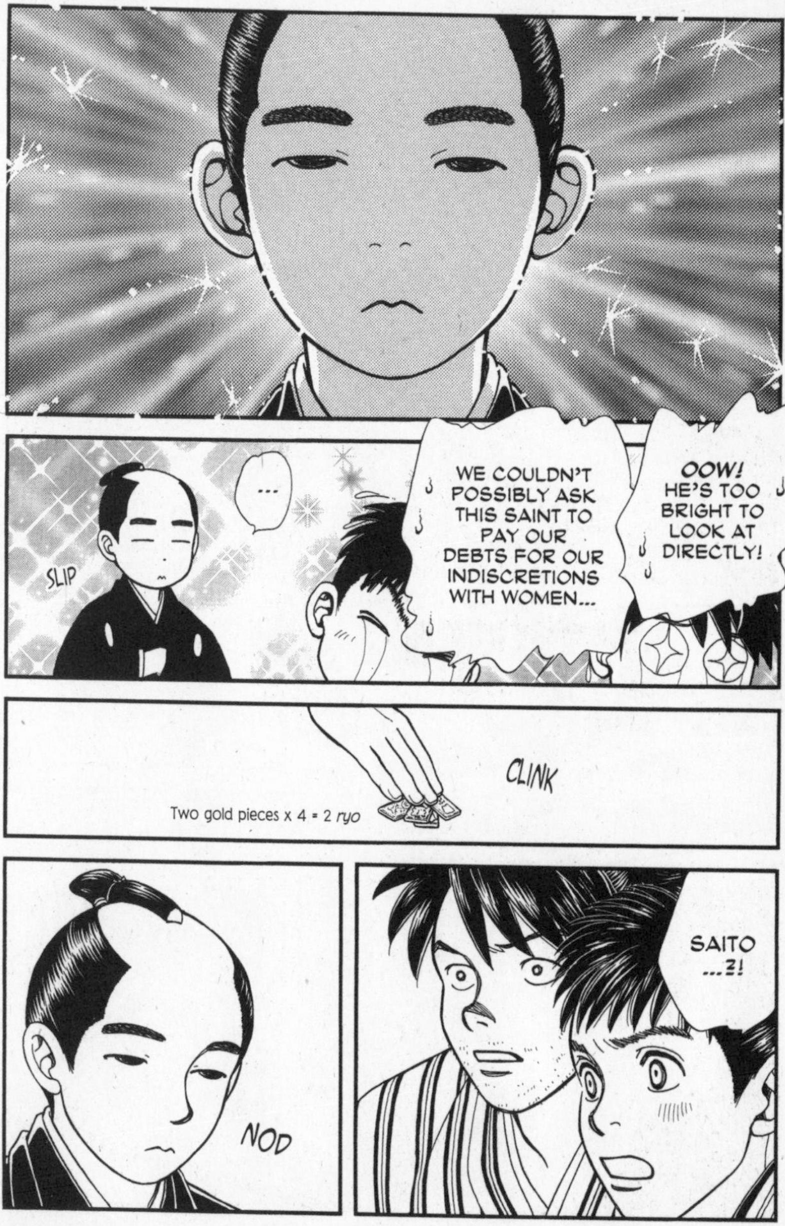
OOW! HE'S TOO BRIGHT TO LOOK AT DIRECTLY!
WE COULDN'T POSSIBLY ASK THIS SAINT TO PAY OUR DEBTS FOR OUR INDISCRETIONS WITH WOMEN...
...
SLIP
CLINK
Two gold pieces x 4 = 2 *ryo*
SAITO ...?!
NOD

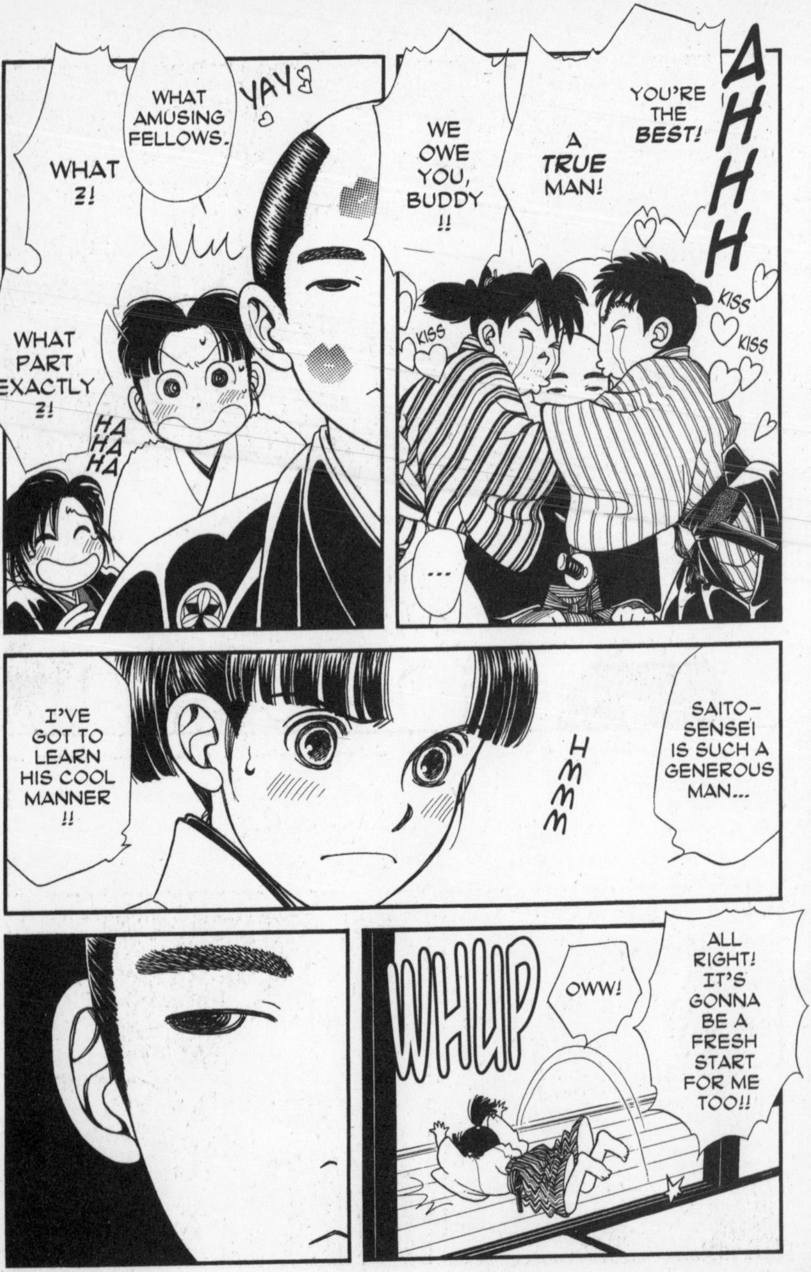
AHHHH
YOU'RE THE BEST!
A TRUE MAN!
WE OWE YOU, BUDDY!!
KISS
KISS
KISS
...
YAY
WHAT AMUSING FELLOWS.
WHAT?!
WHAT PART EXACTLY?!
HA HA HA
SAITO-SENSEI IS SUCH A GENEROUS MAN...
HMMM
I'VE GOT TO LEARN HIS COOL MANNER!!
ALL RIGHT! IT'S GONNA BE A FRESH START FOR ME TOO!!
OWW!
WHUP

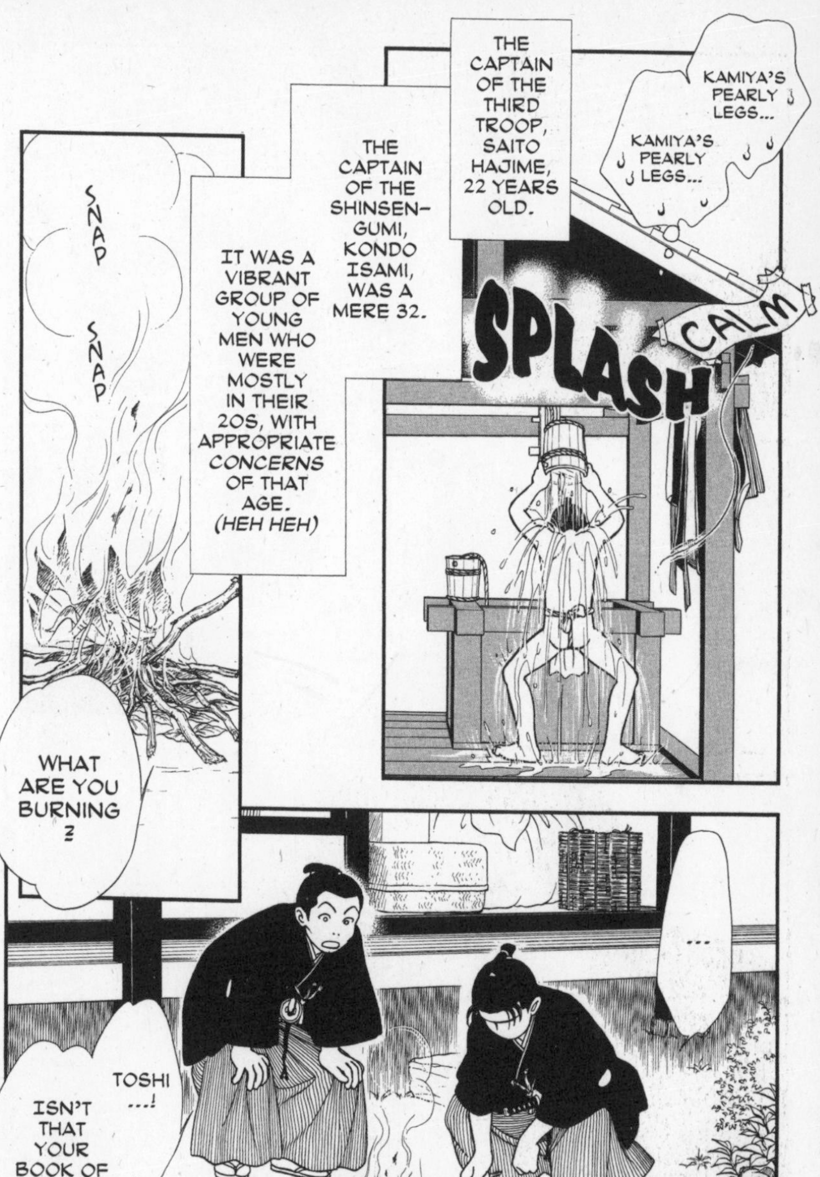
KAMIYA'S PEARLY LEGS...
KAMIYA'S PEARLY LEGS...
THE CAPTAIN OF THE THIRD TROOP, SAITO HAJIME, 22 YEARS OLD.
SPLASH
CALM
THE CAPTAIN OF THE SHINSEN-GUMI, KONDO ISAMI, WAS A MERE 32.
IT WAS A VIBRANT GROUP OF YOUNG MEN WHO WERE MOSTLY IN THEIR 20S, WITH APPROPRIATE CONCERNS OF THAT AGE. (HEH HEH)
SNAP SNAP
WHAT ARE YOU BURNING?
...
TOSHI...!
ISN'T THAT YOUR BOOK OF POEMS?

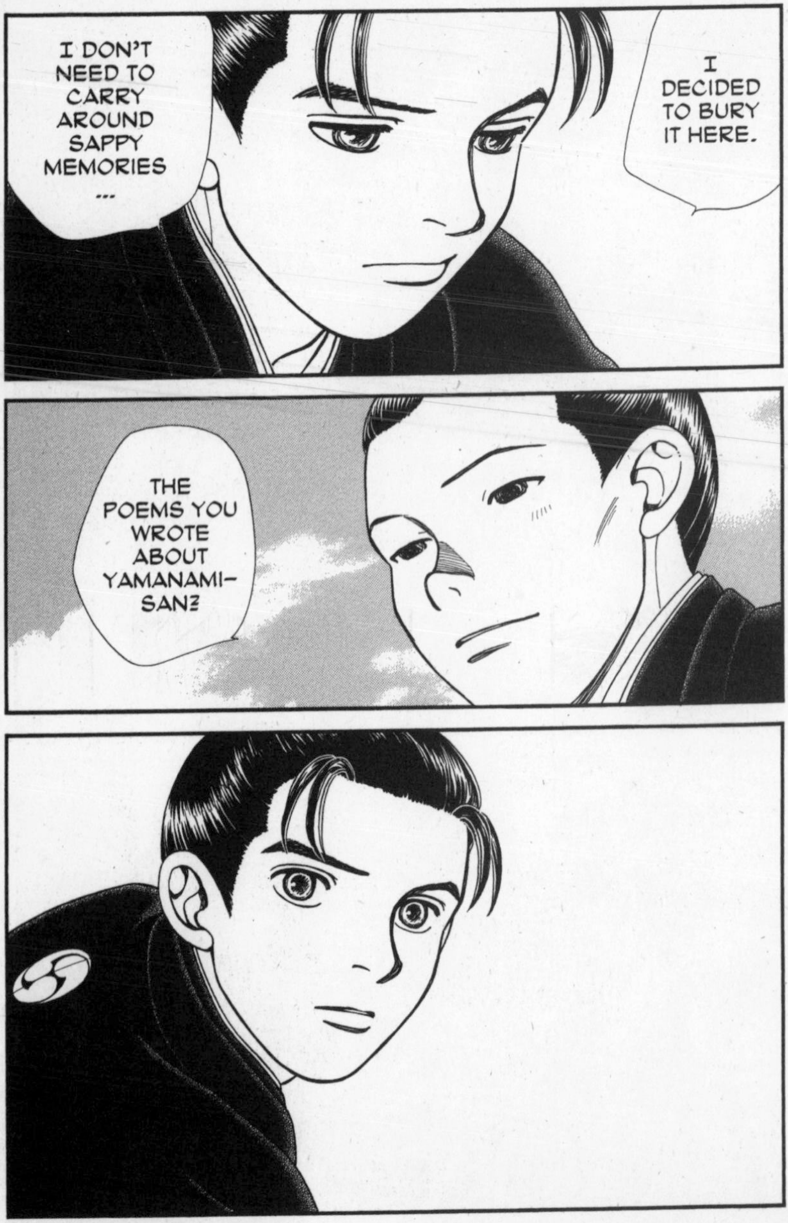
I DECIDED TO BURY IT HERE.
I DON'T NEED TO CARRY AROUND SAPPY MEMORIES ...
THE POEMS YOU WROTE ABOUT YAMANAMI-SAN?

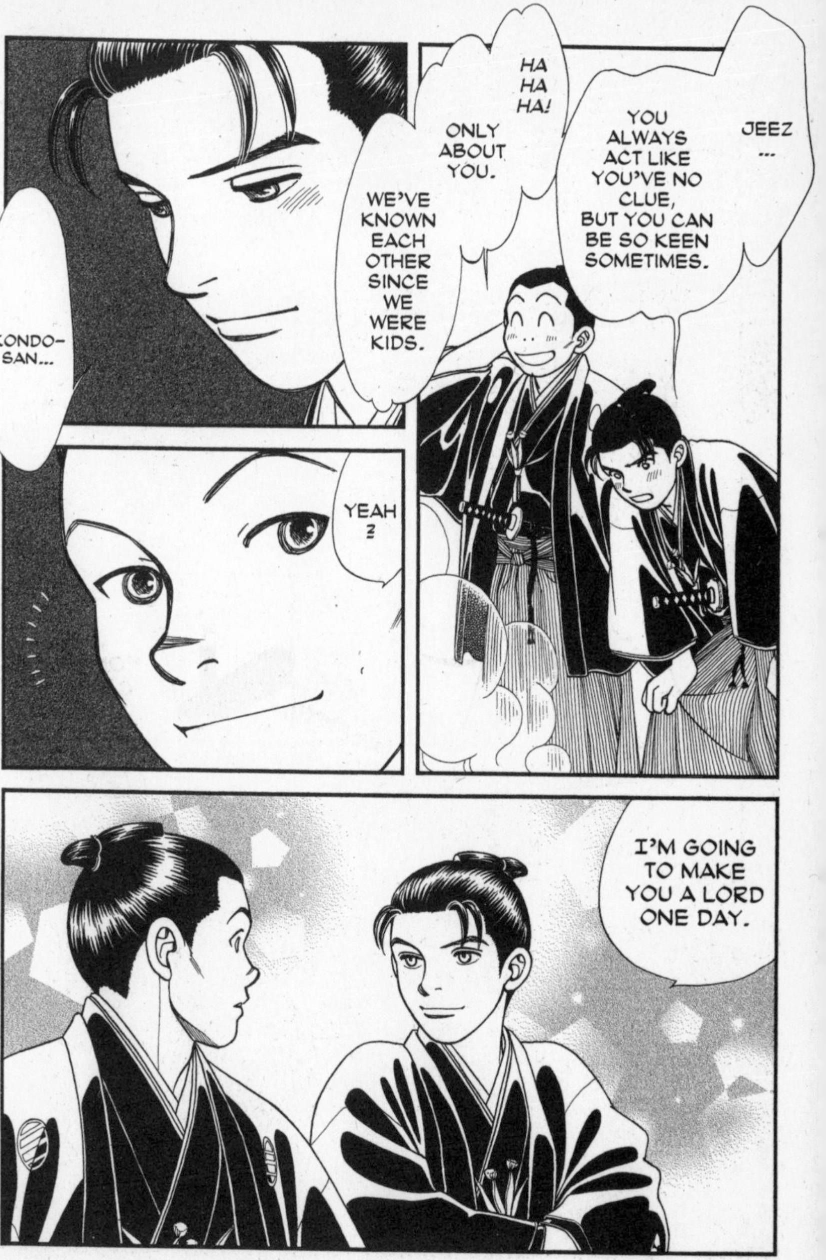
JEEZ ...
YOU ALWAYS ACT LIKE YOU'VE NO CLUE, BUT YOU CAN BE SO KEEN SOMETIMES.
HA HA HA!
ONLY ABOUT YOU.
WE'VE KNOWN EACH OTHER SINCE WE WERE KIDS.
KONDO-SAN...
YEAH?
I'M GOING TO MAKE YOU A LORD ONE DAY.

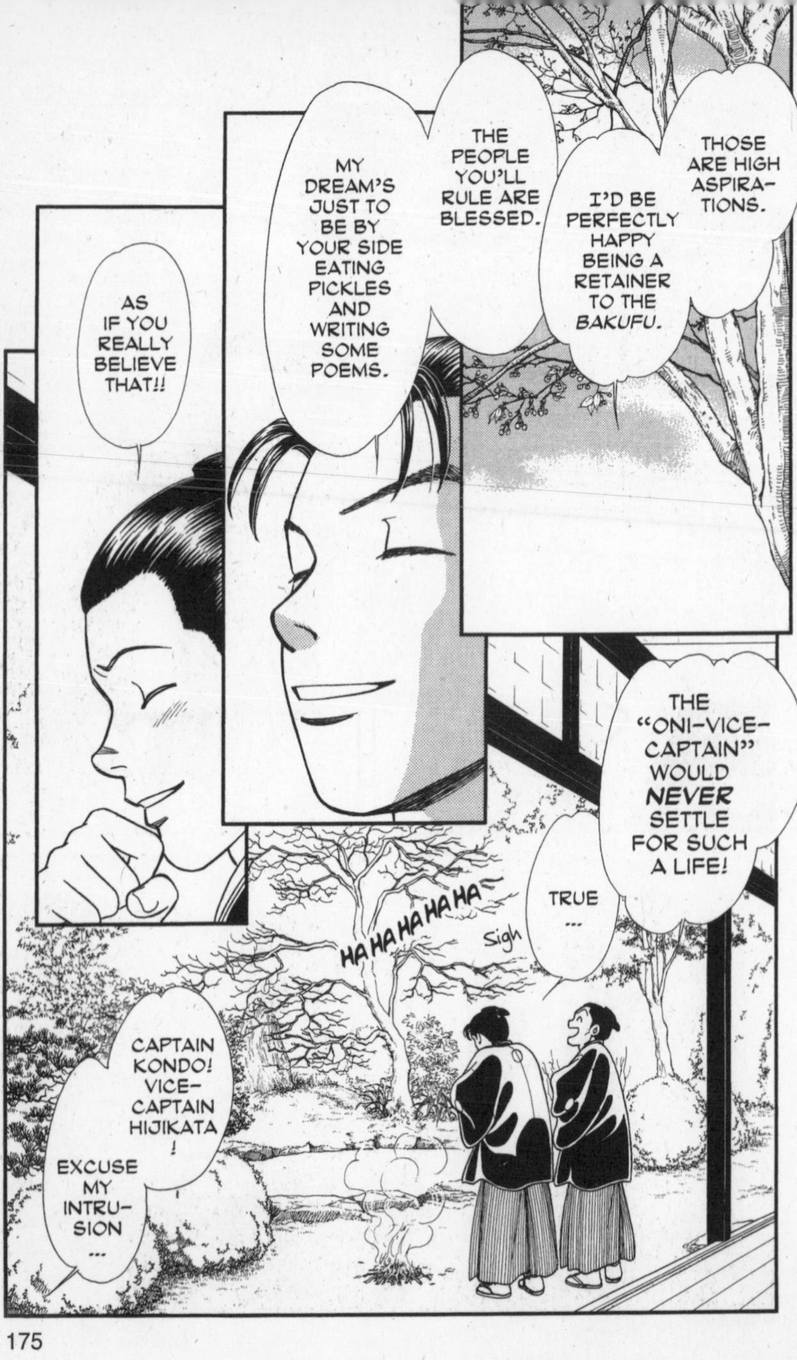
THOSE ARE HIGH ASPIRATIONS.
I'D BE PERFECTLY HAPPY BEING A RETAINER TO THE *BAKUFU.*
THE PEOPLE YOU'LL RULE ARE BLESSED.
MY DREAM'S JUST TO BE BY YOUR SIDE EATING PICKLES AND WRITING SOME POEMS.
AS IF YOU REALLY BELIEVE THAT!!
THE "ONI-VICE-CAPTAIN" WOULD ***NEVER*** SETTLE FOR SUCH A LIFE!
TRUE ...
Sigh
HA HA HA HA HA
CAPTAIN KONDO! VICE-CAPTAIN HIJIKATA!
EXCUSE MY INTRUSION ...

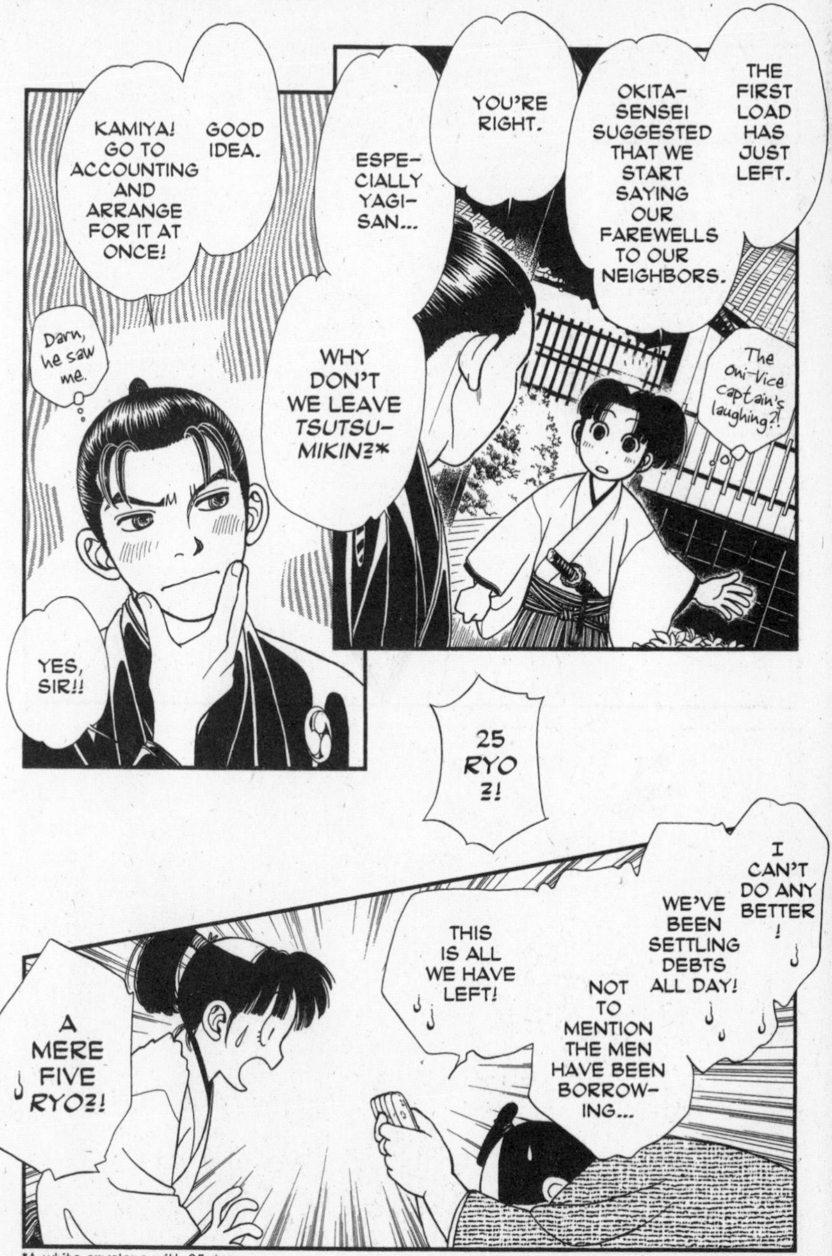
THE FIRST LOAD HAS JUST LEFT.
OKITA-SENSEI SUGGESTED THAT WE START SAYING OUR FAREWELLS TO OUR NEIGHBORS.
YOU'RE RIGHT.
ESPECIALLY YAGI-SAN...
WHY DON'T WE LEAVE *TSUTSUMIKIN*?*
The Oni-Vice captain's laughing?!
GOOD IDEA.
KAMIYA! GO TO ACCOUNTING AND ARRANGE FOR IT AT ONCE!
Darn, he saw me.
YES, SIR!!
25 *RYO* ?!
I CAN'T DO ANY BETTER!
WE'VE BEEN SETTLING DEBTS ALL DAY!
NOT TO MENTION THE MEN HAVE BEEN BORROWING...
THIS IS ALL WE HAVE LEFT!
A MERE FIVE *RYO*?!

*A white envelope with 25 *ryo*

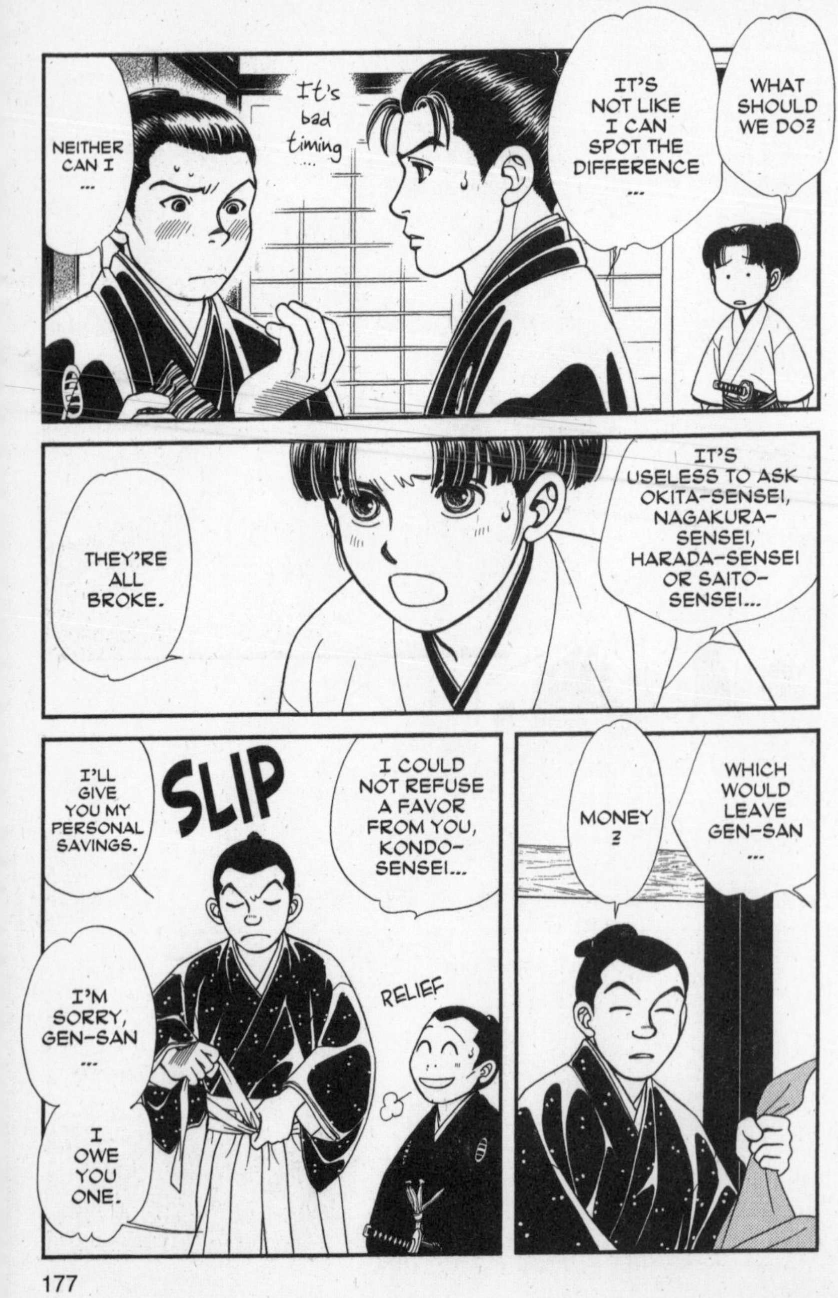
WHAT SHOULD WE DO?
IT'S NOT LIKE I CAN SPOT THE DIFFERENCE ...
It's bad timing ....
NEITHER CAN I ...
IT'S USELESS TO ASK OKITA-SENSEI, NAGAKURA-SENSEI, HARADA-SENSEI OR SAITO-SENSEI...
THEY'RE ALL BROKE.
WHICH WOULD LEAVE GEN-SAN ...
MONEY ?
I COULD NOT REFUSE A FAVOR FROM YOU, KONDO-SENSEI...
SLIP
I'LL GIVE YOU MY PERSONAL SAVINGS.
RELIEF
I'M SORRY, GEN-SAN ...
I OWE YOU ONE.

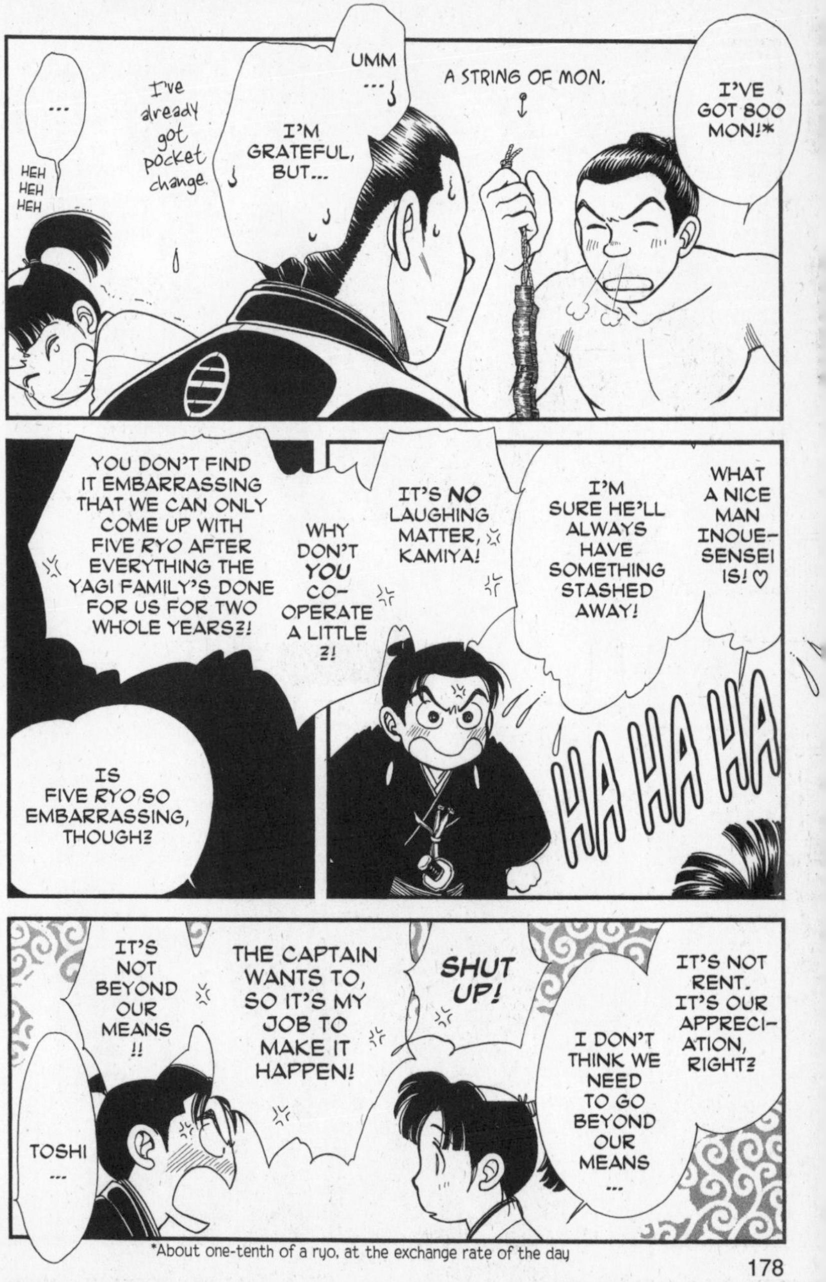
I'VE GOT 800 MON!*
A STRING OF MON.
UMM ...
I'M GRATEFUL, BUT...
I've already got pocket change.
...
HEH HEH HEH
WHAT A NICE MAN INOUE-SENSEI IS! ♡
I'M SURE HE'LL ALWAYS HAVE SOMETHING STASHED AWAY!
HA HA HA
IT'S NO LAUGHING MATTER, KAMIYA!
WHY DON'T YOU CO-OPERATE A LITTLE?!
YOU DON'T FIND IT EMBARRASSING THAT WE CAN ONLY COME UP WITH FIVE RYO AFTER EVERYTHING THE YAGI FAMILY'S DONE FOR US FOR TWO WHOLE YEARS?!
IS FIVE RYO SO EMBARRASSING, THOUGH?
IT'S NOT RENT. IT'S OUR APPRECIATION, RIGHT?
I DON'T THINK WE NEED TO GO BEYOND OUR MEANS ...
SHUT UP!
THE CAPTAIN WANTS TO, SO IT'S MY JOB TO MAKE IT HAPPEN!
IT'S NOT BEYOND OUR MEANS!!
TOSHI ...

*About one-tenth of a ryo, at the exchange rate of the day

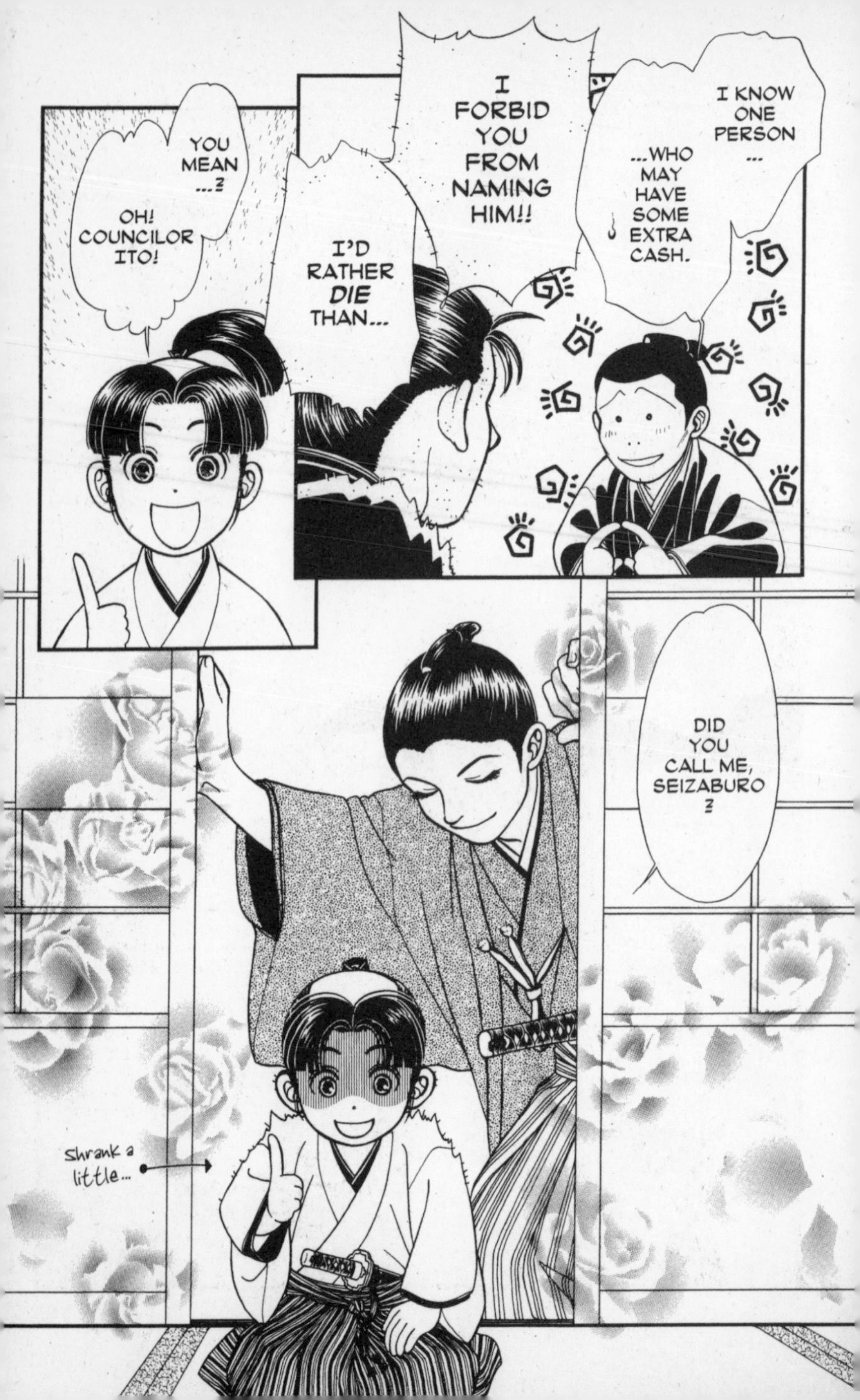
I KNOW ONE PERSON ...
...WHO MAY HAVE SOME EXTRA CASH.
I FORBID YOU FROM NAMING HIM!!
I'D RATHER *DIE* THAN...
YOU MEAN ...?
OH! COUNCILOR ITO!
DID YOU CALL ME, SEIZABURO?
Shrank a little...

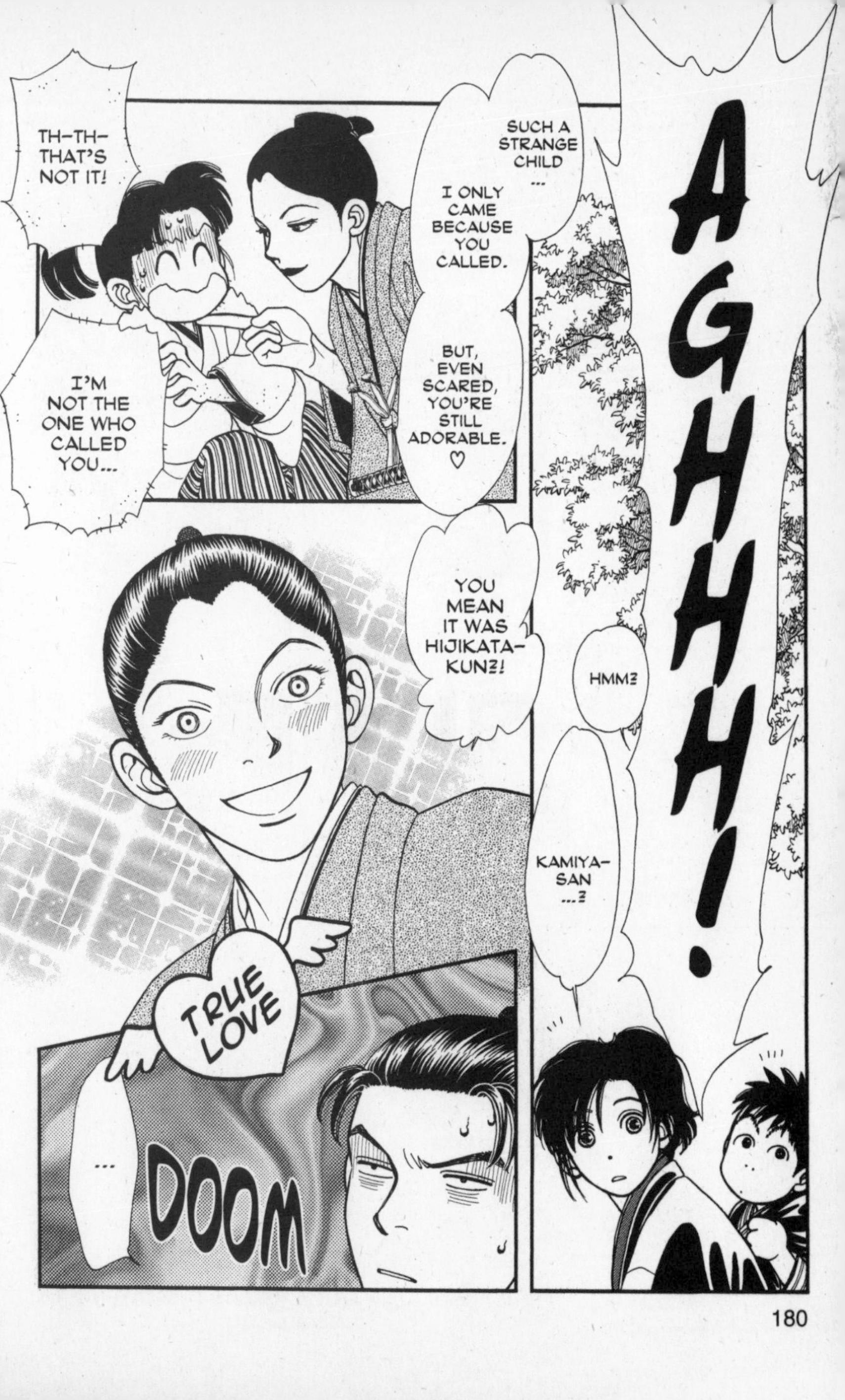
AGHHH!
HMM?
KAMIYA-SAN ...?
SUCH A STRANGE CHILD ...
I ONLY CAME BECAUSE YOU CALLED.
BUT, EVEN SCARED, YOU'RE STILL ADORABLE. ♡
TH-TH-THAT'S NOT IT!
I'M NOT THE ONE WHO CALLED YOU...
YOU MEAN IT WAS HIJIKATA-KUN?!
TRUE LOVE
DOOM
...

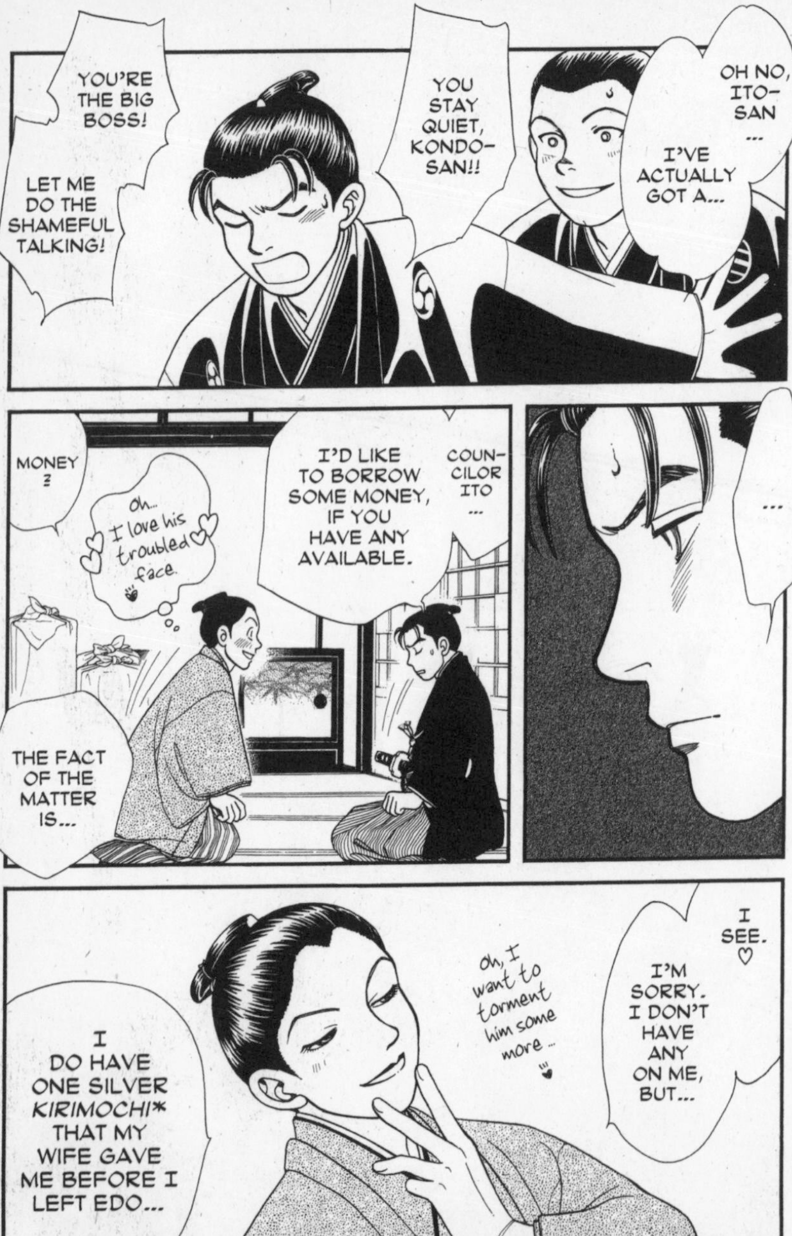
OH NO, ITO-SAN...
I'VE ACTUALLY GOT A...
YOU STAY QUIET, KONDO-SAN!!
YOU'RE THE BIG BOSS!
LET ME DO THE SHAMEFUL TALKING!
...
COUNCILOR ITO...
I'D LIKE TO BORROW SOME MONEY, IF YOU HAVE ANY AVAILABLE.
MONEY?
Oh... I love his troubled face.
THE FACT OF THE MATTER IS...
I SEE. ♡
I'M SORRY. I DON'T HAVE ANY ON ME, BUT...
Oh, I want to torment him some more...
I DO HAVE ONE SILVER KIRIMOCHI* THAT MY WIFE GAVE ME BEFORE I LEFT EDO...

*One bu is a fourth of a *ryo*. A hundred *bu* (25 ryo) in a *tsutsumikin* was called *kirimochi*.

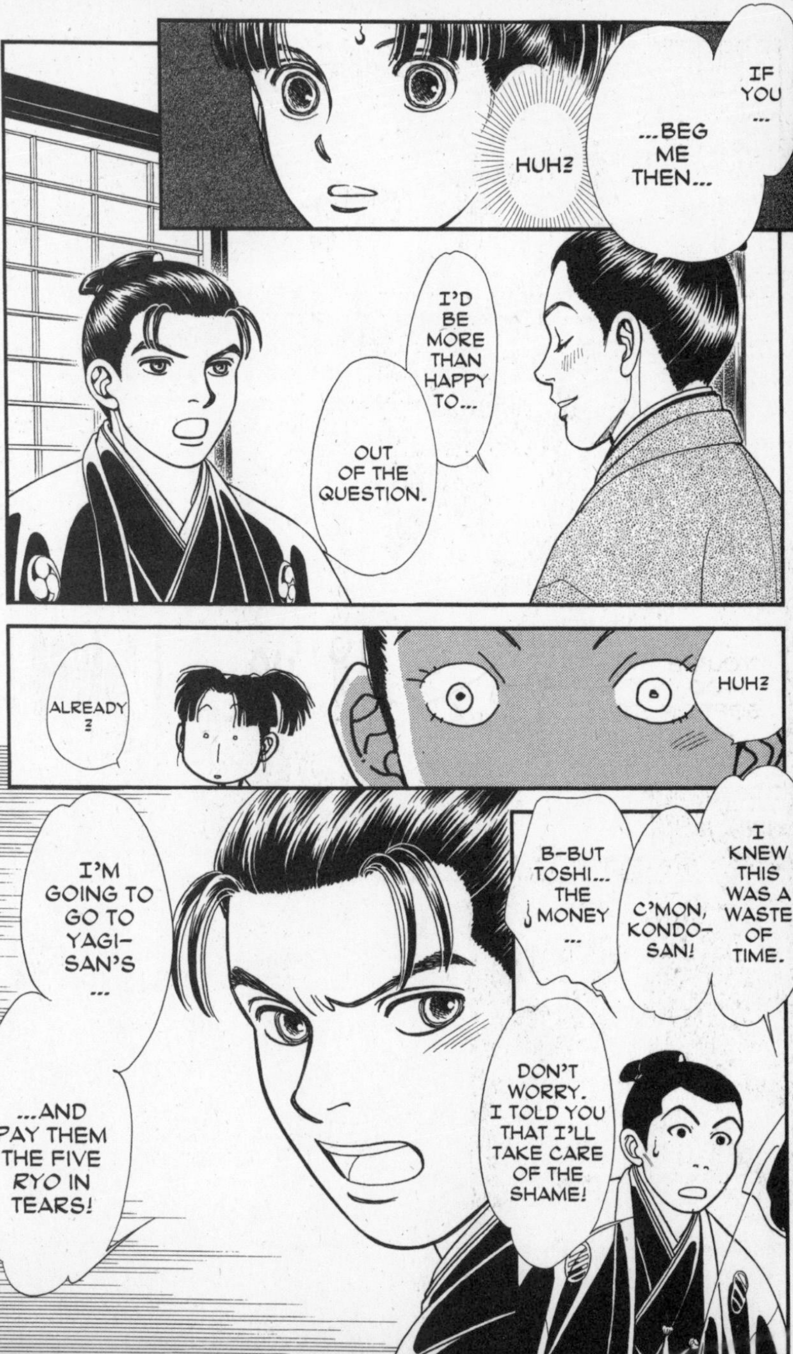
IF YOU ...
...BEG ME THEN...
HUH?
I'D BE MORE THAN HAPPY TO...
OUT OF THE QUESTION.
HUH?
ALREADY?
I KNEW THIS WAS A WASTE OF TIME.
C'MON, KONDO-SAN!
B-BUT TOSHI... THE MONEY ...
I'M GOING TO GO TO YAGI-SAN'S ...
DON'T WORRY. I TOLD YOU THAT I'LL TAKE CARE OF THE SHAME!
...AND PAY THEM THE FIVE *RYO* IN TEARS!

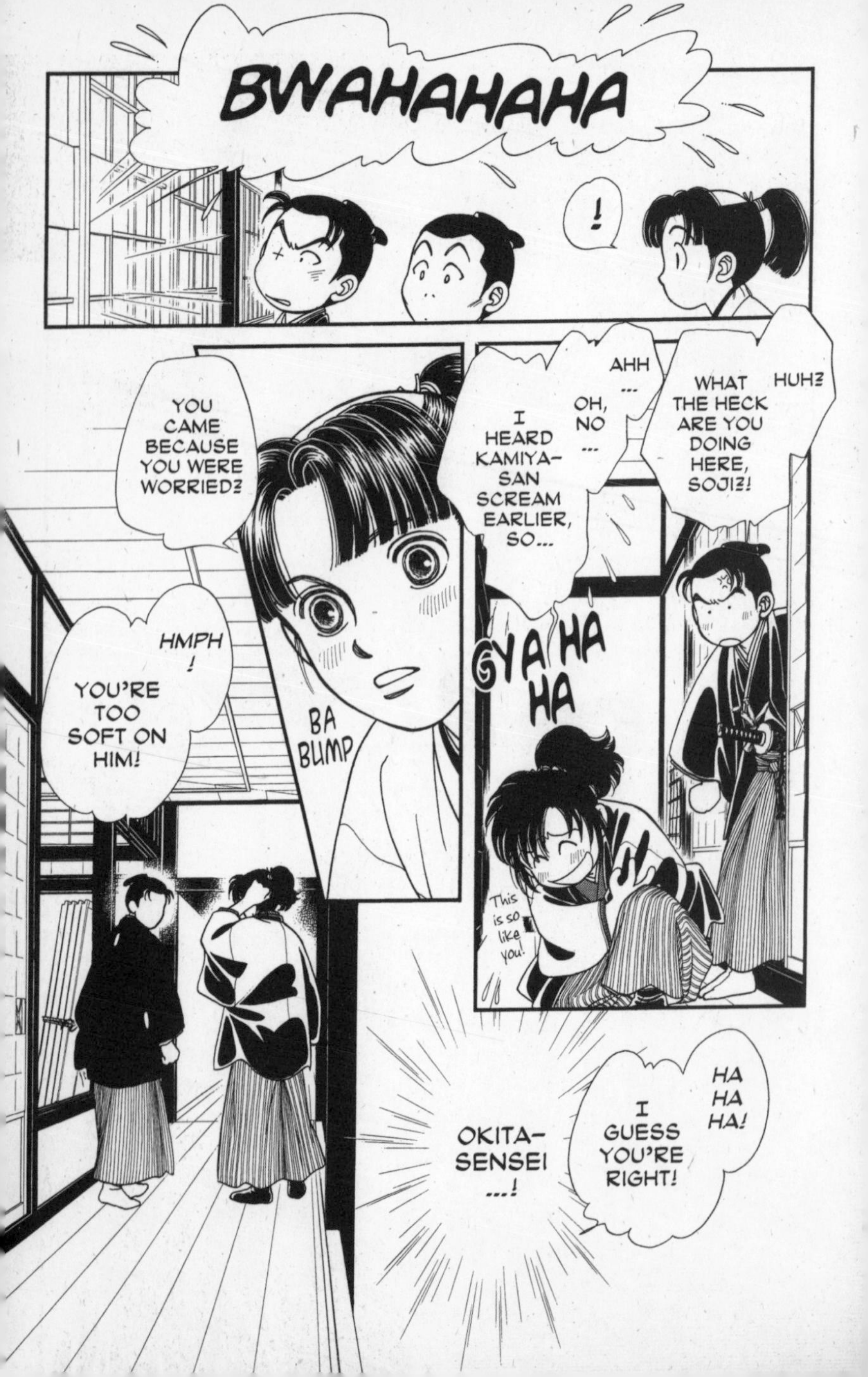
BWAHAHAHA
!
HUH?
WHAT THE HECK ARE YOU DOING HERE, SOJI?!
AHH... OH, NO... I HEARD KAMIYA-SAN SCREAM EARLIER, SO...
GYA HA HA
This is so like you!
BA BUMP
YOU CAME BECAUSE YOU WERE WORRIED?
HMPH! YOU'RE TOO SOFT ON HIM!
HA HA HA! I GUESS YOU'RE RIGHT!
OKITA-SENSEI...!

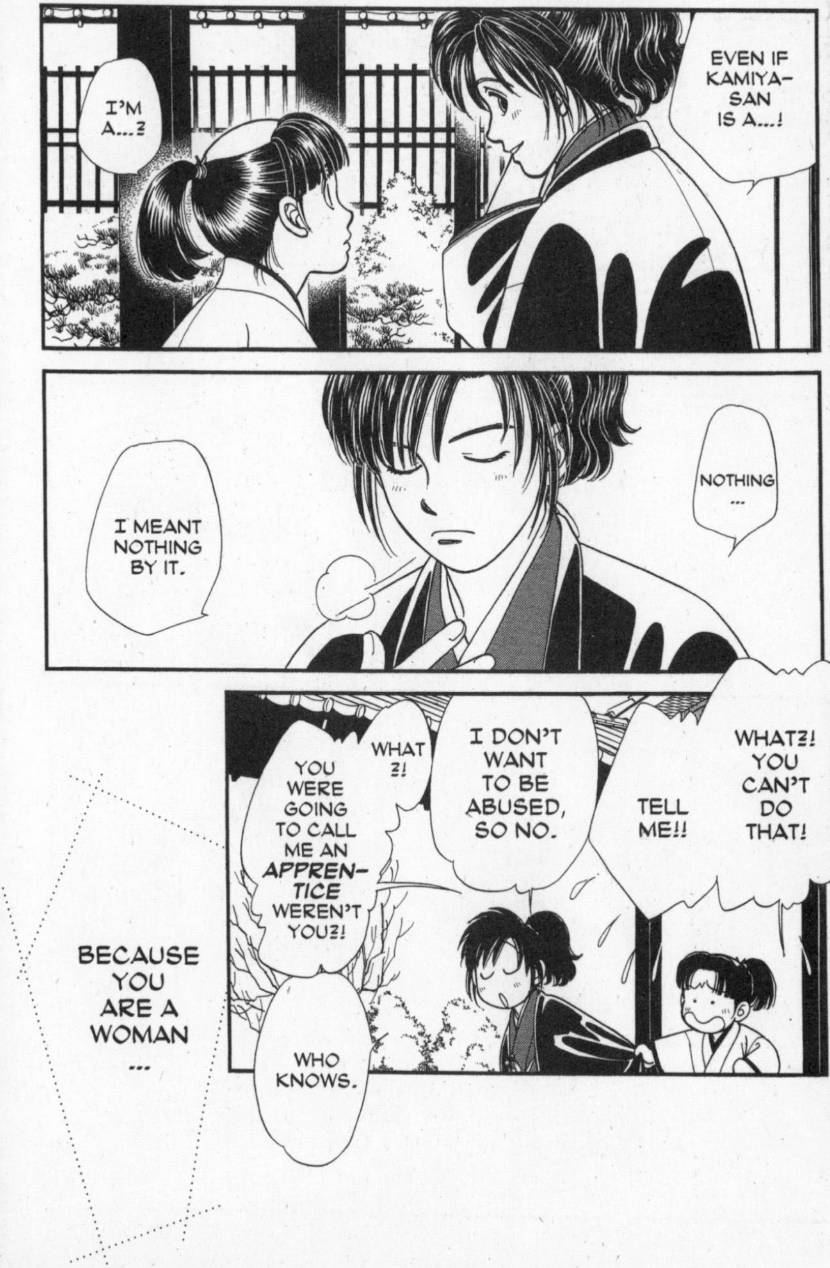
EVEN IF KAMIYA-SAN IS A...!
I'M A...?
NOTHING ...
I MEANT NOTHING BY IT.
WHAT?! YOU CAN'T DO THAT!
TELL ME!!
I DON'T WANT TO BE ABUSED, SO NO.
WHAT?!
YOU WERE GOING TO CALL ME AN *APPRENTICE* WEREN'T YOU?!
WHO KNOWS.
BECAUSE YOU ARE A WOMAN ...

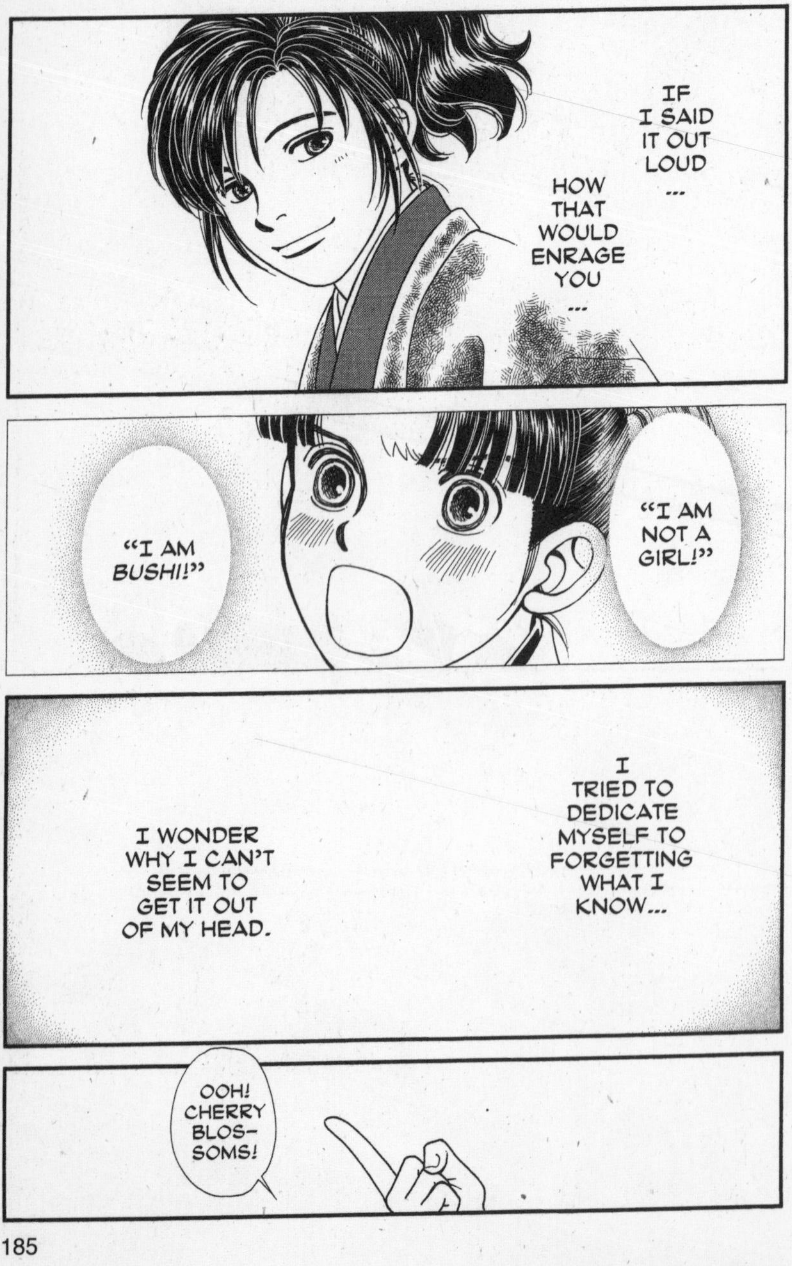
IF I SAID IT OUT LOUD ...
HOW THAT WOULD ENRAGE YOU ...
"I AM NOT A GIRL!"
"I AM *BUSHI*!"
I TRIED TO DEDICATE MYSELF TO FORGETTING WHAT I KNOW...
I WONDER WHY I CAN'T SEEM TO GET IT OUT OF MY HEAD.
OOH! CHERRY BLOS-SOMS!

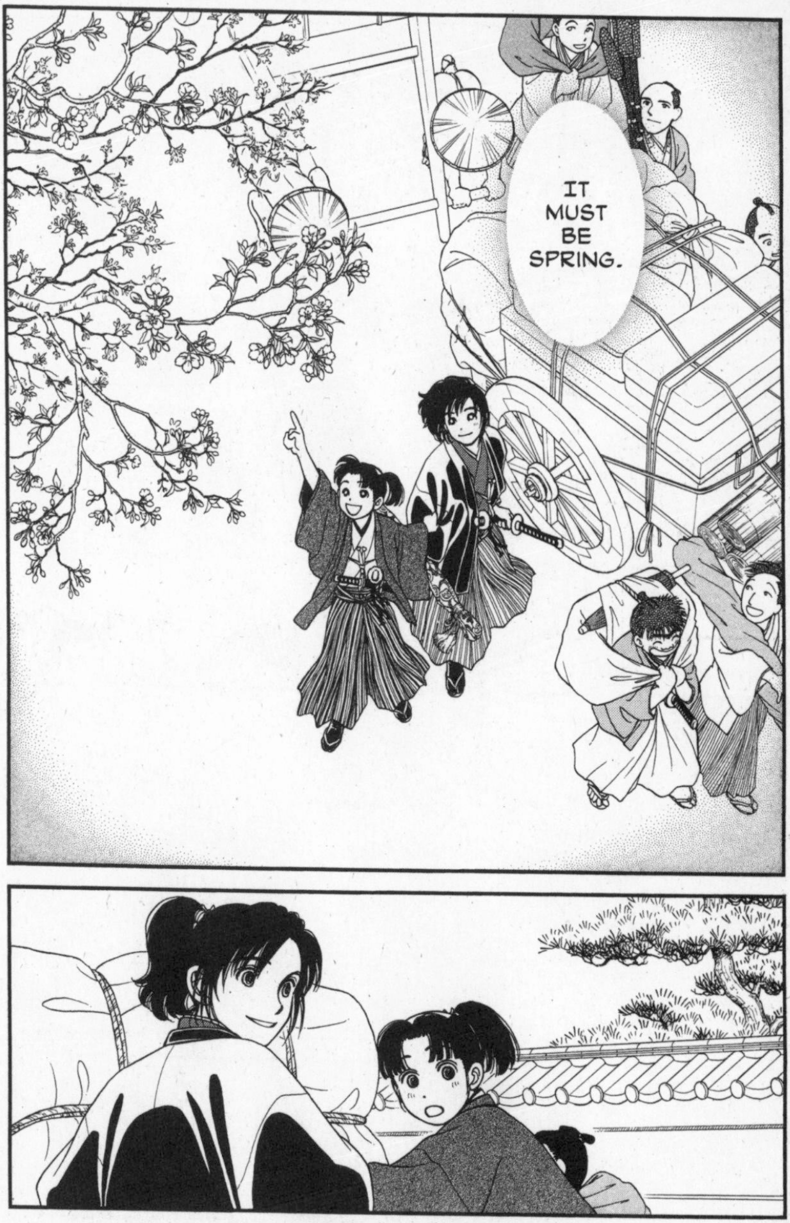
IT MUST BE SPRING.

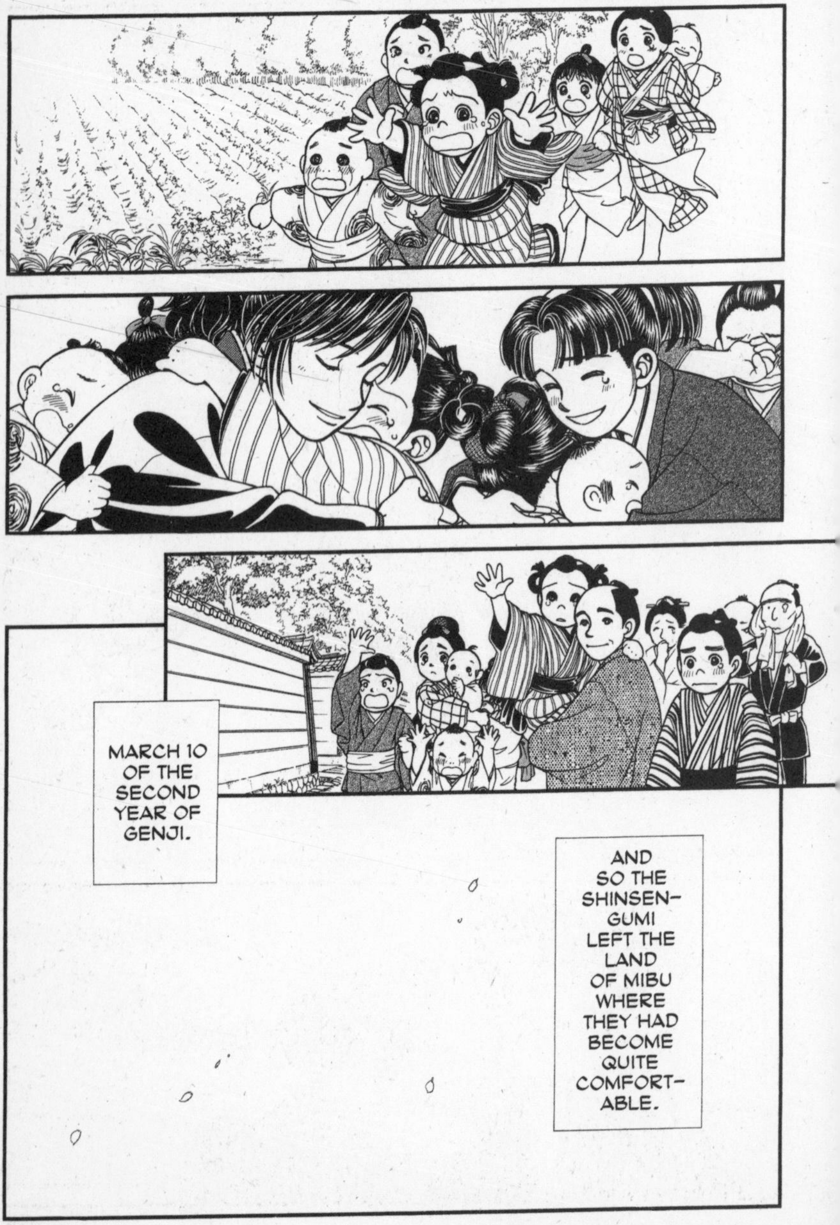
AND SO THE SHINSEN-GUMI LEFT THE LAND OF MIBU WHERE THEY HAD BECOME QUITE COMFORT-ABLE.
MARCH 10 OF THE SECOND YEAR OF GENJI.

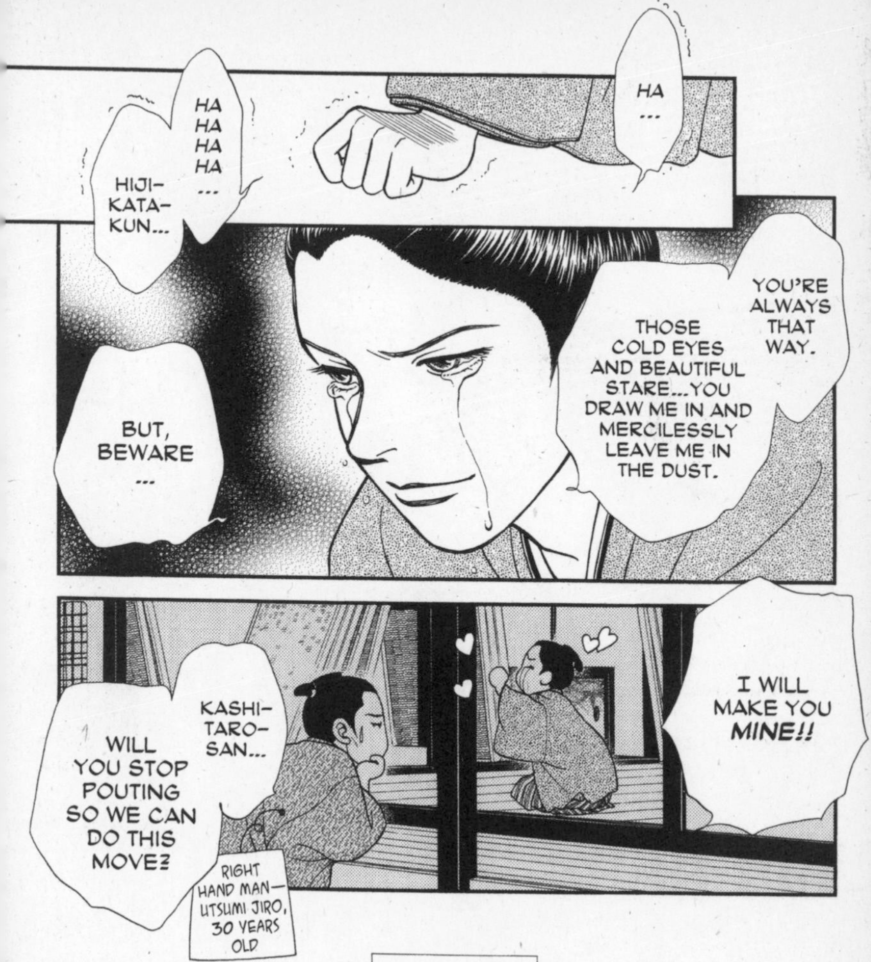
HA ...
HA HA HA HA ...
HIJI-KATA-KUN...
YOU'RE ALWAYS THAT WAY.
THOSE COLD EYES AND BEAUTIFUL STARE...YOU DRAW ME IN AND MERCILESSLY LEAVE ME IN THE DUST.
BUT, BEWARE ...
I WILL MAKE YOU *MINE!!*
KASHI-TARO-SAN...
WILL YOU STOP POUTING SO WE CAN DO THIS MOVE?
RIGHT HAND MAN—UTSUMI JIRO, 30 YEARS OLD

SO OUR STORY WILL CONTINUE AT NISHI HONGANJI.

To Be Continued!

Decoding Kaze Hikaru

Kaze Hikaru is a historical drama based in 19th century Japan and thus contains some fairly mystifying terminology. In this glossary we'll break down archaic phrases, terms and other linguistic curiosities for you, so that you can move through life with the smug assurance that you are indeed a know-it-all.

First and foremost, because *Kaze Hikaru* is a period story, we kept all character names in their traditional Japanese form—that is, family name followed by first name. For example, the character Okita Soji's family name is Okita and his personal name is Soji.

AKO-ROSHI:
The ronin (samurai) of Ako; featured in the immortal Kabuki play *Chushingura* (Loyalty), aka *47 Samurai*.

ANI-UE:
Literally, "brother above"; an honorific for an elder male sibling.

BAKUFU:
Literally, "tent government." Shogunate; the feudal, military government that dominated Japan for more than 200 years.

BUSHI:
A samurai or warrior (part of the compound word *bushido*, which means "way of the warrior").

CHICHI-UE:
An honorific suffix meaning "father above."

DO:
In kendo (a Japanese fencing sport that uses bamboo swords), a short way of describing the offensive single-hit strike *shikake waza ippon uchi*.

RONIN:
Masterless samurai.

RYO:
At the time, one *ryo* and two *bu* (four bu equaled roughly one ryo) were enough currency to support a family of five for an entire month.

-SAN:
An honorific suffix that carries the meaning of "Mr." or "Ms."

SENSEI:
A teacher, master or instructor.

SEPPUKU:
A ritualistic suicide that was considered a privilege of the nobility and samurai elite.

SONJO-HA:
Those loyal to the emperor and dedicated to the expulsion of foreigners from the country.

TAMEBO:
A short version of the name Tamesaburo.

YUBO:
A short version of the name Yunosuke.

-HAN:

The same as the honorific –SAN, pronounced in the dialect of southern Japan.

-KUN:

An honorific suffix that indicates a difference in rank and title. The use of *kun* is also a way of indicating familiarity and friendliness between students or compatriots.

MEN:

In the context of *Kaze Hikaru*, *men* refers to one of the "points" in kendo. It is a strike to the forehead and is considered a basic move.

MIBU-ROSHI:

A group of warriors that supports the Bakufu.

NE'E-SAN:

Can mean "older sister," "ma'am," or "miss."

NI'I-CHAN:

Short for *oni'i-san* or *oni'i-chan*, meaning older brother.

OKU-SAMA:

This is a polite way to refer to someone's wife. *Oku* means "deep" or "further back," and comes from the fact that wives (in affluent families) stayed hidden away in the back rooms of the house.

ONI:

Literally "ogre," this is Sei's nickname for Vice-Captain Hijikata.

RANPO:

Medical science derived from the Dutch.

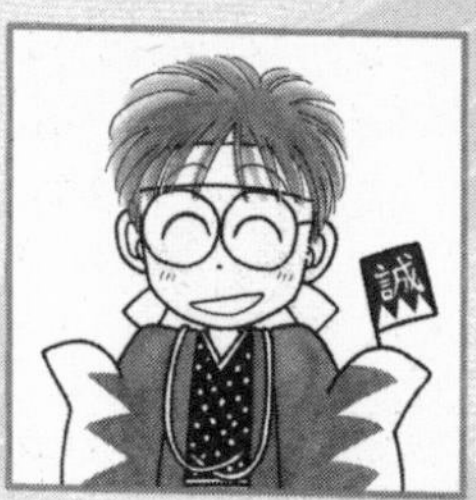
誠

When I decided to do a distant view for the cover, I chose not to do any close-ups for the final season and instead do all the Shieikan members grouped together. Of course I included the heroine, Sei-chan, so it makes a total of nine... What? Do I sense someone getting angry?

A certain "he" is not included as a Shieikan member in *Kaze Hikaru*, but on the historical front, there are theories that "he" was a comrade from the Shieikan days. The unfortunate tenth member has been given the "undercover" role purely to satisfy this author... If you were able to find him hidden in the color illustration, you can call your love for Saito-san the real thing. (*Heh*)

Taeko Watanabe debuted as a manga artist in 1979 with her story *Waka-chan no Netsuai Jidai* (Love Struck Days of Waka). *Kaze Hikaru* is her longest-running series, but she has created a number of other popular series. Watanabe is a two-time winner of the prestigious Shogakukan Manga Award in the girls category—her manga *Hajime-chan ga Ichiban!* (Hajime-chan Is Number One!) claimed the award in 1991 and *Kaze Hikaru* took it in 2003.

Watanabe read hundreds of historical sources to create *Kaze Hikaru.* She is from Tokyo.

Shojo Beat

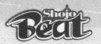

KAZE HIKARU VOL. 12
The Shojo Beat Manga Edition

STORY AND ART BY
TAEKO WATANABE

Translation & English Adaptation/Mai Ihara
Touch-up Art & Lettering/Rina Mapa
Design/Izumi Evers
Editor/Jonathan Tarbox

Editor in Chief, Books/Alvin Lu
Editor in Chief, Magazines/Marc Weidenbaum
VP, Publishing Licensing/Rika Inouye
VP, Sales & Product Marketing/Gonzalo Ferreyra
VP, Creative/Linda Espinosa
Publisher/Hyoe Narita

Printed in Canada

Published by VIZ Media, LLC
P.O. Box 77010
San Francisco, CA 94107

Shojo Beat Manga Edition
10 9 8 7 6 5 4 3 2 1
First printing, February 2009

viz media
www.viz.com

RATED T+ FOR OLDER TEEN

PARENTAL ADVISORY
KAZE HIKARU is rated T+ for Older Teen and is recommended for ages 16 and up. This volume contains realistic violence, alcohol use, and sexual themes.
ratings.viz.com

store.viz.com

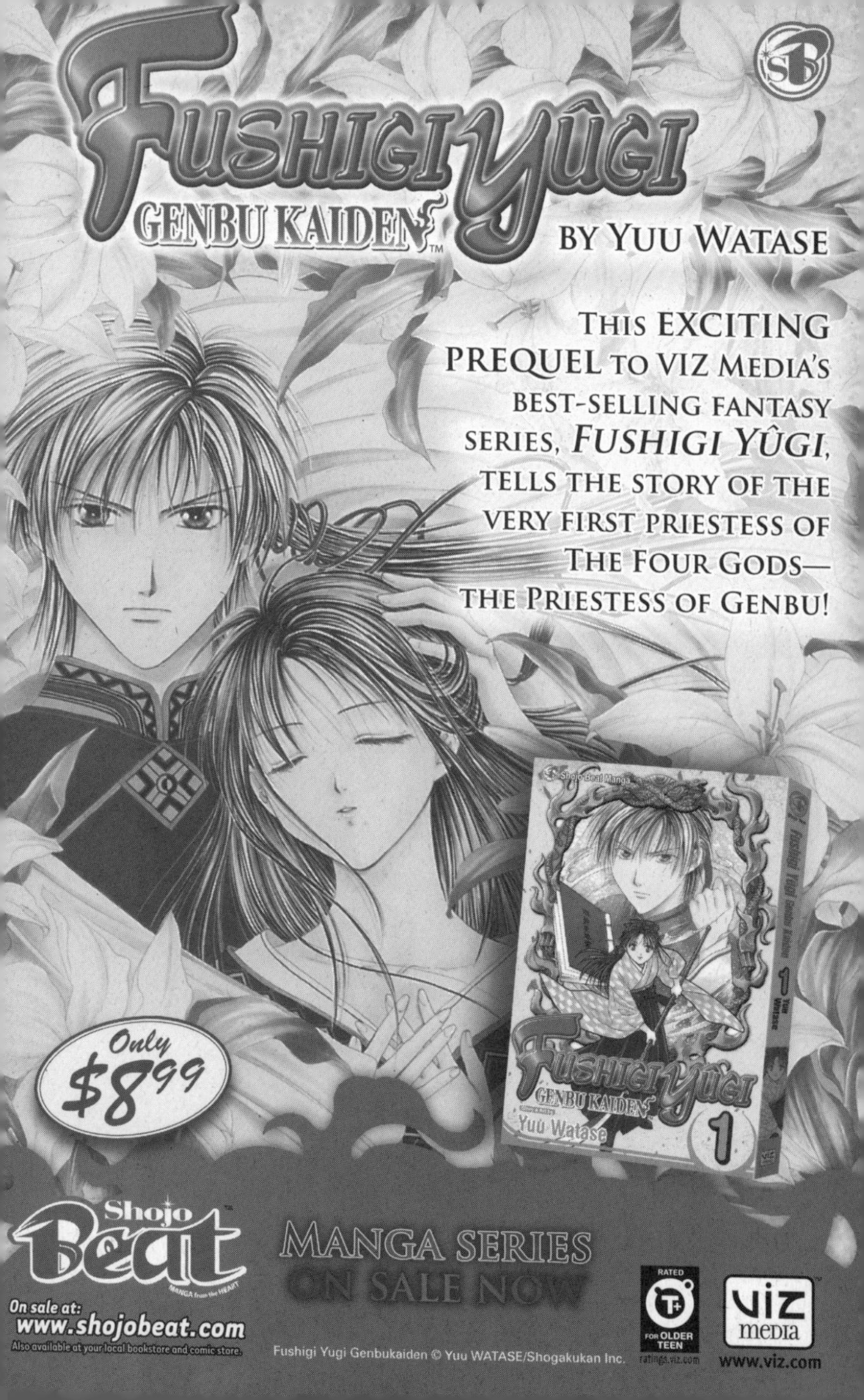
Fushigi Yûgi
Genbu Kaiden™
By Yuu Watase
This EXCITING PREQUEL to VIZ Media's best-selling fantasy series, *Fushigi Yûgi*, tells the story of the very first priestess of The Four Gods—the Priestess of Genbu!
Only $8.99
Shojo Beat Manga
Fushigi Yûgi Genbu Kaiden
Yuu Watase
1
Shojo Beat
MANGA from the HEART
On sale at:
www.shojobeat.com
Also available at your local bookstore and comic store.
MANGA SERIES
ON SALE NOW
Fushigi Yugi Genbukaiden © Yuu WATASE/Shogakukan Inc.
RATED T+ FOR OLDER TEEN
ratings.viz.com
viz media
www.viz.com

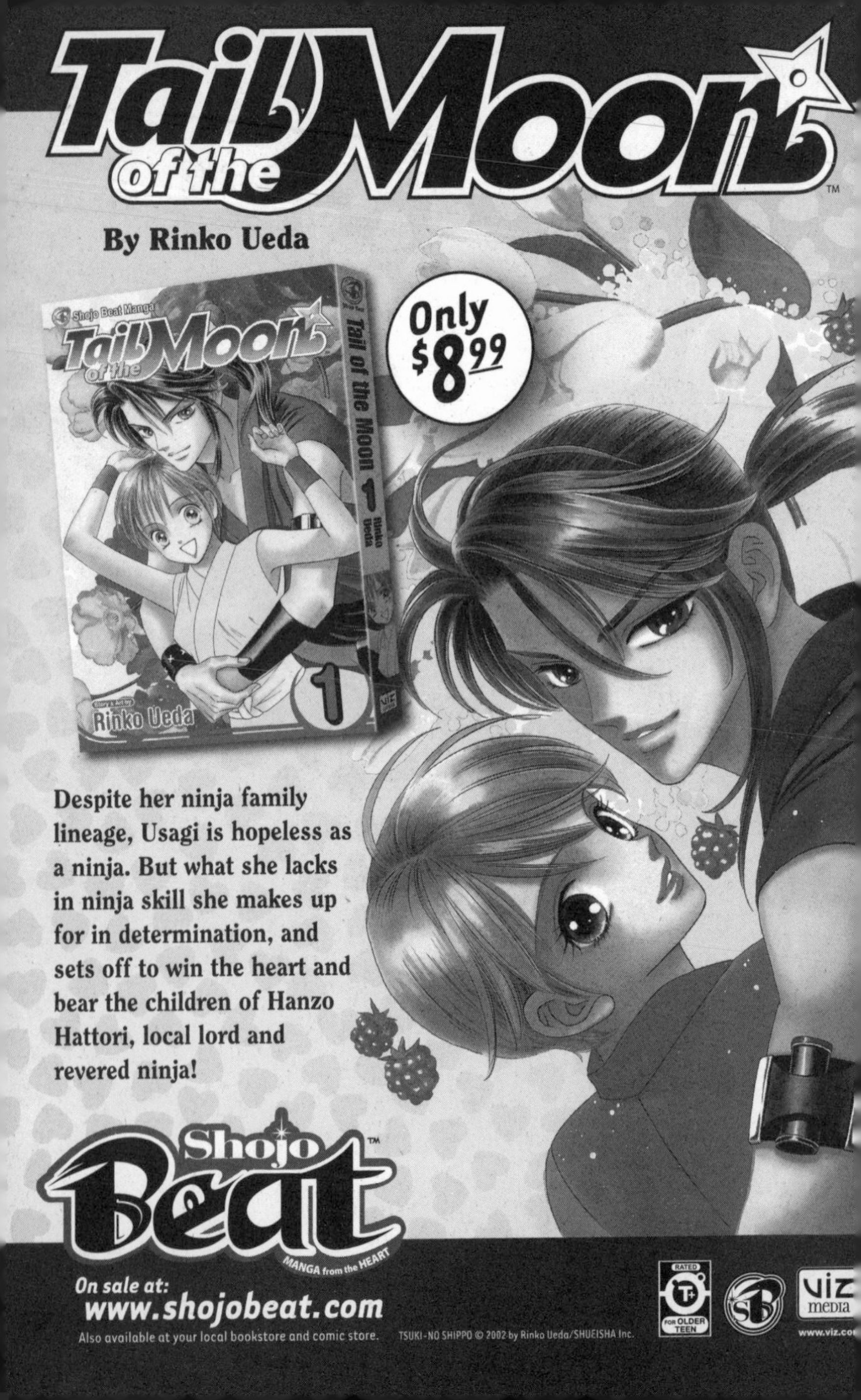
Tail of the Moon™
By Rinko Ueda
Shojo Beat Manga
Tail of the Moon
Tail of the Moon 1 Rinko Ueda
Story & Art by Rinko Ueda
Only $8.99
Despite her ninja family lineage, Usagi is hopeless as a ninja. But what she lacks in ninja skill she makes up for in determination, and sets off to win the heart and bear the children of Hanzo Hattori, local lord and revered ninja!
Shojo Beat™
MANGA from the HEART
On sale at:
www.shojobeat.com
Also available at your local bookstore and comic store.
TSUKI-NO SHIPPO © 2002 by Rinko Ueda/SHUEISHA Inc.
RATED T+ FOR OLDER TEEN
viz media
www.viz.com

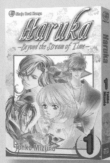
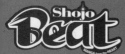
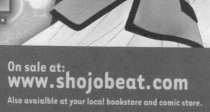

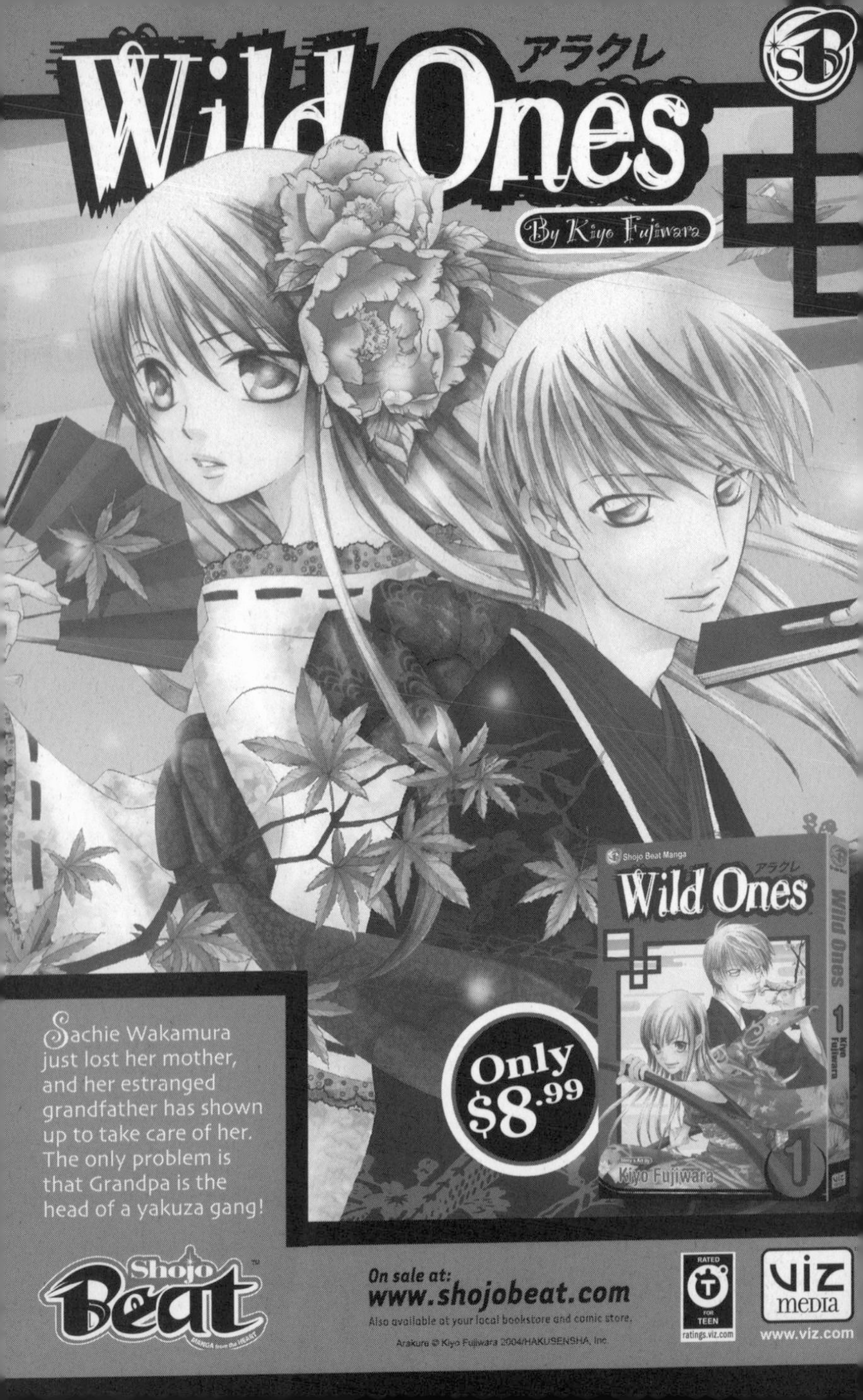
Wild Ones
アラクレ
By Kiyo Fujiwara
Shojo Beat Manga
Wild Ones
アラクレ
Kiyo Fujiwara
1
Only $8.99
Sachie Wakamura just lost her mother, and her estranged grandfather has shown up to take care of her. The only problem is that Grandpa is the head of a yakuza gang!
Shojo Beat
MANGA from the HEART
On sale at:
www.shojobeat.com
Also available at your local bookstore and comic store.
Arakure © Kiyo Fujiwara 2004/HAKUSENSHA, Inc.
RATED T FOR TEEN
ratings.viz.com
viz media
www.viz.com

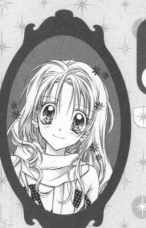
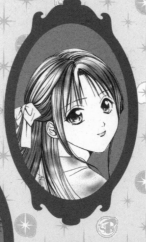

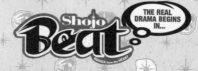

Shojo Beat™

MANGA from the HEART

The Shojo Manga Authority

The most **ADDICTIVE** shojo manga stories from Japan **PLUS** unique editorial coverage on the arts, music, culture, fashion, and much more!

12 GIANT issues for ONLY $34.99*

That's 51% OFF the cover price!

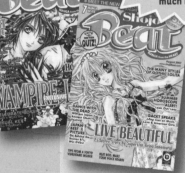

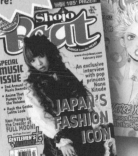

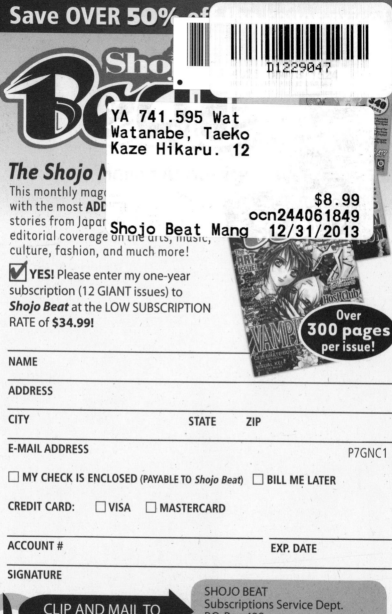

Save **OVER 50%** off

The Shojo M

This monthly maga
with the most **ADD**
stories from Japan
editorial coverage on the arts, music,
culture, fashion, and much more!

☑ **YES!** Please enter my one-year
subscription (12 GIANT issues) to
Shojo Beat at the LOW SUBSCRIPTION
RATE of **$34.99!**

Over 300 pages per issue!

NAME _____

ADDRESS _____

CITY _____ **STATE** ___ **ZIP** ___

E-MAIL ADDRESS _____ P7GNC1

☐ **MY CHECK IS ENCLOSED** (PAYABLE TO *Shojo Beat*) ☐ **BILL ME LATER**

CREDIT CARD: ☐ **VISA** ☐ **MASTERCARD**

ACCOUNT # _____ **EXP. DATE** _____

SIGNATURE _____

CLIP AND MAIL TO →

SHOJO BEAT
Subscriptions Service Dept.
P.O. Box 438
Mount Morris, IL 61054-0438

Canada price for 12 issues: $46.99 USD, including GST, HST and QST. US/CAN orders only. Allow 6-8 weeks for delivery. Must be 16 or older to redeem offer. By redeeming this offer I represent that I am 16 or older.

RATED
T+
FOR OLDER TEEN
ratings.viz.com

Vampire Knight © Matsuri Hino 2004/HAKUSENSHA, Inc. Nana Kitade © Sony Music Entertainment (Japan), Inc. CRIMSON HERO © 2002 by Mitsuba Takanashi/SHUEISHA Inc.